Robert Burns

Patrick Scott Hogg is a leading Burns scholar and co-editor of a recent complete works of Robert Burns. Since 1996, he has contributed groundbreaking research to reveal new poems written by the bard. He is an honours graduate of the University of Stirling and has a postgraduate degree from the University of Portsmouth. During the late 1990s, he was a Leverhulme Trust-funded researcher at the English Studies department of the University of Strathclyde. Patrick writes poetry and songs, and is a well-known speaker on the Burns circuit. He has three children, runs his own business and lives in Cumbernauld

Robert Burns

THE PATRIOT BARD

PATRICK SCOTT HOGG

EDINBURGH AND LONDON

This edition, 2009

First published in Great Britain in 2008 by
MAINSTREAM PUBLISHING COMPANY
(EDINBURGH) LTD
7 Albany Street
Edinburgh EH1 3UG

ISBN 9781845964856

A catalogue record for this book is available from the British Library

Typeset in Caslon and Requiem

Printed in Great Britain by
CPI Cox and Wyman, Reading, RG1 8EX

This work is dedicated with heartfelt gratitude to the memory and contribution made to Scottish literature and Burns studies by the late eminent scholar Professor David Daiches (1912–2005)

Acknowledgements

I owe a considerable debt to the many Burns experts and Burns enthusiasts I have had the pleasure to meet over the last dozen years. First and foremost, for the support they gave to my early archival work, are the late eminent Professor David Daiches, Thomas Crawford and my former boss at the University of Strathclyde, where I was his Leverhulme Trust funded researcher, Dr Andrew Noble, who co-edited the complete works of Burns with me in 2001. For initiating that work, I am grateful to Professors Roderick Watson and Cairns Craig. Also, for her compliments and support I am delighted to thank Professor Carol McGuirk of Florida Atlantic University. Professsor Liam McIlvanney also has been of some encouragement and his recent work on Burns is one of the finest studies written. I am indebted to Professor Bob Harris and the path-breaking historical research he and his colleagues have done on the 1790s period.

I owe a special thanks to Andrew O'Hagan for kind remarks in his recent book on Burns – comparing me to Burns in looks was quite funny. I am also indebted to the late Dr James Mackay for his encyclopaedic biography on Burns. Although his book is somewhat dated in relation to the last years of the poet's life, it is still an invaluable reference. Whatever disagreements James and I had, we shared a love and passion for the works of the bard. It was generous of him to say, the last time we met in public, that my research was 'the way forward'. I hope *The Patriot Bard* sheds some more light on the bard's life and adds to the work of Dr Mackay.

Having spoken at many Burns clubs across Scotland, I am lucky to have met so many of the people who keep the flame of Burns alive. First among Burns clubs is, of course, the Dumfries Burns Howff Club, which kindly conferred Honorary membership on me in 2004. Gentlemen, thank you for that priceless accolade. I am also grateful for the warmth and generosity of various Burns clubs, from Irvine Burns Club, Stranraer and District Burns Club, Bowhill People's Burns Club, Motherwell United Services Burns Club and many others, including my local Cumbernauld Burns Club. There are far too many people to thank, who have encouraged my work on our national poet. Being able to attend regular meetings and discuss ideas with fellow Burnsians has been a pleasure. From Cumbernauld Club, I am grateful to the elder statesman Tom Myles for his advice. Like the incomparable Davie Boyle, Tom sings the songs of Burns with an ability that is awe inspiring. President Jim, Tom Johnston, Dick, Callum, Duncan, Paul, Owen, Ron, Jimmy and the boys all have my admiration. It is regrettable that many of the talented stars of the Burns circuit are not regularly seen performing Burns' work on television.

For help with reading the early drafts and comments on the manuscript, I am indebted to Albert Calder, a man worth gowd, Dr Jim McGregor and the incomparable Scots patriot, Chic Scott, the gaffer. Lord Iqbal Singh was also very supportive. Thanks are due also to Eddie Smith for asking Elaine to type up some of Burns' letters. My thanks also go to Ian Brown for allowing me to look over his private collection, the partly unpublished Burns–Ainslie manuscripts. I am indebted to Willie Johnstone for his research on the poet's ancestry.

All authors owe a debt to the professional skill of librarians. Much of the material used here was consulted over the past years from libraries all over Britain, including the British Library, the Mitchell Library, the National Library of Scotland, Edinburgh University Library and the Scottish Record Office. My thanks also go to staff at Cumbernauld Public Library.

It would have been impossible to write *The Patriot Bard* without the support of Bill Campbell and his highly professional team at Mainstream – especially Graeme Blaikie and Emily Bland – and to my editor Jennie Renton and everyone else who assisted. A huge thank you to Helen for her support and patience.

I hope anyone new to the life and works of Robert Burns enjoys reading this biography and goes on to enjoy his poetry and songs, or vice versa.

As a passionate fan of Burns', I am aware of his failings as a human being and have tried to write an honest, warts and all biography of the real living man with some new, fresh interpretations and insights, if that is possible, 250 years after his birth. It is regrettable there were a few brickbats thrown during a media frenzy in 1996 when my initial research findings were made public on the back of BBC Omnibus programme, *The Ploughboy of the Western World*. If there is a contentious element to *The Patriot Bard* it is hoped discussion is positive and in the manner of genuine Burnsian debate. There is no axe to grind in this biography other than to try to add something to our collective knowledge of our national bard. The bard did once write 'An honest candid enquirer after the truth I revere.'

Patrick Scott Hogg, Cumbernauld,
November 2008

Contents

But still the Patriot, and the Patriot-bard
In bright succession raise, her Ornament and Guard!

'The Cotter's Saturday Night'

Introduction

CELEBRATING THE 250TH ANNIVERSARY

Go, builder of a deathless name!
Thy country's glory and her shame!
Go, and the immortal guerdon claim,
  To Genius due;
Whilst rolling centuries thy fame
  Shall still renew!

William Roscoe, 1796

THE LIFE OF ROBERT BURNS IS THE STORY of remarkable triumph over poverty and adversity. The odds were heavily stacked against a peasant poet bursting onto the scene during the late Enlightenment period. Yet, at 27 years of age, Burns produced his Kilmarnock Edition and became, briefly, the darling of fashionable literary Edinburgh. He was patronised as the 'Heaven-taught ploughman', one of a clutch of iconic myths that continue to obscure the real mettle of the man. Throughout the vicissitudes of his tragically short life, he never totally abandoned himself to bitterness, never shed his social idealism and never lost his innate sense of destiny as a poet. He was sustained through the harshest of times, economically and politically, by an inner certainty that his work would endure down the centuries. His prescience has been amply vindicated.

In *The Patriot Bard*, I set out to strip away the layers of myth to find the real flesh and blood man, poet and visionary democrat. Many of the projections relating to Burns have been far from positive. Was he an alcoholic who drank himself into an early grave? Was he in the grip of an uncontrollable sex addiction? Was he, as some have had it, a 'whore-maister'? These questions are answered. It is a historic irony that those who sought to blast his fame and besmirch his reputation actually enhanced his fame: the ram-stam boy of popular cliché has an alluring, perennial charisma. Too often the myth obscures the real man.

I try to show that many of the apparent contradictions in Burns' personality, as we understand it in the twenty-first century, are contradictions between the real, living man and the popular, iconic myth. Superficially, he is often seen as a simplistic sentimentalist, who, in 'To A Mouse', for example, has empathy for the timid creature's homelessness and hardship. There is, though, a darker union of mice and men, namely the wretched condition of the peasantry living on the margins in rural Scotland – a harsh, brutal back-breaking reality that Burns experienced. Even the shrewd Jeremy Paxman has swallowed the Kailyard myth of Burns as a 'king of sentimental doggerel'.[1] In reality, Burns penned social satire with a dark and deadly pinpoint precision.

Stubbornly independent, Burns resisted all advice to give up composing poetry in the Scots language. He refused to be a part of the cultural capitulation involved in eradicating 'Scotticisms' from the language and so to contribute to the erosion of Scotland's culture and identity. Scots was not a 'vulgar' regional dialect to Burns, it was the native tongue of his country, the voice of the heart. His Scottish poetry, at its best, proves that high literary art could be forged from the language of the people. It was a deliberate, radical and risk-taking decision for Burns to write in the Scots vernacular, following his precursors Ramsay and Fergusson.

With the dominant culture of England flooding and diluting Scottish culture over the centuries since his death, Burns' poetry and songs have become a symbolic touchstone of Scottish identity for generation after generation. The name of Burns should be embedded at the core of Scottish identity, for the simple reason that no other Scot has ever contributed so much to the tapestry of Scottish culture and done so much to preserve the national identity of his country. He was unquestionably a patriotic Scottish bard.

One of the difficulties with Burns the man, for biographers, has been his highly opinionated, hyper-intelligent criticism in verse of the establishment of his day, whether religious or political, local or national. He had a bent for controversy. Living during the age of Enlightenment, he sought to engage in debates and believed in the power of Reason and Common Sense. As a peasant poet, or to be more accurate, a tenant farmer poet – then later, an Exciseman – Burns hailed from a lower rung of society and was meant to avoid topics such as religion and politics. They were no business of his. He was duty-bound to show deference towards his social superiors, keep his head down and mouth shut. The entire notion a peasant could be a hyper-intelligent, articulate, educated poet, especially without university grounding, was not on the radar of the Edinburgh intellectuals of the era. Burns was thus cast in the part of the poet who wrote, miraculously, from pure inspiration. He has rarely been allowed, even nowadays, to own his true intellect.

The genius of Burns, as exemplified in his best poetry, is lauded, while at the same time he has been accused of being semi-confused and contradictory on more serious matters such as the national affairs of his time. Burns' highly opinionated natural bent has been problematic, even to some twentieth-century biographers. A new myth was promulgated during the 1990s, against all literary and historical evidence, that the bard ceased to compose radical or controversial material from 5 January 1793 onwards. This lopsided portrayal of the man's intellect denies Burns' continued radical worldview and tends to distort the underlying values and principles that, as we shall see, permeate all his writings. As DeLancey Ferguson illustrates in 'They Censored Burns', many nineteenth-century writers have misread, failed to take on board or explain his radical values; some have even set out to deny or suppress them.[2] This has allowed an allegedly apolitical Burns to be all things to all people, a point made eloquently by Andrew O'Hagan.[3] When Burns' first main biographer, Dr James Currie, met the poet in Dumfries in 1792, he was so taken by his intellect and conversation, he later described him as a man who, if he had been in the position of power and influence 'might have influenced the history of nations'.[4]

There are five main sections to *The Patriot Bard*. In Part One, I examine Burns' formative years and set out to delineate the values and ideals, essentially moral and religious, engendered by his parents. His early education and literary influences are considered in terms of the growth of his poetic skills and confidence he built as a young man. The mixed strands of influence from the Jacobite cause, the Covenanter tradition and his Presbyterian inculcation are examined. Crucial to his later success in Edinburgh's educated, polite society was his confidence as a public speaker, a skill he developed in the Tarbolton debating society he inaugurated, and the personal connections he accrued from his experience among fellow Masons of various social ranks in Ayrshire, connections he tapped into advantageously when seeking support for his Edinburgh Edition of 1787.

In Part Two, I demonstrate the crucial importance of Robert Fergusson's poetry as a primary motivation in Burns' career as a Scots poet. It was, in a sense, Fergusson who gave life to Burns as a Scots poet and, through respect and poetic imitation, Burns gave life again to Fergusson, raising a headstone to the great Edinburgh poet, who might have been obliterated from the national memory had it not been for the bard. Fergusson was the poet's hero he surpassed in talent. The chronology of the life is stopped temporarily in Chapter Seven, to present what contemporaries thought of Burns and show how he revealed himself as a poet by the decisions he made regarding the poems he allowed into print and those he kept from public view.

Part Three charts the poet's whirlwind successes in Edinburgh, his new edition and subsequent tours around Scotland as Caledonia's bard, plotting the ups and downs of his life in terms of romance and financial problems with his publisher.

Part Four looks at the period in which he and Jean Armour settled down as Mr and Mrs Robert Burns at Ellisland farm, near Dumfries. It was during this period that Burns changed his professional career from tenant farmer to Exciseman. It is also from the Ellisland period onwards that he began to devote more and more creative energy to writing and reshaping Scots song lyrics, having cemented his fame as a poet with the 1787 Edinburgh Edition. After selling the copyright of his poems to his publisher and joining the Excise, Burns began to write more poetry of a controversial nature and indulged in prose compositions for the national press, employing pseudonymous publication to protect his job security.

Part Five covers the years when Burns and his family lived in Dumfries, a time when Britain descended into a political maelstrom that affected every part of the country and profoundly influenced the poet's writings. During this period, sedition laws were brought in to break up the British pro-democracy movement. The tyrannical oppression of the Pitt government brought the Enlightenment movement to its knees and silenced the leading minds of a generation. It was not widely known until the mid-1990s that two of the poet's most famous songs were too seditious for him to print under his own name: 'Scots Wha Hae' and 'A Man's a Man' were both printed anonymously. Burns risked his life and freedom to continue composing such radical material during his last few years. Sheena Wellington, who sang 'A Man's a Man' at the opening of the new Scottish Parliament in 1999, would have been arrested for sedition had she sung the song anywhere in Britain in 1795. Aspirations for the freedoms we take for granted nowadays provoked an ideological war during the 1790s, which resulted in a tyrannical crackdown on those, like Burns, who wished to see democratic reform.

Modern scholarship has given us a new historical perspective on the 1790s period. My own archival findings reveal that a branch of the pro-democracy movement, the Friends of the People in Scotland, existed covertly in Dumfries during 1793 and suggest Burns himself was an active participant. I make very brief mention of the radical poems provisionally attributed to Burns in *Robert Burns: The Lost Poems* (1997), from which around 12 poems were widely accepted by eminent literary scholars and added to the complete works, which I co-edited in a new edition of 2001.[5] Further new attributions, at least two of them genuine variants of known works by Burns, are interwoven into the chronology of the poet's life, as well as new facts, such as Graham of Fintry, the poet's patron and friend, being paid out of the spy network funds in 1793 for pro-Pitt propaganda work. The Dumfries years are presented in a new, more focused historical-biographical context, which reveals the fascinating lengths Burns went to in order to have his say.

The culture of Burns' radical values was framed between the optimism of the American Revolution and the eventual pessimism of the French one. During the 1790s, his views were galvanised by the government crackdown on radicals across Britain, when he himself was ordered to be 'silent and obedient'. The oppressive political atmosphere led to Burns writing as an underground poet to continue expressing his radical sentiments. Given the poet's indignant personality and the fact that his early death left his private papers in chaos, the likelihood is there are more unidentified, radical writings of Burns, buried in dusty archives, still to be found. One would suppose his pseudonymous and anonymous works would be the most difficult area to unravel and piece together, although I have pioneered some progress in this area and engendered debate and other discoveries by scholars such as Dr G. Carruthers.[6] One contentious essay discovered under the known pen name Burns employed 'A Briton' is interwoven into the life-story, where both contextual and textual evidence strongly suggest his authorship. Several eminent scholars now agree that this important essay is the work of Burns. Two further essays that may or may not be by the bard, with less supportive evidence for provenance, are added as an appendix, in order to allow readers to make up their own minds.

There are missing pieces of the jigsaw of Burns' life. Questions will remain unanswered. Poetry and letters have been destroyed, censored and burned, many of them containing controversial radical writings. Are poems such as 'The Poet's Rambles on the Banks of Ayr' or 'The Lucubrations of Henry Dundass, May 1792' still in private hands?

I was allowed to view but not quote from a privately owned manuscript collection, the Burns–Ainslie correspondence – which contains several unpublished letters and two new poems. An interesting feature of the collection is that the manuscripts in it are in transcript, not in the bard's handwriting. Having closely studied the handwriting, I am of the view that the letters appear to be in the same handwriting as that of the copyist who prepared the papers for the treason trials of Thomas Hardy, John Thelwall and Horne Took in London in 1794–95. The copyist who transcribed the papers for the treason trials worked for the Scottish lawyer in London, John Spottiswood, a close friend of Henry Dundas. The current owner of the Burns–Ainslie papers has confirmed that the manuscripts were in the possession of the Spottiswood family in Scotland for well over a century after the poet's death before they came into his hands. This reinforces the likelihood that the handwritten transcripts are by the same copyist, although it would require a specialist handwriting expert to endorse such a conclusion. The manuscript papers show a watermark date of '1793', which means the complete uncensored letters of Burns to Ainslie were copied sometime after 1793 if they were copied by the same legal copyist who prepared the papers for the treason trials in London in 1794–95. Does this mean the Scottish establishment, under Henry Dundas, were preparing to take Burns to trial for sedition? Was Ainslie forced to hand over incriminating letters to legal friends of Dundas? Does the watermark date of '1793' simply indicate that the paper used to copy the letters of the bard was over three years old? It is impossible to answer such questions and speculation would only lead to a maze of possible, probably wrong, conclusions.

It is not a contradiction to describe Burns as a Scottish patriot and a British patriot. There is a qualitative difference between the two. As a British patriot, he identified with the Glorious Revolution of 1688 and held a poet's admiration for the best of English culture, while his Scottish patriotism was of the blood, exerting a passionate, almost unconscious influence on his writings and views. He would have preferred equality between the two nations, not the one-sided, semi-colonial dominance of England over Scotland, politically, economically and culturally. Burns was no Jacobin enemy of Britain, although he loathed the Pitt-Dundas government's oppression of the people and saw through their cynical motives for going to war with France. Burns allied himself with the Whig party in his last years but he did not believe in following a party line and, to the last, maintained the right to think for himself. He had a healthy distrust of politicians, who could readily pretend their actions were motivated by the national interest, when they were acting selfishly and lying to the people. His egalitarian and humanitarian values were anathema to the hidebound establishment, in an era when open expression of dissidence could be expected to result in deportation or possibly death.

Although cerebrally a British patriot, Burns' Scottish patriotism dominated his entire being as a poet. He resented Scotland's lost independence and pragmatically sought the best from the status quo. For him, the Jacobite cause was symbolic of a lost, somewhat romantic past. He was essentially a democrat who opposed the inevitable ascendancy of title and rank.

The fascinating legend of Burns as a ladies' man is placed where it should be, as less important than the message of the bard. Is it not also somewhat ironic that, despite his popular reputation as a male chauvinist, Burns' skill in writing songs in the feminine voice remains unrivalled? He was, in a sense, a reckless romantic who fell in love readily and always kept alive a flame for the women he embraced closest to his heart, namely Ellison Begbie, Margaret Campbell (Highland Mary), Agnes McLehose and his ever-tolerant soulmate, Jean Armour.[7] This is, after all, a life story of a poet, not a Scottish Casanova, hence the poet's romances are considered where they have a bearing on his poetic contribution, mainly in song.

The essential purpose of this biography is to examine, explain and encourage debate about the beliefs and views of Robert Burns. *The Patriot Bard* presents man and poet in all his complexity: he was a patriot to his God, a patriot to his beloved Scotland, and also a patriot to the best of what Britain could have been during his era. A patriot, in the sense of how Burns employs the word, was also someone who would stand up and be counted, be true to core principles, and expose corruption in public affairs. He had become a major poet of the era, greatly admired by his English peers William Wordsworth and Samuel Taylor Coleridge. In the best of his love songs, Burns can be seen to be an even greater Romantic poet than the famous English Romantics group.

The Patriot Bard undertakes a reappraisal of Burns as an underground poet of democracy during the 1790s who risked his freedom, or even his life, for his beliefs, and examines the historical context of the oppression he lived through in his last years, the significance of which is only beginning to be understood by historians and Burnsians.

The spirit of Burns is alive and kicking as long as his writings are being voiced anywhere in the world. Will we continue to praise his remarkable gifts as a wordsmith and condemn his human failings, failings he often tortured himself with in penitential angst? The Burns of *The Patriot Bard* is a highly intense, focused, bookish poet, with behavioural quirks that would probably intimidate many of his modern fans. If the ghost of Burns attends any of the celebrations in 2009, the 250th anniversary of his birth, he will be sizing up the integrity and intellect of those who speak in his name, precisely as the man himself did so many times with his contemporaries. He had almost a magical power of language, not only in poetry but also in personal discourse. This work tries to capture and convey some of the electrical energy and passion of the complex genius his friends knew, whom we today are still striving to comprehend.

Editorial Note

The spelling of words from Burns' poems and letters and from original eighteenth-century documentation has been left as it occurs in the source material.

Part One

The Formative Years

I

A Highland and Lowland Marriage: Jacobite and Covenanter Blood

On 25 January 1759, William Burnes and his wife Agnes (née Broun) celebrated the arrival of their first child, a son: Robert Burnes was born at Alloway, Ayrshire, in the small, two-roomed cottage (the auld clay biggin) that William himself had built. Alloway is situated near the sea on the west of Scotland, adjacent to the town of Ayr. William and Agnes produced a typically large rural family of four sons and three daughters: they were, after Robert, Gilbert (1760), Agnes (1762), Annabella (1764), William (1767), John (1769) and Isabella (1771). It was only after William's death, in 1784, that his eldest son dropped the 'e' from his surname, to become Burns, the Ayrshire spelling of the name.

Agnes Burnes was a local tenant farmer's daughter, born and bred in Ayshire at Craigenton farm, near Kirkoswald. After her mother's early death, she lived as housekeeper with her uncle William Broun (or Brown) at Maybole. As the biographer Dr Chambers records, she was a smallish, vibrant woman with red, gypsy-like hair. Although supposed to have been unable to write, she was able to read – an important distinction in defining literacy among the Scottish peasantry. Her own education consisted mainly of instruction in the Bible and her contribution to the family's education was, amongst other things, through her singing of Scottish traditional songs, whether read or picked up from oral tradition. The poet later remarked that one of the key enjoyments left to William 'Broun' in his last years was to 'sit down and cry', while Agnes sang 'The Life & Age of Man', a beautiful, sad song chronicling the hardships of life from the cradle to the grave.[1] During the first seven years of his life at the 'auld clay biggin', Agnes laid the foundation for her eldest son's lifelong love of Scottish folk songs. Through the oral tradition, she transmitted a spellbinding gift, which later bore fruit in his extraordinary felicity as a song-collector who polished up many dusty old lyrics. The alchemy of Burns' genius in song lyrics originates in the special emotional bond in the voice of a mother to her beloved son.

Agnes also passed on to her children the chilling, religio-political tradition handed down from her Covenanter forebears (a connection that is sometimes disputed, despite the fact that Brown was a name famous to the cause at the Battle of Bothwell Bridge in 1679). Her own mother, Agnes Rainie, had witnessed the 'Killing Times' of the 1690s. Much of central and southwest Scotland was put under the cosh of what was effectively the last blast of the Divine Right of Kings. Religious dissenters were made to swear the Oath of Abjuration to confirm their loyalty first and foremost to the British King rather than to the King of Kings, Jesus Christ. Those who refused to do so were killed. On one occasion, 200 Covenanters drowned below deck off Orkney as they were being transported to the American colonies. In Ayrshire, at the peak of the crackdown by government troops, 1,500 people were executed on the Cassilis Estate near to Maybole. The Kailyard myth of Scotland's romantic sentimental past is often a plaster to cover brutal and bloody events almost too incomprehensible to recall.

Folk memory of the Covenanters was part of rural Ayrshire Presbyterian culture, passed on from one generation to another at the fireside. In 1795, Burns wrote:

> The Solemn League and Covenant
> Now brings a smile, now brings a tear.
> But sacred Freedom, too, was theirs;
> If thou'rt a slave, indulge thy sneer.

The religiosity of 'The Cotter's Saturday Night' is deeply influenced by the Covenanting tradition; the view that the true spiritual link between each individual and God is directly via the human heart and not through the intermediary of a church, minister or institution is a significant motif in Burns' writings.

Agnes was not the only woman who had a formative influence on young Robert's cast of mind. In his autobiographical letter to Dr Moore, he mentions Betty Davidson: 'I owed much to an old Maid of my Mother's, remarkable for her ignorance, credulity and superstition.' She delighted in telling the boy superstitious tales and ghost stories, some of which petrified him:

> She had, I suppose, the largest collection in the county of tales and songs concerning devils, ghosts, fairies, brownies, witches, warlocks, spunkies, kelpies, elf candles, dead-lights, wraiths, apparitions, cantraips, giants, inchanted towers, dragons and other trumpery. This cultivated the latent seeds of Poesy; but had so strong an effect on my imagination, that to this hour, in my nocturnal rambles, I sometimes keep a sharp look-out in suspicious places; and though nobody can be more sceptical in these matters than I, yet it often takes an effort of Philosophy to shake off these idle terrors.[2]

Superstition was still a potent force within rural Ayrshire culture, with fear of the Devil and his variegated troop from Hell commonplace. Had Burns not felt 'idle terrors' in his youthful wanderings near Alloway Kirk and had he not been steeped in its ghostly tales, his greatest epic poem, 'Tam o' Shanter', might never have been written. Burns had the natural fears and imagination of any young child.

It is arguably the case that the most enduring personality traits of the Burnes children, raised as they were in a patriarchal society, would have been ingrained by their father. William Burnes hailed from the Mearns in northeast Scotland and was an incomer to Ayrshire when he met Agnes Broun. He came into the world on 11 November 1721, at Clochnahill farm, situated between Drumlithie and Stonehaven. He was one of ten children born to his father Robert and mother Isabella (née Keith). As a young man, William turned his hand to gardening work and eventually moved to Edinburgh in 1747, where he spent at least two years working near the Meadows, in the south of the city. He moved to Dundonald, after obtaining gardening work from the Laird of Fairlie, then to Doonside, near Alloway, to work for a Mr Crawford.

It was while working at Doonholm that William leased seven and a half acres of land at Alloway from Dr William Ferguson, his landlord, where he built his 'clay biggin'. His plan to make the small feu of land into a market garden did not materialise and necessity forced him to keep working for Dr Ferguson, whose estate was at this time growing considerably. William married Agnes on 15 December 1757 and they moved into the new 'clay biggin'. William was 38 years of age when his first son was born, Agnes 11 years his junior. The young poet emerged into a family that was a union of Highland and Lowland cultures.

It has been suggested that William Burnes was very English in manners, education and speech. If this was indeed so, it was probably due to his itinerant experience. The upper strata of Scottish society were at this time shedding their Scots tongue, dispensing with 'Scotticisms' considered unfit for polite society. William Burnes would have retained his regional Mearns accent and phraseology among friends but would have been 'polite-spoken' to employers, in order that they would understand him. It is a truism of rural life that those who move away from the region of their upbringing often lose their accent in daily discourse (aping those they meet or work for) but are able to revert to their own dialect at ease. He may have appeared 'English' in his civil tongue, but the stories William Burnes passed on to his son about his family being in the 1715 Jacobite Rebellion tell us that he was very much a patriotic Scot.

The notion that his forefathers were involved in the Jacobite cause is often dismissed as a fanciful invention of the bard. James Mackay states in his biography, 'this was little more than a romantic notion, springing out of the erroneous supposition that his ancestors had suffered for the cause in the rebellion of 1715'.[3] Burns, who often let his head follow his heart, is often painted as over dramatic by his biographers – sometimes justifiably so. However, there is no good reason to doubt the poet's claim. The facts are plain. The feudal lords, the Keiths, the Earls of Marischal, forfeited their lands in 1715 and only had them restored in 1759. Burns' ancestors on his father's side rented land from them and, as was the custom, would have followed the landowner in the call to arms. These were times when the landlord was literally the lord of the land and when trouble flared it could be to the death. As the poet later wrote:

> My Fathers rented land of the noble Keiths of Marshal, and had the honour to share their fate . . . Those who dare welcome Ruin and shake hands with Infamy for what they sincerely believe to be the cause of their God or their King 'Brutus and Cassius are honourable men.' I mention this circumstance because it threw my father on the world at large; where after many years' wanderings and sojournings, he pickt up a pretty large quantity of Observation and Experience, to which I am indebted for most of my little pretensions to wisdom.
>
> I have met with few who understood 'Men, their manners and their ways' equal to him; but stubborn, ungainly Integrity, and headlong, ungovernable Irascibility are disqualifying circumstances: consequently I was born a very poor man's son.[4]

Here, he identifies two of the more colourful traits he inherited from William: 'stubborn, ungainly Integrity, and headlong, ungovernable Irascibility'. Burns, of course, did not inherit his taciturn father's reserve about expressing his views in public. The strongest traits of the father, for better or worse, were ingrained in the son.

The last major battle on British soil, at Culloden, in 1746, occurred only 13 years before the birth of Burns. The Jacobite cause was still taboo as a topic of public conversation for the poet's generation. Burns told Lady Winifred Maxwell Constable, whose own family suffered in the Jacobite cause, that his forefathers 'shook hands with Ruin for what they esteemed the cause of their King and their Country'.[5] Charles Edward Stuart, the Young Pretender, lived in exile in France from 1746 until his death in 1791. It was only when the Jacobite cause was a dead one that it began to be seen as a romantic symbol of Scotland's lost freedom, when in reality the Jacobite objective was to regain the British crown, not re-establish Scottish freedom. By Burns' time, those who lamented the Jacobite cause had no desire to see a return to kingship tyranny of any creed or colour.

It is clear that Burns loved his father and saw in him true nobility of mind. The role model of 'The Cotter's Saturday Night' is without doubt William: 'Then kneeling down to HEAVEN'S ETERNAL KING, / The Saint, the Father, and the Husband prays'. Most of his father's associates in Ayrshire were supporters and practitioners of the Presbyterian 'New Licht' faction, which held more liberal views than the extreme Calvinists. William took charge of religious education within his household. He is credited with writing a 'Manual of Religious Belief, in a Dialogue Between Father and Son', in which the father, emphasising New Licht values, responds to sceptical questions posed by his son.[6] The 'Auld Lichts' subscribed to the Westminster Confession of Faith and Calvin's contention that all people were depraved sinners from birth. They believed in predestination, that only those chosen by God, the Elect, would be saved. The poet's letters are peppered with biblical references, especially to the Book of Job, and the fundamental importance of the Bible to the development of his worldview is difficult to overestimate.

New Licht Presbyterian values helped to foster and nourish the emerging democratic sentiments of the young Robert. The view that all people are equal before God and no soul is more important than another, regardless of wealth and status in society, is integral to New Licht values: the contract or covenant between each individual and their God is seen as a direct relationship, not requiring mediation. These fundamental religious principles form the basis of many social criticisms Burns expressed in his poetry: in 'Address to the Unco Guid', for instance, the link between the human heart and God takes precedence over the role of the Church.

Brimming over with knowledge of the Bible and theological matters to such an extent that he could take on clerics in debate, Burns rushed in where angels feared to tread:

> Polemical divinity about this time was putting the country half-mad; and I, ambitious of shining in conversation parties on Sundays between sermons, funerals, &c., used in a few years more to puzzle Calvinism with so much heat and indiscretion that I raised a hue and cry of heresy against me which has not ceased to this hour.[7]

The Kirk Elders, who effectively policed the morals of rural Scotland, were scandalised when Burns privately circulated copies of 'Holy Willie's Prayer', mocking the hypocrisy of the Calvinist 'chosen'. This action

> alarmed the Kirk-Session so much that they held three several meetings to look over their holy artillery, if any of it was pointed against profane Rhymers. Unluckily for me, my idle wanderings led me, on another wide, point blank within the reach of their heaviest metal.[8]

To appreciate the poet's moral universe, it is essential to understand that he held a holistic worldview, perceiving everything as interrelated – morality, religion, God, nature, society and man.

Burns inherited from his father a disdain for the pursuit of wealth for its own end, an attitude which has sometimes been misrepresented as jealousy of wealth or bitter 'class' awareness. In fact, it was a sense of moral outrage at the gap between the privilege enjoyed by the higher echelons of society and the burdensome lot borne by the peasantry. In a letter of 1782 to Thomas Orr, a Kirkoswald friend, Burns wrote indignantly:

> To be rich & to be great are the grand concerns of this world's men, & to be sure if moderately pursued it is laudable; but where is it moderately pursued? the greater part of men grasp at riches as eagerly as if Poverty were but another word for Damnation & misery whereas I affirm that the man whose only wish is to become great & rich; whatever he may appear to be, or whatever he may pretend to be; at the bottom he is but a miserable wretch.[9]

The feudal order was essentially a caste system and the daily reality of the British peasantry in the eighteenth century was not far from slavery – workers in mines in Fife were actually called slaves. Burns described his own experience of working the stony, undrained land at Mount Oliphant and Lochlea as 'the unceasing moil of a galley-slave'.[10] Farm workers were often 'bonded' – meaning that they were owned by their employer for the duration of their contract and accommodated in a 'tied cottage'. The bonding of farm labourers continued, surprisingly, in Scotland into the early twentieth century.

During Burns' lifetime, 'cotters' – many farm labourers who worked seasonally and took on a few acres for their own subsistence – were driven from the larger farms by the advent of enclosures and 'improved' farming techniques. These 'Lowland Clearances', as our leading historian Tom Devine has argued, probably saw more people driven from the countryside in the south and west of Scotland than during the entire Highland Clearances.[11] Cotters were systematically eradicated from the rural countryside by estate factors, who terminated their leases and moved them on.

The odds against a major world poet emerging from the ranks of the downtrodden peasantry in eighteenth-century Scotland were considerable.

The peasants' role was to obey. To think for themselves would be regarded as going beyond their station. Supine obedience to social superiors was mandatory and it required to be signalled by bowing, scraping and forelock-tugging. But Robert Burns was a man whose genius could not be trammelled. He was a 'passionate egalitarian', as the literary critic David Daiches has remarked, and ritual shows of deference were innately repugnant to his values.[12]

It would take courage, conviction, strength of mind and, above all, confidence for a man of Burns' background to write on local and national affairs and step forward in public as a poet. Confidence stems from knowledge and ability, and poking a stick into the hornet's nest of orthodox Calvinist religion, or stirring up radical dissent against the establishment of his day, required knowing his subject chapter and verse.

The Jacobite and Covenanting traditions, fused together in the cultural inheritance Burns received from his parents, may suggest a unity of opposites but both remember and reverence people who laid down their lives for their beliefs and principles – whether for king and country, or for faith. The marriage of Highland and Lowland blood gave Burns a union of passions and historical connections fit for a national poet of Scotland.

2

Educating Rabbie: Of Vice and Virtue

It was a fortuitous choice for William Burnes to arrange for his sons and the children of four neighbouring families to have the services of a university-educated young teacher, John Murdoch, born in Ayr and a former pupil of Ayr Grammar School. (Robert and Gilbert had previously attended a school a mile or so from the clay biggin, run by a William Campbell.) In May 1765, Murdoch commenced as tutor at the Alloway 'school', a small building near the Burnes family home. His employers gave him board and lodgings by turn, and paid his wages.

Murdoch has been seen as a pedantic teacher, who was, in any case, not with the Burnes family long enough to have had a great influence over the young Burns. However, although he was employed for just over two years at Alloway, Murdoch's relationship with the Burns family continued for many years after he had left to take better-paid employment in Ayr. From there, he regularly sent books for his star pupil to read. He later recalled:

> My pupil, Robert Burns, was then between six and seven years of age . . . [He] and his younger brother Gilbert had been grounded a little in English before they were put under my care. They both made a rapid progress in reading, and a tolerable progress in writing. In reading, dividing words into syllables, spelling without book, parsing sentences, &c. Robert and Gilbert

> were generally at the upper end of the class, even when ranged with boys by far their seniors. The books most commonly used in the school were, the Spelling Book, the New Testament, the Bible, Masson's Collection of Prose and Verse and Fisher's English Grammar. They committed to memory the hymns, and other poems of that collection with uncommon facility. This facility was partly owing to the method pursued by their father and me in instructing them, which was, to make them thoroughly acquainted with the meaning of every word in each sentence that was to be committed to memory. By the by, this may be easier done, and at an earlier period, than is generally thought. As soon as they were capable of it, I taught them to turn verse into its natural prose order; and sometimes to substitute synonymous expressions for poetical words, and to supply all the ellipses. These, you know, are the means of knowing that the pupil understands the author.[1]

Well before the age of ten, under the intense and focused scrutiny of Murdoch, Robert was able to understand poetry and transcribe it into prose. The poetry of the age as taught by Murdoch was not the light verse of modern primary schools, but the heavy-duty, heady, serious poetry of major complex poets.

As Burns later wrote, 'I made an excellent English scholar, and against the years of ten or eleven, I was absolutely a Critic in substantives, verbs and particles'.[2] Arthur Masson's *Collection of Prose and Verse* includes many of the poets who were a seminal influence on the bard: Shakespeare, Milton, Thomson, Pope, Gray, Shenstone, Addison and Akenside. Such poets would never be taught to children so young nowadays. Burns' letters written in maturity are peppered liberally with quotations committed to memory from these works. Indeed, the fact he often quoted from these poets in his letters straight from memory suggests that he had more than an encyclopaedic knowledge of verse but also possessed a photographic memory for the poetry he enjoyed most. A love of words and especially of poetry was a predominant feature of the young Robert's passion for learning.

DeLancey Ferguson stresses that Burns had very few books when young, so was able to memorise much of what he read. In adulthood he could recall with fluency a host of quotations from these years.[3] Masson's compilation was so influential on Burns precisely because he went over and over it during his most impressionable youthful years, reading the book day and night. Its importance is broadly acknowledged but commentators rarely state why, or examine the book to analyse the true influence it had on the poet.

Within the pages of Masson is where Burns first met with the poetry of Joseph Addison. This experience fired his ambition to become a poet, as he outlines in his autobiographical letter to Dr Moore:

> The earliest thing of Composition that I recollect taking pleasure in was, The vision of Mirza and a hymn of Addison's beginning 'How are Thy servants Blest, O Lord!' I particularly remember one half-stanza which was music to my boyish ear
>
> 'For though in dreadful whirls we hung,
> High on the broken wave'
>
> – I met with these pieces in Masson's English Collection, one of my school-books.[4]

One of the key texts in Masson is Addison's 'A Letter from Italy to the Right Honourable Charles Lord Halifax', a poem whose theme is the protection of British liberty against corrupt, kingly intervention. In 1794, Burns quoted tellingly from Addison when he sent a letter containing a copy of 'Bruce's Address to his Troops at Bannockburn' ('Scots Wha Hae') to Captain Millar:

> O, Liberty –
> Thou mak'st the gloomy face of Nature gay,
> Giv'st beauty to the sun, & pleasure to the day![5]

It is no coincidence that Burns links the lines he wrote, as spoken by Robert de Bruce in 'Scots Wha Hae', with the lines of Addison. The language of 'A Letter from Italy to the Right Honourable Charles Lord Halifax' made a lasting impression. There are 20 quotes and references from Addison's writings in the poet's letters, including his best-known condemnation of corruption, *Cato, a Tragedy*.[6] Addison's libertarian sentiments and critique of corruption were formative influences. That said, Burns would never have achieved the fame he did had he written only English poetry, for it was when he encountered the Scots poetry of Robert Fergusson in his early twenties that his enthusiasm for his art burst its banks, as we shall see in a later chapter.

The poet's original copy of Masson is in the Birthplace Museum at Alloway, Ayrshire. The first study of its influence on Burns was made in a small booklet by a member of Peterhead Burns Club.[7] While Liam McIlvanney provides interesting commentary on the subject in *Burns: The Radical,* the shaping of Burns' language and attitudes through what he read and studied in Masson has not been fully analysed by biographers and it is important to address this here, in order to evaluate its significance in the detail it deserves.[8] So many of the values and ideals we associate with Burns can be traced to this one seminal school textbook.

There are three main groups of writing in Masson: fables, select poetry and classical oration from Rome and Greece. One of the fables, for example, in discussing order in society, condemns licentiousness, praises diligence and industry and holds up the ideal of 'the public weal' as the highest goal. Meritocracy is seen as a virtue and good citizenship is praised.

In the 'Twelve Caesars' section, it is repeatedly shown, through historical example, that it is the duty of the people to resist and remove any leader who has become tyrannical. Whether from corruption or excessive ambition, Nero, Domitian and Aulus Vitellius abused their position and used their privilege to become tyrants – and merited their fate. As McIlvanney remarks, there is an 'unequivocal endorsement of tyrannicide in Burns' school-reading book'.[9]

It is also demonstrated that kings may be virtuous and public-spirited, as exampled in the virtuous deeds of King Canute and King Alfred. Alfred is shown as a wise king, devoted to his people and prepared to behead judges who behaved corruptly, for his wisdom and for his devotion to the public. The core values taught in Masson are in the mould of Presbyterian libertarianism and blend with Covenanter beliefs, 'No King but Christ', unless, of course, the king is virtuous, principled and for the people.

The third fable in Masson would have appealed to the tenant farmer's son:

> Confidence went directly up to the great house which belonged to WEALTH, the Lord of the village: and without staying for a porter, intruded himself immediately into the innermost apartments where he found VICE and FOLLY well received before him . . . Diffidence, in the mean time, not daring to approach the great house, accepted an

> invitation from POVERTY: and entering the cottage found WISDOM and VIRTUE, who being repulsed by the landlord, retired hither.[10]

In the humble cottage, 'Diffidence' flourished and became 'MODESTY' while in the big house, 'Confidence' became 'IMPUDENCE'. With its moral that riches, or the craving for riches, corrupt, this fable was one of the texts Burns learned to read in his early schooling. Such moral inculcation often serves as the poet's later template when his satire hits at greed and avarice, sentiments which sometimes earned Burns the erroneous accusation of being jealous of wealth.

Also among the fables presented by Masson is the tale 'Alibaeus the Persian', which tells how the civic-minded, patriotic King Cha-Abbas becomes disgusted with the venal flattery he receives at court – a veneer of dishonesty, in his view. He travels, disguised, among the commoners, hoping to discover the real feelings of his people and to 'study that kind of men who are so much despised, but who yet seem to be the prop of human society': the poor. The king encounters Alibaeus, a young shepherd, who responds to his questions 'without sparing anyone in his answers'. Alibaeus, although uneducated, is the honest voice of the common people, whom the king has now realised to be virtuous and decent, not deserving to be looked down upon by his courtly throng. 'I see plainly,' he says, 'that nature is no less pleasing in the lowest than in the highest state of life.' Such sentiments would certainly have resonated with the young Burns and appear to be the precursor to the notion of the common people as the virtuous prop of society as presented in 'The Cotter's Saturday Night', 'The Twa' Dogs' and the poet's blast at court venality in 'A Dream', which caused consternation among readers in London because of its apparent disrespect to the king.[11]

A lifelong hero of Burns from classical times was Demosthenes, who was famed for his honest oratory skills in Athens. He first encountered Demosthenes in Masson in 'The Second Olynthian of Demosthenes'. Critical of the king of Macedonia's avidity for conquest, Demosthenes beseeches the Athenians to assist the Olynthians in their struggle against Philip's designs, remarking how much the public have suffered at the hands of 'Sycophants':

> We have been pestered up by a vile race of hypocrites and Sycophants, who dare not open their mouths till they have learnt their lessons, till

> they have servilely inquired what they shall say, what they shall propose, what they shall vote . . . in a word, advices publickly given, must first be whispered by some great man or minister, and you bespeak it as it were and prepare your own poison, how can it otherwise happen, but your debates must be corrupted, your counsels ineffectual, your reputation blasted, and disgrace accumulated upon disgrace, while those illustrious parasites flourish and prosper by their country's ruin.[12]

The final sentiment, the notion of leaders flourishing by the ruin of their country, is one Burns repeats several times in his letters during 1793–94 and first encountered in Masson.

The ancient more worthy leaders of Athens are then contrasted with the current, corrupt crew: they did not seek self-aggrandisement, their ambition was only for the public benefit and their 'honours, dignities' were 'disposed by the voice and favour of the people'. Such forthright favouring of honest plain-speaking over sycophantic venality finds eloquent voice in many of Burns' poems. In 'The Author's Earnest Cry and Prayer' he condemns the sell-out of 'Honourable Scotch Representatives to the House of Commons' to patronage and the bribe of post and pension, comparing them unfavourably with his childhood heroes, Demosthenes, whose oratorical skill, honesty, integrity and courage in speaking out in the face of danger made a deep impression on Burns.

Particularly in terms of shaping the poet's radical values, this may have been underestimated hitherto. Demosthenes' life bears a chilling parallel to that of Burns during the reactionary blast of the 1790s, when sedition laws were introduced to curb what could be said in public, outlawing open criticism of the government. A further part of Demosthenes' speech could readily apply to the time of Thomas Muir's trial for sedition in 1793:

> honest men dare not speak plain . . . for what freedom of speech can you expect, if while you honour with your protection, and encourage with your favour, such sycophants only as humour your fancy and flatter your inclinations, though never so contrary to your interests or your honour, the true patriot who has no other view but the public good shall be suspected and impeached and delivered up a sacrifice to the hatred and fury of the people.[13]

The duty of a 'true patriot' to stand up and speak for the greater good of the people is central to the views of Burns – it is in this sense of a patriot's duty he describes himself as 'the patriot bard' in 'The Cotter's Saturday Night' . The absence of such integrity among MPs made them a target for his satirical pen. Demosthenes goes on to ask, who would stand forth a friend to Rome, when he will be treated as an enemy? Burns himself in 1795 hoped a time was 'not far distant when a man may freely blame Billy Pitt' without being deemed 'an enemy to his Country'.[14] Within Burns' moral universe, Demosthenes was the ideal orator, statesman and patriot, a standard by whom to judge contemporary politicians.[15]

A further example of the influence of Masson's *Collection* on Burns is to be found in the story of the incorruptible senator, Fabritius. Shunning the offer of silver and gold, Fabritius considers his 'wealth' not in monetary terms but to be in his vocation as a senator and in his civic duty to Rome: 'I have a mind free from SELF-REPROACH and I have an HONEST FAME,' he says. Burns could easily have written such a line as his letters reveal and must surely have identified strongly with Fabritius. From the publication of the Kilmarnock Edition in 1786, Burns aspired to maintain his own 'HONEST FAME' in the same way Fabritius did.

Robert was, as his brother Gilbert noted, an avid reader from an early age. He borrowed the book of William Wallace's lifestory from 'the blacksmith that shod our horses'. As the poet recalled:

> The two first books I ever read in private, and which gave me more pleasure than any two books I ever read again, were, the life of Hannibal and the history of Sir William Wallace. Hannibal gave my young ideas such a turn that I used to strut in raptures up and down after the recruiting drum and bagpipe, and wish myself tall enough to be a soldier; while the story of Wallace poured a Scottish prejudice in my veins which will boil along there till the flood-gates of life shut in eternal rest.[16]

While most of the poet's early education was in the English language, his highly charged reaction to the tale of William Wallace's glorious struggle for Scottish freedom – his victories, his betrayal and defeat – shows his juvenile patriotism already rooted in a deep emotion that would never diminish.

DeLancey Ferguson refers to the 'stormy emotions that were his to the grave', referring to an anecdote recounted by John Murdoch about reading *Titus Andronicus* to the Burnes family.[17] During a particularly gory scene (a girl has her hands cut off and her tongue cut out), the children began to cry and demanded that Murdoch stop reading. The book had been intended as a present for the family but Robert had exclaimed in a burst of indignation that if he dared to leave the book, he would burn it. On another occasion, witnessing a young servant girl being unceremoniously ejected from her pew in church to make way for an aristocratic youth, Burns was outraged. He was without doubt a highly emotional young man with a burning sense of right and wrong.

Wrongs and injustices aroused passionate feelings, which often resulted in outbursts. The ready indignation of the poet is best understood in terms of the fundamental importance he sets on having a moral worldview, as he describes in one of his letters:

> There are not any first principles or component parts of the Human Mind, more truly radical than what is meant by, OUGHT, and OUGHT NOT; which all Mankind (a most respectable Suffrage!) have, for several thousand years, agreed are synonymous terms with Virtue, Vice. – But, except our Existence here, have a reference to an Existence hereafter, Virtue & Vice are words without a meaning.[18]

So much that we associate with Burns originates in Masson's *Collection*: this one school textbook was, in a sense, a mini liberal arts course that helped shape his sense of integrity (a trait inculcated by his father), his desire for honest fame, his criticism of corruption, his proclivity towards forthright expression of his views in public, his courage in representing the welfare of the people, his distrust of political ambition and his belief that it was a right to choose whether to praise or criticise kings.

The extracts of poetry in Masson served as models he emulated in style, diction and verse, until he found his own poetic voice, from mimicry to maturity. And while there are many strands of influence within the writings of Burns from earlier poets, one of the most profound was the verse of Joseph Addison. It was this main school textbook that served to shape Burns' values and writings, poetry and prose, probably more than any other he read. Encouraged greatly by his father, Burns was fortunate to have the services and enthusiastic spark of the young idealist Murdoch as his tutor. The special bond between pupil and teacher fuelled Robert's insatiable hunger for learning and his eagerness to shine. Murdoch, as we shall see, would return briefly in a few years to further enhance his star pupil's education. With Masson's textbook, Murdoch had laid the literary foundation upon which most of Burns' artistic skills were based, in both prose and poetry.

3

The Lochlie Years: From Village Rhymer to Public Speaker in Tarbolton

IN 1765, WILLIAM BURNES TOOK ON THE LEASE of Mount Oliphant farm some two miles southeast of Alloway. Provost Fergusson, for whom he worked as a gardener, had recently purchased Mount Oliphant. At a lease of £40 per annum, the farm was in a poor state, with only one steading building. Hilly, stony ground made it a difficult farm to work. The two eldest boys were compelled to labour with their father: childhood labour was a normal part of rural peasant life. Fergusson, in the style of the 'improving', innovative times, allocated £100 to stock the farm. This was a debt William was due to repay if he gave up the farm.

The family was unable to move to the new farmhouse until a year later in 1766. When they did move, the two eldest boys marched back and forth to Murdoch's Alloway school. After Murdoch moved to Ayr in 1768, William enrolled his eldest boys in Dalrymple Parish School to improve their writing and grammar. They went to the school at alternate times, Robert first, for a period, then Gilbert, but only when labour demands allowed. Education and work were an integral part of life and rarely separate experiences. Learning to work was part of learning how to live. At work or at home, the education of Robert and Gilbert continued, their father teaching them arithmetic by candlelight during the winter evenings.

In the summer of 1773, Murdoch was back in Ayr and William allowed Robert, now 14 years of age, to spend three weeks with his former tutor, who recalled:

> I told him, that as now he was pretty much master of the parts of speech, &c, I should like to teach him something of French pronunciation . . . immediately we attacked the French with great courage. Now, there was little else to be heard but the declension of nouns, the conjugation of verbs, &c. When walking together and even at meals, I was constantly telling him the names of different objects . . . he was hourly laying in a stock of words and sometimes little phrases. In short, he took such a pleasure in learning, and I in teaching, that it was difficult to say which of the two was most zealous in the business.[1]

This one-to-one tutoring was intense, day and night. As to how good a French tutor Murdoch was is difficult to tell. The poet was able to read French and his letters contain occasional French phrases. One of his heroes during his impressionable youth was the French Enlightenment author Jean Jacques Rousseau. In his 'Elegy On the Death of Robert Ruisseaux', Burns cleverly adapts the French word 'ruisseaux' (plural for streams, brooks or, in Scots, burns) to associate himself with the French author. Burns also read the works of Voltaire although it is not known if he did so in the original French.[2]

In January 1783, Burns wrote affectionately to Murdoch, who was then in London:

> You will wish to know what has been the result of all the pains of an indulgent father, and a masterly teacher; I have indeed, kept pretty clear of vicious habits; & in this respect I hope, my conduct will not disgrace the education I have gotten; but, as a man of the world, I am most miserably deficient . . . I seem to be one sent into the world, to see, and observe; and I very easily compound with the knave who tricks me of my money . . . In short, the joy of my heart is to 'Study men, their manners, and their ways;' and for this darling subject, I cheerfully sacrifice every other consideration . . .
>
> I forget that I am a poor, insignificant devil, unnoticed and unknown, stalking up and down fairs and markets when I happen to be in them,

> reading a page or two of mankind, and 'catching the manners living as they rise' . . .[3]

In the long winter nights, reading, conversation and song were the main leisure pursuits of the eldest boys. Gilbert later commented, 'we rarely saw anybody but the members of our own family' while at Mount Oliphant.[4] Gilbert wrote of the family hardship:

> To the buffetings of misfortune we could only oppose hard labour and the most rigid economy. We lived very sparingly. For several years butchers' meat was a stranger in the house, while all the members of the family exerted themselves to the utmost of their strength, and rather beyond it, in the labours of the farm . . . to think of our father growing old (for he was now about fifty) broken down with the long continued fatigues of his life . . . these reflections produced in my brother's mind and mine sensations of the deepest distress.[5]

Work on the farm was often backbreaking. Draining muddy land on a wet, windy day, fingers numb with cold, could not be farther from the idyll presented in the Kailyard myth of Burns' life. Ploughing stony land, and feeling the shudder and shock run up through hands and arms each time the plough hit a large stone was not an enjoyable experience, as Burns later recalled:

> We lived very poorly; I was a dextrous Ploughman for my years; and the next eldest to me was a brother, who could drive the plough very well and help me to thrash. – A Novel-Writer might perhaps have viewed these scenes with some satisfaction, but so did not I . . .[6]

No amount of hard work guaranteed the farm would be profitable. It could take years to cultivate the land and make it fertile. Even with a healthy crop in prospect, there was always the risk that inclement weather might destroy the harvest. While they worked together, William would engage his sons in conversation and test their knowledge on various subjects. Engrossed as the adolescent Robert's physical energies were in work, his thoughts often wandered to literary ideas stimulated by his reading habits.

It was during harvest, in his sixteenth year, 'a little before which period

I first committed the sin of RHYME', that Burns had his first experience of 'love', a state of innocent rapture which intoxicated his entire being. He later wrote:

> You know our country custom of coupling a man and woman together as Partners in the labors of Harvest. – In my fifteenth autumn, my Partner was a bewitching creature who just counted an autumn less . . . she altogether unwittingly to herself, initiated me in a certain delicious Passion . . . I did not well know myself, why I liked so much to loiter behind with her, when returning in the evening from our labors; why the tones of her voice made my heartstrings thrill like an Eolian harp; and particularly, why my pulse beat such a furious ratann when I looked and fingered over her hand, to pick out the nettle-stings and thistles. – Among her other love-inspiring qualifications, she sung sweetly; and 'twas her favorite reel to which I attempted giving an embodied vehicle in rhyme . . .
>
> Thus with me began Love and Poesy; which at times have been my only, and till within this last twelvemonth have been my highest enjoyment.[7]

The song, his first in the genre of matching Scots tunes to heart-melting lyrics, was 'Handsome Nell' (to the tune 'I Am a Man Unmarried'), its heroine was Nellie Kilpatrick. Burns copied it into his First Commonplace Book. Murdoch could not have been more wrong in thinking that Burns did not have much of an ear for music. Much of Burns' lyrical juvenilia penned over the next few years formed the raw material he used for the Kilmarnock Edition.

William sent Robert to the parish school of Kirkoswald in the summer of 1775. The headmaster, Hugh Rodger, was a well-reputed teacher of mathematics. The exact duration of the stay is not known. During this period Robert lodged with his uncle, Sam Brown, a farm labourer at Ballochniel farm near Kirkoswald. It was a far cry from the isolated life he was used to at Mount Oliphant and he made the most of the opportunity to socialise and observe:

> I spent my seventeenth summer on a smuggling coast a good distance from home at a noted school, to learn Mensuration, Surveying, Dialling, &c. in which I made a pretty good progress. But I made greater progress

> in the knowledge of mankind. – The contraband trade was at that time very successful; scenes of swaggering riot and roaring dissipation were as yet new to me; and I was no enemy to social life. – Here, though I learned to look unconcernedly on a large tavern-bill, and mix without fear in a drunken squabble, yet I went on with a high hand in my Geometry; till the sun entered Virgo, a month which is always a carnival in my bosom, a charming Fillette who lived next door to the school overset my Trigonometry and set me off in a tangent from the sphere of my studies. – I struggled on with my Sines and Co-sines for a few days more; but stepping out to the garden one charming noon, to take the sun's altitude, I met with my Angel,
>
> *Like Proserpine gathering flowers,*
> *Herself a fairer flower.*
>
> It was vain to think of doing any more good at school . . . I did nothing but craze the faculties of my soul about her, or steal out to meet with her; and the two last nights of my stay in the country, had sleep been a mortal sin, I was innocent.[8]

The charming 'fillette' was Peggy Thomson. He affectionately presented a copy of the Kilmarnock Edition to her in later years with a verse inscribed, referring to her as the 'Sweet early object of my youthful vows'.

The bustling trade in smuggling along the Carrick shore and its spoils fascinated Burns. It was in Kirkoswald area that he first experienced the temptations of alcohol and, no longer under his father's disciplinarian eye, was able to associate more with the opposite sex. Even so, it appears that romance with the lassies was kept strictly within moral bounds in his late teens. As Burns would find out first-hand before too long, the 'sin' of sexual intercourse brought social shame and disgrace to the individuals involved and to their families. From the evidence of his letters, it would appear that he was a virgin until his late teens, if not into his early twenties. This, of course, does not square with the reputation posterity has given him.

Kirkoswald is best known for its association with characters from 'Tam o' Shanter'; Souter Johnnie's house is still there today, and it was while at Kirkoswald that Burns visited the Shanter farm. It was also there that he met William Niven; his letters to Niven, which date from 1780 onwards, are his earliest on record. In them, Burns pursues a variety of heady philosophical topics: he discusses the 'human soul' and how 'Pride' can be a virtue if combined with honesty but how, when mixed with other more selfish motives '& disingenuous inclinations, it enters largely into the composition of many vices'.[9] These early letters show a keenly observant, studious young man finding his way in the world, rationalising his experience against the register of values and principles inculcated during his upbringing.

Burns' experience at Kirkoswald boosted his confidence and fuelled his motivation for self-education:

> I returned home very considerably improved. – My reading was enlarged with the very important addition of Thomson's and Shenstone's works; I had seen mankind in a new phasis; and I engaged several of my schoolfellows to keep up a literary correspondence with me. – This last helped me much in composition. I had met with a collection of letters by the Wits of Queen Ann's reign, and I pored over them most devoutly. – I kept copies of any of my own letters that pleased me, and a comparison between them and the composition of most of my correspondents flattered my vanity.[10]

Thomas Orr, whom Burns met at Hugh Rodger's school, was one of his first literary correspondents, along with Niven. Not only did Burns size himself up against his peers. A story is told that he took Rodger on in debate one lunchtime and that his oratory won the class over.

He continued to read voraciously, as he recounted in his autobiographical letter to Dr Moore:

> My knowledge of ancient story was gathered from Salmon's and Guthrie's geographical grammars; my knowledge of modern manners, and of literature and criticism, I got from the Spectator. – These, with Pope's works, some plays of Shakespear, Tull and Dickson on Agriculture, The Pantheon, Locke's Essay on the human understanding, Stackhouse's history of the bible . . . Boyle's lectures, Allan Ramsay's works, Taylor's scripture doctrine of original sin, a select Collection of English songs, and Hervey's meditations had been the extent of my reading. – The Collection of Songs was my vade mecum. I pored over them, driving my cart or walking to labor . . . carefully noting the true tender or sublime from affectation and fustian. – I am convinced I owe much to this for my critic-craft such as it is.[11]

He carried his pocket Milton with him everywhere and read it so much it fell apart. Bookishness was by now part of his personality and image. Burns was constantly absorbed in harvesting ideas, images, stories, legends and storing poetry and phrases he liked or could adapt. He may have been an introvert in bookish learning but he was also an extrovert in social behaviour, all the while watching, learning and taking notes about human nature and experience – and enjoying the company of the fairer sex:

> In my seventeenth year, to give my manners a brush, I went to a country dancing school. – My father had an unaccountable antipathy against these meetings; and my going was, what to this hour I repent, in absolute defiance of his commands. – My father, as I said before, was the sport of strong passions: from that instance of rebellion he took a kind of dislike to me, which, I believe was one cause of that dissipation which marked my future years. – I only say, Dissipation, comparative with the strictness and sobriety of Presbyterian country life; for though the will-o'-wisp meteors of thoughtless Whim were almost the sole lights of my path, yet early ingrained Piety and Virtue never failed to point me out the line of Innocence.[12]

This streak of rebelliousness against his strict father's 'strong passions' appears to have changed William's mind on the topic of dancing – Gilbert records that he and his sisters were permitted to go the following month. The poet's definition of 'Dissipation' meant consuming any alcohol whatsoever. A bottle of claret between two would have been dissipation to the young Burns, given the strictness of his religious father.

In 1776, Provost Fergusson died and his estate was broken up among his daughters. Having been on amiable terms with his former landlord, William Burnes now had to contend with the scourge of tenant farmers: the 'factor' (generally a lawyer acting on behalf of the landowner):

> My father's generous Master died; the farm proved a ruinous bargain; and, to clench the curse, we fell into the hands of a Factor who sat for the picture I have drawn of one in my Tale of two dogs . . .
>
> My indignation yet boils at the recollection of the scoundrel tyrant's insolent, threatening epistles, which used to set us all in tears.[13]

In 'The Twa Dogs', Burns sketches the 'factor' as villain:

> Poor tenant bodies, scant o' cash,
> How they maun thole a *Factor*'s snash.
> He'll stamp an' threaten, curse an' swear
> He'll *apprehend* them, *poind* their gear;
> While they maun staun', wi' aspect humble,
> An' hear it a', an' fear and tremble!

Evictions were commonplace during the eighteenth century. For William Burnes his days of dealing with a landlord who was sympathetic to the difficulties of tenant farming were over.

Burns later wrote to his cousin in Montrose about the lot of tenant farmers in Ayrshire:

> Farming is also at a very low ebb with us. Our lands, generally speaking, are mountainous & barren; and our Landholders, full of ideas of farming gathered from the English, and the Lothians and other rich soils in Scotland; make no allowance for the odds of the quality of land, and consequently stretch us much beyond what, in the event, we will be found able to pay. We are also much at a loss for want of proper methods in our improvements of farming: necessity compels us to leave our old schemes; & few of us have opportunities of being well informed in new ones.[14]

William's next move, in 1777, is somewhat puzzling, given his struggles at Mount Oliphant on a rent that had risen to £45. He took on the 130-acre Lochlie farm, which he must have believed to have some real potential, agreeing to pay £130 per annum (20 old shillings per acre, or £1 per acre) to his new landlord, David McClure. William obtained some funding from McClure to stock the farm. Lochlie is situated to the northeast of Tarbolton and just over three miles northwest of Mauchline. While these small, thriving market villages were to play a significant part in the poet's life and light up in his poetry, the farm proved ruinous and hastened William to an early death. Burns comments on the transition from Mount Oliphant to Lochlie:

> My father struggled on till he reached the freedom in his lease, when he entered on a larger farm about ten miles farther in the country. – The nature of the bargain was such as to throw a little ready money in his hand at the commencement, otherwise the affair would have been impractible. – For four years we lived comfortably here; but a lawsuit between him and his Landlord commencing, after three years tossing and whirling in the vortex of Litigation, my father was just saved from absorption in a jail by phthisical consumption, which after two years promises, kindly stept in and snatch'd him away – 'To where the wicked cease from troubling, and where the weary be at rest'.[15]

The litigation over the farm ended up in the Court of Session. In short, William's landlord fell into financial problems following the collapse of a local bank and in 1781 tried to extract more rent than was due from the Burnes family. Denying there had ever been a written agreement specifying how much could be offset against improvements to the boggy land of Lochlie, McClure demanded around £500 back rent, which William refused to pay. Doggedly determined, principled, honest and independently minded, William stood his ground and eventually paid less than half of his exploitative landlord's demands. However, being under the yoke of legal visitation and local shame broke William's spirit and ageing body; 'Misfortune's undeserved blow' and 'legal rage' had beaten him 'low'.[16] The experience profoundly scarred Robert, implanting a deep-seated fear of a debtors' jail.

It is highly regrettable that the character of William Burnes has been maliciously stained by some nineteenth-century biographers of his son, who, after condemning the so-called failings of the poet, sourced them genetically to the father and blamed him as the wrongdoer in the litigation with McClure. Alexander Peterkin, in his 1816 reprint of Currie's edition of Burns' *Works*, writes bitterly of a particularly mendacious 'life' by an alleged friend of the poet, Mr Walker of Perth:

> No better illustration can be given of this unsatisfactory style of biography, than the 'suspicion' which is excited against the unspotted worth of William Burnes, the poet's father. We are instructed . . . that the misfortunes of that worthy man must probably have arisen from some radical defect in his own character . . . How silly and cruel are such insinuations? . . . We have known individuals possessing every quality that we can conceive of

> human worth, destined, like William Burnes, to drink deeply in the cup of affliction – to struggle through life with poverty and disappointment and sorrow; and to descend, like him, into the grave with few other consolations than the prospects beyond it . . . He had not money: that was his defect. And the want of capital alone fettered him to all the disasters which he experienced in his affectionate anxiety to keep his family around him in their tender years.[17]

It was the tenacious determination of William that finally saw the litigation settled in his favour but the price of being put through this hell was that he would not live to witness his son's rise to fame. Although the eldest of a growing family and a determined worker – 'At the plough, scythe or reap-hook I feared no competitor, and set Want at defiance' – Burns was free of financial responsibility for the family; these, his patriarchal father carried.

It was in Tarbolton and Mauchline that Burns began to gain a reputation as a rebel, who spoke his mind on topics generally outwith the usual ken of most tenant farmers' sons:

> I saw my father's situation entailed on me perpetual labor. – The only two doors by which I could enter the fields of fortune were, the most niggardly economy, or the little chicaning art of bargain-making: the first is so contracted an aperture, I never could squeeze myself into it; the last, I always hated the contamination of the threshold. – Thus, abandoned of aim or view in life; with a strong appetite for sociability, as well from native hilarity as from a pride of observation and remark; a constitutional hypochondriac taint which made me fly solitude; add to all these incentives to social life, my reputation for bookish knowledge, a certain wild, logical talent, and a strength of thought something like the rudiments of good sense, made me generally a welcome guest; so 'tis no great wonder that always 'where two or three were met together, there was I in the midst of them'.[18]

His 'wild, logical talent' and confidence in his own views made him a leader among his peers and a controversial troublemaker to many of the more reactionary Auld Lichts pillars of rural society.

In 1780, Burns formed the Tarbolton Batchelors' Club, a social club and debating society for young men.[19] Among the inaugural members were Gilbert Burns, Walter Mitchell, Thomas Wright, William McGavin, Hugh Reid and Alexander Brown. Over the next few years the club thrived and new members enrolled, including Matthew and his brother James Patterson, John Orr and David Sillar. Burns' hand is certainly in the rules which bar membership to any

> haughty, self-conceited person, who looks upon himself as superior to the rest of the club, and especially no mean-spirited, worldly mortal, whose only will is to heap up money, shall on any pretense whatever be admitted.

Debating various subjects, such as the benefits of a good education compared to an average education, Burns was in his element. The variety of topics allowed him the stage he craved to develop his skills as an orator – already begun in Kirkoswald – to build his confidence and leadership skills, and drink in the applause.

A previously uncollected quatrain introducing the Batchelors' Club, identified as being in the poet's handwriting, was found among papers passed on to Dr James Currie, the poet's first biographer:

> Of birth or blood we do not boast
> Nor Gentry does our club afford;
> But ploughmen and mechanics we
> In Nature's simple dress record.[20]

It is unlikely that Burns would have copied such mediocre lines from elsewhere; they are in all probability his own work, although they have never featured among his collected poetry.

In the same room where the Batchelors' Club met, on 4 July 1781, Burns joined his local Masonic group as an apprentice member, at the St David's Tarbolton Lodge, paying a joining fee of 12s 6d. He was, in Masonic language, 'passed and raised' on 1 October 1781. The following year in June, a breakaway group reformed themselves into the St James's Lodge, Tarbolton, which had been the original name of the Lodge when it was set up in 1771. In November 1782, Burns wrote to the Master of the Lodge, Sir John Whitefoord, concerned at the disarray of the lodge's financial status and sought to remedy the situation, stressing the importance to members 'who are of the lower orders of mankind, to have a fund in view on which we may with certainty depend to be kept from want should we be in circumstances of distress or old age'.[21] Sir John, a local agricultural improver, was one of the first aristocrats Burns met and an intimate friend of James, Earl of Glencairn, who was to play a pivotal role in the success of the Edinburgh Edition.

On 27 July 1784, Burns was made Depute Master of the St James's Lodge. Here too was another platform for his oratorical skills in discussion and debate which enhanced his self-confidence in public speaking. Rising through the ranks of the Masonic movement eventually opened doors for his poetic career. Burns' Masonic connections, as we shall see, played a considerable role in the success of the Kilmarnock Edition in 1786. Burns continued as an active Mason during his last years in Dumfries where he was elected Senior Warden of the St Andrew's Lodge on 30 November, 1792.[22] The Masonic movement was radical in the sense that it allowed men of all ranks to meet quite literally on one level, where they were, for meetings at least, on equal terms as 'brothers'; those with ability and oratory skills such as Burns were often rewarded on merit with promotion. As a movement it possessed a social fraternity and fluidity between classes that the feudal order did not.

Burns has immortalised many of the close friends he made in this period. These include David Sillar, who joined the Batchelors' Club a year after its inauguration. Celebrating genuine friendship is a common motif throughout the poetry of Burns and, in 'Epistle to Davie, a Brother Poet', his radical contempt for rank is already evident in stanza five:

It's no in titles nor in rank:
    It's no in wealth like *Lon'on* Bank,
To purchase peace and rest.
It's no in makin muckle, mair:
It's no in books, it's no in Lear,
To make us truly blest:
If happiness hae not her seat
    An' centre in the breast,
We may be wise, or *rich*, or *great*,

But never can be *blest*:
Nae treasures nor pleasures
Could make us happy lang;
The *heart* ay's the part ay
That makes us right or wrang.

At this period, Sillar shared relative deprivation with Burns. He went on to have a mixed career: a failed teacher, he eventually inherited the family farm, Spittleside, Tarbolton, and died a rich Irvine magistrate. A competent fiddler and composer – he wrote the music to Burns' 'The Rosebud' – he published his own mediocre *Poems* at Kilmarnock in 1789. Sillar has left a fascinating description of Burns, which reveals his growing, almost swashbuckling confidence. Although not yet known widely as a poet, he was evidently keen to be seen as the sophisticated local intellectual:

> He wore the only tied hair in the parish; and in the church, his plaid, which was of a particular colour, I think *fillemot*, he wrapped in a particular manner round his shoulders. These surmises and his exterior, had such a magical influence on my curiosity as made me particularly solicitous of his acquaintance . . . we frequently met at Sundays at church, when, between sermons, instead of going with our friends or lassies to the Inn, we often took a walk in the fields.[23]

Sillar goes on to observe that, however fascinating their conversation, it always ended abruptly if they encountered a member of the opposite sex. Like any young man, Burns was not always successful in his amours. Gilbert states that in their seven years at Lochlie, he never once saw his brother drunk and that, in relation to women, Burns' conduct never deviated from 'the strictest rules of virtue and modesty' until 'his 23rd year'.

In 1781, Burns courted Ellison Begbie, the heroine of his song 'On Cessnock Banks a Lassie Dwells'. A handful of his letters are addressed to her under the heading 'Dear E'. Ellison (or Allison) Begbie was a farmer's daughter from Galston, Ayrshire.[24] (The letters were once erroneously believed to have been written to an Elizabeth Gebbie, who went on to marry a Hugh Brown.) These letters, which DeLancey Ferguson also believed to be to Begbie in his 1931 edition of the poet's letters, abound with high moral language and wooden clichés such as 'the love

I have for you is founded on the sacred principles of virtue and honor'. Burns made a proposal of marriage to her and refers to her jilting him in his autobiographical letter 'a belle-fille whom I adored and who had pledged her soul to meet me in the field of matrimony, jilted me with peculiar circumstances of mortification'.[25] The letters are devoid of the mature eloquence of his later compositions to Agnes McLehose. Although attracted to the opposite sex with a glint in his eyes, Burns seems to have been a rather dreamy, serious, romantic young man looking for marriage.

Poetry and love were his twin passions:

> My life flowed on much in the same tenor till my twenty-third year. – Vive l'amour et vive la bagatelle, were my sole principles of action. – The addition of two more Authors to my library gave me great pleasure; Sterne and Mckenzie. – Tristram Shandy and The Man of Feeling were my bosom favorites. – Poesy was still a darling walk for my mind, but 'twas only the humour of the hour . . . My Passions when once they were lighted up, raged like so many devils, till they got vent in rhyme; and then conning over my verses, like a spell, soothed all into quiet.[26]

Here Burns gives an insight into his peculiar 'rhyming mania': how he let the creative energies of his imagination possess him when he was composing poetry.

Gilbert Burns mentions that he and Robert tried their hand at growing and dressing flax, having sub-leased around three acres of land at Lochlie from their father.[27] In doing so Robert began to see a way out of farming:

> Partly thro' whim, and partly that I wished to set about doing something in life, I joined with a flax-dresser in a neighbouring town, to learn his trade and carry on the business of manufacturing and retailing flax. – This turned out a sadly unlucky affair. – My Partner was a scoundrel of the first water who made money by the mystery of thieving; and to finish the whole, while we were given a welcoming carousal to the New year, our shop, by the drunken carelessness of my Partner's wife, took fire and was burnt to ashes; and left me like a true Poet, not worth sixpence . . .[28]

The flax partner is supposed to have been Alexander Peacock and the clumsy fire-raiser, his wife, Sarah. Burns stayed in the loft of the flax shop for several months then found better lodgings near the town centre in the Vennel. Flax-dressing was no easy task. The flax seed or flower destined to be processed into oil had to be separated from the main plant, then the stalks were stripped and treated and the fibres were separated with a heckling comb so that they could be spun into yarn. It was laborious, dusty work and flax-dressing shops tended to suffer a higher rate of accidental fire damage than most workplaces. After the notorious fire, Burns stayed on in Irvine until around March 1782.

In the late autumn of 1781, he became unwell. The illness was acute enough to require five visits in eight days from Dr Charles Fleeming. Biographers have speculated on the nature of this illness. Smallpox, malaria and typhoid have all been postulated and dismissed. Whatever his diagnosis, Dr Fleeming prescribed a combination of medicines, which appear to have been effective. He administered ipecacuanha and 'sacred elixir' – the former, a South African root powdered for emetic purposes and the latter, a laxative derived from aloes and rhubarb. During his last visits, Fleeming gave Burns an opiate painkiller to lower his fever – cinchona, a powdered alkaloid from an Andes evergreen bark. If it was rheumatic heart disease that eventually killed Burns, was this the episode of rheumatic fever which precipitated that condition?

At Irvine, Burns met Captain Richard Brown who was six years older than the poet; the two young men formed a 'bosom-friendship'.

> He was the son of a plain mechanic; but a great Man in the neighbourhood taking him under his patronage gave him a genteel education with a view to bettering his situation in life. – The Patron dieing . . . the poor fellow in despair went to sea; where after a variety of good and bad fortune . . .
>
> This gentleman's mind was fraught with courage, independance, Magnanimity, and every noble, manly virtue. – I loved him, I admired him, to a degree of enthusiasm; and I strove to imitate him . . . His knowledge of the world was vastly superiour to mine, and I was all attention to learn. He was the only man I ever saw who was a greater fool than myself when WOMAN was the presiding star; but he spoke of a certain fashionable failing with levity, which hitherto I had regarded with horror. – Here his friendship did me a mischief; and the consequence was, that soon after I resumed the plough, I wrote the WELCOME inclosed.[29]

It would appear that Brown, who was the first person to urge Burns to get his poems into print, also advised the would-be Lothario to get beyond verbal romancing and give the lassies what they wanted, and to hell with the consequences. In other words, he set about initiating Burns into the world of the predatory male.

The two young men often went for walks in the local Eglinton Woods, which according to local legend had been visited by Sir William Wallace. To a patriotic Scot like Burns, places such as a woodland where William Wallace had walked, or the bore stone at Bannockburn marking the victory of King Robert de Bruce were sacred places and inspired the powerful emotional bond which inspired some of his best work.

The poet's father had visited him at Irvine during his illness. From the morbid tone of the only surviving letter from son to father, dated 27 December 1781, it appears that Burns was then in the grip of a severely debilitating depression:

> My principal, and indeed my only pleasurable employment is looking backwards & forwards in a moral & religious way – I am quite transported at the thought that ere long, perhaps very soon, I shall bid an eternal adieu to all the pains, & uneasiness & disquietudes of this weary life; for I assure you I am heartily tired of it, and, if I do not very much deceive myself I could contentedly & gladly resign it . . .
>
> I foresee that very probably Poverty & Obscurity await me & I am, in some measure prepared & daily preparing to meet and welcome them. I have but just time & paper to return you my grateful thanks for the many Lessons of Virtue & Piety you have given me . . . I am Honoured Sir, your dutiful son, Rob't Burns.[30]

The most death-obsessed verse Burns ever wrote dated to his stay in Irvine, or not long afterwards. Mackay may indeed be right to suggest that what the poet went through was a type of nervous breakdown; his physical illness certainly seems to have contributed to an anxiety neurosis.

However, Burns arrived back at Lochlie to find that McClure had obtained an injunction against his father, which resulted in an audit of William's possessions and the townspeople of Tarbolton being warned not to buy his goods or stock. It was an unjust public shaming the family simply had to live through, the family name tarred and feathered for what was essentially McClure's financial loss and chicanery.

Burns lost 'the best of fathers' on 13 February 1784 and William Burnes was taken back to Alloway to be buried. His son's lines on him, printed in the Kilmarnock Edition, are etched on his headstone, beginning, 'O ye whose cheek the tear of pity stains'. Burns uses a direct quote from Goldsmith's *The Deserted Village* in the final line: 'ev'n his failings lean'd to Virtue's side'. Some editions of the *Complete Works* drop Burns' own footnotes and quotation marks, making it appear that the final line is his.

One of the best songs from Burns' early period is 'My Father Was a Farmer', a eulogy to William Burnes. Two sample verses illustrate the values passed on from father to son:

> My father was a farmer upon the Carrick border, O,
> And carefully he bred me in decency and order, O;
> He bade me act a manly part, though I had ne'er a farthing, O;
> For without an honest manly heart, no man was worth regarding, O.
> . . .
> All you who follow wealth and power with unremitting ardour, O,
> The more in this you look for bliss, you leave your view the farther, O:
> Had you the wealth Potosi boasts, or nations to adore you, O,
> A cheerful honest-hearted clown I will prefer before you, O.

This song conveys the honestly held sentiment that there is an innate worth to the common peasantry – a motif which runs through all his poetry.

Dr John MacKenzie, who attended William Burnes, eventually became a family friend and a confidant of the poet. According to MacKenzie, Robert and Gilbert 'both possessed great abilities, and uncommon information', Gilbert being the more approachable, talkative brother. When MacKenzie first met them, Robert, at first, sat sullenly in a dark corner of the room, watching him with a 'distant, suspicious' glower. His habit of 'observing men and their manners' may have made some feel a little ill at ease but it was not until Burns was sure of someone that he would freely engage in conversation. 'I frequently detected him scrutinising me,' MacKenzie commented. He soon warmed to Burns, impressed by his 'dexterity of reasoning and ingenuity of reflection':

> I took a lively interest in Robert Burns, and before I was acquainted with his poetical power, I perceived that he possessed very great mental abilities, an uncommon, fertile and lively imagination, a thorough acquaintance with many of our Scottish poets, and an enthusiastic admiration of Ramsay and Fergusson. I have always thought that no person could have a just idea of the extent of Burns' talents who had not an opportunity to hear him converse. His discrimination of character was great beyond that of any person I ever knew.[31]

It was MacKenzie who personally introduced Burns to Sir John Whitefoord, whom Burns had only known as a fellow Mason and not as a friend. MacKenzie is also reputed to have introduced him to Professor Hugh Blair of Edinburgh University, who would later pave the way for Burns to display his talents amongst Scottish academics in the capital in 1786–87. It was also MacKenzie who, in a time of crisis, provided a hiding place for Burns and Jean Armour a few years later, when their relationship was in turmoil. Hence, the family doctor was an important part in the chain of connections that led to the poet's success.

Britain's war against America in the Wars of Independence brought economic chaos to the west coast of Scotland, as Burns describes to his Montrose cousin James Burness:

> This country, till of late, was flourishing incredibly in the Manufactures of Silk, Lawn & Carpet Weaving, and we are still carrying on a good deal in that way but much reduced from what it was; we had also a fine trade in the Shoe way, but now entirely ruined & hundreds driven to a starving condition on account of it . . . In short, my dear Sir, since the unfortunate beginning of this American war, & its as unfortunate conclusion, this country has been, & still is decaying very fast.[32]

Parochial self-interest did not deter Burns from supporting the American settlers and one of his earliest known radical songs, probably written in 1784, is his 'Ballad on the American War', sometimes known as 'When Guilford Good', which he kept out of the Kilmarnock Edition but, daringly, brought into print in the Edinburgh Edition of 1787. 'Ballad on the American War' is remarkable for its condensed narrative of events. In nine stanzas, starting with the Boston Tea Party, this shrewd, provocative ballad records the genesis of the war, highlights the politically significant campaigns – including places and military names – and the disruption provoked in British politics by the loss of America. With this work, Burns graduates from regional Ayrshire poet and becomes a player in the more dangerous macrocosm of British politics. The key figures in the ballad, leading politicians and soldiers of the era, include General Gage, Charles Cornwallis, Charles James Fox, William Pitt the Younger and Henry Dundas. To bring such personages before the bar of vernacular Scots and treat them without deference was a risky step. Henry Dundas was certainly none too pleased to be caricatured as 'slee' (sly), nor was the comment that Pitt's Whig opponents had 'Gowff'd Willie like a ba', man' likely to make Burns friends in high places. This ballad reveals that Burns was already an expert in transmuting material from national newspaper reports into poetry. The satirical provocative song brings the great and the good in British politics to the level of ordinary people.

It was not long before his father's death that Burns first encountered Fergusson's poetry and 'strung anew' his 'wildly-sounding, rustic lyre with emulating vigour'.[33] Already soaked in the *oeuvre* of the English poets, Burns was now under the spell of Fergusson, whose influence triggered the burst of creativity which would catapult him from regional bard to national and international fame. The realisation that Scots could be used for high literary art was one that changed his life.

[illegible]

[illegible]

[illegible]

Part Two

From Tenant Farmer to Literary Fame

4

Mossgiel Farm: The Ram-stam Boy under the Influence of Robert Fergusson

Farm labour may have occupied his days, but Burns' mind was now elsewhere, focused on his new-found hero, Robert Fergusson. In Fergusson's rich Scots verse, he recognised the language of his own heart. He saw that his passionate feelings for his country, his zest for people and events – his sense of who and what he was – could now be fully expressed in his natural voice.

After their father's death, Burns became the family's chief breadwinner, although Gilbert was more the natural farmer and well capable of taking responsibilities on his shoulders; he was also the sounding board for most of his brother's new compositions. Their next move, to Mossgiel farm, had been prompted by their father's warning to prepare for the worst. Robert and Gilbert had signed the lease the previous Martinmas. Mossgiel, 118 acres, leased at £90 per year, lay about two miles southeast of Lochlie, in the adjacent parish of Mauchline. Mossgiel also had a lot of clay-sealed soil and was in a poor state of drainage. Crucial in the decision to move there was the fact that it was owned by a family friend, local lawyer Gavin Hamilton – an ally who might give them some flexibility in hard times – and there would be no factor to deal with. Hamilton, who had advised William through the litigation, was a liberal-minded adherent of the New Licht religious faction and, like Burns, a Freemason.

Burns took his responsibilities as head of the family seriously. But although he had no fear of hard work, the first years at the new farm were not a success:

> I entered on the farm with a full resolution, 'Come, go to, I will be wise!' I read farming books; I calculated crops; I attended markets; and in short, in spite of 'The devil, the world and the flesh,' I believe I would have been a wise man; but the first year from unfortunately buying in bad seed, the second from a late harvest, we lost half of both our crops; this overset all my wisdom, and I returned 'Like the dog to his vomit, and the sow that was washed to her wallowing in the mire.'[1]

Daily work on the farm provided a fertile area for ideas Burns could turn into poetry. A poem based on actual events, 'The Death and Dying Words of Poor Mailie, the Author's Only Pet Yowe: an Unco Mournfu' Tale' is one of his first works in Scots.[2] In the poem, Mailie dies but in reality was saved by the poet and Gilbert, after the herdsman from the neighbouring farm, Hughoc, informed them that the yowe had been strangled by its own tether. The comic pathos is derived from Hughoc's overreaction. Burns would have been aware of Fergusson's very funny parody of Henry Mackenzie's *The Man of Feeling* (1771), his Milton-burlesquing 'The Sow of Feeling' (1773). The sequel to this animal monologue, 'Poor Mailie's Elegy', is probably based on Fergusson's 'Elegy on the Death of Mr David Gregory' with its repetitive, end-line stem, 'Sin' Gregory's dead'. The lively, friendly, devoted Mailie was one of several pet animals Burns kept, including a lamb at Ellisland. An early stanza (dropped by Burns from the published poem because it was unsuitable for the genteel palate of the sentimental era) suggests Mailie's eventual fate was more realistic in the farming world of eighteenth-century Scotland:

> She was nae get o' runted rams,
> Wi' woo' like goat's an' legs like trams;
> She was the flower o' Fairlee lambs,
>   A famous breed:
> Now Robin, greetin', chows the hams
>   O' Mailie dead.[3]

With only his conscience for a moral compass – in place of his father's sterner advice – Burns' sexual restraint was soon abandoned. In 1784 he was 25 years of age, a fit young man, with sainthood never an option. His reputation as a poet was on the rise as well. He mentions his growing reputation as a poet in his autobiographical letter to Dr Moore:

> I now began to be known in the neighborhood as a maker of rhymes.
>
> The first of my poetic offspring that saw the light was a burlesque lamentation on a quarrel between two reverend Calvinists, both of them dramatis personae in my Holy Fair. – I had an idea myself that the piece had some merit; but to prevent the worst, I gave a copy of it to a friend who was very fond of these things, and told him I could not guess who was the Author of it, but that I thought it pretty clever. – With a certain side of both clergy and laity it met with a roar of applause. – Holy Willie's Prayer next made its appearance, and alarmed the kirk-Session so much that they held three several meetings to look over their holy artillery, if any of it was pointed against profane Rhymers. – Unluckily for me, my idle wanderings led me, on another side, point-blank within the reach of their heaviest metal.[4]

'Idle wandering' refers to his romance with Elizabeth Paton, who, by August 1784, was pregnant. She was a maid who had helped on the farm at Lochlie but was not kept on at Mossgiel, which means that Burns must have kept seeing her once he moved. Elizabeth lived only a few miles away, at Largieside. On 22 May 1785 she gave birth to their daughter, Elizabeth, his 'Dear-bought Bess'. This led to gossip around the area and eventually to Burns being hauled before the Kirk Elders and made to sit before them on the stool of repentance wearing the black sackcloth robe of a fornicator. Sex outwith marriage was bad enough to the 'houghmagandie squad' but children outwith wedlock was a black sin. The Elect were obviously rubbing their hands in glee that the rebellious Burns was now before them wearing the robes of shame.

This experience led to the song, 'The Fornicator', in which Burns is unashamedly untroubled and unrepentant at the finger-wagging of his clerical masters. He shows his disdain by going through the procedure as respectfully as he can before the Kirk with a defiant lustful look down at the attractive legs of his co-accused, partner in crime:

Before the Congregation wide
    I pass'd the muster fairly,
My handsome Betsy by my side
    We gat our ditty rarely;
But my downcast eye by chance did spy
    What made my lips to water,
Those limbs so clean where I, between,
    Commenc'd a Fornicator.

Tarbolton Kirk Session's public shaming was not enough, they also fined the poet a guinea, a taxation duty he wittily termed a 'buttock-hire'. According to the poet's niece Isabella Begg (daughter of his sister Isabella Burns), it was Gilbert and his sisters, not Mrs Burnes, who prevented Burns from marrying Elizabeth, deeming her unsuitable. Why his family did so may never be completely determined but it left a raw wound, with Burns longing to find himself a wife. 'Dear-bought Bess' was eventually brought to Mossgiel and raised as part of the Burnes family.

Burns used his experience with Elizabeth for a bawdy lyric, composing 'My Girl She is Airy' to the tune of 'Black Joke', which ends with the triple exclamatory 'And oh, for the joys of a long winter night!!!' Elizabeth appears to have inspired the song 'Corn Rigs', which ends:

I hae been blythe wi' comrades dear;
    I hae been merry drinking;
I hae been joyfu' gath'rin gear;
    I hae been happy thinking:
But a' the pleasures e'er I saw,
    Tho' three times doubl'd fairly –
That happy night was worth them a',
    Amang the rigs o' barley.
    Corn rigs, &c.

The simple beauty of this song, both in its description of nature and of romance, cloaks a subtext of lustful passion in a corn field. It is, in a sense, a bawdy song with its clothes on.

While he kept the sexual innuendo of 'Corn Rigs' simmering below the surface, he dared to go even further in his 'Epistle to John Rankin'. Rankin was a tenant farmer in Adamhill, Tarbolton and knew Burns from his Lochlie years. John's sister Margaret was the wife of the poet John Lapraik. Both Lapraik and Rankin belonged to the anti-clerical, 'ram-stam' Ayrshire lads. The specific occasion of the poem is Burns' 'allegorical' account of his impregnation of Elizabeth Paton, represented in terms of the poacher and his gun. When the poem was published, Hugh Blair was horrified when he eventually realised the true nature of its meaning:

> The description of shooting the hen is understood, I find, to convey an indecent meaning tho' in reading the poem . . . I took it literally, and the indecency did not strike me. But . . . the whole poem ought undoubtedly to be left out of the new edition.[5]

Burns kept the poem in his edition but was guaranteed to raise more than just a few eyebrows:

> The poor, wee thing was *little hurt*;
> I *straikit* it a wee for sport,
> Ne'er thinkan they wad fash me for't;
> But, Deil-ma-care!
> Somebody tells the *Poacher-Court*
> The hale affair.
>
> Some auld, us'd hands had taen a note,
> That *sic a hen* had got a *shot*;
> I was suspected for the plot;
> I scorn'd to lie;
> So gat the whissle o' my groat,
> An' pay't the *fee* . . .
>
> . . . As soon's the *clockin-time* is by,
> An' the *wee pouts* begun to cry,
> Lord, I'se hae sportin by an' by
> For my gowd guinea;
> Tho' I should herd the buckskin kye
> For 't, in Virginia!

The 'Poacher-Court' is the Kirk Session, which punished fornicators, as already mentioned.

Engaging the reactionary Calvinists of Ayrshire was beginning to become a habit for the young tenant farmer, as his reputation as a poet grew. The 'burlesque lamentation on a quarrel' he mentions to Dr Moore was actually a public row between two Auld Licht Ministers, which escalated into a public scandal. The poet sets up the two preachers in 'The Twa Herds', or 'The Holy Tulzie'– 'tulzie' meaning a brawl. The Revd John Russell, ('Black Jock' to Burns) and the Revd Alexander Moodie had been good friends before they fell out over a dispute about parish boundaries. Russell was known for his bellowing oratory. The dispute was settled before the Presbytery at Irvine: the two protagonists tore at each other like strutting cockerels, showing little Christian forbearance. The poem was too contentious to include in the Kilmarnock Edition, as was Burns' next ecclesiastical satire, 'Holy Willie's Prayer'.

The target of 'Holy Willie's Prayer' was not a minister but a member of the laity: William Fisher, tenant farmer at Montgarswood, a Kirk Elder in Mauchline parish from 1772. Burns explains in his own head notes to the poem that Fisher was noted for his drinking habits:

> In a sessional process with a gentleman in Mauchline – a Mr Gavin Hamilton – Holy Willie and his Priest father Auld, after full hearing at the Presbytery of Ayr, came off but second best; owing partly to the oratorical powers of Mr Robert Aiken, Mr Hamilton's counsel, but chiefly to Mr Hamilton being one of the most irreproachable and truly respectable characters in the country. On losing his process, the Muse overheard him at his devotions.

O Thou, that in the Heavens dost dwell!
Wha, as it pleases best Thysel',
Sends ane to Heaven, an' ten to Hell
  A' for Thy glory!
And no for ony gude or ill
  They've done before thee!

Each subsequent stanza, in the first-person voice, exposes Willie as a spiteful, hypocritical drunkard. The poem was occasioned by a dispute between Gavin Hamilton and the local Kirk Session. Hamilton had been collector of the parish 'stent', or poor tax, since around 1778. Being found to be short of around six pounds, William 'Daddy' Auld, the Auld Licht minister of Mauchline, charged him with fiddling the books and demanded the money. Hamilton defended himself by arguing that he was short because there were parishioners who could not afford the levy.[6] The more Holy Willie damns Hamilton and others, including Aiken, for their 'sins', the more he elevates himself on his tottering pedestal as one of the Elect whom God has chosen, even going as far as blaming God for making him get 'fu' and fornicate with 'Leezie's lass'. It is a masterful satire, in which Willie knocks himself off his own pedestal in a tirade of self-destruction. The more serious he becomes, the more ridiculous and absurdly funny he is, with the irony that he is the only person who cannot see this fact.

Hamilton was accused of Sabbath-breaking and, amongst other things, of causing a servant to dig potatoes on a Sunday. It does not take a Billy Connolly to eke laughter out of such absurd, man-made rules. After being found guilty at local level, Hamilton eventually won his case at the Presbytery of Ayr and was exonerated. With 'Holy Willie's Prayer', Burns graduates as a great poet in the Scots vernacular, displaying savage, satirical wit as a weapon against his enemies in the Auld Lichts.

Fisher had the misfortune to die during a blizzard on his way home, supposedly drunk, and his frozen body was found the next morning. Although Burns circulated the poem, he never printed it under his own name during his lifetime. In Ayrshire, no one needed to ponder who the author was, or whom its target. The Kirk Session were, as Burns commented, highly agitated and 'alarmed' at the satire, so much so that they pored over 'their holy artillery' to see if it included powers to deal with a 'profane' poet. Local occasional poems so often lose their impact through time and rarely reach the level of quality literature; 'Holy Willie's Prayer', a rare exception, has never lost its power to ridicule arrogant hypocrisy.

By 1785, Burns had a coterie of fraternal, like-minded spirits around him. These 'ram-stam' Ayrshire lads were making a name for themselves, especially among the clergy. 'The Epistle to John Rankin' has already been mentioned, along with the role of Gavin Hamilton and David Sillar and the poems they engendered. James Smith and John Richmond both fathered children out of wedlock. Smith's child was born to a servant of his mother's, Christian Wilson, and Richmond's to Jenny Surgeoner, whom he married four years later. The 'Epistle to James Smith' shows Burns rooting his poetic muse in Ayrshire soil. He makes a carefree dismissal of his lack of formal literary training:

The star that rules my luckless lot,
Has fated me the russet coat,
An' damn'd my fortune to the groat;
    But, in requit,
Has blest me with a random-shot
    O' countra wit.

This while my notion's taen a sklent,
To try my fate in guid, black prent;
But still the mair I'm that way bent,
    Something cries, 'Hoolie!
I red you, honest man, tak tent!
    Ye'll shaw your folly:

. . . Nae hair-brained, sentimental traces
In your unletter'd, nameless faces!
In *arioso* trills and graces
    Ye never stray;
But *gravissímo*, solemn basses
    Ye hum away.

Ye are sae *grave*, nae doubt ye're *wise*;
Nae ferly tho' ye do despise
The hairum-scairum, ram-stam boys,
    The rattling squad:
I see ye upward cast your eyes –
    Ye ken the road!

It was with one of the 'rattling squad', John Richmond, that Burns went into Mauchline on visits to Poosie Nancy's tavern, where he witnessed a scene, which, legend has it, inspired him to write 'Love and Liberty', a cantata known now as 'The Jolly Beggars'. It is, however, far from being merely an occasional piece inspired by a passing event. Burns takes as his model songs in Ramsay's *Tea-Table Miscellany* (1724–27), such as 'Jolly Beggars', 'Merry Beggars', and 'Scots Cantata', or possibly from Gay's *The Beggar's Opera* (1728). The critic Matthew Arnold, who was sometimes disparaging about Burns, considered this one of his finest works, comparable with Shakespeare's best. Hugh Blair thought it unfit for publication in the Edinburgh Edition. Being supposedly too licentious, lewd and radical to publish, it remained in private circulation until after the poet's death and only appeared in 1799, printed by Stewart and Meikle in Glasgow. When the song collector George Thomson enquired about the cantata in September 1793, Burns tactfully informed him that he could hardly remember any of it, bar the last few lines.[7] Daiches rightly states that Burns could not have forgotten his 'wildly radical cantata'.[8]

Through a liberation in which 'Freedom and whisky gang the gither', the sexually liberated voices of the lead characters celebrate the chaos of their lives with salty bravado and earthy revelry, that might have shaken the feudal order to its core, had the denizens of every alehouse in Scotland sung along, banging their jugs of frothing brew:

Chorus:
A fig for those by law protected!
LIBERTY'S a glorious feast
Courts for cowards were erected,
Churches built to please the PRIEST.

What is TITLE, what is TREASURE,
What is REPUTATION'S care?
If we lead a life of pleasure,
'Tis no matter HOW or WHERE.
  A fig for those &c . . .

Life is all a VARIORUM,
We regard not how it goes;
Let them cant about DECORUM,
Who have character to lose.
  A fig for those &c . . .

The point is not whether Poosie Nancy's drinking den actually witnessed this weekend storm of chaotic human flotsam, it is that Burns realises his characters so brilliantly, investing in them such vitality and bold honesty. 'Love and Liberty' is a celebration of the innate worth of the poor – a theme that runs through his work – and it is his least performed masterpiece.

Although David Sillar may have temporarily been one of the ram-stam boys, he was of a more exclusive group who encouraged Burns to set his ambitions beyond the boundaries of Ayrshire. They included William Simpson, a Glasgow University graduate who taught at Ochiltree and, later, at Cumnock. His relationship with Burns started when he sent him a now lost verse epistle praising his anti-clerical satire 'The Twa Herds'. The inspiring, bardic fraternity of Ayrshire was on the march:

> Auld COLIA, now, may fidge fu' fain,
> She's gotten *Bardies* o' her ain,
> Chiels wha their chanters winna hain,
>   But tune their lays,
> Till echoes a' resound again
>   Her weel-sung praise.

Yet it is really a march of one, the often self-effacing, sometimes excessively confident 'Rab Mossgiel' himself. Flattered by Simpson comparing him to the best of Scottish poets, Burns plays it down:

> My senses wad be in a creel,
> Should I but dare a *hope* to speel,
> Wi' *Allan*, or wi' *Gilbertfield*,
>   The braes o' fame;
> Or *Fergusson*, the writer-chiel,
>   A deathless name.
>
> (O *Fergusson*! thy glorious parts
> Ill suited law's dry, musty arts!
> My curse upon your whunstane hearts,
>   Ye Enbrugh Gentry!
> The tythe o' what ye waste at *cartes*
> Wad stow'd his pantry!)

Blasting the Edinburgh gentry for their treatment of Fergusson might not have been wise in a poem published in the Kilmarnock, then the Edinburgh Edition, but Burns was hell-bent on being true to his poetic muse and damn the consequences. Having read MacKenzie's *The Man of Feeling*, he was ready to show his readers that a peasant could have feelings, too, and display them in poetry:

We'll sing auld COLIA'S plains an' fells,
Her moors red-brown wi' heather bells,
Her banks an' braes, her dens an' dells,
  Whare glorious WALLACE
Aft bure the gree, as story tells,
  Frae Suthron billies.

At WALLACE' name, what Scottish blood
But boils up in a spring-tide flood?
Oft have our fearless fathers strode
  By WALLACE' side,
Still pressing onward, red-wat-shod,
  Or glorious dy'd!

Braveheart passion aside, Burns' knack of turning out a phrase to describe gory detail is witnessed here in 'red-wat-shod', meaning *blood-spattered boots*. In the postscript of the epistle to Simpson, Burns creates a burlesque satire on the Auld Licht Calvinists who, by their own lunatic-fringe determination to prove their view of cosmology to be true, decide to go up in a balloon to observe the last moment of the fading old moon and bring it back down to earth (in their pocket!) in order to show it does not change into a new moon. Setting up his opponents for ridicule was part of the strategy employed by Burns in his poetic guerrilla warfare with the forces of Auld-Licht Calvinism, to the applause of many New Licht adherents.

It was both the depth of Burns' biblical knowledge and his satirical bent that rattled Auld Licht cages. As a tenant farmer, he had gone way beyond accepted parameters of speech and action for one of his station; he had stepped into the ring with the Calvinist Elect heavyweights to fight the good fight on behalf of the New Lichts and laity. He single-handedly ridiculed and routed the ecclesiastical reactionaries – initially to entertain himself and friends. The victories he had, if they can be termed that laughter and applause born of ridicule – were temporary gratification only, and won him friends and enemies alike.

Among the New Lichts, too, his reputation preceded him. An Ayrshire cleric of the New Licht persuasion and a friend of Josiah Walker (who became Professor of Humanity at Glasgow University in 1815), admitted he was deeply affected by the presence of 'Burns, who was of a different parish', when he saw him 'unexpectedly enter the church'. His reading was 'instantly affected with a tremor and embarrassment' because he knew 'the depth of his discernment, the force of his expressions and the authoritative energy of his understanding'.[9] He told Walker he had met Burns socially and had obtained first-hand a 'sense of his power' that the poet himself, as yet unpublished, was apparently unaware of. Evidently, even some New Licht ministers felt the eye of scrutiny upon them when the rebel-rousing poet came to prayer. Clerical allies may have viewed Burns as a remarkably bright, critical-thinking believer with a verve for satire that they quietly envied but those who bore the brunt of his satirical sallies considered him an outrageous heretic and irreligious blasphemer.

Another versifier recruited by Burns in his hoped for renaissance in his native Ayrshire, was the older, almost father-figure of John Lapraik, whose 'Poems on Several Occasions' was published in 1788. Lapraik was postmaster at Muirkirk when he received the first of three epistles from Burns. (The first two were written in April 1785; the third was left unpublished.) Given his own family's recent experiences, Burns would have had sympathy for Lapraik on account of his fiscal fate: the Ayrshire bank failure of 1773 had caused him to lose his farm at Dalfarn and led to his imprisonment for debt in Ayr in 1785. The poet warmed to Lapraik after hearing an alleged song of his: Gilbert Burns states that he and his brother heard 'When I Upon Thy Bosom Lean' sung at a 'rocking' at Mossgiel, when a dozen young folk with their distaffs for spinning were at work outside the farmhouse. Authorship of the song has been questioned, however, and it appears that the 'King o' Hearts' may indeed have been a 'Knave o' Spades', who lifted the song from the *Weekly Magazine*.[10] Burns described Lapraik as 'a worthy, facetious old fellow' who 'often told me that he composed [the song] one day when his wife had been fretting o'er their misfortunes'.[11] It is probable that Burns eventually knew the song was not by Lapraik but did not wish to dislodge his little claim to fame. Burns writes in his 'Epistle to J. Lapraik':

I am nae *Poet*, in a sense;
But just a *Rhymer* like by chance,
An' hae to Learning nae pretence;
Yet, what the matter?
Whene'er my Muse does on me glance,
I jingle at her.
. . .
A set o' dull, conceited Hashes,
Confuse their brains in *Colledge-classes*!
They *gang* in Stirks, and *come out* Asses,
Plain truth to speak;
An' syne they think to climb Parnassus
By dint o' Greek!

Gie me ae spark o' Nature's fire,
That's a' the learning I desire;
Then, tho' I drudge thro' dub an' mire
At pleugh or cart,
My Muse, tho' hamely in attire,
May touch the heart.

The self-denigration here is, of course, tongue-in-cheek. Burns' comments about the formalities of literary education, although clothed in humour, harbours a serious point about the nature of poetic inspiration and creativity.

In the 'Second Epistle to Lapraik', Burns comments, 'Now comes the sax an twentieth simmer / I've seen the bud upo' the timmer', but despite all the gossip and trouble he has been through, 'I, Rob, am here'. The poem goes on to advise Lapraik never to envy the wealthy sons of Mammon, then inverts the oppressive nature of poverty, suggesting that having enough to survive, untainted by greed, is sufficient:

Were this the *charter* of our state,
'On pain o' *hell* be rich an' great,'

Damnation then would be our fate,
  Beyond remead;
But, thanks to *Heav'n*, that's no the gate
  We learn our *creed.*

For thus the royal *Mandate* ran,
When first the human race began:
'The social, friendly, honest man,
  Whate'er he be,
'Tis *he* fulfils great *Nature's plan*,
  And none but *he*.'

The poem, something of a prelude to the more overtly political 'A Man's a Man', concludes with an extraordinary image of the poor but poetically creative inheriting Heaven, while Mammon's sons are suitably rewarded for their bestial conduct to their fellow human beings.

Early 1785 also saw the production of 'Death and Doctor Hornbook'. Gilbert Burns explained the origin of the poem to Dr Currie:

> The Schoolmaster of Tarbolton parish, to eke out its scanty subsistence allowed to that useless class of men, had set up a shop of grocery goods. Having accidentally fallen with some medical books, and become almost hobby-horsically attached to the study of medicine, he had added the sale of few medicines to his little trade . . . and advertised that 'Advice would be given in common disorders at the shop gratis'.[12]

John Wilson was the schoolmaster at Tarbolton. He had advertised his medical prowess to a Masonic meeting in Burns' presence. Despite the burlesque, Wilson and Burns remained friends. When he left the Tarbolton school, Wilson wrote to the poet for help and Burns' reply is kindly constructive.[13] He subsequently became a prosperous session clerk in Govan.

'Hornbook' refers to the hornbook used in Scottish schools: lettered pieces of parchment inserted between a wooden back and a transparent bone front, for learning ABCs. In the poem, the poet, heading home one evening, meets Death, who whines that his career of six thousand years of mayhem has been ruined by Dr Hornbook's more lethal talents. A burlesque on ignorance masquerading as medical science, the poem contains a comic caricature of Wilson's medical cures, based on a fragile knowledge of Buchan's *Domestic Medicine*, and brings forth our sympathy towards the Grim Reaper, who is so distraught at this do-gooder quack, whose supposed cures 'poison, kill, an' slay'. A young girl, looking to hide 'her shame' of being pregnant, tries Dr Hornbook's medicine to abort her unwanted child and ends up dead – he 'sent her aff to her lang hame'. The dark underbelly of the piece, though, is its commentary on how exposed poor communities were to illness and death by a mixture of folk-remedies and a general lack of adequate medical knowledge – the newspapers of the period were peppered with miracle cures. The reputation of Burns as a 'king of sentimental doggerel' could not be more wrong.[14]

Visits into Mauchline were always providing Burns with subject matter for his writings. One such work is a mini-tapestry of the human condition, 'The Holy Fair', also written in 1785. The Fair was an annual religious event. Although perhaps not quite the equivalent of today's T in the Park, it was a carnival celebration of the capacity of the Scottish people to resist the rantings of their clerical masters. The lineage of open-air preaching comes from the long Covenanter Scottish tradition deeply rooted in the west of Scotland. The audience gathered together was upwards of 2,000 (four times the population of Mauchline), of whom 1,200 were communicants. 'The Holy Fair' takes its form from Fergusson's 'Leith Races', adapted from the nine-line Scottish medieval 'brawl' poem.

Burns places an epigraph at the start of the poem from *Hypocrisy À-La-Mode*, a play written in 1704 by Tom Brown, whose contribution to liberal, satirical English literature, like Henry Fielding's, is an attempt to sweep away institutionalised religious hypocrisy, a theme which binds them to Burns' ecclesiastical satires and epistles. The satire in 'The Holy Fair' is not quite as fierce as in some other radical works by Burns:

Upon a simmer *Sunday morn*,
  When Nature's face is fair,
I walked forth to view the corn,
  An' snuff the caller air:
The rising sun, owre GALSTON Muirs,
  Wi' glorious light was glintan;
The hares were hirplan down the furs,

The lav'rocks they were chantan
Fu' sweet that day.

As lightsomely I glowr'd abroad,
To see a scene sae gay,
Three *hizzies*, early at the road,
Cam skelpan up the way.
Twa had manteeles o' dolefu' black,
But ane wi' lyart lining;
The *third*, that gaed a wee a-back,
Was in the fashion shining
Fu' gay that day.

The three allegorical wenches are Superstition, Hypocrisy and their gorgeous sister, Fun, a victorious Cinderella whose spirit permeates the poem. If not promiscuous, Fun is a decidedly erotic young lass, as are the young women running barefoot, to save their shoes, towards the thronging excitement, carrying gifts, which might be for the satisfaction of various appetites. The savage forces of religious repression do not get their way at the Mauchline fair. There are giggling girls, leering whores and weavers from Kilmarnock among the crowd. Indeed, the whole poem is infused with the way in which the people convert the clerical event into a carnival opportunity for their multiple – especially sexual – appetites:

O happy is that man an' blest!
Nae wonder that it pride him!
Whase ain dear lass, that he likes best,
Comes clinkan down beside him!
Wi' arm repos'd on the *chair back*,
He sweetly does compose him;
Which, by degrees, slips round her *neck*,
An's loof upon her *bosom*,
Unkend that day.

The first gig on stage is Sawney Moodie, with his old-time, Auld-Licht undiluted gospel of damnation. Moodie was minister of Riccarton near Kilmarnock. The comic narrator wittily informs us that Moodie's hell-fire roaring, with his 'stampan' and his 'jumpan!', is enough to send the Devil himself, 'Hornie', back to his hot hell, 'het hame', in fright. He is followed by the 'New Licht' George Smith, minister of Galston, whose approach is moderate and reasonable; the bored crowd head for refreshments. Then, as the clerical tag-team changes back to the Auld Licht heavyweights, Smith's position is assaulted by William Peebles of Newton-upon-Ayr, who inflames the passions of the congregation and drives Common Sense – a central value of the new, more liberal Christianity – from the field. Next into the fray is the expedient Alexander Miller, who, in the guise of an orthodox Auld Licht preacher, merely mouths his words unconvincingly because he wants a manse. (He actually blamed Burns and this poem for a dispute with parishioners of Kilmaurs, who subsequently attempted to stop him getting a post.) Whatever he is saying, no one is listening, as alcohol (always a release for repressive forces in Burns' lyrics) and fleshly thoughts divert attention:

Leeze me on Drink! it gies us mair
  Than either School or Colledge;
It kindles Wit, it waukens Lear,
  It pangs us fou o' Knowledge:
Be't *whisky-gill or penny wheep*,
  Or onie stronger potion,
It never fails, on drinkin deep,
  To kittle up our *notion*,
      By night or day.

The lads an' lasses, blythely bent
  To mind baith *saul* an' *body*,
Sit round the table, weel content,
  An' steer about the *Toddy*:
On this ane's dress, an' that ane's leuk,
  They're makin observations;
While some are cozie i' the neuk,
  An' formin *assignations*
      To meet some day.

Then, to galvanise the motley crowd, the headliner, top of the bill, 'Black' John Russell, minister at Kilmarnock, mounts the stage. His capacity to terrify, indeed traumatise, his congregation was notorious and his booming voice – with probably double the decibels range of the legendary Reverend Dr Ian Paisley of Belfast in modern times – echoes back from the nearest hills:

A vast, unbottom'd, boundless *Pit*,
    Fill'd fou o' *lowan brunstane*,
Whase ragin flame, an' scorchin heat,
    Wad melt the hardest whun-stane!
The *half-asleep* start up wi' fear,
    An' think they hear it roaran;
When presently it does appear,
    'Twas but some neebor *snoran*
        Asleep that day.

The rollicking pastiche of everything but the gospel ends on a note of spontaneous eroticism. In defiance of every railing rant, Fun has her way and even if it means eternal damnation – if only the Elect could be saved, then the youthful revellers would be damned if they did and damned if they did not – so, sex is on the agenda: 'An' monie jobs that day begin, / May end in *Houghmagandie* / Some ither day'. 'Houghmagandie', of course, means sexual intercourse.

In work and play, Burns found material from daily experience – subject matter and characters he could shape into poetic composition and, although he sought to emulate Fergusson, he was often excelling the standards set by his heroic predecessor. Confident, with a rebellious streak, his primary aim as a poet was to stay true to his inner voice, his so-called 'Muse'.

5

The Poetic Calling of 'The Vision': Coila's Anointed Bard

To step up to become a national poet, Burns had both to make Ayrshire his own and to lift his work to embrace larger Scottish themes. 'The Vision' is one of his most ambitious works and, psychologically, probably his most important during this phase of his poetic development. The genesis of this panegyric to an Ayrshire revitalised through a renaissance of its progressive forces, present and historic, can be traced in his Commonplace Book notes:

> I am pleased with the works of our Scotch Poets, particularly the excellent Ramsay, and the still more excellent Fergusson, yet I am hurt to see other places of Scotland, their towns, rivers, woods, haughs &c. immortalised in such celebrated performances, while my dear native country, the ancient Baileries of Carrick, Kyle & Cunningham, famous both in ancient & modern times for gallant, and warlike race of inhabitants; a country where civil, and particularly religious LIBERTY have ever found their first support, & their last asylum; a country the birthplace of many famous Philosophers, Soldiers, & Statesmen, and the scene of many important events recorded in Scottish history, particularly a great many of the actions of the GLORIOUS WALLACE, the SAVIOUR of his country; yet, we

> have never had one Scotch Poet of any eminence, to make the fertile banks of Irvine, the romantic woodlands & sequestered scenes of Aire, and the heathy, mountainous source, & winding sweep of Doune emulate Tay, Forth, Etterick, Tweed, & c. This is a complaint I would gladly remedy, but Alas! I am far unequal to the task, both in native genius & education.

'The Vision' is energised by the power and beauty of Ayrshire's landscape and rivers with its organic, living connection to its celebrated heroic dead and to the pioneering, positive men of virtue, who are listed in the poem. 'The Vision' is split into two Duans, a term derived from James Macpherson's *Ossian*, where it signifies different sections within a digressive poem. Critics agree that the first Duan, mostly in Scots, shows Burns at his best in scene-setting:

> The Sun had clos'd the *winter-day*,
> The Curlers quat their roaring play,
> And hunger'd Maukin taen her way,
> To kail-yards green,
> While faithless snaws ilk step betray
> Whare she has been.
>
> The Thresher's weary *flingin-tree*,
> The lee-lang day had tired me;
> And when the Day had clos'd his e'e
> Far i' the West,
> Ben i' the *Spence*, right pensivelie,
> I gaed to rest.
>
> There, lanely by the ingle-cheek,
> I sat and ey'd the spewing reek,
> That fill'd, wi' hoast-provoking smeek,
> The auld clay biggin;
> An' heard the restless rattons squeak
> About the riggin.

The appearance of the supernatural muse Colia, the feminine spirit of his native Ayrshire is, in a sense, the moment of the poet's true calling:

When click! the *string* the *snick* did draw;
And jee! the door gaed to the wa';
And by my ingle-lowe I saw,
Now bleezan bright,
A tight, outlandish *Hizzie*, braw,
Come full in sight.

Ye need na doubt, I held my whisht;
The infant aith, half-form'd, was crusht;
I glowr'd as eerie's I'd been dusht,
In some wild glen;
When sweet, like *modest Worth*, she blusht,
And stepped ben.

Green, slender, leaf-clad *Holly-boughs*
Were twisted, gracefu', round her brows;
I took her for some SCOTTISH MUSE,
By that same token;
And come to stop those reckless vows,
Would soon been broken.

A 'hair-brain'd, sentimental trace'
Was strongly marked in her face;
A wildly-witty, rustic grace
Shone full upon her;
Her *eye*, ev'n turn'd on empty space,
Beam'd keen with *Honor*.

Down flow'd her robe, a *tartan* sheen,
Till half a leg was scrimply seen;
And such a *leg*! my bonie JEAN
Could only peer it;
Sae straught, sae taper, tight an' clean
Nane else came near it.

Nowadays, a young man claiming to have visitation from a feminine Muse clad in a multicoloured, ever-changing, almost cinematic dress, would be sectioned under the Mental Health Act; but such was the normal mechanism in eighteenth-century poetics to convey creative inspiration of the revelatory kind. The following verses, in which Coila's dress reveals an animated history of Ayrshire scenery and heroics, contain tantalising imagery, which reveals the intensity of Burns' imagination:

Her *Mantle* large, of greenish hue,
My gazing wonder chiefly drew;
Deep *lights* and *shades*, bold-mingling, threw
  A lustre grand;
And seem'd, to my astonish'd view,
  A well-known Land.

Here, rivers in the sea were lost;
There, mountains to the skies were tosst;
Here, tumbling billows mark'd the coast,
  With surging foam;
There, distant shone *Art*'s lofty boast,
  The lordly dome.

Here, DOON pour'd down his far-fetch'd floods;
There, well-fed IRWINE stately thuds:
Auld hermit AIRE staw thro' his woods,
  On to the shore;
And many a lesser torrent scuds
  With seeming roar.

Low, in a sandy valley spread,
An ancient BOROUGH rear'd her head;
Still, as in *Scottish Story* read,
  She boasts a *Race*
To ev'ry nobler virtue bred,
  And polish'd grace . . .

The second Duan is devoted to Coila's monologue, in which she not only reassures the poet about the nature and success of his creative career but integrates this individual success into an Ayrshire full of land-owning local heroes, whose talents are directed to the nation's common good. 'The

Vision' reflects Burns' growing confidence in the liberal-minded, progressive elite of his native region, many of whom he was beginning to count as friends. The influence on his values from texts encountered in the Masson *Collection* rings clear:

'They SCOTIA'S Race among them share:
Some fire the *Sodger* on to dare;
Some rouse the *Patriot* up to bare
Corruption's heart;
Some teach the *Bard*, a darling care,
The tuneful Art.

''Mong swelling floods of reeking gore,
They, ardent, kindling spirits pour;
Or, 'mid the venal Senate's roar,
They, sightless, stand,
To mend the honest *Patriot-lore*,
And grace the hand.

Coila, aided by her accompanying spirits, pours a cornucopia of gifts not only on the head of her chosen poet but over all of Ayrshire. After merging past heroics with present deeds and invoking the immortal, ever-present hero, William Wallace, Coila consoles her newly crowned poet:

'When ripen'd fields and azure skies
Call'd forth the *Reapers'* rustling noise,
I saw thee leave their ev'ning joys,
And lonely stalk,
To vent thy bosom's swelling rise,
In pensive walk.

'When *youthful Love*, warm-blushing, strong,
Keen-shivering, shot thy nerves along,
Those accents grateful to thy tongue,
Th' adorèd *Name*,
I taught thee how to pour in song
To soothe thy flame.

'I saw thy pulse's maddening play,
Wild-send thee Pleasure's devious way,
Misled by Fancy's *meteor-ray*,
By Passion driven;
But yet the *light* that led astray
Was *light* from Heaven.

It may have been this last phrase, 'light from Heaven', that led to Henry Mackenzie's wholly inappropriate tag for Burns, 'Heaven-taught ploughman' – meaning he wrote from pure inspiration.

With the second Duan, Burns changes to neo-classical English, rarely in his best manner, and 'The Vision' is hence sometimes regarded as rather broken-backed. The literary critic Thomas Crawford, however, judges the poem to be a masterpiece, also dismissing the idea that Burns is involved in any kind of sycophancy in the second Duan:

> To regard these stanzas as flattery of the local nobility and nothing more would be to misunderstand Burns' intention completely. The Vision is the work, above all others, in which Burns shows himself aware of the contemporary national renaissance: a movement which, in many spheres of life, from agricultural improvement to moral philosophy, was led by the most energetic and forward-looking of the landed gentry.[1]

In 'The Vision', more than in any other early poem, Burns sets out his ambition to pursue his poetic calling and his 'patriot' values: to fight the good fight. The poem is the result of his Fergusson-inspired epiphany and his muse, Coila, a symbol of this revelation, when she anoints him as her chosen Scottish bard. Burns felt that true poets were gifted with the second-sight and now began to feel his passion for Scottish history pulse through his veins, a feeling that would soon flourish into a life-changing sense of his own immortality as a poet.

6

From Fugitive to Celebrity

With so many fine compositions under his belt, Burns' self-belief was on the ascent. In March 1786, he received a request from John Kennedy, (then working at Dumfries House, Cumnock), a brother of Gavin Hamilton's wife, Helen Kennedy, to send a copy of 'The Cotter's Saturday Night' to him. Through friends and relations, the fame of his poetry was spreading beyond Ayrshire and that spring, he set his mind to getting it published. On 17 February, he wrote to his old friend John Richmond, now living in Edinburgh:

> I have been very busy with the muses since I saw you, and have composed, among several others, The Ordination, a poem on Mr McKinlay's being called to Kilmarnock, Scotch Drink, a poem; The Cotter's Saturday Night, An Address to the Devil, &c. I have likewise compleated my Poem on the dogs, but have not shown it to the world. – My chief patron now is Mr Aiken in Ayr, who is pleased to express great approbation of my works.[1]

Robert Aiken heard from Burns in early April that he planned to publish his poetry. On 3 April, Burns wrote to him stating 'My Proposals for publishing I am just going to send to the Press.'

This is an important date for several reasons. It is the date on which Burns sets out to get his work into print. At this point there is no sign of any plan to flee the country to Jamaica or elsewhere and, as we can see from the letter to Richmond of mid-February, most of the key poems featured in the Kilmarnock Edition were already written; albeit some may have required final touches and improvements for publication. While it is certainly true that many of Burns' best poems were written between 1784 and up until the early summer of 1786, the best of his songs and his classic work 'Tam o' Shanter' were yet to be written. Things were about to take a turn for the worse before they would get better.

From April 1786, Burns' life became, for six months, almost cyclotronic, taking him from being a fugitive from the law to celebrity status. Looking back at the situation, he told Dr Moore that he was beside himself during this period, unable to maintain a balanced perspective on life:

> This is the unfortunate story alluded to in my printed poem, The Lament. 'Twas a shocking affair, which I cannot bear yet to recollect; and had very nearly given [me] one or two of the principal qualifications for a place among those who have lost the chart and mistake the reckoning of Rationality.[2]

Here he refers to his deep anguish at the forced break-up of his relationship with Jean Armour, whom he had apparently first seen in Mauchline in late 1784, becoming personally acquainted with her in 1785. In conversation with John McDiarmid in 1827, Jean later recollected:

> The first time I ever saw Burns was in Mauchline. His family then lived in Mossgiel, about a mile from the village. I was then spreading clothes on a bleach-green along with some other girls, when the poet passed on his way to call on Mr Hamilton. He had a little dog that ran on the clothes, and I scolded and threw something at the animal. Burns said, 'Lassie if ye thought ought of me, ye wadna hurt ma dog!' – I thought to myself – 'I wadna think much o' you at ony rate!' I saw him afterwards at a dancing room, and we fell acquainted.[3]

She does not give an exact date when they met. Most biographers agree it was probably in April 1785 and then at Morton's ballroom in Mauchline, where fiddle music was played to the dancing crowd. When they began their courtship is not exactly known either. An entry in the poet's Commonplace

Book, dated August 1785, suggests that the relationship had started:

When first I came to Stewart Kyle
  My mind it was nae steady,
Where e'er I gaed, where e'er I rade,
  A Mistress still I had ay;
But when I came roun' by Mauchline town,
  Not dreadin any body,
My heart was caught before I thought
  And by a Mauchline Lady.

Jean, the 'Mauchline Lady', around six years younger than Burns, was about 20 years old when they met. By all descriptions, she was an attractive, dark-haired lass with a fine singing voice; and, more appropriately from the poet's eye-view, a fine pair of legs. She was not, though, Burns' first amour in Mauchline.

After his affair with Elizabeth Paton and the birth of their child, Burns became infatuated with Helen Miller, who was for a period 'the Tenant of my heart' but Helen was already committed to another and 'huffed my Bardship in the pride of her new Connection'.[4] Resenting this treatment, he burlesqued her brother William's marriage that summer to a rich widow, Agnes Bell, in the song 'The Mauchline Wedding'. This was not the first time Burns had tried his art in courtship and failed. He inscribed in his Commonplace Book some notes regarding his song 'Montgomerie's Peggy', recording that she was:

> ... my Deity for six, or eight months. She had been bred, tho' as the world says, without any just pretence for it, in a style of life rather elegant ... I began the affair, merely in a gaiete de coeur, or to tell the truth, what would scarcely be believed, a vanity in showing my parts in Courtship, particularly my abilities as a Billet doux, which I always piqu'd myself upon, made me lay siege to her; and when, as I always do in my foolish gallantries, I had battered myself into a very warm affection for her, she told me, one day in a flag of truce, that her fortress had been for some time before the rightful property of another ... she offered me every alliance, except actual possession ... it cost me some heart Achs to get rid of the affair.[5]

In laying siege on the object of his desire, Burns sometimes uses language that can make him seem coldly calculating but it was more that he was a romantic, who naively thought he had the magic formula to woo the lassies.

Burns probably wrote 'The Mauchline Lady' around the same time as 'The Belles of Mauchline', which mentions six young women, including Helen Miller and Jean Armour, with Jean coming out on top as 'the jewel for me of them a''. He had fallen in love with her. By late December 1785, Jean was pregnant. This was the last thing the Burnes family needed. They had not long buried Robert's younger brother John, who died on 28 October 1785 from an unknown cause, aged only 16. The second pregnancy plunged Burns into an emotional crisis. By mid-February, he was hinting to Richmond in the letter quoted above, 'I have some very important news with respect to myself, not the most agreeable, news that I am sure you cannot guess, but I shall give you the particulars another time'.[6] Trying to do the right thing by Jean, he entangled himself in what has become known as an 'irregular marriage'. This involved a written pledge that they were husband and wife. Both partners believed that under Scots Law and in the view of the Church, such a written pledge was legally binding. That Burns considered himself and Jean to be married is plain from 'The Lament', written after the break up:

Encircled in her clasping arms,
    How have the raptur'd moments flown!
How have I wished for Fortune's charms,
    For her dear sake, and her's alone!

And, must I think it! is she gone,
    My secret heart's exulting boast?
And does she heedless hear my groan?
    And is she ever, ever lost?

Oh! can she bear so base a heart,
    So lost to Honour, lost to Truth,
As from the *fondest lover* part,
The *plighted husband* of her youth?

. . .

From ev'ry joy and pleasure torn,
 Life's weary vale I wander thro';
And hopeless, comfortless, I'll mourn
 A faithless woman's broken vow!

Whether Jean was faithless and broke the vow they pledged together is hard to determine. The marriage paper has not survived. This matter has engendered much overheated debate. Were these verses written in pique at temporarily losing her?

The poet's rakish reputation came home to roost. Fathering a child to Elizabeth Paton was black gossip enough to his potential in-laws. As a poor tenant farmer, he had little prospect of finding the wherewithal to provide a home for his spouse. And this time, Burns had been sleeping with the enemy's daughter. Jean's father, James Armour, was of the Auld Licht persuasion. A reasonably well-to-do master stonemason, he had worked on many of the stately homes in Ayrshire. It is indicative of his sense of his own social position that he paid for one of the most expensive pews in church. The Armour house was situated just behind the Whitefoord Arms. James Armour and his wife Mary had certainly heard of Rab Mossgiel and his heretical sallies in verse against their good friends in the Kirk. It seems most likely that James Armour did not just dislike Burns but hated him with a passion and would rather have had the Devil wed his favourite daughter than Burns; it is said that he fainted with shock when Jean informed him that she was pregnant to Burns.

Armour now went to war against the apparently irreligious troublemaker. There would be no shotgun wedding for his lass. He went to an Ayr lawyer (Robert Aiken, as it happened), with the 'marriage' paper taken from Jean and had the names cut away to annul the paternal vows. Whatever assurances Burns had given to Jean in the missive as to their matrimony, their relationship was now to end; Jean was made to pledge she would not wed the rascal Burns. The poet got wind of this action almost immediately, as a letter to Gavin Hamilton written on 15 April suggests:

> Apropos, old Mr Armour prevailed with him to mutilate that unlucky paper, yesterday. – Would you believe it? tho' I had not a hope, nor even a wish, to make her mine after her conduct; yet when he told me, the names were all cut out of the paper, my heart died within me, and he cut my very veins with the news. – Perdition seize her falsehood and perjurious perdify!

> but God bless her and forgive my poor, once-dear, misguided girl. She is ill-advised. Do not despise me, Sir: I am indeed a fool, but a *knave* is an infinitely worse character than any body, I hope, will dare to give.[7]

As a Kirk Session minute dated 2 April indicates, the 'houghmagandie pack' of 'holy beagles' went into action on the first whiff of gossip. It reads: 'Jean Armour, an unmarried woman, is said to be with child and that she has gone off from the place of late, to reside elsewhere.' A further report, of 9 April, records that Mrs Armour had been spoken to and had denied that her daughter was pregnant, saying she had gone to Paisley 'to see friends'. However, the Armours were more prepared for the disgrace of their daughter being a single mother than of her marrying Burns. Jean's removal to Paisley to live temporarily with Andrew Purdie, husband of her aunt Elizabeth Smith, suggests she had little choice in the matter. She was the victim of her father's actions as much as Burns felt he was, although, in the heat of the moment, it appears Burns blamed Jean almost as much as he blamed her father. The notion of her faithlessness might have derived from a rumour that while resident at Paisley she was seeing a weaver named Robert Wilson. It should be borne in mind that James Armour himself could have been the source of this rumour.

During his estrangement from Jean, Burns found himself on the rebound with an old flame he met sometime in 1785. The renewal of the affair with 'Highland Mary' has been turned into mythology due to her tragic death in late 1786. As James Mackay's fine research has shown, Highland Mary was actually one Margaret Campbell, first celebrated in the poet's song 'Montgomerie's Peggy' as noted earlier.[8] In notes to 'The Highland Lassie O', Burns wrote:

> My Highland lassie was a warm-hearted charming young creature as ever blessed a man with generous love. After a pretty long tract of the most ardent reciprocal attachment we met by appointment, on the second Sunday of May, in a sequestered spot by the Banks of Ayr, where we spent the day in taking farewell, before she should embark for the West Highlands to arrange matters among her friends for our projected change of life. At the close of Autumn following she crossed the sea to meet me at Greenock, where she had scarce landed when she was seized with a malignant fever, which hurried my dear girl to the grave in a few days, before I could even hear of her illness.[9]

At their last meeting on that May Sunday, Burns presented Margaret with a pair of small bibles as a parting gift. Due to speculation based on the gift of the bibles and the songs 'Will Ye Go to the Indies My Mary' and 'Highland Mary' (written in 1792), some believe that Burns intended taking Margaret Campbell to Jamaica with him, if he was serious about leaving Scotland. The Train manuscripts (which contain information provided by the poet's friend Richmond) suggest Margaret Campbell was not the pure-hearted maiden of myth.[10] It seems that, for a spell in 1785, she was the mistress of James Montgomerie and Burns at the same time, a point Richmond and friends made clear to the poet to encourage him to stop seeing her. With Jean off the scene, the 'on-off affair' as Mackay rightly terms it, was back on in the spring of 1786, until their May parting. Sadly, Margaret died of a fever, possibly typhus, and was buried in Greenock.

More heat than light was cast on the myth of Highland 'Mary', when, in 1920, her burial site was dug up and the remains of an infant were discovered. This provoked wild speculation. It was found that the infant's remains were interred with Margaret Campbell almost 40 years *after* she died. It is therefore bewildering that more recently the biographer McIntyre made calls for the infant's remains to be exhumed and tested to verify if Burns was the father. It does not take a Sherlock Holmes to work out that this could not have been the case.

In the spring of 1786, Burns therefore was temporarily back in the arms of Margaret Campbell. Whether or not they ever planned a life together is impossible to determine. Burns would not have been the first male to be in the arms of one girlfriend while still pining for another. It seems clear, though, that Burns would have chosen to be the settled, married man, with Jean, if events had gone his way. With his life spinning out of control, Highland 'Mary' or Margaret provided temporary comfort.

Burns tried to push on with publishing his poems and sent out further subscription bills to friends and associates – one to John Ballantine, an Ayr banker, with a copy of 'Death and Dr Hornbook' and another to John Kennedy. He was aware of Aiken's role in assisting Armour.[11] Contemplating sending subscription bills to Aiken, he wrote to Gavin Hamilton on 15 April: 'If he is now reconciled to my character as an honest man, I would do it . . . but I would not . . . if he imagined me a rascal.'[12] Aiken came through for him later in the summer by obtaining

145 subscribers to the Kilmarnock Edition; almost a quarter of the print run.

In a letter of April 1786 to John Arnott, the poet's emotions pour out, cloaked in a mix of braggadocio and self-mockery:

> I have lost, Sir, that dearest earthly treasure, that greatest blessing here below, that last, best gift which compleated Adam's happiness in the garden of bliss, I have lost – I have lost – my trembling hand refuses its office, the frighted ink recoils up the quill. – Tell it not in Gath – I have lost – a – a – a Wife!
>
> Fairest of God's creation, last & best!
> How art thou lost.[13] . . .
>
> I had long had a wishing eye to that inestimable blessing, a wife . . .
>
> There is a pretty large portion of bedlam in the composition of a Poet at any time; but on this occasion I was nine parts & nine tenths, out of ten, stark staring mad. – At first I was fixed in stuporific insensibility, silent, sullen, staring, like Lot's wife besaltified in the plains of Gomorrha. – But my second paroxysm chiefly beggars description . . .
>
> My chained faculties broke loose; my maddening passions, roused to ten-fold fury, bore over their banks with impetuous, resistless force, carrying every check & principle before them. – Counsel, was an unheeded call to the passing hurricane; Reason, a screaming elk in the vortex of Moskoe strom; & Religion, a feebly-struggling beaver down the roaring of Niagara . . .
>
> A storm naturally overblows itself. – My spent passions gradually sank into a lurid calm; & by degrees, I have subsided into the time-settled sorrow of the sable widower, who, wiping away the decent tear, lifts up his grief-worn eye to look – for another wife . . .
>
> Already the holy beagles, the houghmagandie pack, begin to snuff the scent; & I expect every moment to see them cast off, & hear them after me in full cry: but as I am an old fox, I shall give them dodging and doubling for it; & by & bye, I intend to earth among the mountains of Jamaica.[14]

Having planned to do the right thing with Jean, to declare their marriage to her parents, Burns was clearly intent on publishing his poems to obtain some urgently needed cash. As scandal engulfed him, Burns began to think Ayrshire was too claustrophobic and in desperation he considered fleeing overseas. It was primarily his lack of money, his inability to be the independent man he desired to be that effectively delivered him back into the hands of his enemy – Willie Fisher's Auld Licht 'holy beagles' – to face public shaming for the second time. It was largely his poverty that provoked the Armours' rejection of Burns; his apotheosis into the Bard of Caledonia caused an eventual volte-face.

Burns was deeply in love with Jean Armour and it was his internal war to rid himself of the feelings he had for her that made him lose the 'chart and mistake the reckoning of Rationality'. In June, Burns confessed to David Brice, a close friend from Mauchline, who had moved to Glasgow to be a shoemaker:

> Poor, ill-advised, ungrateful Armour came home on Friday last . . . one thing I know, she has made me completely miserable. – Never man lov'd or rather ador'd, a woman more than I did her: and, to confess a truth between you and me, I do still love her to destraction after all, tho' I won't tell her so, tho' I see her which I don't want to do. – My poor, dear, unfortunate Jean! How happy have I been in her arms! – It is not the losing her that makes me so unhappy; but for *her* sake I feel most severely. – I foresee she is on the road to, I am afraid, *eternal* ruin; and those who made so much noise, and showed so much grief, at the thought of her being *my wife*, may, some day, see her connected in such a manner as may give them more real cause of vexation. I am sure I do not wish it: may Almighty God forgive her ingratitude and perjury to me, as I from my very soul forgive her! And may His grace be with her, to bless her in all her future life! . . .
>
> I have tried often to forget her: I have run into all kinds of dissipation and riot, Mason-meetings, drinking matches, and other mischief, to drive her out of my head, but all in vain: and now for a grand cure, the Ship is on her way home that is to take me out to Jamaica, and then, farewell, dear old Scotland, and farewell dear, ungrateful Jean, for never, never will I see you more![15]

He could not muffle his feelings for Jean with alcohol – his finances at this time would not stretch to drowning his sorrows. In Masonic meetings, he could advise friends of his impending publication, as he did Brice:

> You will have heard that I am going to commence Poet in print: and tomorrow, my work goes to the press. – I expect it will be a Volume about two hundred pages. – It is just the last foolish action I intend to do; and then turn a wise man as fast as possible.[16]

As someone who tended to let his heart rule his head, Burns was unlikely to become a wise man overnight. It would take until 31 July before his poetry was published. Rumours of his possible departure to Jamaica and impending publication were by now circulating widely in Ayrshire.

It was on 13 June that Jean contacted the Kirk Session to apprise them of her predicament, which could not be hidden if she returned to Mauchline: 'I acknowledge that I am with child and Robert Burns in Mossgiel is the father.' When 'Daddy' Auld and his deputies, who included Willie Fisher, received this information they demanded that Burns appear before them, which he duly did on 25 June, and admitted his role. The punishment, delivered gleefully, with much hand-wringing and high moral rectitude, was three public appearances before the Kirk to make penance as a fornicator. Burns explained his 'irregular marriage' to them. In a letter to John Richmond, he records that the Kirk agreed to give him a certificate as a bachelor if he accepted the punishment they gave. He went to see Jean, not from 'any the least view of reconciliation but merely to ask for her health' and 'a foolish hankering fondness'. On 17 July, he informed David Brice that he had 'already appeared' publicly in church, 'to get a certificate as a batchelor, which Mr Auld has promised me'.[17] His last two appearances to be shamed as a fornicator were set for 23 July and 6 August.

His meeting with Jean had alerted Burns to her father's next move. Armour was in the process of obtaining a writ *in meditatione fugae*, meaning *in meditation of flight*, to prevent the poet from fleeing the country and force him to provide for Jean's child. Burns details the implications to Richmond on 30 July, writing from Old Rome Foord, near Kilmarnock, the address of his uncle and aunt James and Jean Allan, where he was in hiding (and busily preparing his poems for publication):

> Armour has got a warrant to throw me in jail till I find security for an enormous sum. – This they keep an entire secret, but I got it by a channel they little dream of; and I am wandering from one friend's house to another, and like a true son of the Gospel 'have no where to lay my head' . . .

> . . . may all the Furies that rend the injured, enraged Lover's bosom, await the old harridan, her Mother, until her latest hour! . . . For Heaven's sake burn this letter, and never show it to a living creature. I write it in a moment of rage . . . exiled, abandoned, forlorn . . . [18]

It would appear that James Armour, hell-bent on fleecing every penny from the black sheep of Mossgiel, decided that Burns would not be fleeing the country with any profits from his book. Having seen his father go through the hell of litigation at Lochlie, Burns immediately tried to cover his own back and, in a Deed of Assignment dated 22 July 1786, dispossessed himself of any worldly goods in the Burnes family home, signing over the farm, lock, stock and barrel, to Gilbert, who became sole tenant; he also assigned to his brother the legal right to all profits from his impending book publication and the copyright thereof.[19] Additionally, Gilbert accepted the responsibility of bringing up and providing for Robert's daughter by Elizabeth Paton.

Burns was now living the life of a fugitive. He later recorded, 'I had for some time been skulking from covert to covert under all the terrors of a Jail; as some ill-advised, ungrateful people had uncoupled the merciless legal Pack at my heels.'[20] This language is somewhat dramatic, since he was not actually being chased over the countryside, although his fear of arrest was genuine and, if he could not pay up, jail was a real possibility. He goes on to explain to Dr Moore his reasons for signing the Deed of Assignment and, from the oasis of a contented mind, looks back at this manic period with relative calm:

> I gave up my part of the farm to my brother, as in truth it was only nominally mine; and made what little preparation was in my power for Jamaica. Before leaving my native country for ever, I resolved to publish my Poems . . . It is ever my opinion that the great, unhappy mistakes and blunders, both in a rational and religious point of view, of which we see thousands daily guilty, are owing to their ignorance, or mistaken notions of themselves. – To know myself had been all along my constant study . . . I was pretty sure my Poems would meet with some applause; but at the worst, the roar of the Atlantic would deafen the voice of Censure, and the novelty of west-Indian scenes make me forget Neglect.[21]

This retrospective rather conflates events, given that he had contemplated publication in 1785 and was heavily engaged in writing new works from the December of that year through till February 1786 – before the notion of fleeing Scotland entered his head. His long-gestated efforts bore fruit on 31 July 1786: the Kilmarnock Edition, *Poems, Chiefly in the Scotch Dialect*, appeared on sale at the price of three shillings. The tide had turned. The publication of the Kilmarnock Edition, comprising 30 poems and 14 songs and epigrams, was Burns' saving grace.

> I threw off six hundred copies, of which I had got subscriptions for about three hundred and fifty. My vanity was highly gratified by the reception I met with from the Publick; besides pocketing, all expences deducted, near twenty pounds. – This last came very seasonable, as I was about to indent myself for want of money to pay my freight. So soon as I was master of nine guineas, the price of wafting me to the torrid zone, I bespoke a passage in the very first ship that was to sail, for 'Hungry ruin had me in the wind'.[22]

Burns rode all over Ayrshire, distributing copies of his book and collecting subscription monies. A letter to James Smith in Mauchline shows that on 12 or 13 August he was in Ayr, visiting Dr Patrick Douglas, who had two friends from Jamaica with him, a Mr and Mrs White. There ensued a conversation which 'derang'd my plans altogether'. Informed that the total cost of sailing might be upwards of fifty pounds (given that the ship was to travel indirectly to Jamaica), Burns was cautioned that the journey could throw him 'into a pleuritic fever in consequence of hard travelling in the sun'.[23] His new projected departure, after so many last farewells to friends, would now be from 'Greenock the first of Sept.', at a cheaper fare. Was he truly wishing to leave Scotland?

Daringly – there was still a warrant out for his arrest – he asked Smith to meet him in Mauchline, 'Thursday morning, if you can muster as much self-denial as be out of bed about seven o'clock, I shall see you as I ride thro' to Cumnock.' Whether or not there was a genuine chance Burns would be arrested due to the warrant, he was taking no chances – the fear of being thrown in jail made him a moving target and he wanted to be one step ahead. Hence, Burns' early bird visit to Mauchline was a swift in-out and away visit. He had stayed with his old friend William Niven in Maybole, where he had given one of his bawdy songs to a 'worthy knot of lads' he was introduced to. A letter to Niven, dated 30 August, promises extra copies of his book would be delivered personally by Burns.

The sailing date arrived and Burns was not ready to leave Scotland. He does not say so but it is likely he had not delivered books to all subscribers at this point; he was relying heavily upon friends to facilitate this, particularly through the organisation of Masonic lodges in the west of Scotland. He had been an active Mason since joining in July 1781 and the Masonic movement subsequently opened many doors for him. As Depute Master of the St James's Lodge in Tarbolton, he had a social standing within the movement and dedicated a song to them in the Kilmarnock Edition, 'The Farewell to The Brethren of St James's Lodge, Tarbolton'. He was well known at the Newmilns Lodge, which he had attended in March with Gavin Hamilton. The poet's friends John Rankin and John Arnot were both members. Burns also attended the St John's Lodge, Kilwinning. The Masonic lodges of the west of Scotland disseminated news of his work as a poet and many educated, professional men of the movement gave much-needed support to their somewhat wayward bard.

On sailing day, 1 September, Burns wrote to Richmond from Mossgiel, having been reassured by Jean that her father would probably not pursue the warrant for his arrest:

> I well expected to have been on my way over the Atlantic by this time. The Nancy, in which I was to have gone, did not give me warning enough. Two days notice was too little for me to wind up my affairs and go for Greenock. I now am to be a passenger aboard the Bell, Captn Cathcart, who sails the end of this month. I am under little apprehension now about Armour. The warrant is still in existence, but some of the first Gentlemen of the county have offered to befriend me; and besides, Jean will not take any step against me, without letting me know, as nothing but the most violent menaces could have forced her to sign the Petition.[24]

He goes on to state that Jean would take him back but is adamant that he would never do so. Who the 'first Gentlemen' are is not specified. He then goes on to chastise his friend for dumping Jenny Surgeoner, who still loved Richmond. Burns must have wished his own romance was as straightforward.

On 3 September, Jean gave birth to twins, a girl and a boy. They were named Jean and Robert, following the Kirk Session protocol of naming children out of wedlock with the names of the parents.[25] Burns received news of the birth from Adam Armour, Jean's younger brother, and went to the Armour house that Sunday evening with a peace offering of tea, sugar and a guinea. The effect of seeing Jean and their children was profound. He wrote to Richmond later that evening, 'Wish me luck, dear Richmond! Armour has just brought me a fine boy and girl at one throw. God bless the little dears!' He broke the news to Robert Muir, a friend and wine merchant in Kilmarnock, on 8 September: 'Armour has repaid my amorous mortgages double. A very fine boy and girl have awakened a thousand feelings that thrill, some with tender pleasure, and some with foreboding anguish, thro' my soul.'[26] His elated mood is expressed in exuberant, religious terms in a letter to John Kennedy of Dumfries House, dated 26 September:

> . . . man feels a consciousness of something within him, above the trodden clod! The grateful reverence to the hoary, earthly Authors of his being. –
>
> The burning glow when he clasps the Woman of his Soul to his bosom – the tender yearnings of heart for the little Angels to whom he has given existence. – These, Nature has poured in milky streams about the human heart, and the Man who never rouses them into action by the inspiring influences of their proper objects, loses by far the most pleasurable part of his existence.
>
> My departure is uncertain; but I do not think it will be till after harvest.[27]

Burns' inner conflict is evident in many letters written around this time. He told John Smith he was 'fix'd as Fate' about staying in Scotland 'and owning her conjugally. The first by heaven I will not do! The last by Hell I will never do!' In the very same letter, there is a quatrain the first line of which gives a rather different message:[28]

> O Jeany, thou hast stolen away my soul!
> In vain I strive against the lov'd idea:
> Thy tender image sallies on my thoughts,
> My firm resolves become an easy prey![29]

His heart was evidently at war with his head. In early October, Burns listed to Robert Aiken the reasons that 'urged' him to leave the country:

> . . . and to all these reasons I have only one answer – the feelings of a father. This, in the present mood I am in, overbalances everything that can be laid in the scale against it . . .
>
> How should I, in the presence of that tremendous Being, the Author of existence, how should I meet the reproaches of those who stand to me in the dear relation of children, whom I deserted in the smiling innocency of helpless infancy? O thou Great Unknown Power! Thou almighty God! Who hast lighted up reason in my breast, and blessed me with immortality! . . . Thou hast never left me nor forsaken me![30]

It is a striking feature of Burns' letters that his most tender, genuine feelings towards his children are expressed naturally to his male friends and rarely, even for effect, to female correspondents. It does seem that his paternal feelings outweighed his love for any woman, even for Jean. The Kilmarnock Edition is peppered with evidence of the poet's fraught emotions. In 'On a Scotch Bard Gone to the West Indies', he writes:

> He saw Misfortune's cauld *Nor-west*
> Lang-mustering up a bitter blast;
> A Jillet brak his heart at last,
> Ill may she be!
> So, took a berth afore the mast,
> An' owre the Sea!

The 'Jillet' is, of course, Jean. In 'The Farewell to The Brethren of St James's Lodge, Tarbolton', Burns likewise projects making his last goodbyes with a dramatic tear in his eye:

> And *YOU* farewell! whose merits claim
> Justly that *highest badge* to wear:
> Heav'n bless your honour'd, noble Name,
> To MASONRY and SCOTIA dear!
> A last request permit me here,
> When yearly ye assemble a',

One *round*, I ask it with a *tear*,
To him, the Bard, that's far awa.[31]

Some of the material in the Kilmarnock Edition reads almost like a cry for help. In 'A Bard's Epitaph', it is possible to detect his father's voice and the workings of a Presbyterian conscience:

Is there a man, whose judgment clear
Can others teach the course to steer,
Yet runs, himself, life's mad career
Wild as the wave,
Here pause – and, thro' the starting tear,
Survey this grave.

The poor Inhabitant below
Was quick to learn and wise to know,
And keenly felt the friendly glow
And softer flame;
But thoughtless follies laid him low,
And stain'd his name!

Reader, attend – whether thy soul
Soars Fancy's flights beyond the pole,
Or darkling grubs this earthly hole,
In low pursuit,
Know, prudent, cautious, *self-control*
Is Wisdom's root.

The rapid sales of the Kilmarnock Edition suggested that a second issue would be viable and, to this end, Burns asked John Wilson to print another 1,000 copies, only to be told that an advance of £27 for the paper would be necessary. He did not have the money. He remarks to Robert Aiken, in a letter dated 8 October, 'so farewell hopes of a second edition till I grow richer! An epoch, which, I think, will arrive at the payment of the British national debt. There is scarcely anything hurts me so much in being disappointed of my second edition'.[32] The pages set up in type for the first edition would already have been broken up and by October the printer would have had to typeset the entire book from scratch. Mackay rightly asserts the profits from the first edition should have been around £54, assuming the poet obtained the cover price from every subscriber and sale, which, given his generosity, is highly improbable. The proceeds from the seventy copies Gilbert managed to sell to subscribers would most likely have gone into family funds; there was the expense of distribution and Burns, a giver, not a taker, would have purchased a few pints for friends out of his profits and forked out for his digs.

In the same letter to Aiken, Burns mentions the possibility of joining up as an Excise Officer, which would require the support of patronage and a report on his good character. Naturally, this concerned him. However, this is the first time he talks of obtaining a new career within Scotland; his wild scheme of fleeing to the West Indies was now effectively shelved.

Distribution of the Kilmarnock Edition was predominantly in the west of Scotland. Its success had been steady and accumulative, and members of the aristocracy, including Mrs Alexander Stewart of Stair and Sir William Cunninghame of Robertland, had begun to invite Burns into their homes.

The contact which made a second edition a reality came through a New Licht cleric, the Reverend George Lawrie, minister of Loudon Parish, who counted among his Edinburgh friends Thomas Blacklock and Hugh Blair. On receiving a copy of the Kilmarnock Edition from Lawrie, Blacklock, who had been blind since childhood due to smallpox, requested Dugald Stewart to read them to him. Stewart, a leading Enlightenment author, was Professor of Moral Philosophy at the University of Edinburgh. A competent poet himself, Blacklock promptly discussed with Lawrie the possibility of a reprint, 'as it appears certain that its intrinsic merit, and the exertions of the authors friends, might give it a more universal circulation than any thing of the kind which has been published within my memory'.[33] This letter was passed to Gavin Hamilton, who showed it to Burns. It electrified his ambitions:

> I had taken the last farewell of my few friends; my chest was on the road to Greenock; I had composed my last song I should ever measure in Caledonia. 'The gloomy night is gathering fast,' when a letter from Dr Blacklock to a friend of mine overthrew all my schemes by rousing my poetic ambition. The Doctor belonged to a set of Critics for whose applause I had not even dared to hope. His idea that I would meet with

> every encouragement for a second edition fired me so much that away I posted to Edinburgh without a single acquaintance in town, or a single letter of introduction in my pocket. The baneful Star that had so long shed its blasting influence in my Zenith, for once made a revolution to the Nadir.[34]

Dr John MacKenzie, who had tended William Burnes in his last illness, arranged for Burns to have lunch with Dugald Stewart on 23 October, at Caterine Bank, Stewart's country retreat situated on the banks of the River Ayr, south of Mauchline. Also present was Viscount Daer, Basil William Hamilton Douglas, son of the Earl of Selkirk, who lived in Galloway. In 'The Extempore Verses On Dining With Lord Daer', Burns parodies his nervousness – 'knees on ane anither knoited, / As faultering I gaed ben', continuing:

> I sidling shelter'd in a neuk,
> An' at his Lordship staw a leuk,
> Like some portentous omen;
> Except GOOD SENSE, and SOCIAL GLEE,
> An' (what surpris'd me) MODESTY,
> I marked nought uncommon.
>
> I watch'd the symptoms o' the GREAT,
> The GENTLE PRIDE, the LORDLY STATE,
> The arrogant assuming;
> The feint o' pride, nae pride had he
> Nor sauce, nor state, that I could see
> Mair than an honest Ploughman.
>
> Then from his Lordship I shall learn,
> Henceforth to meet with unconcern,
> One rank as well 's another;
> Nae honest, worthy man need care,
> To meet wi' NOBLE, youthfu' DAER,
> For he but meets a BROTHER.

It was not simply because Daer was a Mason that Burns called him 'BROTHER'; the same age as Burns, a fellow democrat and passionately patriotic Scot, Daer became a leading advocate for parliamentary reform when the Friends of the People was set up in mid-1792.

Burns was now gaining access to social circles from which he would automatically have been excluded in the recent past. However, he could hold his own in conversation, as Dugald Stewart later remarked, deeply impressed by the 'fluency, and precision, and originality of his language, when he spoke in company'.[35]

On 15 November, Mrs Frances Anna Dunlop, whose estate in Stewarton was almost sixteen miles from Burns' home, dispatched a servant to Mossgiel bearing a letter requesting six copies of the Kilmarnock Edition and a personal meeting with the poet. A widow in her mid-forties, originally from Lochryan House by Cairnryan, Wigtownshire, Mrs Dunlop counted William Wallace among her ancestors (via one of his brothers). On reading 'The Cotter's Saturday Night', she had been delighted by references to the great Scottish hero. Burns, who had not been present when her servant arrived, wrote to her that night:

> You could not have touched my darling heart-chord more sweetly than by noticing my attempts to celebrate your illustrious Ancestor, the SAVIOUR OF HIS COUNTRY, 'Great patriot hero! Ill-requitted Chief'[36] . . . I have only been able to send you five Copies: they are all I can command. – I am thinking to go to Edinburgh in a week or two at farthest, to throw off a second Impression of my book . . . [37]

This was the start of a friendship which lasted a decade – their voluminous correspondence is a testament to the significance of their bond. Mrs Dunlop is often called Burns' Mother Confessor. Throughout their friendship, she did everything in her power to assist him. Burns was not always amenable to taking her advice. His outbursts of radicalism finally caused a rift between them in 1795.

Burns' self-publishing venture had paid off. The positive response to the Kilmarnock Edition reignited his ambition and he now sought a larger stage. Literary fame would be his ticket to a new world – that of the Athens of the North, not Jamaica. The call of Caledonia's capital proved irresistible.

[illegible]

[illegible]

[illegible] wrote to her that night.

He could not be reconciled [illegible]

[illegible]

[illegible]

7

The Kilmarnock Edition: Reviewers, Patronage and the Myth of the Heaven-taught Ploughman

> Critics! – appalled, I venture on the name –
> Those cut-throat bandits in the paths of fame.
>
> *Burns*

How did contemporary literary critics view Burns' poetic talents? The first review of the Kilmarnock Edition appeared in the *Edinburgh Magazine* in October 1786, written by its editor, James Sibbald. Burns was the talk of the Edinburgh literati and, to satisfy their appetite, Sibbald published extracts from his poetry in the October, November and December issues. On 9 December, *The Lounger* carried a review by Henry Mackenzie, having been introduced to the Kilmarnock Edition by Dugald Stewart. Famously, Mackenzie praised Burns as a 'Heaven-taught ploughman'.

'Who are you, Mr Burns?' asks Sibbald; 'At what university have you been educated? What languages do you understand?' He answers his own catechism: 'I am a poor country man; I was bred up at the school of Kilmarnock; I understand no languages but my own; I have studied Alan Ramsay and Fergusson . . . I have not looked on mankind through the spectacle of books.' Sibbald, unaware of quite how off the mark he was, continues:

> He is said to be a common ploughman . . . Those who view him with the severity of lettered criticism, and judge him by the fastidious rules of art, will discover that he has not the Doric simplicity of Ramsay, nor the brilliant imagination of Fergusson . . . His observation on human characters are acute and sagacious . . . He . . . often startles us with a dash of libertinism, which will keep some readers at a distance.[1]

He then goes on to quote Horace's *Satires* in Latin, comparing Burns to Ofellus – a peasant, a philosopher unschooled and of rough mother-wit.[2] Sibbald was not the only Edinburgh sophisticate to be hoodwinked by Burns.

The myth of Burns as the unlettered instinctive can be traced back to the image of himself conveyed in the Preface to the Kilmarnock Edition, in which he deliberately plays down his literary acumen: his poems are 'trifles', 'little creations of his own fancy'; he claims that he does not have the advantages of 'learned art' and knows nothing about 'Theocritus or Virgil'. It was, we are told, his friends who pushed him to consider publication. He even fibs that 'none of the following works were ever composed with a view to the press'. Then, with the strategic finesse of a chess master, he outmanoeuvres possible critics and averts criticism by dishing it out against himself – dismissing the criticism as invalid. A skilful dance of irony and rhetoric, every last word controlled and choreographed with a fluidity of language that effaces the calculation it embodies, the Preface to the Kilmarnock Edition truly ought to be performed at Burns Clubs.

That Burns had confidence in his own skill as a writer is amply shown in his letters but in his Preface he avers that he appears before his public in 'fear and trembling', in danger of being branded as 'an impertinent blockhead, obtruding his nonsense on the world; and because he can make a shift to jingle a few doggerel, Scotch rhymes together, looks upon himself as a Poet of no small consequence forsooth'.

After mentioning Shenstone, he goes on to suggest he himself might indeed have some ability, after all. He acknowledges the genius of Ramsay and Fergusson, merely hoping to 'kindle at their flame', although not with 'servile imitation'. The best is kept for last:

> He begs his readers, particularly the Learned and the Polite . . . that they will make every allowance for Education and Circumstances of Life: but, after a fair, candid, and impartial criticism, he shall stand convicted of Dulness and Nonsense, let him be done by, as he would in that case do by others – let him be condemned, without mercy, to oblivion.

It is remarkable that Enlightenment Edinburgh fell for his pose as an uneducated rustic, given that this Preface itself reveals a hyper-intelligent mind at work. Burns was well aware the literati might speculate as to whether a peasant could feel and think like superior members of society, such as themselves.[3]

Henry Mackenzie's review was the most influential the poet received in his lifetime. Mackenzie was a leading literary critic and a close friend of both Robert and Henry Dundas. His 'Surprising Effects of Original Genius', as exemplified in the poetical productions of Robert Burns, contains a preening discourse on what constitutes 'genius'. Mackenzie, like Sibbald, swallows the author's image as promoted in the Preface, hook, line and sinker. He pronounces Burns 'a genius of no ordinary rank', suggesting that there should be a 'verdict of his country on the merit of his works, and to claim for him those honours which their excellence appears to deserve'. He regrets most of the poems are written in Scots, a 'provincial dialect', which would act as a barrier to fame, praising mainly those written in English. (The collective advice Burns received in Edinburgh was to cease writing in Scots. Fortunately, he was not susceptible to such asinine advice.)

Readers, says Mackenzie, will find 'a high tone of feeling, a power and energy of expression, particularly and strongly characteristic of the mind and the voice of a poet' within 'The Vision'; 'Despondency, an Ode', 'The Lament', 'Winter, a Dirge' and 'To Ruin' are 'solemn and sublime'; 'Man Was Made to Mourn', 'The Cotter's Saturday Night', 'To a Mouse' and 'To a Mountain Daisy' have a 'tender and moral' aspect; 'far from meaning to compare our rustic bard to Shakespeare', readers will 'perceive with what uncommon penetration and sagacity this Heaven-taught ploughman, from his humble and unlettered station, has looked upon men and manners'. In making these observations, Mackenzie reflects the incapacity of most of the Edinburgh literati to grasp that Burns was no less than an informed, intellectual, self-aware, poetic genius. For such a phenomenon to emerge from the ranks of the peasantry was beyond their comprehension.

Mackenzie was, however, perceptive in seeing Burns to be a 'champion of morality, and the friend of virtue'. In relation to Sibbald's criticism of libertinism, he suggests that 'exceptionable parts of the volume . . . caution would have suppressed', concluding: 'I do my country no more than justice, when I suppose her ready to stretch out her hand to cherish and retain this native poet, whose "wood-notes wild" possess so much excellence.'[4] Mackenzie's praise was a major boost but, despite his influence and connections, he was unable to find the hand in Scotland willing to support Burns in his quest for patronage.

If Mackenzie thought that some poems should have been left out of the Kilmarnock Edition, he would have blanched at some of those Burns had omitted – 'Holy Willie's Prayer', a savage blast at religious hypocrisy, and 'Love and Liberty, a Cantata' were kept from view. And Mackenzie, who later became President of the Highland Society, would have choked on his claret at 'The Address of Beelzebub', a monologue in Scots, which damns the Society for trying to stop 500 Highlanders from emigrating to America because they were their 'property':

> Get out a HORSE-WHIP, or a JOWLER,
> The langest throng, the fiercest growler,
> An' gar the tatter'd gypsy's pack
> Wi' a' their bastarts on their back!

The two bawdy lyrics Burns is known to have written at this point were also omitted and 'The Court of Equity', a wildly funny burlesque on the Kirk Session's punishment of fornicators, remained unpublished until Catherine Carswell's *Life* appeared in 1930.

What must have surprised more than a few of Burns' supporters and detractors alike in the literary world was that he had the confidence to speak as a national bard, on behalf of Scotland. In the midst of pastoral, elegiac work are bold, radical poems such as 'The Author's Earnest Cry and Prayer', 'Scotch Drink' and, most controversial of all, 'A Dream'. It was probably this latter work which evoked Sibbald's charge of libertinism.

If any poem during his life did Burns' prospects of patronage harm, it was 'A Dream'. A well-heeled, loyalist bard might well have found himself an easy life to dedicate to literary pursuits. Dundas's silence towards Burns during and after his visit to Edinburgh is ominously significant.

The poet imagines himself having fallen asleep, then suddenly awakening at the King's birthday celebration in London; he delivers the poem as an address.

GUID-MORNIN to your MAJESTY!
  May Heaven augment your blisses,
On ev'ry new *Birth-day* ye see,
  A humble Poet wishes!
My Bardship here, at your Levee,
  On sic a day as this is,
Is sure an uncouth sight to see,
  Amang thae Birth-day dresses
          Sae fine this day.

I see ye're complimented thrang,
  By monie a *lord* an' *lady*;
'God Save the King' 's a cuckoo sang
  That's unco easy said ay:
The *Poets*, too, a venal gang,
  Wi' rhymes weel-turn'd an' ready,
Wad gar you trow ye ne'er do wrang,
  But ay unerring steady,
          On sic a day.

For me! before a Monarch's face,
  Ev'n *there* I winna flatter;
For neither Pension, Post, nor Place,
  Am I your humble debtor:
So, nae reflection on YOUR GRACE,
  Your Kingship to bespatter;
There's monie *waur* been o' the race,
  And aiblins *ane* been better
          Than You this day.

Whether the last phrase refers to King Alfred or to Charles Edward Stuart is uncertain. In tones that echo his early readings from Alibaeus, Fabritius and Demosthenes, Burns proposes that the king would be better off with

William Pitt working in a byre, due to his punitive fiscal problems and naval cuts: 'Ye've trusted 'Ministration / To chaps wha in a barn or byre/ Wad better fill'd their station, / Than courts yon day'. He then cheekily assures the king, he is 'no mistrusting Willie Pit, / When taxes he enlarges' and prays, with irony, for Pitt to keep spending plenty of public money and not suffer a 'saving fit' which could threaten the royal 'barges'. After hoping the king will hang corrupt ministers by the neck, he launches into an assault on the royal household, starting with the 'Potentate o'Wales', who was reportedly involved in whoring and gambling with some of 'Charlie' Fox's Opposition Whigs:

> But some day ye may gnaw your nails,
> An' curse your folly sairly,
> That e'er ye brak *Diana's pales*,
> Or rattl'd dice wi' Charlie
> By night or day.

Distilling the media gossip into poetry, Burns mentions that King George III's son, the 'right rev'rend Osnaburg', Frederick Augustus, had taken up with Letitia Derby, the ex-mistress of Rann the highwayman. Then with blatantly lewd overtones, he caricatures Prince William as 'Royal TARRY-BREEKS'. William had a naval, *navel* encounter with Sarah Martin, daughter of the commissioner of the Portsmouth dockyard and is advised to throw a chain and grapnel upon her 'An', large upon her quarter, / Come full that day'. This was a satirical hit well below the royal belt.

Mrs Dunlop warned him of the consequences of publishing political satire. On 26 February 1787, she urged that 'A Dream' should be excluded from the second edition: 'I ought to have told you that numbers at London are learning Scots to read your book, but they don't like your address to the King, and say it will hurt the sale of the rest.'[5] It is a remarkable phenomenon that the Scots language, which was being phased out in Scotland as 'barbaric', was, for a brief moment, in the ascendancy in London circles purely to read Burns.

The literary critic David Daiches has remarked that 'A Dream' would be a rude poem, even if it were an address from one farmer to another. Burns' response to Mrs Dunlop is an unyielding declaration that he would be true to his art, his values and ideals: 'I am determined to flatter no created being, either in prose or verse, so help me God. I set as little by kings, lords, clergy, critics, &c as all these respectable Gentry do by my Bardship.'[6] He was determined not to sell out the integrity of his guiding inner voice as a poet, in Ayrshire or in Edinburgh.

Part Three

All Hail!
The Bard of Caledonia

8

Caledonia's Bard – Walking the Tightrope[1]

On 27 November 1786, Burns borrowed a pony from George Reid of Barquarrie farm, near Ochiltree, and started to make his way eastward towards the capital. It took him two days over the winding, country roads. He made a stop halfway with a friend of Reid, Archibald Prentice, at Covington Mains farm.

On his arrival in Edinburgh, Burns made his way through the city to Baxter's Close off the Lawnmarket, where his friend John Richmond, a solicitor's clerk who had previously worked for Gavin Hamilton, rented a room. The landlady, a Mrs Carfrae, upped the weekly rent to three shillings, now that she had a second lodger. Burns agreed to pay half the rent. After the long journey, a late night at Covington Mains and catching up with Richmond, he spent the next day in bed, recovering.

Edinburgh was a bustling ancient city with parts of the New Town still under construction. The ghost of William Burnes must have smiled over his son's shoulder as he walked the same streets his father had known years before. Edinburgh's population had grown considerably since the 1750s. Its tenement flats were home to a rich social mélange – the wealthiest inhabiting the upper storeys and all sharing the same common entrance to the street. The taverns and coffee shops on the Royal Mile, from the Lawnmarket down to the Canongate, were where the Old Town pulsed; Burns' meandering discovery of Edinburgh would have been an exhilarating experience.

❖❖❖

In his first month in the capital, Burns showed himself to be an assiduous correspondent, despite being caught up in a whirlwind of social appointments. His Ayrshire enemies had friends in Edinburgh and, since bad news travels faster than good, gossip had followed him from Ayrshire too. On 1 December Burns wrote to Sir John Whitefoord, the former Master of Tarbolton Masonic Lodge, to thank him for defending his reputation in relation to James Armour's writ and his problems with Jean. Whitefoord, formerly of Ballochmyle Estate, was now living in Edinburgh after his losses in the Ayr banking disaster of the company Douglas Heron & Co. Burns told Sir John it was an outrage a gentleman would 'stoop to traduce the morals of such a one as I am, and so inhumanly cruel, too, as to meddle with that late, most unfortunate, unhappy part of my story'.[2]

Burns provides a colourful description of his landlady in a letter to John Ballantine. She, and no doubt Richmond and himself, could hear their upstairs neighbours carousing by night:

> I have just now had a visit from my Landlady who is a staid, sober, piously-disposed, sculdudery-abhoring Widow, coming on her grand climacterick. She is at present in sore tribulation respecting some 'Daughters of Belial' who are on the floor immediately above . . . as our floors are low and ill-plaistered, we can easily distinguish our laughter-loving, night-rejoicing neighbors – when they are eating, when they are drinking, when they are singing, when they are &c., my worthy Landlady tosses sleepless & unquiet, 'looking for rest but finding none' the whole night.[3]

Hearing her rail on about the terrors of Hell that awaited the miscreants must have raised a wry grin of recognition in Burns who was well used to the wagging finger of Calvinist damnation. While Richmond was at work, Burns got down to his own task. By 8 December, his first run of subscription bills was ready.

Under the guidance of an Ayrshire landowner, James Dalrymple of Orangefield, Burns attended a Masonic meeting at the Canongate Kilwinning Lodge, where he met, among others, the former Lord Advocate and current Dean of Faculty, Henry Erskine, a leading Whig. Henry was younger brother to the Earl of Buchan and older brother to the brilliant, radical lawyer Thomas Erskine. By far the most important connection made on behalf of Burns was his introduction to James Cunningham, Earl of

Glencairn. Lord Glencairn was also related via his younger brother, the Reverend John Cunningham, to the Erskine family; John's wife was Lady Isobella Erskine. Burns' letter to Gavin Hamilton of 7 December begins with buoyant, tongue-in-cheek wit:

> I am in a fair way of becoming as eminent as Thomas à Kempis or John Bunyan; and you may expect henceforth to see my birthday inserted among the wonderful events, in the poor Robin's and Aberdeen Almanacks, along with the black Monday, & the battle of Bothwell bridge.[4]

Full of the exciting news of Glencairn's efforts on his behalf, he declares triumphantly,

> My Lord Glencairn & the Dean of Faculty, Mr H. Erskine, have taken me under their wing; and by all probability I shall soon be the tenth Worthy, and the eighth Wise man, of the world. Through my Lord's influence it is inserted in the records of the Caledonian Hunt, that they universally, one & all, subscribe for the 2d Edition. My subscription bills come out tomorrow.[5]

Events taken at the flood, as Shakespeare wrote, may lead to great things. Glencairn, through this one act, guaranteed the success of the Edinburgh Edition, in financial terms at least. The Caledonian Hunt represented the landed elites, who conspicuously frequented city life; the upper echelons of Scottish society, who mingled, of a Sunday, on the Meadows. It was a marketing *coup de grâce* and a circulation dream to receive a bulk subscription order from the opinion-shakers and leading socialites of Scotland's capital.

Glencairn's influence extended further than the capital, as Burns makes clear to Robert Aiken:

> His Lordship has sent a parcel of subscription bills to the Marquiss of Graham with downright orders to get them filled up with all the first Scottish names about Court. He has likewise wrote to the Duke of Montague and is about to write to the Duke of Portland for their Graces' interest in behalf of the Scotch Bard's Subscription.[6]

With the London-based Scottish elite being told to sign up and support the bard, it is no surprise that Burns wrote of Glencairn with gushing praise in his Commonplace Book, dedicated poetry to him and later named his fourth son after him. (His 'Lament for James, Earl of Glencairn', a heartfelt tribute, appeared in the 1793 revised Edinburgh Edition, following Glencairn's untimely death in 1791.) The Enlightened and liberal-minded men of the square and compass, like James Cunningham and James Dalrymple, were 'friend(s) that sticketh closer than a Brother' to Burns.

Any detractors now paled in significance to the elites who embraced Burns in Edinburgh, as he informed John Ballantine:

> I have been introduced to a good many of the noblesse, but my avowed Patrons & Patronesses are, the Duchess of Gordon – the Countess of Glencairn, with my lord & lady Betty – the Dean of Faculty – Sir John Whiteford. I have likewise warm friends among the Literati, Professors Stewart, Blair, Greenfield, and Mr McKenzie the Man of feeling. An unknown hand left ten guineas for the Ayrshire Bard in Mr Sibbald's hand, which I got. I have since discovered my generous unknown friend to be Patrick Miller Esq. brother to the Justice Clerk . . .
>
> I was, Sir, when I was first honoured with your notice, too obscure, now I tremble lest I should be ruined by being dragged to [*sic*] suddenly into the glare of polite & learned observation.[7]

The surprise gift of ten guineas was from Patrick Miller, who would eventually become Burns' landlord at Ellisland farm near Dumfries.

Burns knew that his poetical skills had elevated him only temporarily to these circles. The mask of Heaven-taught ploughman would eventually slip. Fundamentally, this was a social world he was allowed to observe rather than to enter fully and, as he told Aiken, 'I look down on the future as I would into the bottom-less pit.'[8]

The Duke and Duchess of Gordon – George Alexander and his Galloway-born wife, Jane Maxwell of Monreith, whose sister Betty married a son of Mrs Dunlop – were showy socialites; the fun-loving, boisterous sisters were reputed to have ridden down the High Street on the back of a pig. The Duchess, remarking on Burns' finesse in conversation, said that he was the first male ever to have swept her completely off her feet, a comment that has engendered speculation as to whether they were on physically intimate terms. This is unlikely. Burns would have been aware that such a liaison risked the sort of scandal that might have imperilled his second edition.

It became well known that Burns' favourite Edinburgh belle was Eliza Burnett, a daughter of James Burnett, Lord Monboddo, a highly eccentric Lord of Session and philosopher of language. She obtains mention in the poet's rather turgid, Augustean 'Address to Edinburgh', which Daiches has rightly described as a 'duty poem' of public gratitude for the hospitality he received. It serves to demonstrate that, unless composing from the internal spark of his own inspiration, Burns could write mediocre poetry; great poets, as he himself would later comment, do not always write in their best manner.

In a letter of 27 December to lawyer William Chalmers, in Ayr, he rhapsodises about Eliza's charms:

> One blank in the address to Edinr – 'Fair B–', is the heavenly Miss Burnett, daughter to lord Monbodo, at whose house I have had the honor to be more than once. There has not been anything nearly like her, in all the combinations of Beauty, Grace and Goodness the great Creator has formed, since Milton's Eve on the first day of her existence.[9]

Eliza succumbed to tuberculosis in 1790 and is memorialised by Burns in the elegy 'On the Late Death of Miss Burnett'.[10]

Now rubbing shoulders with the aristocracy, accepting their respect as his due based on the merit of his poetic achievements, Burns had no inclination to make a show of empty obeisance purely on grounds of birth. However, it was not he who wrote:

> The disposition to admire, and almost to worship, the rich and the powerful, and to despise, or at least, to neglect persons of poor and mean condition . . . is, at the same time, the great and most universal cause of the corruption of our moral sentiments. That wealth and greatness are often regarded with the respect and admiration which are due only to wisdom and virtue; and that the contempt, of which vice and folly are the only proper objects, is often most unjustly bestowed upon poverty and weakness, has been the complaint of moralists in all ages.[11]

The author of the above passage is economist and moral philosopher Adam Smith, the most eminent luminary of the late Enlightenment, whose lopsided posthumous reputation tends to stress his role purely as an economist. There is no evidence that he and Burns ever met but it was Smith's *Theory of Moral Sentiments* that inspired him to try his hand at Shakespearian blank verse in the poem 'Remorse'. Burns writes, in his Second Commonplace Book, which he started in Edinburgh, 'There are few of the sore evils under the sun give me more uneasiness and chagrin than the comparison how a man of genius – nay, avowed worth – is everywhere received with the reception which a mere ordinary character, decorated with the trappings and futile distinctions of Fortune meets.'[12] Although Smith's comments are couched in more detached terms, they are addressing the same issue. On an everyday basis, this was more than theory to Burns, who was expected to show deference and respect to everyone of title, whether or not they had any valid claim to his respect.

Smith argues that it is contrary to good morals 'to say, that mere wealth and greatness, abstracted from merit and virtue, deserve our respect' and his comment, 'The profligacy of a man of fashion is looked upon with much less contempt or aversion, than that of a man of meaner condition,' applies aptly to Burns' predicament.[13] Many of Burns' remarks on the behaviour of his so-called superiors are strikingly similar to Smith's social commentary. While both men had a strongly moral view of the world, the poet sparks with indignation more readily.

The duality of being a national poet and a peasant irked Burns till his dying day. He did not enjoy being treated as an oddity, and on one occasion, on being invited to a lady's soirée, he is supposed to have quipped he would appear if the 'Learned Pig' then on display at the Grassmarket was to be included (the porcine celebrity performed tricks for a shilling). In a letter to Mrs Dunlop he gives vent to a blast against social vanity:

> . . . often, as I have glided with humble stealth through the pomp of Princes street, it has suggested itself to me as an improvement on the present Human figure, that a man, in proportion to his own conceit of his consequence in the world, could have pushed out the longitude of his common size, as a snail pushes out his horns, or as we draw out a perspective. – This trifling alteration, not to mention the prodigious saving it would be in the tear & wear of the neck and limb sinews of

> many of his Majesty's liege subjects in the way of tossing the head and tiptoe strutting, would evidently turn out a vast advantage in enabling us at once to adjust the ceremonials in making a bow or making way to a Great Man, and that too within a second of the precise spherical angle of reverence, or an inch of the particular point of respectful distance, which the important creature itself requires; as a measuring-glance at its towering altitude would determine the affair like instinct.[14]

The best-known example of Burns letting the mask of the Heaven-taught ploughman slip relates to derogatory remarks made by the Reverend William Robb about Thomas Gray's 'Elegy in a Country Churchyard'. Burns let him rave on, then cut in with 'Sir, I now perceive a man may be an excellent judge of poetry by square and rule, and after all, be a damned blockhead!' Burns gritted his teeth as much as he could but the odd snarl escaped. Like it or not, each person he met was a potential subscriber and so alienating anyone was unwise.

Unlike the all-in-one publishing package provided by John Wilson in Kilmarnock, the Edinburgh Edition became a tripartite arrangement. William Creech agreed to act as the publisher and deal with subscription bills, William Smellie was the printer and typesetter and William Scott was responsible for stitching and binding. This arrangement, with the notoriously tight-fisted Creech as the money-handler, incurred three separate costs and caused delays in the final payment to the poet. Creech, the city's leading publisher, had been to school with Lord Glencairn and it was probably the latter's introduction that brought him on board, although he was shrewd enough to see that publishing the work of Burns would be a lucrative venture.

More congenial to the poet was William Smellie, a leading author in the field of natural history, who had published the first volumes of the *Encyclopaedia Britannica*. He was a member of the Crochallan Fencibles, a somewhat radical gentlemen's drinking club, which met in the tavern at Anchor Close.[15] Its leading lights held mock military titles after the groups of Fencibles set up like home-guard battalions during the war for American independence. Smellie's son Alexander destroyed his correspondence with Burns, due to the comments they contained about high-ranking individuals who were still alive at the time. It is a loss to be lamented. The one extant letter, from Smellie to Burns (quoted in Robert Kerr's *Memoirs* of William Smellie, 1811), addresses the bard as 'Dear Rabbie' and informs him that he is sending the letter personally via a painter, a profession, Smellie asserts, that is the same as a poet's, in that they are 'both liars'. Burns' side of the correspondence must remain a mystery.

As part of Burns initiation into the Crochallan Fencibles, 'Colonel' William Dunbar, a Writer to the Signet, tested his temper by making him suffer a satirical verbal onslaught – a 'flyting', or, as Burns put it, 'literary scolding'.[16] Other friends made at the Fencibles were William Nicol, Classics teacher at the Edinburgh High School and Alexander Cunningham, a lawyer, both of whom had already met Burns at Masonic meetings in Edinburgh. It was among the Crochallan Fencibles that Burns indulged his propensity for bawdry and laid the foundation for what was to become *The Merry Muses of Caledonia*, a collection of lewd songs.

Alexander Smellie left a fascinating description of how eccentrically Burns behaved in his father's printing offices while the Edinburgh Edition was being typeset and proofed:

> Burns would walk up and down the room three or four times, cracking a whip which he carried, to the no small surprise of the men. He paid no attention to any of his own copy that might be in hand, but looked at any others which he saw lying in the cases . . . There was a particular stool in the office which Burns uniformly occupied while correcting his proof-sheets; as he would not sit on any other, it always bore the name of Burns' Stool.[17]

He goes on to explain that Sir John Dalrymple came into Smellie's offices to check proofs of his *Essay on the Properties of Coal Tar* and sat upon Burns' Stool. The poet came in and gave him a stare of territorial disdain. Staff took Burns aside, then asked Dalrymple to relinquish the stool. He refused:

> 'I will not give up my seat to yon impudent staring fellow.' Upon which it was replied: 'Do you not know that that staring fellow, as you call him, is, Burns the poet?' Sir John instantly left the stool, exclaiming 'Good gracious! Give him all the seats in your house!' Burns was then called in, took possession of his stool, and commenced the reading of his proofs.[18]

A variety of other reminiscences have survived, revealing the impression Burns made during his first stay in Edinburgh. While he was observing his variegated hosts and taking notes in his Second Commonplace Book – 'never did four shillings purchase so much friendship since Confidence went first to market, or Honesty was set to Sale'– they, too, were passing judgement on him.[19] Dugald Stewart commented that the attention Burns received would have 'turned any head but his own':

> He retained the same simplicity of manners and appearance which struck me so forcibly when I first saw him in the country; nor did he seem to feel any additional self-importance to the number and rank of his new acquaintances. His dress was perfectly suited to his station, plain and unpretending, with a sufficient attention to neatness. If I recollect right, he always wore boots; and, when on more than usual ceremony, buck-skin breeches.[20]

Regarding the rumour, that Burns had a 'predilection for convivial and not very select society', Stewart observes, 'I should have concluded in favour of his habits of sobriety.'

On show among the literati, Burns knew he might be called to perform his poetry at any moment and, for that reason alone, was unlikely to become intoxicated in such company; Alicia Cockburn (authoress of the Scots ballad 'Flowers of the Forest') wrote on 10 January 1787, 'The town is at present agog with the ploughman poet, who receives adulation with native dignity.'[21] On the poet's 28th birthday, Alexander Dalziel, the Professor of Greek at Edinburgh University, observed:

> We have got a poet in town just now, whom everybody is taking notice of . . . a man of unquestionable genius, who has produced admirable verse, mostly in the Scottish dialect, though some of them are nearly in English. He is a fellow of strong common sense, and by his own industry has read a good deal of English, both prose and verse . . . Everybody is fond of showing him everything here that the place furnishes . . . he behaves wonderfully well; very independent in his sentiments . . .[22]

Even Walter Scott, at 16 years of age, got in on the act. He encountered Burns at the home of Adam Ferguson, in the company of Ferguson's eldest son (also Adam). Scott observed Burns looking at a painting by Bunbury, showing a soldier lying dead in the snow, his widow kneeling beside him with a child in her arms and the dead soldier's dog pining by his master, and later said that the scene so moved Burns that he 'actually shed tears'. When Burns asked whose lines of poetry were printed beneath the painting, it was Scott who whispered to the professor's son that the lines were from Langhorne's 'The Justice of the Peace'. Burns 'rewarded me with a look and a word, which, though of mere civility, I then received and still recollect, with very great pleasure,' Scott remembered, going on to describe Burns as having the appearance of a 'sagacious country farmer', adding perceptively, with a strange use of language:

> ... the eye alone, I think, indicated the poetical character and temperament. It was large and of a dark cast, and glowed (I say literally glowed) when he spoke with feeling or interest. I never saw such another eye in a human head, though I have seen the most distinguished men in my time.[23]

However, this was not quite the passing of the torch from one generation of writers to another, as has sometimes been suggested.

By mid-January, Burns knew his second edition would be a runaway success. His celebrity as Scotland's national bard can be gauged by the fact that at the St Andrew's lodge meeting on 12 January, in front of all the senior Masons of the country and all the members of lodges around Edinburgh, a toast was drunk to:

> 'Caledonia, & Caledonia's Bard, brother Burns!' Which rung through the whole Assembly with multiplied honors and repeated acclamations . . . I was downright thunderstruck, and, trembling in every nerve, made the best return in my power. Just as I had finished, some of the Grand Officers said so loud as I could hear, with a most comforting accent, 'Very well indeed!' which set me something to rights again.[24]

The notion that Burns was officially inaugurated as the Poet Laureate of the Canongate Kilwinning Lodge probably stems from the events at the St Andrew's lodge meeting, given that there is no record of the ceremony at the former. The Masonic movement in Scotland and America was progressive – most of the leading members of the first American government were

Freemasons. Although the Master Mason of a lodge was usually of the aristocracy, senior positions within lodges were open to all – making them far more democratic than was the case in the general social order in Scotland in the eighteenth century.

Not wanting to alienate friends, Burns asked Lord Glencairn if he thought 'The Ballad on the American War' should be included in the Edinburgh Edition. Glencairn sidestepped the issue, suggesting Burns should seek the view of Henry Erskine:

> I showed the inclosed political ballad to my lord Glencairn, to have his opinion whether I should publish it; as I suspect my political tenets may be rather heretical in the opinion of some of my best Friends. I have a few first principles in Religion and Politics, which I believe, I would not easily part with . . .
>
> I would not have a dissocial word about it with any one of God's creatures, particularly an honored Patron, or a respected Friend. His Lordship seems to think the piece may appear in print, but desired me to send you a copy for your suffrage.[25]

Burns' political sentiments were already clearly delineated in 'A Dream' and no amount of etiquette could unpublish that poem. Glencairn and Erskine were of the Whiggish persuasion and had no problems with the sentiments expressed in 'The Ballad on the American War'. He printed the radical song.

In deciding what material he ought to exclude from the Edinburgh Edition, while not wishing to compromise his principles or poetic integrity, Burns heeded a great deal of the advice given by Hugh Blair. Surprisingly, Blair only wished to amend one stanza of 'A Dream', believing that the description 'Young Royal Tarry Breeks' was a bit 'coarse' and should be omitted. He also condemned two poems, now supposedly missing, as 'burlesquing the Scriptures': Blair's notes record that 'The Prophet' and 'God's Complaint' took their origin from Jeremiah 15.[26] Part of the missing poetry, three verses based on Jeremiah 15, but with the title adapted from the biblical text, 'Ah Woe is Me My Mother Dear', appeared in the 1835 Hogg and Motherwell edition of Burns. These are probably an early draft of the first part of the two poems previously supposed missing and if so, the identification is a disappointing anti-climax.

Blair's put-down of the poet's radical sentiments, 'Burns' politics always smell of the smithy', is indicative of the professor's mindset. Burns remarked in a letter to Mrs Dunlop on 22 March, 'I sometimes find it necessary to claim the priviledge of thinking for myself.'[27]

Interestingly, Burns declared in a letter to the Reverend William Greenfield that his meteoric rise would be short-lived and also foretold that there would be those who would try to destroy his fame and name – a scenario that actually occurred in terms of posthumous character assassinations during the vicious Loyalist counter-attack on Scottish radicalism:

> I am willing to believe that my abilities deserved a better fate than the veriest shades of life; but to be dragged forth, with all my imperfections on my head, to the full glare of learned and polite observation, is what, I am afraid, I shall have bitter reason to repent. 'When proud fortune's ebbing tide recedes' you may bear me witness, when my bubble of fame was at the highest, I stood, unintoxicated, with the inebriating cup in my hand, looking forward, with rueful resolve, to the hastening time when the stroke of envious Calumny, with all the eagerness of vengeful triumph, should dash it to the ground.[28]

Greenfield was one of the finest, most 'engagingly charming' preachers Burns had ever heard; he comments in his Second Commonplace Book on his 'joyous hilarity'. The two songs Burns sent him, supposedly written by 'two Ayrshire mechanics', were probably his own bawdy lyrics.

Edinburgh's door of fame had opened to welcome Burns and he had slipped through it, wearing the mask of the Heaven-taught ploughman. He had played the part well, holding up to close scrutiny among what he termed 'the permanent lights of genius and literature'.[29] Fame, as any poet knows, is about going into the culture and staying there. When Wordsworth later wrote of Burns, after visiting the poet's grave, 'Deep in the general heart of men, / His power survives', he was describing the living phenomenon of genuine fame, the immortality a great poet dreams of among the general public. Edinburgh's progressive liberal-minded elite had welcomed Burns with open arms but they were, in the long term, a stepping stone for him – as Burns was a curiosity to many of them. When Dr John Moore, a friend of Mrs Dunlop, to whom she sent a copy of the

Kilmarnock Edition, wished to give Burns his pennyworth of advice on the Edinburgh Edition, Burns informed him the work was in the press and too late to change, then expanded on his ambitions for poetic fame:

> The hope to be admired for Ages is, in by far the greater part of what are even Authors of repute, an unsubstantial dream. – For my part, my first ambition was, and still my strongest wish is, to please my Compeers, the rustic Inmates of the Hamlet, while everchanging language and manners will allow me to be relished and understood.[30]

Burns here realises that lasting fame would depend on the general public's view of him, not on that of his Edinburgh patrons. The bread-and-butter mission to Edinburgh would seal his fame during his lifetime but it could have been at a far greater price, had he not stuck to his instincts. Most of his advisers there suggested he should avoid writing in Scots. Blair, Mackenzie and others were leading proponents of eradicating 'Scotticisms' from polite society; preferring to ape their English counterparts and consign the Athens of the North to the cultural dominance of the Union's powerbase in London, they considered Scots a barbarous, regional dialect. Burns was too patriotic a Scot and too single-minded in purpose to take their feeble advice. He knew he was minting literary art in the Scots tongue and that his art would be appreciated in ages to come.

It appears to have been some advice and an 'epistle of criticisms' from the Earl of Buchan that planted the idea in Burns' head that he should tour parts of Scotland and 'fire my Muse at Scottish story and Scottish scenes'. The pompous earl had pretensions to poetry and sent a windbag missive to Burns, dressed in such high-falluting, flowery language, that the bard (who was obviously meant to be deeply impressed) must have almost spewed. One example is enough: 'may the Apollo of my Nypa who sits on the fork of Eildon enable you to produce the genuine offspring of Genius'. The poet's generous reply informs Buchan that he would probably not have the time to wander Scottish scenes at will, merely to write poetry, but that he will eventually have to 'return to my rustic station, and, in my wonted way woo my rustic Muse at the Plough-tail'[31] in order to stay a step away from the 'veriest Poverty'. However, Burns did, after all, take up the earl's suggestion of a tour immediately following the publication of the Edinburgh Edition.

With a knack of finding the depressing cloud to any silver lining, Burns periodically turned his attention to his future: to Robert Muir in Kilmarnock, he wrote, on 15 December, 'I have now neither house nor home that I can call my own.'[32] A moth to the light of fame in Edinburgh, Burns had placed his home-based problems on the back burner during his visit to the capital.

One possibility was to take on the lease of a farm at Ellisland, which had been offered to him by its owner, Patrick Miller. In a letter to John Ballantine, he expresses his concern about going back into farming and his repugnance at the thought of living in claustrophobic, Calvinist Ayrshire again:

> Some life-rented, embittering Recollections whisper me that I will be happier anywhere than in my old neighborhood, but Mr Miller is no Judge of land; and though I dare say he means to favour me, yet he may give me, in his opinion, an advantageous bargain that may ruin me. I am to take a tour by Dumfries as I return and have promised to meet Mr Miller on his lands some time in May.[33]

To be a full-time poet was beginning to look like an idle dream. Henry James Pye, the Poet Laureate, obtained his annual stipend for writing loyalist gush; Scotland had no such post, then or now.[34] Burns took up the lease at Ellisland farm after a prolonged period in which he found it almost impossible to extract from Creech the monies he was owed.

Burns' warmth towards Jean had not been extinguished among the glittering city belles, as he informed Gavin Hamilton: 'To tell the truth among friends, I feel a miserable blank in my heart, with want of her, and I don't think I shall ever meet with so delicious an armful again,' going on philosophically, 'She has her faults; and so have you and I; and so has every body,' then admitting:

> I have met with a very pretty girl, a Lothian farmer's daughter, whom I have almost persuaded to accompany me to the west country, should I ever return to settle there . . .
>
> We had dined all together at a common friend's house in Leith, and danced, drank, and sang till late enough. The night was dark, the claret had been good, and I thirsty . . .[35]

The letter ends abruptly and the manuscript has not been preserved, nor has the identity of the young woman been satisfactorily ascertained. DeLancey Ferguson assumes she was Margaret Chalmers, who later claimed Burns had proposed marriage to her but, as Mackay rightly points out, that Margaret Chalmers was not the daughter of a Lothian farmer. In a letter addressed laconically to 'My Dear Countrywoman', also believed to be to Chalmers, it is evident that she (or the unknown woman) kept their relationship on a strictly friendly basis. Burns admits to her, 'You know the black story at home. My breast has been widowed these many months.'[36] He was not averse, though, to trying the art of courtship. Mackay postulates that the woman was actually Archibald Lawrie's sister Christina, but her father was not a Lothian farmer either. He was the Reverend George Lawrie from near Kilmarnock, a friend and correspondent of Burns. The poet mentions Miss Lawrie as 'the daughter of a reverend friend of mine in the West country'.[37] Burns was obviously a close friend of Miss Lawrie and it would appear that the unknown object of his amours was a friend of Christina and Archibald Lawrie.

In February, the poet's flirtatious interests focused upon another lady, again unidentified. He confessed his amorous feelings to Lord Glencairn and appears to have regretted doing so, as he informs James Dalrymple of Orangefield:

> I have compromised matters with his godship of late by uncoupling my heart and fancy, for a sight-chace, after a certain Edinr Belle. My devotions proceed no farther than a forenoon's walk, a sentimental conversation, now and then a squeeze of the hand or interchanging an oeillade, and when peculiar good humor and sequestered propriety allow.[38]

Burns' infatuation with his Edinburgh belle appears to have been little more than a flirtatious friendship. It may have been an attempt to woo the society beauty Eliza Burnett, given the evidence of his earlier crush upon her. Burns was, in a sense, a moth to the light of the educated, mannered, 'bewitching sex'. Whatever physical attraction might occur, he was unlikely to find himself snuggly berthed with a wealthy 'Edinr Belle'. It would have been taboo for any lady of standing to descend and marry a peasant, not even if he was the famed poet, Robert Burns.

❖❖❖

During the eighteenth century, it was generally only politicians, the nobility or leading authors who had their portrait painted or their silhouette done. Burns joined this select group at Creech's behest: his publisher arranged a meeting with Alexander Nasmyth, as Burns proudly announced to John Ballantine: 'I am getting my phiz done by an eminent engraver, and if it can be ready in time, I will appear in my book, looking like all other fools, to my title-page.'[39] Nasmyth's bust-portrait was passed on, unfinished, to the engraver John Beugo for a final copperplate engraving for the Edinburgh Edition. Both Nasmyth and Beugo became intimate friends of the bard. Two sketches of Burns by Nasmyth are in the collections of the National Galleries of Scotland and the other is in the possession of Irvine Burns Club. It was Nasmyth's son James who recorded the story of his father and Burns marching to Roslin Castle after a late night in a High Street tavern in June 1787, to meet the early rising summer sun.[40] Had Burns been the dissipated rogue of legend, he would have been incapable of a 500-yard stagger, let alone a walk of several miles.

The poet had opened a dialogue with the literati by touting his poetry around for their criticisms. Believing themselves more intelligent than Burns, they dished up their views. He writes to Gavin Hamilton on 8 March, complaining angrily:

> My two Songs on Miss W. Alexander and Miss P. Kennedy were likewise tried yesterday by a jury of Literati, and found defamatory libels against the fastidious Powers of Poesy and Taste; and the author forbidden to print them under pain of forfeiture of character. – I cannot help almost shedding a tear to the memory of two Songs that had cost me some pains, and that I valued a good deal, but I must submit. –
>
> ... My poor unfortunate Songs come again across my memory – Damn the pedant, frigid soul of Criticism for ever and ever![41]

The problem for Burns was he did not have permission from the ladies to print the songs. The literati pointed out this simple etiquette. He had strived to obtain the notice of Miss Wilhelmina Alexander, an Ayrshire aristocrat, heroine of 'The Bonnie Lass of Ballochmyle' in a letter to her in November 1786, where he asked permission to print the song with her name added. 'She was too fine a lady to notice so plain a compliment,' Burns writes in the Glenriddell Mss of his attempt to impress her with his 'ADMIRATION'. His letter and the song were ignored, as Burns himself was, by her brother, the laird of Ballochmyle, Claud Alexander, when they subsequently met. Burns wrote stingingly: 'As to her great Brothers, when Fate swore their purses should be full, Nature was equally positive their heads should be empty.' The poet believed there could be no offence if the ladies' names were dashed out, in the manner of the times, so his frustrations are understandable. Fortunately, the songs were preserved.

DeLancey Ferguson compares Burns' visit to Edinburgh with the reception given to Benjamin Franklin in Versailles ten years before, emphasising that Burns, like Franklin, was the intellectual equal of any of his patrons.[42] The letter from Burns to the Reverend George Lawrie shows that the so-called Heaven-taught ploughman knew his own intellectual prowess: 'I had been at a good deal of pains to form a just, impartial estimate of my intellectual Powers before I came here; I have not added, since I came to Edinr, anything to the account; and I trust, I shall take every atom of it back to my shades.'[43] By the time the second edition appeared he realised that he had let too many 'experts' meddle in his writings:

> You are right in your guesses that I am not very amenable to counsel . . . I set as little by kings, lords, clergy, critics, &c. as all these respectable Gentry do my Bardship. I know what I may expect from the world, by and by; illiberal abuse and perhaps contemptuous neglect.[44]

Robert Fergusson died prematurely and penniless in the Edinburgh madhouse. On 6 February, Burns wrote to the magistrates of the Canongate for permission to erect a headstone at Fergusson's grave. They passed his letter to the managers of the Canongate Kirkyard, who duly gave permission. The poet commissioned an Edinburgh architect named Robert Burn to design the headstone, which was to 'remain an unalienable property to his deathless fame'.[45] Burns complained that it took the architect two years to erect the headstone. He, therefore, took two years to pay him, 'so he and I are quits,' he told Creech's assistant, Peter Hill, in a letter of February 1792.[46] The elegiac lines Burns inscribed on the stone are:

> No sculptur'd marble here, nor pompous lay,
>   'No story'd urn nor animated bust;'

This simple stone directs pale SCOTIA'S way
To pour her sorrows o'er her POET's dust.[47]

Further stanzas were composed but remained unpublished in the poet's lifetime. The very fact that Fergusson lay in the Canongate Kirkyard, his grave neglected, without even a headstone, was probably what triggered Burns' fear that he, too, would eventually suffer the same neglect. The so-called 'libertine' in Burns had already slighted many of his new subscribers when he wrote, 'My curse upon your whunstane hearts. / Ye Enbrugh Gentry! / The tythe of what ye waste at cartes / Wad stow'd his pantry' in the 'Epistle to William Simpson'. Ironically, the very same Edinburgh gentry were now stowing Burns' pantry.

It was an old patron and friend of Robert Fergusson, the well-known actor William Woods, who invited Burns to write a Prologue for the actors benefit night at the Theatre Royal in Edinburgh on 16 April 1787. (He later became a leading patron of the Theatre Royal in Dumfries and composed several works for espousal from the 'humble boards' of the small town.) The Prologue is a finer work than the hidebound 'Address to Edinburgh' and patriotically acknowledges Scotland's leading role in the Enlightenment:

But here an ancient nation, fam'd afar,
For genius, learning high, as great in war.
Hail, CALEDONIA, name for ever dear!
Before whose sons I'm honour'd to appear!

Where every science – every nobler art –
That can inform the mind, or mend the heart,
Is known; as grateful nations oft have found,
Far as the rude barbarian marks the bound.
Philosophy, no idle pedant dream,
Here holds her search by heaven-taught Reason's beam;
Here History paints with elegance and force
The tide of Empire's fluctuating course;
Here *Douglas* forms wild Shakespeare into plan,
And *Harley* rouses all the God in man . . .[48]

The final passage prays for Scotland to rise up against any future tyranny and be 'Self-dependent in her native shore':

> O Thou, dread Power! whose empire-giving hand
> Has oft been stretch'd to shield the honour'd land!
> Strong may she glow with all her ancient fire;
> May every son be worthy of his sire;
> Firm may she rise, with generous disdain
> At Tyranny's, or direr Pleasure's chain;
> Still Self-dependent in her native shore,
> Bold may she brave grim Danger's loudest roar,
> Till Fate the curtain drop on worlds to be no more!

The poet was by now in receipt of what can only be termed fan mail, some in the form of verse epistles. Probably the best of these received during this period came from the elderly Mrs Elizabeth Scott of Wauchope House, by Jedburgh – a niece of the poetess Mrs Cockburn. She shows a perceptive appreciation of Burns' satire.

> An' then sae slee ye crack yer jokes
> O' Willie Pitt and Charlie Fox.
> Our Great men a' sae weel descrive,
> And how to gar the nation thrive,
> Ane maist wad swear ye dwalt amang them,
> An' as ye saw them, sae ye sang them.[49]

It was a piece worthy enough to provoke, by way of reply, 'To the Guidwife of Wauchope House', in which Burns refers to his wish to 'write a book' or 'sing a sang at least' for 'Scotland's sake'. Mrs Scott extended an open invitation to the poet to visit and promised to make him a checked plaid – Burns eventually met her and her husband Walter on 10 May on his Borders tour. Her poem praising Burns was printed in the Scottish press in early 1796, probably submitted by the poet himself.

It was Robert Heron, in his biographical sketch of Burns (1797), who first made the accusation that the poet frequented brothels and was regularly drunk when in Edinburgh. Heron was born in Galloway, the son of a weaver, and a graduate from Edinburgh University. He worked as an assistant to Professor Blair. The biographer McIntyre quotes as fact Robert Heron's accusations that, while in Edinburgh, Burns began to associate with a 'race of miserable beings' who encouraged the poet into 'drunkenness, in the tavern, in the brothel, on the lap of the woman of pleasure'.[50] Are these accusations true, or scurrilous gossip invented by Heron?

Heron's reliability and honesty are called into question for two main reasons. On a later visit to Burns at Ellisland farm, the poet asked Heron to pass a letter to Dr Blacklock but the quasi-clerical scribbler Heron stole it. During the 1790s, Heron was, as my recent research has shown, a paid government hack who received on at least one occasion a £50 payment from Henry Dundas via Henry Mackenzie for his attacks on radicals in the press.[51] Further patronage was bestowed upon Heron for his bootlicking servility in the form of a post as a writer to assist the French loyalists in London, with a handsome wage of £300 per annum. It should be borne in mind that deliberate character assassination was dished out to almost every radical writer during the late 1790s and afterwards.

It was the American scholar DeLancey Ferguson who argued in the 1930s that Burns did not have the finances to be a boozy drunk when in Edinburgh, even if he were so inclined. When Burns wrote to Patrick Miller in early spring 1787, remarking, 'I thank my God, Dissipation or Extravagance have never been part of my character,' he was being honest. Burns was not on a social visit to the capital. He was working. This holds true even when he was a guest of honour at social events. He was in the spotlight. From extant reports by Blair (as quoted earlier) and other members of the literati, Burns put his best foot forward. The bulk of his working week consisted of collating and brushing up older material for publication, writing new poetry and seeing his material from typesetting to proof sheets and making amendments. He had, indeed, been cracking the whip rather than cracking open the claret. All evidence from this period proves the poet's relative sobriety.

If Burns ever did frequent Edinburgh brothels, he would only have had the finances to do so while the money was coming in from the new Edinburgh Edition, during his last weeks in the city, not before. Since we do not have CCTV footage, it cannot be said with absolute certainty that the bard did not take advantage of everything the city had to offer. His letters show he was sympathetic to the women who were forced through poverty to engage in such activity. He advised his younger brother to avoid the temptation to use prostitutes for a host of reasons, including the danger of contracting a sexual disease. Burns' alleged impregnation of Meg Cameron is a topic dealt with in the next chapter.

There is a mystery surrounding the disappearance of a collection of the poet's manuscripts during this period. In a letter to George Reid, a few days after the Edinburgh Edition appeared in print, Burns informed him a thief had stolen a letter containing derogatory remarks about some important politicians and other persons,

> I had taken to pieces rt Honorables, Honorables, and Reverends not a few but it, with many more of my written things were stolen from my room, which terrified me from 'scauding my lips in ither folks kail' again. By good luck the fellow is gone to Gibraltar, and I trust in Heaven he will go to the bottom for his pains.[52]

The identity of the thief is not known. It is known that Burns withheld various poems from publication such as 'Love and Liberty', the 'Cantata' and possibly other poems such as 'The Address of Beelzebub'. The stolen material might have been dumped. Yet if the thief was after the poet's private papers and poetry, the unanswerable question is, why? Were his papers stolen and passed on to someone in authority? The political powerbrokers of the Dundas dynasty appear never to have paid him any attention whatsoever.

Caressed as the darling 'Bard of Caledonia', albeit as a 'Heaven-taught ploughman', Burns walked the social tightrope of Edinburgh's fashionable literary elite, playing the part of the inspired rustic with panache. Only rarely did he fall off. If he let his hair down among friends with the Crochallan Fencibles, it was because he had something to celebrate: his Edinburgh Edition was a major success.

9

THE EDINBURGH EDITION, 1787

THE NEW EDINBURGH EDITION APPEARED ON 17 APRIL 1787. Subscribers paid five shillings, while those who bought from a bookshop or privately, paid six shillings. It irked the poet a little that he was compelled to append a list of subscribers' names, adding to his printing costs. Subscribers, though, wanted to be seen as patrons of literature. There were a few hiccups before final publication. Many subscription bills came in late and some were misplaced, a potentially serious problem. Due to a shortage of type, Smellie began to break up the set pages early to prepare for other work, then found he had to reset part of the book again because insufficient copies had been printed, which resulted in a few sloppy proof errors creeping into what was in effect a second imprint of the Edinburgh Edition.[1] This affected around 1,000 copies. The print run was 3,000, of which 1,500 people subscribed for around 2,800 copies, although they did not take away 2,800 books. Burns was advised by Dr Moore that subscribers did not always expect to receive the number of books which precisely equated with what they had paid. However, he was certain to have had surplus copies – from subscribers who paid for several copies but only wanted one or two – which could be sold on again.

Moreover, Burns did not have to run himself ragged distributing books as he had done with the Kilmarnock Edition. He parcelled off a number of copies to Robert Aiken and John Ballantine in Ayrshire. He eventually received over twenty-two pounds for ninety copies of his *Poems*, sold by Mr Pattison, the Paisley bookseller.[2] The bulk of orders were dealt with by Creech's assistant, Peter Hill, who became a close friend of Burns' over the next few years.

The poet's celebrity did not translate itself into immediate financial returns. Creech dangled a carrot before him on the very day his poems appeared and offered to buy his copyright for 100 guineas.[3] The hand of Henry Mackenzie may be discerned here, as a 'friend' of both and in his formal role as a lawyer. The first sentence of the agreement reads, 'By advice of friends, Mr Burns having resolved to dispose of the property of his *Poems*, and having consulted with Mr Henry Mackenzie upon the subject, Mr Creech met with Mr Burns at Mr Henry Mackenzie's house.' Whose idea this was is not known, but Burns, naïve enough not to take advice from his lawyer friend Aiken or others on this matter, gave little thought to the future consequences – he would live to regret his decision – and signed away his copyright. The legal document was drawn up by Mackenzie. Creech, in his subsequent dealings with Burns, could certainly not be termed a 'friend'. Mackenzie may have smiled at Burns, but he was no friend either. Indeed, in later life, Burns represented everything Mackenzie loathed, although Mackenzie's mendacious involvement in efforts to crush radicalism in Scotland in the 1790s was something he preferred to keep quiet.

Whether or not this *coup de grâce* delivered upon Burns was intended to make him a literary gelding – neuter him and control what was henceforth printed under his name – is impossible to determine. It is difficult to avoid the conclusion that Mackenzie and Creech shafted Burns. They denied him income he could have benefited from greatly later in life, when he needed it most. But in the short term, at least, it made Burns richer than he had ever been.

Creech believed he could seek agreement with the publishers Cadell and Davies in London for an edition there, so his motives appear to have been primarily self-interest. Certainly, he would not have made the offer unless he was going to benefit by it.

The notion in the memorandum that 'Scotland was now amply supplied' was somewhat inaccurate, given the speed at which copies sold. Creech, having agreed to pay Burns the £105 (100 guineas) for his copyright, took until 30 May 1788 to pay out. Even worse, it took until 25 March 1789 before all accounts for subscriptions were paid to Burns – almost two years after publication.

Burns' short-term gain was also his long-term loss. He never got a penny from Creech for the next Edinburgh Edition, in 1793, despite its including new poems to which Creech had no legally binding rights – in particular, 'Tam o'Shanter'. It must have been a bitter pill to swallow, to write the best poem in Scottish literary history and receive nothing for it other than praise.

The poet calculated he had cleared between £440 and £450 for the first Edinburgh Edition.[4] This was a handsome sum for any tenant farmer's son, but it came in dribs and drabs. Generous to a fault, Burns helped save the Mossgiel household from ruin and gave a loan of £180 to Gilbert to clear rent arrears and help the family improve their standard of living. There are no proper accounts extant for the costing of the Edinburgh Edition and so it is problematic to work out an objective balance-sheet, especially when bookstore sellers took what Burns termed their 'unconscionable, Jewish tax of 25 per Cent by way of agency', as he wrote to John Ballantine.[5] Mackay tries to suggest Burns was not too good at arithmetic (despite being meticulous with figures as an Exciseman later) and obtained a larger profit from Creech but it is almost impossible to determine the exact amount, due to the lack of concrete figures.

The Edinburgh Edition contained 22 additional works, a 50 per cent increase on the Kilmarnock Edition. There was a considerable increase in pagination, from 235 to 343 pages, plus a 24-page glossary and 38 pages of subscribers names. In comparing the times taken to produce the Kilmarnock Edition with the time taken to produce the Edinburgh Edition, it took just over two weeks more to have the second edition off the press than the time dedicated to the smaller Kilmarnock Edition. The list of subscribers was a roll-call of the great and the good (and old friends who had supported the Kilmarnock Edition) patronising the newly anointed, if not appointed, Bard of Caledonia. The Earl of Eglington, Archibald Montgomerie, who sent ten guineas to Burns after he arrived in the city, paid for 36 copies. Archibald Prentice of Covington Mains took 20, while Robert Muir of Kilmarnock was down for 40 copies. Lord Glencairn paid for 24 and the Duchess of Gordon, 21. The final product, a huge success, was bound in French grey paper boards; overall, it was more professionally produced than the earlier, self-published edition.

The largest bulk subscription was from the Caledonian Hunt. It was to them the edition was dedicated, with tongue-in-cheek obsequiousness that simmers with dislike of sycophancy, tempered with the requirement to acknowledge the level of patronage he had successfully obtained. It is dressed in high-flown, poetic language:

> A SCOTTISH BARD, proud of the name, and whose highest ambition is to sing in his Country's service, where shall he so properly look for patronage as to the illustrious Names of his native Land; those who bear the honours and inherit the virtues of their Ancestors? The Poetic Genius of my Country found me as the prophetic bard Elijah did Elisha – at the *plough* . . . She bade me sing the loves, the joys, the rural scenes and rural pleasures of my native Soil, in my native tongue . . .
>
> . . . I do not approach you, my Lords and Gentlemen, in the usual stile of dedication, to thank you for past favours; that path is so hackneyed by prostituted Learning, that honest Rusticity is ashamed of it. – Nor do I present this Address with the venal soul of a servile Author, looking for a continuation of those favours: I was bred to the Plough, and am independent. I come to claim the common Scottish name with you, my illustrious Countrymen; and to tell the world that I glory in the title. – I come to congratulate my Country, that the blood of her ancient heroes still runs uncontaminated; and that from your courage, knowledge, and public spirit, she may expect protection, wealth and liberty . . .
>
> . . . may Pleasure ever be of your party; and may Social-joy await your return! When harassed in courts or camps with the justlings of bad men and bad measures, may the honest consciousness of injured Worth attend your return to your native Seats; and may Domestic Happiness, with a smiling welcome, meet you at your gates! May Corruption shrink at your kindling indignant glance; and may tyranny in the Ruler and licentiousness in the People equally find you an inexorable foe!

The feudal order, as described in this quasi-religious, utopian blessing, was not quite the blissful land Burns pretended. Yet it was the liberal-minded Edinburgh literati, many of who were either Masonic or from dissenting elements of Scottish society, who buoyed up support for Burns and, therefore, his fame as a poet.

Many of the poems first included in the Edinburgh Edition were older poems, from 1786. 'The Ballad on the American War' appeared along with other poems such as 'The Brigs of Ayr', dedicated to John Ballantine.

Other worthy additions were 'The Ordination', the brilliant 'Address to the Unco' Guid', 'Death and Doctor Hornbook', the boisterous 'Tam Samson's Elegy' and the witty piece, 'The Calf'. A plethora of religious verse, some rather mundane and with few real flashes of genius, serves to illustrate Burns' deep inculcation in religion and ability to versify biblical texts.

These include 'A Prayer Under the Pressure of Violent Anguish', 'The Nineteenth Psalm Paraphrased', 'Paraphrase of the First Psalm', 'Prayer: O Thou Dread Power' and 'Stanzas Written in the Prospect of Death'. Recent compositions included 'Address to Edinburgh', 'Address to a Haggis' and the Shakespeare-inspired blast at the desolation of economic forces that keep the peasantry poor, 'A Winter Night'. Among new songs were the timeless hymn to feminine beauty, 'Green Grow the Rashes O', followed by 'John Barleycorn', 'My Nanie O', 'The Gloomy Night is Gathering Fast' and 'No Churchman Am I'. The best of Burns as songwriter was still to come.

A tantalising new song, 'There Was A Lad', sometimes known as 'Rantin' Rovin' Robin', was apparently composed too late for inclusion. It is a remarkable song, which is almost prescient in its celebration of the poet's life. As his fame spread posthumously, so the popularity of this song grew, though it only appeared in print in 1808. The second line of the last stanza is blatantly sexual: 'You'll gar the lasses lie aspar', which means Robin will make the lasses lie with their legs apart. The last verse is usually discreetly dropped nowadays.

Another piece composed during the spring of 1787 was 'Epistle to Wm Tytler of Woodhouselee, Author of A Defence of Mary Queen of Scots'. William Tytler was a Writer to the Signet and author on various subjects, including music and antiquities. On enquiring into the evidence in defence of Mary Queen of Scots, Tytler provoked the wrath of David Hume, who remarked that a 'sound beating or a Rope too good for him' and blasted anyone who maintained the innocence of Mary as being beyond the reach of sound reason.[6] The pro-Jacobite verses, with their anti-Hanoverian slights, were only partially published by Currie in 1800, the lines offensive to the throne having been dropped. Burns told Tytler, who, like him, collected songs for Johnson's *Scots Musical Museum*, 'Burn the above verses when you have read them, as any little sense that is in them is rather heretical.'[7] The contentious and somewhat portentous lines were:

But why of that Epocha make such a fuss,
 That gave us th' Electoral Stem?
If bringing them over was lucky for us,
 I'm sure 'twas as lucky for them!

But Politics, truce! We're on dangerous ground;
 Who knows how the fashions may alter:
The doctrines today that are loyalty sound,
 Tomorrow might bring us a halter.

The poet's final act before leaving Edinburgh on his Borders tour was to write a series of farewell and thank you letters to Lord Glencairn, Hugh Blair, Henry Mackenzie, William Tytler and other individuals, whose help, advice and friendship he deemed indispensable.

The bard's fame was now spreading well beyond Scotland. An appraisal of Burns' work appeared in the *Critical Review* in May 1787, stating that the poet's name would be 'transmitted to posterity with honour'. The *Universal Magazine* of May 1787 lauded Burns, printing 'A Winter Night' and 'Epistle to Davie, a Brother Poet' as examples of his genius. In August, the *New Town and Country Magazine* praised the 'powerful genius' of Burns, quoting with approval a stanza of 'The Cotter's Saturday Night'. James Anderson returned almost a year after his first review with a follow up in December 1787 to praise the new edition, hoping the 'change in his circumstances will prove beneficial to the cause of literature, or productive of greater happiness to the individual'.

By 5 July 1787, Creech saw his venture with Thomas Cadell and A. Strahan bear fruit. A London edition appeared, followed by Belfast and Dublin editions. In 1788, an edition was printed in Philadelphia. By the end of the year, a New York edition appeared. It is generally believed that the Irish editions were pirated, although there is no evidence of Creech, the copyright holder, taking legal action; the same is true of the American editions. By the start of 1789, Burns was an internationally recognised Scottish poet. He had sneaked through Fame's door while no one was looking; while his readers admired the mask of the Heaven-taught ploughman poet.

10

His Bardship on Tour: The Borders Journal

Burns made two tours during 1787, the first through the Borders and briefly into England, then through the Highlands. Despite being celebrated in households across Scotland as the Bard of Caledonia, Burns kept his feet on the ground, sure that his old companion, poverty, had not gone for good. He knew he would have to return to farming or join the Excise to eke out a living. He hoped to meet Patrick Miller on his lands north of Dumfries in June, to look over the farmland Miller proposed renting. A few days prior to departing Edinburgh, Burns purchased himself a new horse for four pounds, which he named Jenny Geddes, after the woman who threw a cutty-stool at Bishop Lindsay's head at St Giles Cathedral in 1637. It was a typical gesture, the rebel with a cause, naming his horse after a notorious rebel.

His companion for part of the Borders tour was Robert Ainslie, a trainee lawyer several years younger than himself. They headed off through East Lothian towards Haddington on Saturday 5 May and continued on to Berrywell, near Duns, where Ainslie had arranged their first overnight stop, with his parents – his father worked as a steward for Lord Douglas. Burns purchased a new journal in which to write up his thoughts on 'men and manners' while on his peregrinations. The first entry states: 'Left Edinr. – Lammermuir hills miserably dreary but at times very picturesque.' He describes Ainslie's father as 'an uncommon character', quite knowledgeable on 'Agriculture natural philosophy & politics' and Rachel Ainslie as 'an angel'.

On the Sunday, Burns attended a church service with the Ainslies. The minister, a Dr Bowmaker, was 'a man of strong lungs and pretty judicious remark'. On observing Rachel's agitation during his rant about sinners, Burns inscribed in the fly-leaf of her Bible:

> Fair maid, you need not take the hint,
>   Nor idle texts pursue;
> 'Twas guilty sinners that he meant,
>   Not angels such as you.

He is supposed to have remarked to her that Bowmaker meant him as the prime sinner, 'I am found out wherever I go.' Wit and humour abound in the poetry and the man.

Ainslie's reminiscence of their jaunt, written after the poet's death, recounts that, on reaching Coldstream, he suggested they cross to the English side of the Tweed in order that Burns could say he had been in England. Ainslie went first. On setting foot on foreign soil for the first time, Burns took off his hat, fell to his knees and, in patriotic fervour, declaimed to his native country the last two stanzas of 'The Cotter's Saturday Night'.[1] It was a spontaneous gesture; he was, after all, the Bard of Caledonia.

At Coldstream, they dined with a Robert Foreman; Burns noted in his journal that he 'beat' Foreman in a dispute over Voltaire. His depth of acquaintance with the work of Enlightenment authors was no doubt a surprise. At Lennel House, Burns met the author Patrick Brydone, author of *A Tour Through Sicily and Malta*. Burns found him and his wife to be good-hearted but with a propensity to admire 'every thing that bears a splendid title or possesses a large estate'. Such an attitude might well have triggered his condemnation but their hospitality tempered his views.

The following morning, they travelled on, Burns noting a 'fine bridge over Tweed'. At the ruins of Roxburgh Castle, he saw 'a holly bush growing where James 2nd of Scotland was accidentally killed by the bursting of a cannon . . . a fine old garden planted by the religious, rooted out and destroyed by an English Hottentot.' With a farmer's eye, he observes: 'climate & soil of Berwick shire & even Roxburgh shire superior to Ayrshire – bad roads – turnip & sheep husbandry their great improvement'. They reached Jedburgh on Wednesday 9 May and decided to spend a few days there, at 27 Canongate. They breakfasted with a James Fair, a blind lawyer, his wife and sister. On a short excursion outside Jedburgh, they met and dined with a Captain John Rutherford, who told them he had been a soldier in America and had once been a captive of the native American Indians. Back in Jedburgh, Ainslie and Burns were taken a walk to be shown 'Love-lane and Black-burn' where they met a lawyer, Mr Potts, and the Reverend Dr Thomas Somerville. The cleric, according to Burns, required medical help to eradicate a verbal disease – he was 'sadly addicted to punning'. Apparently, when Somerville read this remark by Burns in Currie's 1800 edition of Burns, the cleric's addiction was miraculously cured.[2]

The next morning, they journeyed to Wauchope to meet Elizabeth Scott. Burns observes in his journal, 'breakfast by the way with Dr Elliot', a retired army doctor, who, acting as a guide, accompanied them 'almost to Wauchope'. Delighted by Mrs Scott, Burns observes that she had 'all the sense, taste, intrepidity of face, & bold critical decision which usually distinguish female Authors'; but her husband, although 'shrewd in his farming matters' was a 'complete Hottentot', with a leathery, sun-beaten face like Sancho Panza of Cervantes' *Don Quixote*. That evening they went back to Jedburgh and arranged events for the next day, Burns hoping Miss Lindsay would appear for breakfast, which she did. The group, including James Fair, went off to visit Esther Easton, 'a very remarkable woman for reciting Poetry of all kinds . . . She can repeat by heart almost every thing she has ever read, particularly Pope's Homer from end to end . . . A woman of very extraordinary abilities'. Burns mentions she was suspected of having been a prostitute in her pre-marriage days, or in his uncharacteristically tactful phrase, one of the 'Cytherean Deesse'.

In Esther's garden, Burns took Miss Lindsay aside and, to use his own words, 'I presented her with a proof-print of my nob' as a parting gift. (It was, of course, a copy of Beugo's engraving.) His attraction to Miss Lindsay is clear: 'Sweet Isabella Lindsay, may peace dwell in thy bosom . . . That love-kindling eye must beam on another, not on me' – despite the mischievous journal reference to his 'nob', Burns acted the part of a gentleman, hardly the behaviour of the rampant Rabbie of myth. The poet was 'presented with the freedom of the burgh' by the town Magistrates before making a 'melancholy' farewell to Jedburgh.

At Kelso, Burns and Ainslie dined with the farmers' club, then stayed over with Gilbert Kerr of Stodrig farm, a man who reminded Burns of his Kilmarnock friend Robert Muir. On 12 May, they dined with Sir Alexander Don and his 'divine lady' Harriet Don, the sister of James, Earl of Glencairn. After a second night at Stodrig farm, they set out for Melrose, visited the ruins of Dryburgh Abbey, then made their way along the Ettrick water to Selkirk in awful weather, arriving soaked to the skin. They spent the rest of the day at an inn. (Surprisingly, Burns does not mention Selkirk's links with William Wallace in his journal.)

In his 1838 edition of Burns' *Works*, the Ettrick Shepherd, James Hogg, recounts the story told to him by Dr Clarkson, who had been enjoying a Sunday evening drink with a few friends at Veitch's Inn, Selkirk, when they were asked if two travellers might join them. The landlord described the newcomers as 'twa drouket craws', a 'drover-looking chap' and 'one who spoke rather like a gentleman'.[3] Clarkson thought them unworthy of their company, unaware that one of the men was Robert Burns, whose works he greatly admired.

On 14 May, Burns and Ainslie reached Innerleithen, where they stayed at the inn. The following day, they dined at Earlston, which Burns notes to be 'the birth-place and residence of the celebrated Thomas A Rhymer'. Back with Ainslie's parents, Burns was pestered by Simon Gray, a retired local businessman, who had already sent him some dull verse; a third parcel awaited his arrival at Duns. Burns gave Gray what he requested, his honest opinion:

> We auld wives' minions gie our opinions,
>   Solicited or no';
> Then of its fau'ts my honest thoughts
>   I'll give – and here they go.
>
> Such damned bombast no time that's past
>   Will show, or time to come,
> So, Cimon dear, your song I'll tear
>   And with it wipe my bum.

At Berrywell, Burns received £22 7s. from Alexander Pattison in Paisley for 90 books sold. Planning to be in Dumfries by the start of June, he thereafter directed friends to send his mail to Dumfries post office. On 18 May, he and Ainslie rode to Berwick, then on to Eyemouth, where they stayed over with William Grieve, a leading local freemason. Grieve's brother Robert took them for a sail and later they were both welcomed to the St Abbs Lodge, where they were honoured as Royal Arch Masons. Ainslie at this point had to leave the excursion and return to work in Edinburgh.

Burns now records that a Miss Nancy Sherriff, daughter of George Sherriff, with whom they had dined, decided to accompany him to Dunbar 'by way of making a parade of me as a sweetheart' to her relations in the town. They had talked of love and romance the night before and suddenly Burns found his flirtatious conversation being taken seriously by the limpet-like Miss Sherriff. He was having none of it. He tried to shake her off by riding Jenny Geddes like the wind, hoping she would fall behind but, although Nancy was on an 'old cart horse as huge and as lean as a house', he did not outrun her. She asked Burns to call in to see her uncle but 'I refused to call with her, and so we quarrelled & parted.'[4]

At Dunbar, Burns dined with Provost Robert Fall. The next morning he had breakfast at Skateraw, four miles southeast of Dunbar, with Mr Lee, a local farmer, who detained him an extra day. There he met up again with the Reverend Dr Bowmaker and a host of others for dinner, including two sea Lieutenants and a Dr Brown from Dunbar. He headed back to Duns the next morning with a Mr Lorimer, Collector of Customs. At Berrywell, Burns found Miss Rachel Ainslie alone. He was like a thief in a bank vault who dares not touch the cash. His journal reads, 'Heavenly Powers who know the weaknesses of human hearts support mine! What happiness must I see only to remind me that I cannot enjoy it!' He adds, 'I could grasp her with rapture on a bed of straw, and rise with contentment to the most sweltering drudgery of stiffening Labour!'

A friend of Ainslie senior, Gilbert Kerr, agreed to accompany the bard on the next leg of his jaunt, to Newcastle. Robert Ainslie stayed behind. They dined at the home of a Mr Thomas Hood on 24 May. Burns suddenly felt unwell: 'I am taken extremely ill with strong feverish symptoms, & take a servant of Mr Hoods to watch me all night.' Despite 'Remorse' scaring his 'fancy at the gloomy forebodings of death', he survived the night. This may, again, have been a bout of rheumatic fever. Mr Hood decided to accompany Burns and Kerr on their journey. On 27 May, the three travellers crossed the Tweed and made their way, via narrow moorland drover byways, to Alnwick and slept at Morpeth the following night, before heading into Newcastle. From there, Burns wrote to Ainslie complaining that his older companions would not appreciate his talking nonsense so he could not relax and be himself: 'Here am I, a woeful wight on the banks of Tyne . . . I have not had one hearty mouthful of laughter since that merry-melancholy moment we parted'.[5]

From Newcastle, Burns, Kerr and Hood set off for Hexham, then moved on to Longtown where, after dinner, his fellow travellers said farewell. At Carlisle, at the end of May, Burns was shown around a printing company. In the town, he met up with 'a strange enough romantic adventure . . . with a girl and her married sister', which, he frivolously suggests, might have led to a 'Gretna-green affair', if he had been 'gull' enough to fall for it. The journal ends with the remark, 'Come by the coast to Annan. – Overtaken on the way by a curious old fish of a shoemaker, and miner from Cumberland mines.'

From Carlisle, Burns sent his only surviving letter in the Scots vernacular, a letter which for most of the nineteenth century was printed in English translation. It is addressed to William Nicol, the Latin master of the High School in Edinburgh and wittily dated the 1st June, 'or I believe the 39th o' May':

> Kind, honest-hearted Willie,
>
> I'm sitten down here, after seven and forty miles ridin, e'en as forjesket and forniaw'd as a forfoughten cock, to gie you some notion o' my landlowper-like stravaguin sin the sorrowfu' hour that I sheuk hands and parted wi' auld Reekie . . .[6]

The letter gives a fascinating description of how his hardy horse coped with the rough byways and an anecdote about the two women he met in Carlisle, all in guid, braid, often poetical Scots.

The next stop on the tour was Dumfries, where he had an appointment to meet Patrick Miller at Dalswinton to discuss renting a farm, possibly Ellisland, several miles north of the town. When Burns called at Dumfries post office to pick up mail, he found, to his horror, a letter from 'Meg' or Peggy Cameron, a servant from Edinburgh with whom he had had sexual intercourse in April. She believed herself to be pregnant by him. According to her letter (written on her behalf by the wife of a James Hogg) she had been turned out of her job and was destitute. Her pleading letter, dated 26 May 1787, states:

> Youl excuse this trouble but my present situation of health has grown every day worse ever since you left the town . . . my Mrs told me I best to seek another place to be in for now as I was growing observable to be with child. They for their Characters' sake could not keep me in their House so I was obliged to leave there this forenoon . . . I have not got a penny from my own people. – Out of quarters without funds my situation at present is nearly deplorable. I beg for God's sake you will write immediately & let me know how I am to do . . . Your Sincere Wellwisher, Meg Cameron.[7]

Burns took immediate action. He wrote an undated letter to Robert Ainslie, enclosing the letter he received from Peggy and sent an unsigned letter to her. He explained to Ainslie:

> My first welcome to this place was the enclosed letter. – I am very sorry for it, but what is done is done. – I pay you no compliment when I say that except my old friend Smith there is not any person in the world I would trust so far. – Please call at the James Hogg mentioned, and send for the wench and give her ten or twelve shillings . . . Call for God's sake, lest the poor soul be starving. Ask her for a letter I wrote her just now, by way of token. – It is unsigned. Write me after the meeting.[8]

This letter to Ainslie is sometimes misdated for 1788 in editions of the poet's letters but Burns was not in Dumfries in early June 1788 and so it was obviously written in June 1787. The Chambers-Wallace edition (1896) was the first to quote Miss Cameron's letter and fixed the date of Burns' letter to Ainslie correctly as June 1787. The Chambers-Wallace edition also mentions a writ in *meditatione fugae* being taken out against Burns in August 1787 by Peggy Cameron.

In a further letter to Ainslie dated 25 June 1787, relating to the Cameron episode, Burns mentions that his last meeting with Peggy was in mid-April; he puzzles at her pregnancy being visible so quickly: 'I begin from that, and some other circumstances to suspect foul play'; unfortunately, how the letter ends is unknown – the remainder of the manuscript has been torn away. It seems highly possible, as Mackay suggests, that 'Robert would have been quite right to suspect that he was now taking the blame for someone else.'[9] Surprisingly, after Burns dealt with the legal writ later in the year – the details are explained in a later chapter – there is no record of Miss Cameron giving birth or pursuing Burns for any further support.

On a more positive note, he was given the freedom of the Burgh of Dumfries on 4 June 1787 and was made an Honorary Burgess of the town. During his stay in Dumfries, he travelled up to Dunscore parish to meet Patrick Miller and look over the farms he had to rent. He told William Nicol two weeks later, 'From my view of the lands, and his reception of my Bardship, my hopes in that business are rather mended.'[10] Undecided about taking on a farm, Burns agreed to meet Miller again in August. He chirpily told Nicol in the same letter, 'I am quite charmed with Dumfries folks,' unaware he would spend his last years among them.[11]

11

You Can't Go Home Again: Rantin', Rovin' Around the Highlands

The poet's homecoming to Mossgiel on 8 June 1787 raised a painful reality for Caledonia's bard: celebrity or not, he had responsibilities he could not run away from for ever. On the first night, he stayed at John Dow's tavern, where he took up the pen to write to his old friend John Smith, then at Linlithgow:

> I slept at John Dow's, and called for my daughter; Mrs Hamilton and family; your mother, sister and brother; my quondam Eliza, &c., all, all well. If anything had been wanting to disgust me completely at Armour's family, their mean servile compliance would have done it.[1]

The Armours threw down the red carpet for the recently despised prodigal now that he was a published author and Scotland's bard. Burns, who could not resist his 'delicious armful' – Jean was soon pregnant again – did not forgive her parents' previous bitterness towards him. He imputed his restlessness partly to 'the servility of my plebeian brethren', who had 'nearly put me out of conceit altogether with my species'.[2]

On 24 June, Burns wrote to Creech from Glasgow, where he was visiting John Smith's, booksellers, requesting that he forward 50 books for subscribers in Glasgow. With money from his second edition, Burns purchased some material to be made into bonnets and cloaks for his sisters and mother while he was in Glasgow. He later paid out to have carpets on the floors at Mossgiel, a luxury for any tenant farmhouse.

In response to the many invitations from all over Scotland, Burns now planned his next excursion, to the West Highlands. On 25 June, he wrote to Robert Ainslie from Arrochar, in Argyll, 'where savage streams tumble over savage mountains, thinly overspread with savage flocks, which starvingly support as savage inhabitants'.[3] The letter is incomplete in the standard editions; a hitherto unpublished lengthy paragraph, mostly in Scots vernacular, is extant in transcript within a private collection.[4]

At Inveraray, Burns hoped to be received by the Duke and Duchess of Argyll. The Duke, John Campbell, was in the midst of business as President of the British Fisheries Society, with an entourage at his estate that spilled over into the local tavern. Although a subscriber to the Edinburgh Edition, he was too busy to meet Burns – his business associates were heading to the Isle of Mull the next morning. To make matters worse, the local tavern owner was also too busy to serve a wandering poetic minstrel and friend of Burns, Dr George Grierson. Vexed at the lack of Highland hospitality, Burns is reputed to have taken his pen and etched two verses on a window-pane of the inn. The final quatrain is stinging:

> There's naething here but Highland pride,
>   And Highland scab and hunger;
> If Providence has sent me here,
>   'Twas surely in an anger.

It is known that Burns did, on several other occasions, use his diamond stylus – a present from Lord Glencairn – to inscribe verse on windows. Cheeky vandalism it may have been, but these windows became hot memorabilia after his death.

A more amenable Highland welcome for Burns and guest occurred at a mansion near Loch Lomond where they were embraced into a good Scottish ceilidh:

> . . . a merry party and danced 'till the ladies left us, at three in the morning. Our dancing was none of the French or English insipid formal

> movements; the ladies sung Scotch songs like angels, at intervals: then we flew at Bab the Bowster, Tullochgorum, Loch Erroch side, &c. like midges sporting in the mottie sun . . . we went out to pay our devotions to the glorious lamp of day peering out over the towering top of Benlomond.[5]

On their departure for Dumbarton the next day, Dr Grierson and Burns met up with a galloping Highlander on horseback and decided to race him. The Highlander's horse stumbled in front of Jenny Geddes and the poet fell off his horse, cut and bruised almost as badly as his competitor, who landed head-over-heels in a hedge of gorse. Burns was still suffering the ill effects when he wrote from Mossgiel to John Richmond on 7 July – 'a skinful of bruises and wounds'.[6] His condition was serious enough to prevent him from travelling to Edinburgh for at least four weeks. However, it did not slow his pen: he wrote an elegy to mark the death of the Lord Provost of Edinburgh, Sir James Hunter Blair, an Ayrshire man, and sent it to Robert Aiken in mid-July. As Burns wrote in the Glenriddell Mss, Hunter Blair was a friend and his 'grief was sincere':

> My Patriot falls – but shall he lie unsung,
> While empty Greatness saves a worthless name?
> No: every Muse shall join her tuneful tongue,
> And future ages hear his growing fame. –

While recovering from his injuries, Burns took stock of his meteoric changing life during the last year and composed his autobiographical letter to John Moore, the longest prose work he is known to have composed.

Before returning to Edinburgh, Burns received the news that Robert Ainslie, at twenty-one years of age, had become a father. He replies to his friend, 'Welcome, Sir, to the society, the venerable society, of FATHERS!!!', boasting, that Jean was 'certainly in for it again' (pregnant) and fantasising, 'Peggy will bring a gallant half-Highlander – and I shall get a farm, and keep them all about my hand, and breed them in the fear of the Lord and an oatstick, and I shall be the happiest man upon earth.'[7] He enclosed a bawdy song, 'My Girl She's Airy', and ended with his usual note to Ainslie on how he could write creative 'zig-zag' nonsense to him without losing his esteem as a friend.

After the various letters from his Mother Confessor, Mrs Dunlop, Burns eventually made his way to Dunlop House to meet her, thinking that his

'Bardship' and their friendly correspondence permitted him to treat her as an equal. It was a mistake. She had sent a servant to Mossgiel to request he attend her stately home but, when they met, she was piqued at his lack of what she deemed appropriate deference. Burns casually wandered into her stately home, gave her his customary sizing-up, then acted the part of the famed poet. Even so, Mrs Dunlop still adored him and they subsequently kept up their correspondence.

On his arrival in Edinburgh, around 7 August, Burns spent a few days with Richmond in Baxter's Close, Lawnmarket. William Nicol then offered him more spacious accommodation and probably a more comfortable bed at his house, near St Patrick Square.

For Burns, this was a very different experience of Edinburgh: the cards inviting him to the houses of the rich and powerful had dried up. Hugh Blair, in his wisdom, had warned him not to feel neglected when his unprecedented peak of fame subsided. That it did affect his mood is clear from his letter to Archibald Lawrie, dated 14 August:

> Here am I – that is all I can tell you of that unaccountable Being – myself. What I am doing no mortal can tell; what I am thinking I myself cannot tell; what I am usually saying is not worth telling. The clock is just striking one, two, three, four, – , –, – , –, – , –, –, twelve forenoon; and here I sit, in the attic storey, alias the garret, with a friend on the right hand of my Standish . . . a friend who has more of the milk of human kindness than all the human race put together . . . he is without the least alloy, a universal Philanthropist; and his much beloved name is – a BOTTLE OF GOOD OLD PORT! In a week, if whim and weather serve, I shall set out for the North – a tour of the Highlands.[8]

Characteristically, he overplays the drunken bard role. Burns was more often tipsy than drunk.

The following day, Burns received a shock. He was arrested under a writ in *meditatione fugae* taken out by Peggy Cameron and was forced to deal with it immediately by paying a fixed sum. From evidence within a set of newly discovered manuscripts in private hands, which contain all the letters written by Burns to Robert Ainslie with many hitherto unpublished passages of biographical interest, it is clear the poet paid the required sum and was freed of the affair then and there. He saw Peggy that very day after resolving the matter but there is no corroborative evidence in the new manuscripts to suggest she was visibly pregnant. A meeting that occurred between Miss Cameron and Burns is described in detail within an unpublished letter to Ainslie but the private owner of the letter has not given permission to divulge the details.

Before leaving on a tour of the Highlands with William Nicol, Burns sent his apologies to the St James's Lodge, Tarbolton, care of James Manson, the innkeeper, stating he was unable to attend the quarterly meeting. Ainslie received a letter from him dated 23 August, which complained of Nicol proof-reading a thesis in Latin so loudly, 'I cannot hear what my own soul is saying in my own scull.' Burns said they intended to leave Edinburgh the next day 'in a chaise: Nicol thinks it more comfortable than horse-back, to which I say, Amen; so Jenny Geddes goes home to Ayrshire, to use a phrase of my Mother's, wi her finger in her mouth'.[9] In his mid-forties, 'Kind, honest hearted Willie' was probably not as fit for riding horseback as the younger Burns and, as the poet was about to find out, his pro-Jacobite friend could take umbrage easily and throw a bad tempered strop like a spoiled child. As with the Borders tour, Burns kept a Journal of this part of his Highland sojourn. Again, it mostly consists of anecdotal sketches, phrases and names.

The first stop was Linlithgow, where they visited 'the room where the beautiful, injured Mary Queen of Scots was born'. The 'old Gothic church' was, to Burns' mind, a 'fine but melancholy ruin'. The travellers stopped over at Falkirk and tried to visit the Carron Ironworks the following day but its caretaker turned them away, as it was a Sunday and he would not break the Sabbath.[10]

In a letter to Robert Muir dated 26 August, Burns describes his feelings on reaching Bannockburn:

> This morning I knelt at the tomb of Sir John the Graham, the gallant friend of the immortal WALLACE; and two hours ago I said a fervent prayer for Old Caledonia over the hole in a blue whinstone, where Robert de Bruce fixed his royal standard on the banks of Bannockburn.[11]

The passionate fervour he felt for places steeped in Scotland's history is evident. On reaching Stirling, he stood at dusk on the esplanade at Stirling

Castle, taking in the glorious view of the sun setting over the windings of the River Forth 'through the rich Carse of Stirling'.

The next morning, Burns visited relations of Gavin Hamilton, who lived on the Harvieston estate in Clackmannanshire along the area known as the hillfoots near to the Devon Valley. The entire family was there bar Margaret Chalmers, the one person he had hoped to see. He later wrote from Stirling to Gavin Hamilton to update him on the 'Ayrshire folks at Harvieston', informing him that his stepsister, Charlotte, had gladdened his eye and that he had spent 'one of the most pleasant days I ever had in my life'.[12] Back in Stirling, Burns and Nicol visited Stirling Castle where Scotland's kings once presided and parliamentary business had been conducted. The ruinous neglect of the old Palace at the Castle provoked the following verse, inscribed on a window pane:

HERE Stewarts once in triumph reign'd,
And laws for Scotland's weal ordain'd;
But now unroof'd their Palace stands,
Their sceptre's fall'n to other hands;
Fallen indeed, and to the earth,
Whence grovelling reptiles take their birth. –
The injur'd STEWART-line are gone,
A Race outlandish fill their throne;
An idiot race, to honor lost;
Who knows them best despise them most.

These biting anti-Hanoverian lines were left anonymous. Copies were eventually made and on 5 October they found their way into the *Edinburgh Evening Courant* under the poet's initials 'R.B.' The Paisley poet James Maxwell published them in a pamphlet as lines by Burns, to attack the bard as a disloyal troublemaker. By the end of January 1788, it was widely known they were his lines. Certain editors of Burns tried to pin the verse on William Nicol in order to cleanse the bard's image of Jacobite patriotism; Cunningham, in 1834, was too timid to print the final couplet. Censoring and sanitising the radical sentiments of Burns has been a meddler's pastime for a few centuries now.

From Stirling they moved on to Crieff, then the next day went to visit Ossian's grave by Glen Almond. At Kenmore, Taymouth, Burns wrote 'Verses Written with a Pencil', beginning 'Admiring Nature in her wildest grace', which later appeared in the *Edinburgh Evening Courant* on 6 September, sent to the newspaper by a mysterious 'O.B. of Kenmore'. The fine scenery poem appeared in the Edinburgh Edition of 1793.

On the way to Dunkeld, Burns and Nicol passed through Aberfeldy, where the poet stood admiring the Falls of Moness and later composed 'The Birks of Aberfeldy', which appeared in the *Scots Musical Museum* in February 1788. It was autumn, the propitious season for the bard – his favourite time of year – and he was on song.

At Dunkeld, a historic meeting occurred between Scotland's greatest poet and, arguably, her greatest fiddle music composer, Neil Gow. Burns, an amateur fiddler who could scrape a decent slow air, was in the company of a musical genius. Gow's hauntingly beautiful lament for his second wife is probably one of the most emotionally evocative melodies ever created. What Burns could do with words, Gow could do with his fiddle. Burns describes the fiddler as 'a short, stout-built Highland figure with his greyish hair shed on his honest social brow'. He dedicated 'Amang the Trees' to the great musician – a song which sets Scots bagpipe and fiddle music above the 'squeels' of German and Italian music which was then popular among Scots aristocrats. It was probably his Highland tour which awoke in him the deep-seated desire to set new words to many great old Scots melodies over the coming years, when he not only wrote wonderful lyrics for Scots airs, he also helped preserve many old Scots fiddle tunes that would have evaporated into misty obscurity without his aid.

On their way to Blair Atholl, with Burns carrying a letter of introduction to the Duke of Atholl from Hugh Blair, Burns and Nicol traversed the intimidating pass of Killicrankie, where Graham of Claverhouse led the Highland army to victory in 1689. On sending word to Blair Castle of their arrival, Josiah Walker, tutor to the Duke's son, arrived to greet them bearing an invitation for Burns, *only*, to stay over. The snub, deliberate or not, did not go down well with Nicol, who had to put up in the local inn, although Walker thoughtfully arranged some fine fishing for him the next day, while the bard was entertained at the big house.[13] The Duke was away but returned the following day to join the party at the Castle.

Among the guests was Robert Graham of Fintry, a recently appointed Commissioner on the Board of Excise. With the poet's notion of the

Excise as a safety-net job, he had made the acquaintance of a key figure, whom he could approach in future.

A more powerful individual than Graham of Fintry was due the following day, but an intemperate spat by Nicol forced Burns, against the wishes of his hosts, to cut short his stay. The family at Atholl tried every trick to keep Burns another day. The visitor was Henry Dundas, who had the power of every patronage job in Scotland in his pocket. Burns was well aware that Dundas was not among the Edinburgh Edition subscribers. And his patronage was never forthcoming, for reasons already outlined. Also, Dundas had delusions that he himself was a poet of some worth and so his cold neglect of Burns might possibly have arisen from jealousy.

Walker boasts in a letter to Dr Currie the biographer that it was his idea Burns should celebrate his visit to Atholl House by paying tribute to his hosts in verse and to send the final product to the Duke and Duchess, when composed. Burns would probably have done so without being prompted. Indeed, Burns remarked to Walker that if his poetic Muse had not paid a worthy compliment to the people of Atholl House, he would 'with unrelenting vengeance throw her into the House of Correction and finally banish her to Botany bay'.[14] 'The Humble Petition of Bruar Water', written in the voice of the running burn, which pleads to be adorned with 'lofty firs, and ashes cool / My lowly banks o'erspread', is dedicated to the Duke; it appeared in the 1793 Edinburgh Edition.

Burns and Nicol arrived in Inverness on 4 September, having travelled up through Aviemore into Strathspey and Findhorn, via Cawdor Castle of Macbeth fame. During their two-day stay in Inverness, they visited the shores of Loch Ness, the Falls of Foyers and Culloden battlefield. They dined with William Inglis on their second evening at Kingsmills House. Inglis was a friend of William Dunbar of the Crochallan Fencibles who gave the poet a letter of introduction to the local bailie. Regarding the battle of Culloden, Burns merely wrote, 'Reflections on the field of battle'. It is difficult to believe these could be his thoughts on the land where the Jacobites were cut to their knees by English, German and Scottish troops and where Drumossie Moor ran red with Scottish patriot blood to become a desolate green grave of a nation. The most patriotic of all patriotic poets Scotland ever bred must have been emotionally numb in his private 'reflections'. Any written commentary has not survived.

From Findhorn to Forres, then on to Elgin and Fochabers, the chaise rattled its way to Castle Gordon, home to the Duke and Duchess of Gordon. Burns, who had met the Duchess in Edinburgh in December 1786, was made very welcome by his 'princely . . . affable . . . charming, witty and sensible' hosts. The poet's journal does not mention the incident which triggered an early departure from Castle Gordon. Burns left Nicol to himself for most of the day at a local inn and ventured to the castle alone but on sitting down to supper, indicated to the Duke and Duchess he had a travelling partner, whom they then asked to join them. Burns went to meet Nicol with the invitation. It was too late. The huffing puffing Nicol punctured a blood vessel with pique and threw down the gauntlet to Burns to either go back alone to the castle or to continue their journey immediately, in the chaise. A local man, Dr Robert Couper, later passed on what he had witnessed of this exchange to Currie, corroborating that Nicol was the offender. Torn rudely from Castle Gordon, Burns cursed Nicol in an apologetic letter to the Duke's librarian, James Hoy, written when he was back in Edinburgh on 20 October:

> I shall certainly, among my legacies, leave my latest curse to that unlucky predicament which hurried me, tore me away from Castle Gordon. May that obstinate son of Latin Prose be curst to Scotch-mile periods, and damn'd to seven league paragraphs; while Declension & Conjugation, Gender, Number, and time, under the ragged banners of Dissonance and Disarrangement eternally rank against him in hostile array!!!!!![15]

It was rare for Burns to use his triple exclamatory, but six exclamation marks hint that he was more than slightly peeved. Nicol's knot of obstinate behaviour in feeling neglected by Burns soured the remainder of their journey and embarrassed Burns by making him appear ungrateful and inconsiderate. The poet's links were tenuous enough among his landed and titled 'friends' and Nicol's selfishness made it less likely that the Duke and Duchess would assert themselves on the poet's behalf.

The travellers stayed at Cullen for the evening then rode along the roads by the Moray Firth the next morning. Burns jotted down notes in his journal on the barren view from the chaise: 'The country is sadly poor & unimproven, the houses, crops, horses, cattle etc., all in unison.' At Banff, they breakfasted with a friend of Nicol's, Dr George Chapman, who arranged for them to see Duff House, owned by the Earl of Fife. From there they moved on to the ancient town of Old Deer, near Mintlaw, towards Peterhead on the coast and eventually to Aberdeen, where they stayed at the New Inn, Castle Street. Here they met with Professor John Ross of King's College and Professor Thomas Gordon of the University of Aberdeen, plus the editor of the *Aberdeen Journal*, James Chalmers. The meeting that appears to have excited the poet was with Bishop John Skinner, son of the famous Reverend John Skinner, a clerical scholar and lyricist who penned, among other well-known songs, a favourite of Burns', 'Tullochgorum'; Burns describes the song as 'the best Scotch song ever Scotland saw'.[16] It grieved the poet considerably to hear from John junior that they had travelled past his father's home by only four miles on their way to Aberdeen. Burns later wrote to him to inform him of the gathering of Scots songs for Johnson's *Scots Musical Museum*; it is clear from this letter that the poet had been gathering notes about songs and melodies everywhere he travelled. They formed a seed stock of melodies he would later craft lyrics to and harvest for posterity.

The poet gave advance notice in a letter to his cousin James Burness of when he and Nicol would arrive at the Stonehaven inn; there, he would meet his namesake, Robert Burness, aunts and other family members. The poet later described his relations as hearty and decent folk in a letter to his brother Gilbert, sent from Edinburgh. It appears that Nicol, once again, ushered Burns away sooner than he would have wished. After visiting James in Montrose, they travelled to Auchmithie, on to Dundee and eventually down to Perth, where they visited Scone Palace. The tour journal concludes laconically: 'Pass through a cold barren country to Queensferry – dine – cross the ferry, and on to Edinburgh.' It had been 'a tour of 22 days, and travelling near 600 miles; windings included'.[17]

From Edinburgh, Burns dispatched nine copies of the Edinburgh Edition to James Burness, probably gratis. In a letter to Patrick Miller, Burns apologised for not being able to meet him again in Dumfriesshire as arranged, and included some poetry as a part apology stating he hoped to see him in Edinburgh soon.

Burns went to see William Creech to find out if he could settle accounts. All that is known at this time is he had no luck; he was probably fobbed off and told to come back in a few weeks' time. Whatever arrangements were made, Burns decided to escape Edinburgh and go on a few social visits.

Sir William Murray of Auchtertyre, Strathearn, near Crieff, gave an invitation to the poet to visit his estate when they met at Blair Atholl. Burns had also been invited to the home of John Ramsay of Ochtertyre, the same place-name but over four miles north of Stirling on the River Teith. The primary motive for the excursion would seem to have been to visit and woo Margaret Chalmers at Harvieston. This time, the poet's travelling companion was the amiable Dr James Adair, son of an Ayr surgeon and a relative of Mrs Dunlop.

Burns and Adair went first to see Ramsay of Ochtertyre near Stirling. It was Ramsay who suggested that Burns should turn his hand to longer works, such as a play, or more substantial poems like Thomson's 'The Seasons'. Like many others who met Burns, Ramsay left a reminiscence of the bard for Dr James Currie, describing him as possessing 'flashes of intellectual brightness' he had never before witnessed.

The two men next headed into Clackmannanshire, to Harvieston. If Burns was intent on wooing Margaret Chalmers, he was outdone by Adair, who subsequently married Charlotte Hamilton in November 1789 after this first introduction to her from Burns. During their eight days at Harvieston, they made various excursions, including a visit to an elderly lady, Mrs Catherine Bruce of Clackmannan, who was said to hail from the family of Robert the Bruce and had in her possession what she claimed to be the helmet and broadsword of the last Scottish king. The story goes that the elderly Lady Bruce knighted both men using the broadsword. The current Lord Balfour, also Robert Bruce, asserts that this story is true – and that a Lord Elgin visited Mrs Bruce when she was elderly and somewhat confused and conned her out of the priceless sword and helmet.[18] Burns and Adair also visited Dunfermline Abbey, where Burns knelt and kissed the flagstones over King Robert the Bruce's grave.

Most of the correspondence between Burns and Margaret Chalmers has not survived; possibly it was destroyed to preserve her blushes or privacy, given that she married Lewis Hay in December 1788. A hitherto unpublished poem by Burns in the private Burns–Ainslie Mss collection mentions a visit to see 'Lucky Chalmers' sometime in 1787, which proved less lucky for the poet, as he galloped through a storm of thunder and lightning and got himself soaked to the skin.[19] Burns, by this time, had developed a knack of pursuing women already emotionally attached to another suitor. Margaret, highly literate, a talented musician, and singer of

Scots songs, was made the subject of two of Burns' songs, 'Where, Braving Angry Winter Storms' and 'My Peggy's Charms'. If an offer of marriage was made by Burns, she would have explained that she was already seeing Hay, a banker. Burns refers to her in a letter of January 1788, stating that she was 'surrounded by the blandishments of Flattery and Courtship' but was still registered in his 'heart's core'.[20] Looking back, Burns described his time at Harvieston as eight of the happiest days of his life.

After leaving Harvieston, Burns and Adair went on to Strathearn to visit Sir William Murray. Here Burns wrote 'On Scaring Some Water-Fowl in Loch Turit'. Murray's family were of Jacobite lineage; his wife had been born in the Tower of London, when her own mother visited relations who were taken to Tower Hill and hanged after the 1746 Rebellion. Sir William's young cousin Euphemia, known locally as 'the flower of Strathearn', was made the subject of the pastoral lyric 'Blythe Was She': Burns seemed to think it was his duty as a poet to flatter young women with word portraits but he was sometimes a little overfamiliar, creating in song what was an intimate personal description.

Burns and Adair now made their way back to Edinburgh. Scotland's bard had made some leisurely excursions across his native land, laying in store many seeds of ideas for songs and poetry. He no longer had to imagine what it would feel like to walk over Culloden Moor or stand on the Banks of Bannockburn: he now knew how it felt. He had travelled and surveyed his heartland; felt the angst, sorrow, pain and the lively hope still within the people he met and talked and sang and drank with. In all his touring jaunts through Scotland, it is clear Burns valued, above all else, his fame and reputation as a Scottish bard.

12

Back in Auld Reekie: Sex and the City?

Back in Edinburgh by 20 October, Burns took accommodation with a colleague of William Nicol's, William Cruikshank, at no. 2d St James's Square. He had a front and back room with bay windows, one looking over St Andrew's Square, the other over St James's Square. He was hoping it would be a short stay to settle accounts with Creech since he now had plans to lease a farm. A secondary objective was to get into the Excise, or to be exact, placed on what was known as the 'expectant' list of qualified Officers. He spent the first two days in bed with a severe cold and sensibly used the time to catch up on correspondence. To business, he dashed off a letter to Patrick Miller:

> I want to be a farmer in a small farm . . . under the auspices of a good landlord. I have no foolish notion of being a Tenant on easier terms than another. To find a farm where one can live at all, is not easy . . . The banks of the Nith are as sweet, poetic ground as any I ever saw . . . I would wish to call you landlord sooner than any landed gentleman I know.[1]

Before the end of October Burns made a hurried visit to Dalswinton to see Miller. He wanted the advice of his father's friend James Tennant of Glenconner regarding the lands at Dalswinton estate, so waited for Tennant's advice before committing himself to a lease. It took until mid-

March 1788 before Burns signed the lease for Ellisland farm at Miller's solicitor's office in Edinburgh.

Burns was now severely shaken to receive the news his baby daughter Jean had just died, having just seen her first birthday on 3 September. How she died is not known nor is it known how he was informed. It may have been through news from his brother Gilbert. To Richmond, on 25 October he wrote, 'By the way, I hear I am a girl out of pocket and by careless, murdering mischance too, which has provoked me and vexed me a good deal.'[2] Such language can make him seem unfeeling but the apparent casualness of the first phrase gives way to his true emotion. He also asked Richmond in the same letter to enquire after Jean if her pregnancy was showing and whether there was talk on the subject around Mauchline. He was still in the good books of the Armours but feared that might change on the news of her second pregnancy.

While he waited on Creech to keep his side of the bargain, Burns found himself becoming engrossed in what was essentially an Enlightenment project in antiquarian culture – the process of gathering together old Scots songs to preserve them in the face of cultural erosion. The person in charge of the project was James Johnson; the first volume of his *Scots Musical Museum* (1787) included two original songs by Burns and two he collected and improved. Burns informed the Duke of Gordon's librarian, James Hoy:

> An Engraver, James Johnson, in Edinr has, not from mercenary views but from an honest Scotch enthusiasm, set about collecting all our native Songs and setting them to music . . . Clarke, the well-known Musician, presides over the musical arrangement; and Drs Beattie & Blacklock, Mr Taylor, Woodhouslee, and your humble servt to the utmost of his small power, assist in collecting the old poetry, or sometimes for a fine air to make a stanza, when it has no words . . .[3]

Enlisting the help of Reverend John Skinner, Burns told him he was 'absolutely crazed about it, collecting old stanzas, and every information regarding their origin'.[4] The second volume of the *Scots Musical Museum* (abbreviated to *SMM* hereafter) was ready by spring 1788. Burns had contributed around 34 songs. Johnson deferred to Burns in deciding what was best in the collection and effectively allowed him to become the editor of the series. By the time of his death, Burns had contributed 160 original songs and amended or improved many others. Each volume was to contain 100 Scotch songs. In July 1796, volume five was at the press. It took a further seven years after the poet's death before the last volume, number six, appeared. Burns' contribution to Scottish song was a singular achievement of historic significance. It was also a labour of patriotic love for his country, given the bard did not ask for one penny for all his efforts.[5]

On 23 October, Burns managed to get a written agreement from Creech stating that he would pay on demand 100 guineas for his copyright. It would not be until 30 May 1788 that Burns would receive payment from the slippery Creech, who took his cut for subscription copies without having to lay out a penny. Due to the speed of book sales and the large subscribers list, Creech ought to have paid up for copies sold no later than six months after publication. Moreover, the Memorandum of Agreement on the poet's copyright was payable from the date the agreement was made. To make matters worse, there were rumours that Creech had secretly published another edition. He certainly acted in his own self-interest, to the detriment of the poet, with his deceit and endless deferment of payment. He was probably waiting on profits from the London edition to accrue before squaring accounts. He kept Burns in Edinburgh for several months more than planned, whittling his patience to the wire.

With a knack of complicating his own life – 'I am the luckless victim of mad tornadoes, which blow me into chaos'[6] is how he put it himself – the extended winter visit to Edinburgh resulted in his becoming embroiled in a new romance he would find it difficult to extricate himself from. Around 4 December he was invited to Miss Erskine Nimmo's – whom Burns had met the previous winter – where he was introduced to a woman of his own age who was already a fan of his poetry. She was the daughter of a Glasgow surgeon and had an intermittent education, although she attended boarding school in Edinburgh at the age of fifteen. Buxom, vivacious, lively, intelligent and with a passion for poetry, Agnes Craig McLehose appeared to be the sophisticated woman of heart, mind and soul Burns had been searching for since his first visit to Edinburgh. Her marriage in 1776 to a Glasgow lawyer, James McLehose, had fallen apart due to abuse on his part: they had four children; only two survived by 1787. James McLehose ended up in a debtors' jail in London before fleeing in shame and disgrace to Jamaica, leaving Nancy – as she was known to friends – to fend for herself on an annuity of ten shillings per week from her deceased father's estate. Nancy was still legally married to McLehose and genteel Edinburgh society would have been scandalised by a new romantic liaison.

Nancy invited Burns around to her flat in Potterrow on 6 December. The poet could not make it and promised he would appear on Saturday the 8th but fate stepped in and prevented the meeting. An accident occurred late on the Friday night; Burns badly hurt a knee. He originally blamed a drunken coachman for the mishap but later told Nancy it was an 'unlucky fall from a coach'.[7] The bruised, dislocated kneecap was reset by his friend Alexander Wood. The injury kept him housebound for a few weeks. He wrote to Margaret Chalmers on 12 December, 'I am here under the care of a surgeon, with a bruised limb extended on a cushion . . . I have taken tooth and nail to the Bible, and am got through the five books of Moses, and half way in Joshua. It is really a glorious book.'[8] On the same day, he wrote to Nancy remarking that 'Tomorrow, and every day, till I see you, you shall hear from me.'[9] This was the beginning of one of the most prolific episodes in the poet's romantic letter-writing as he laid siege – to put it in the language he once employed to Brown of such an affair – to Nancy's voluptuous, embattled defences. There were just too many 'baited hooks' for the knight errant in Rab Mossgiel not to rise to the challenge. The inveterate romantic seems to have thought that here, at last, was his Heaven-sent soulmate.

During the next six, housebound weeks, Burns engaged in an extraordinary correspondence with Nancy. Edinburgh benefited from a penny post system offering deliveries every hour between nine in the morning and nine at night, anywhere in the city centre. Both correspondents were ideally situated to benefit from this. Over the next three months, from 6 December onward, 80 or more letters went to and fro between Nancy and Burns, with at least 42 being from Burns. It is known a few letters on both sides were either censored or did not survive; the majority were published in the mid-nineteenth century, after Mrs McLehose's death. Taken as a whole, they form a fascinating window into the mind of the poet at this crossroads in his life. They reveal the confused psyche of a genius in poetry who also thought himself a master in the art of romantic gamesmanship, becoming entangled in the web of his own chat-up lines. Once again, Burns fell in love with a woman he could never marry.

In her first letter of adulation to her poet-hero, Nancy let it be known that, were she his sister, 'I would call and see you; but 'tis a censorial world this.'[10] Before long, the semi-caged, frustrated pair were engaged in heavy prose-petting. Nancy chose romantic Arcadian names for their often daily missives, in the naïve assumption that pen-names might protect her anonymity if any letters went astray: she adopted the name Clarinda and Burns, Sylvander. From a flicker to a flame, their correspondence evolved into a mixture of semi-erotic innuendo, flights of defensive religiosity and poetic exuberance, always burning with an impatience for their next meeting. She was also fond of issuing cautionary rebukes at his probing advances, reminding him that she was after all, a married woman. For his part, Burns played the part of the gentleman, supposedly too gallant to be searching for a breach in her defences.

By the close of the year, Burns was writing to his old friend Richard Brown that he was 'ready to hang myself for a young Edinr widow, who has wit and beauty more murderously fatal than the assassinating stiletto of the Sicilian banditti, or the poisoned arrow of the savage African'.[11] Had she been a 'widow' the relationship might have been less encumbered by social pressures. He enclosed for Brown some stanzas written by Clarinda beginning 'Talk not of Love, it gives me pain' and ending in a rhapsody of Platonic love and bliss, which would be destroyed if she were to grant to him the one 'odious' request she 'must deny'. Burns had already broken the decorous boundaries by declaring he was in love with her and was a little disingenuous when he declared he, too, was merely being Platonic: 'Don't think I flatter you or have a design upon you, Clarinda; I have too much pride for the one, and too little cold contrivance for the other.'[12] He went on to explain his key constituent elements of personality were a 'Pride and Passion', assuring her confidently the latter held the former in check. It was surely tongue-in-cheek to conclude 'I may take a fort by storm, but never by Siege.' In truth, Sylvander now had Clarinda under complete siege and her replies suggest she was loving every minute of it. Burns cursed the 'etiquette' that prevented Clarinda from visiting him. On 4 January 1788, he wrote a phrase to her, 'He who sees you as I have done and does not love you' – which later flowered into the lyric, 'But to see her is to love her' which is from one of his most heart-melting songs of parting, 'Ae Fond Kiss'.[13] Meanwhile, meeting with his poetess – as soon as he was fit to walk – was at the top of Burns' agenda.

Other friends were trying to keep Burns busy with his muse. On 13 December the death was announced of Robert Dundas of Arniston – a brother of Henry Dundas, Lord Melville, who ruled Scotland from London although he was periodically in Edinburgh. Wood suggested that Burns compose an elegy in his memory. The final product was a clever enough work, with Scotland's 'mortal wound' turning the flood waters red, 'a wound degenerate ages cannot cure'. The poet wrote a letter to Lord Arniston's son, also named Robert Dundas, the Solicitor General and sent the poem via Wood to the son. Burns recalled this in a letter a few years later 'with gnashing of teeth . . . His Solicitorship never took the smallest notice of the Letter, the Poem, or the Poet. From that time . . . I never see the name, Dundas, in the column of a newspaper, but my heart seems straightened for room in my bosom'.[14] Burns was right to comment that had his poem been the work of some 'Lord or Baronet, they would have been thought very clever'. As the poet remarked to Charles Hay, Advocate, the Muster-Master-General of the Crochallan Fencibles: 'I have done the best I could.'[15] It was not good enough to stir even a polite acknowledgement from Robert Dundas junior. It seems evident by this point the Dundas family had already decided that the Glencairn-sponsored, Ayrshire bard was not to their liking.

Indeed, the contents and subject matter of the bard's next poem, written to mark the birthday of Charles Edward Stuart on 31 December 1787, would not have pleased the Dundas family if they had read it. James Steuart (an old spelling of the surname) of Cleland Gardens, a short walk (on crutches) from St James's Square, invited Burns to attend a Jacobite Club to celebrate the Young Pretender's 67th birthday on the last day of the year. The king 'o'er the water', whose name was not to be spoken in Scotland after 1746, was still living in exile in France. 'A Birthday Ode, December 31st 1787' was printed only as a censored fragment by Dr James Currie in 1800 because of its potent, anti-Hanoverian sentiments. Even the 1896 edition of Henderson and Henley deliberately toned down its death wish for the Duke of Brunswick. Burns paints a scene in which 'Vengeance's arm' assails the foes of Jacobitism to right their wrongs until 'Brunswick's head shall lowly lay': that is, his head was to be cut off. Most nineteenth-century editors rendered it as Brunswick's 'pride' rather than 'head', to tone down its political message. Brunswick was the brother-in-law of King George III. Critics are divided on the merits of this partly

Pindaric Ode, which ends in an adapted form of the Scottish stanza taken from Alexander Montgomerie's *The Cherry and the Slae*:

Perdition, baleful child of night!
Rise and revenge the injur'd right
  Of Stewart's ROYAL RACE:
Lead on the unmuzzled hounds of hell,
Till all the frighted echoes tell
  The blood-notes of the chase!
Full on the quarry point their view,
Full on the base usurping crew,
The tools of Faction, and the Nation's curse!
  Hark how the cry grows on the wind;
  They leave the lagging gale behind,
Their savage fury, pitiless, they pour;
With murdering eyes already they devour;
  See Brunswick spent, a wretched prey,
  His life one poor despairing day,
Where each avenging hour still ushers in a worse!
  Such havock, howling all abroad,
Their utter ruin bring,
The base apostates to their God,
Or Rebels to their KING!

No one at the birthday celebration wished to see a despotic dynasty back on the British throne. Jacobitism had evolved into a romantic, patriotic longing for Scotland's lost independence, laced with a grudging disdain towards the 'traitors' who sold out the Parliament of 1707 and an implacable resentment at England's dominance over Scotland in economic and cultural terms. The dominant English culture was supposedly eradicating Scotland of its 'barbaric' culture and its native tongue. Burns' 'Birthday Ode' takes its place in the long lineage of Scots songs cursing those who sold out Scotland's freedom in 1707 but, for him, Jacobitism was more of a source of Scottish inspiration, a poetical theme or motif, than a political creed per se.

Burns had by now realised that there was no prospect of long-term patronage materialising. That well had dried up with the sales of his second book. Having met Robert Graham of Fintry at Atholl House, he decided to tax his goodwill and on 7 January he wrote to explain that he had already applied to join the Excise:

> You know, I daresay, of an application I lately made to your Board, to be admitted an Officer of Excise. I have according to form, been examined by a Supervisor, and today I give in his Certificate with a request for an Order for instructions.[16]

He suggests in dramatic terms that the Excise represents his strongest hope for providing a future livelihood and that:

> I had intended to have closed my late meteorous appearance on the stage of Life, in the country Farmer; but after discharging some filial and fraternal claims, I find I could only fight for existence in that miserable manner, which I have lived to see throw a venerable Parent in the jaws of a Jail; where, but for the Poor Man's last and often best friend, Death, he might have ended his days.[17]

Entry to the Excise was competitive and character references were essential to obtain the stamp of acceptance from the Board. Entrants had to be under 30 years of age and, if married, have no more than three children. Burns, technically still single, was coming up for 29 years: time for pursuing this avenue was running out. He was aware that if his application was successful, he would have to swear an Oath of Allegiance to George III – which would obviously stick in the throat of the author of the blatantly anti-Hanoverian 'A Dream'. For reasons of self-protection, he never signed his name to any of the pro-Jacobite songs he wrote after he eventually joined the Excise.

Indeed, the poet's publicly avowed radical sentiments were potentially a bar to his being allowed into the Excise, the lowest rung and most despised of the crown employee jobs – the lines he had inscribed on a Stirling window were brought up during his character and loyalty assessment. He descended to business prose in a letter to Clarinda:

> I have almost given up the Excise idea. I have been just now to wait on a great Person, Miss Nimmo's friend, Mrs Stewart. Why will Great

> people not only deafen us with the din of their equipage, and dazzle us with their fastidious pomp, but they must also be so very dictatorially wise? I have been question'd like a child about my matters, and blamed and schooled for my Inscription on Stirling window.[18]

Had Burns adhered to the social etiquette of Edinburgh's genteel society, he would probably have written no poetry worth reading after 1787, although naturally cautious in some respects, he was never prepared to join the fashionable herd in terms of his political opinions, any more than he had been prepared to toe the line and keep his mouth shut in Calvinist Ayrshire. For a radical poet to become an Exciseman was to force a square peg into a round hole: his first loyalty would always be to his poetic 'muse'.

To help smooth his way through the rites of passage into the Excise, Burns turned to James, Earl of Glencairn. In February, he wrote bluntly: 'I wish to get into the Excise.' The plan he then outlined to Glencairn was one with which Burns probably lived to wish he had stuck:

> After what I have given and will give [Gilbert] as a small farming capital to keep the family together, I guess my remaining all will be about two hundred pounds. Instead of beggaring myself with a small dear farm, I will lodge my little stock, a sacred deposite, in a banking-house.[19]

Whatever Burns said in favour of joining the Excise, at a deeper level the thought of being a 'gauger' revolted him; it would be a compromise of necessity over principle.

The second, long-awaited meeting between Clarinda and Sylvander, to consummate their emotional communion of letter writing, occurred on 4 January. Burns arrived at Potterrow, perhaps to save the stress on his recuperating knee, in a sedan chair. The starry-eyed pair did as all courting couples do at the commencement of an affair, swapped life stories, compared their understanding of the world and enjoyed each other's company. To Burns, it was probably Heaven to be with a woman so much more his equal, at least in terms of poetry and education, than the Mauchline Belles. But he swiftly became aware of the gulf between them: she was a Calvinist and believed she could convert Burns to her beliefs but his thinking on religion was far too well advanced and thorough to be modified.

Mentioning Milton's Satan as a favourite hero of his must have disturbed her considerably, since he had to explain the next day, in writing, that he merely identified with the stoical perspective of the fictional character, 'his manly fortitude in supporting what cannot be remedied'[20] in life. Burns had some cause to identify with a 'noble, exalted mind in ruins'; the ghost of his father's voice never quite left his conscience and for him that was the stern measure of his own fall from grace.

Clarinda told Burns she wished the situation with Jean Armour truly over after Burns explained their child, little Bobbie, was still living. He was candid enough to tell her about Margaret Chalmers, who was 'worthy of a place in the same bosom with my Clarinda'.[21] Religion, he explained, came from the heart, not from the Bible, although the tenets of the Bible might guide such feelings. To reassure her that he took religion seriously, he emphasised that religion was his 'favourite topic'.

Clarinda was hooked and even took to making the odd visit down to St James's Square in order that her Sylvander might see her from his attic window and she could give him a smiling nod. The partly crippled Romeo might have wished for a role reversal for his Juliet but etiquette and chin-wagging scared her from making a proper visit. On being asked in a letter if he had seen her in the Square, Burns may have been merely polite in replying in the affirmative, hoping not to dissuade her from any potential visit. Six visits by Sylvander to Clarinda occurred in January and it would seem some physical contact occurred beyond a polite hug and goodnight kiss.

It is clear that by the poet's 29th birthday – 25 January 1788 – he had tried to seduce Clarinda more than once but it seems his advances stopped short of triumph. In mid-January, he exhorts her, 'You wound my soul by hinting that last night must have lessened my opinion of you. True, I was behind the scenes with you; but what did I see? . . . I saw the noblest immortal soul creation ever showed me.'[22] She had evidently breached her own parameters of decorum and restraint. Reproach is explicit in his next letter:

> Now, my Love, do not wound our next meeting with any averted looks or restrained caresses: I have marked the line of conduct, a line I know exactly to your taste, and which I will inviolably keep; but do not you show the least inclination to make boundaries: seeming distrust, where you know you may confide, is a cruel sin against Sensibility.

> The Man who adores you: who would die a thousand deaths before he would injure you; and who must soon bid you a long farewell![23]

Clarinda might have experienced what she termed 'the most exquisite' night of her life with Burns but he was a dog without his bone. With letters missing from the correspondence, it is almost impossible to surmise what is meant in one extant letter by Burns being 'behind the scenes'. Could this allude to some kind of passionate frolic and were the missing letters suppressed to preserve Nancy's blushes?

With the hot-blooded poet's frustration at a fever pitch, Clarinda's decision to save on the penny post led him into temptation which eventually did injure his beloved poetess: she asked her maidservant, Jenny Clow, to deliver a letter to Burns and the same day, to collect his reply. Jenny, a pretty lass of 20 years, was unencumbered by the restraints of Calvinism or genteel etiquette. In sending her to the poet's garret rooms, Clarinda had unwittingly sent a birthday present.

Jenny was soon pregnant, although the first Burns heard of this was in the June of that year. Burns' intentions toward Nancy McLehose are not altogether clear. He may have entertained the possibility of marriage – no formal proposal is documented or hinted at – but, with Jenny Clow involved at the end of January 1788, the end was now inevitable, sooner rather than later. If Burns was head-over-heels in love with Clarinda, why did he have sex with her maid? Had he decided, sometime in mid-January, that he was Ayrshire-bound, to be with Jean, and there was no future for him with Clarinda in Edinburgh? Did Burns himself know, given he so often let his head follow his heart? It is almost impossible to draw a fixed conclusion.

After a meeting with Mary Peacock and Robert Ainslie at Clarinda's on 26 January, word got out among Edinburgh gossips about the romance between Burns and Mrs McLehose. (Ainslie, originally the poet's friend, became Clarinda's lawyer and reported as a confidant on Burns to her over the next few years.) Clarinda had been to sit for the artist John Miers, who had done the poet's silhouette – at Burns' request, since he wanted a breast-pin love pendant of her silhouette as a reminder of her. Chins wagged and the clatter was heard by the Reverend John Kemp, Clarinda's minister. Her cousin, Lord William Craig was informed, as was her lofty-minded, puritanical second cousin, John McLaurin, Lord Dreghorn, himself a bit of a playwright and poet. They would have known about Burns' children to Jean Armour and Betty Paton and, possibly, of the writ taken out by May, or Meg, Cameron. It appears that Kemp wrote a 'Puritanical scrawl' of 'Damned sophistry' (Burns' description) to Mrs McLehose, reminding her of her marriage and the rules of the Church regarding associating with another man while still married. The hypocritical Kemp, who eventually had three different wives, demanded Nancy stop seeing Burns, who continued seeing her during the last weeks of his stay in Edinburgh.

Burns later brushed up Nancy's lyrics, 'Talk Not of Love' and 'To A Blackbird' and had them printed in the *SMM*. His own 'Sylvander to Clarinda' was mediocre compared to his later song for Nancy, lyrics wrung out of the longing and angst of what might have been: 'Ae Fond Kiss'.

Burns had tried again in late January to extract monies from Creech, to no avail. He informed Margaret Chalmers on 22 January that he had 'broke measures' with Creech 'and last week wrote him a frosty, keen letter'. The slippery publisher 'promised me upon his honour that I should have the account on Monday; but this is Tuesday, and yet I have not heard a word from him'.[24] The fragment of a letter closes with, 'my limb will soon be sound, and I shall struggle on.' In early March, Burns had been to visit Ellisland farm with James Tennant and agreed to lease the farm from Patrick Miller. The necessity of settling accounts with Creech became more urgent when the poet returned to Edinburgh in mid-March to sign the farm lease. On 19 March, his patience was worn out:

> I have just now written Creech such a letter, that the very goose-feather in my hand shrunk back from the line, and seemed to say, 'I exceedingly fear and quake!' I am forming ideal schemes of vengeance. O for a little of my will on him![25]

The following day, Burns informed Richard Brown that he had at least got Creech to look at the paper work:

> I have been racking shop accounts with Mr Creech; which, both together, with watching, fatigue, and a load of Care almost too heavy for my shoulders, have in some degree actually fever'd me . . . I was convulsed with rage a good part of the day . . . these eight days I have been positively crazed.[26]

A few days before Burns wrote this letter, James Grierson of Dalgoner, Dumfriesshire – who became a friend of the poet after he took the lease of Ellisland farm – was informed that Burns was seen marching up Leith Walk with a branch of a tree in his hand and 'violence in his face & manner'. When asked what was the problem, Burns is supposed to have snapped, 'I am going to smash that Shite Creech.'[27] It would appear that Creech managed to placate Burns with some subscription money but the poet had to wait until the end of May for him to cough up the 100 guineas for his copyright.

When Burns left Edinburgh in mid-February, it was to travel to Glasgow to meet with his younger brother William (who was bringing his horse, Jenny Geddes, up from Mossgiel) and to see his old friend, the sailor Richard Brown. They met the poet off the coach at Argyle Street and went to the Black Bull Inn where they spent the night before saying goodbye to Brown the next morning. The brothers journeyed on together to Paisley and Kilmarnock, en route to Ayrshire. He had promised to write daily to Clarinda, suggesting that the further apart they were, the fonder they would be, cleverly inverting Sir Isaac Newton's observation that the closer objects are the stronger forces attract. He partly kept his promise, writing from Glasgow then Kilmarnock, Cumnock then Mossgiel. With the farm lease of Ellisland safely in his pocket he was also set on getting his name on the Excise list, as a safety net if farming proved precarious.

He told Margaret Chalmers of his plans regarding the Excise:

> You will condemn me for the next step I have taken: I have entered into the Excise. I stay in the West about three weeks, and then return to Edinburgh for six weeks' instructions; afterwards, for I get employ instantly . . . The question is not at what door of fortune's palace shall we enter in; but what doors does she open to us?[28]

For Burns, due to the poverty of his upbringing, the contrast between a stable, regular income in the Excise and the hardship of farming, notably during the worst winter months each year, was considerable. Indeed, the notion of a regular wage was a luxury he had never known before.

Over the next few weeks, Burns fell into the mire of trying to run two relationships in tandem, telling Clarinda what she wanted to hear rather than the truth. On 2 February, he lies:

> Now for a little news that will please you. I, this morning as I came home, called for a certain woman. I am disgusted with her; I cannot endure her! I, while my heart smote me for the profanity, tried to compare her with my Clarinda: 'twas setting the expiring glimmer of a farthing taper beside the cloudless glory of the meridian sun . . . I have done with her, and she with me.[29]

The opposite was true. Burns arrived back in Mauchline in early March to find Jean heavily pregnant and banished from her parents' house. She had found accommodation with William Muir of Tarbolton Mill, a friend of the poet's family. Burns went straight there before going to Mossgiel farm. On 7 March, he reported to Richard Brown:

> I found Jean with her cargo very well laid in; but unfortunately moor'd, almost at the mercy of wind and tide: I have towed her into convenient harbour where she may lie snug till she unload; and have taken the command myself – not ostensibly, but for a time, in secret.[30]

On 3 March, Burns wrote to Ainslie what is now known as the infamous 'horse-litter letter':

> Jean I found banished like a martyr – forlorn, destitute, and friendliness; all for the good old cause: I have reconciled her to her fate: I have reconciled her to her mother; I have taken her a room; I have taken her to my arms; I have given her a mahogany bed: I have given her a guinea; and I have f[ucke]d her till she rejoiced with joy unspeakable and full of glory. But – as I always am on every occasion – I have been prudent and cautious to an astounding degree; I swore her, privately and solemnly, never to attempt any claim on me as a husband, even though anybody should persuade her she had such a claim, which she has not, neither during my life, nor after my death. She did all this like a good girl, and I took the opportunity of some dry horse-litter, and gave her such a thundering scalade that electrified the very marrow of her bones. O, what a peacemaker is a guid weel-willy p---le! It is the mediator, the guarantee, the umpire, the bond of union, the solemn league and covenant, the plenipotentiary, the Aaron's rod, the Jacob's staff, the prophet Elisha's pot of oil, the Ahasuerus' sceptre, the sword of mercy, the philosopher's stone, the horn of plenty, and Tree of Life between Man and Woman.[31]

According to modern medical knowledge, such sexual activity could in no way have harmed the babies Jean was carrying, although it may have hastened their birth.[32] The twin girls were born and died a few days apart, around the middle of March, when Burns was in Edinburgh. The exact cause of death is not known.

While back in Edinburgh, Burns once again met Nancy McLehose and both were reconciled to parting as friends. Kemp had paid her a visit while Burns was in Ayrshire and threatened to end his friendship with her unless she stopped seeing the poet. Clarinda had persuaded him it was over. Geography and circumstances had intervened. Clarinda appealed to the poet's heart and mind but the solace she found in pious religiosity was a prison-house of the mind that Burns had long outgrown. On 18 March, Burns wrote to her affectionately, 'I thank you for all the happiness you bestowed on me yesterday. – The walk – delightful; the evening – rapture.'[33] Before leaving Edinburgh, he presented her with 'To Clarinda' and a pair of drinking goblets as a farewell present.

During his second extended stay in Edinburgh over the winter of 1787–88, Burns' life witnessed a rollercoaster of emotions. He was kept waiting in the city by his publisher, who postponed payment of the poet's copyright and monies owed for books until Burns was beside himself with anger at his prevaricating postponements. He felt the unspeakable loss of his only daughter, baby Jean. He was laid up, a cripple in pain, for a few weeks after an accidental fall that badly damaged a knee. And while recuperating he fell in love and engaged in a whirlwind romance with Nancy McLehose, his 'Clarinda'. All the while Jean was waiting in the wings at home in Ayrshire pregnant, out of sight although not out of mind. When it looked like there was no future between him and Clarinda, Burns went home to Jean, his ever-patient, devoted lover. For the moment at least, during late spring and into the early summer of 1788, the affair with Jenny Clow was kept secret. Then, during a brief trip back to Edinburgh he discovered Jean had lost their newly born twins. It is difficult to see Burns in a favourable light during this period given his infamous 'horse-litter' letter. The penitential Burns soberly reflected at home in Mauchline and on 31 March wrote to Robert Cleghorn (a fellow Crochallan Fencible and farmer at Saughton Mills, near Edinburgh) expressing a deep sense of torment: 'The world sits such a load on my mind that it has effaced almost every trace of the image of God in me.'[34]

Part Four

Farmer to Exciseman – Songs of a Nation

13

Farming Ellisland: The Riddles of Creation

Ellisland farm, situated in Dunscore parish, just under six miles north of Dumfries on the banks of the River Nith, was in a rundown state and without a farmhouse or decent outbuildings. On the positive side, the annual rent of £50 was less than half what they had paid for Lochlie Farm, for more land – 170 acres – albeit unfertile, stony and hilly. The land required to be drained and limed and required enclosures erected to delineate fields. Ploughed stony ground tends to yield more and more stones – hence, Ellisland farm has aptly been described as the riddles of creation. James Tennant's report on its viability had been surprisingly favourable and Miller, who looked like being a hands-off, friendly landlord, was prepared to provide some £300 for improvement work.

Additionally in Ellisland's favour was its appeal to the romantic patriot in Burns: these were lands once owned by Robert the Bruce, who took the lands from the Red Comyn, his main contender for the Scottish crown. To the north of Ellisland, it is reputed that the Roman general Agricola made an encampment. Burns was evidently aware of this when he employed the pen name 'Agricola' over the next few years for radical poetry he published in the press.

With his mind fixed on obtaining an Excise commission as a back-up, Burns was entering a new phase in his life and coming down to earth from the heights of literary fame. In early April, he wrote to William Dunbar: 'I am earnestly busy to bring about a revolution in my own mind . . . my late scenes of idleness and dissipation have enervated my mind to an alarming degree. Skill in the sober science of life is my most serious and hourly study.'[1] The 'revolution' was an oblique reference to being once again attached to Jean Armour. By the end of the month it is clear Burns had entered into a formal but, it appears, secret civil marriage with Jean, whom he was now calling 'Mrs Burns': he let his old friend James Smith in Linlithgow know on 28 April:

> So to let you into the secrets of my pericranium, there is, you must know, a certain clean-limbed, handsome, bewitching young hussy of your acquaintance, to whom I have lately and privately given a matrimonial title to my corpus . . .
>
> Now for business. – I intend to present Mrs Burns with a printed shawl, an article of which I daresay you have variety: 'Tis my first present to her since I have irrevocably called her mine . . . Mrs Burns ('Tis only her private designation) begs her best compliments to you.[2]

One reason for this covert behaviour may have been that he had still to arrange for six weeks' instruction in the routine procedures, paperwork and legalities of the Excise before he could be placed on the waiting list as an 'expectant' Exciseman. On application he had signed himself a bachelor and maybe did not wish to upset the process by informing them of his changed status where he would have to supply his spouse's and children's details. The second reason may have been to do with a desire not to upset Agnes McLehose so soon after his departure from Edinburgh. Indeed, Burns was highly cautious even about informing his Mother Confessor, Mrs Dunlop, about his matrimonial status and eventually did so via her son Andrew. No formal record of this marriage exists but evidence from the Joseph Train Mss suggests Burns and Jean were married in Gavin Hamilton's office by a local magistrate, John Farquar-Gray.[3] It was 5 August before the local minister, William Auld, acknowledged Jean and Robert Burns as man and wife, 'to adhere to one another as Husband & Wife all the days of their life'.

Although he planned to commence farming on Whitsunday – 25 May – the start of his lease, Burns did not actually begin work at Ellisland until the second week in June. His priority was to complete his period of instruction in Excise duties. Rather than in Edinburgh, he had managed to arrange for this to be with James Findlay, Excise Officer in Tarbolton, under George Johnston, the Supervisor of Excise in Ayr. With Graham of Fintry notified, Adam Pearson, the Secretary of Excise in Edinburgh, rubber-stamped the change. Burns had to pay both Findlay and his Ayr Supervisor for his training in keeping Excise books and learning how to gauge barrels and measure and monitor brewing processes. Excise work covered a multitude of sellable materials, from candles to animal skin hides. Each officer had to prove he could afford to purchase a horse and was liable to carry his own pistol or an Excise sword – it was not unknown for an Excise officer to be killed or almost beaten to death by smugglers – as happened in the case of Duncan Henderson, an Excise Officer in Dumfriesshire, who was attacked by an Edgar Wright.[4]

The exact dates of the poet's Excise instruction are not known. However, by 28 April it is clear he was going through his training period, as a letter to Mrs Dunlop mentions his desire to complete instruction prior to 25 May: 'I am at present attending these instructions, to have them completed before Whitsunday.' The salary when Burns began his training was modest but any stable income was welcome. He wrote to Mrs Dunlop: 'I thought five-and-thirty pounds a-year was no bad dernier ressort for a poor poet, if Fortune in her jade tricks should kick him down from the little eminence to which she has lately helped him up.'[5] It was not until 14 July that he received his certified commission from the Excise in Edinburgh, signed by three members of the Board of Excise, Commissioners James Stoddart, George Brown and Thomas Wharton.

Despite Burns' romantic involvements in Edinburgh and the fact that there are remarks to the contrary in some of his letters, it would appear that he had kept Jean on tenterhooks with promises that he would return. While courting Agnes McLehose, he had got news of Jean being thrown out by her parents and had made arrangements for accommodation for her, as he later explained to Mrs Dunlop: 'As I was at that time laid up a cripple in Edinr she was turned, literally turned, out of doors, and I wrote to a friend to shelter her, till my return.'[6] Now Burns moved Jean from Tarbolton Mill to live with him in the two upstairs rooms of Dr MacKenzie's house at the Back Causeway, Mauchline. With their only living child, Bobbie, based at Mossgiel, Jean was regularly out at the farm where she was initiated in the ways of farm work, assisting the poet's brother, three sisters and mother, in preparation for the move to Ellisland.

In a host of letters written in the first week of May, to James Johnson, Alexander Cunningham and other friends in Edinburgh, Burns set about acknowledging his marriage to Jean, to explain he was simply facing up to responsibilities. To James Johnson, he wrote: 'I found I had a long and much loved fellow-creature's happiness or misery among my hands,' a phrase repeated almost verbatim to several other correspondents.[7] Ainslie was told the news on 26 May. Marriage was in a sense an antidote to Burns' previous rakish behaviour, as he told his old partner in crime: 'I am truly pleased with this last affair . . . it has given a stability to my mind & resolutions, unknown before.'[8]

It was 11 June before Burns began to farm Ellisland. He required labourers to clear stones, plough, drive lime, drain fields, sow seeds, plant crops and build enclosures. Potatoes were now becoming a staple of diet in Scotland. (It was Patrick Miller himself who brought turnips – 'swedes' – from Sweden to Scotland for the first time. He also introduced the threshing mill and drill plough to Scotland.) A stranger in the parish of Dunscore, Burns originally sought the help of William Stewart, factor to the nearby estate of Closeburn, to find local workers. Stewart's father owned the Inn at Brownhill, near Closeburn, where the poet had lodged during his first few visits to Ellisland. Burns hired two male and two female servant workers; they were paid off in November, at Martinmas, as was the custom.

While first at Ellisland, from June 1788 onwards, Burns lodged with Agnes and David Cullie in their cottage at the southern border of Ellisland, near the ruin of the Isle Tower. He was travelling between Dumfries and his family in Ayrshire regularly, hoping to get his new house erected at Ellisland. He wrote to Peggy Chalmers on 16 September:

> I am building my house; for this hovel that I shelter in, while occasionally here, is pervious to every blast that blows, and every shower that falls; and I am only preserved from being chilled to death, by being suffocated with smoke.[9]

The damp conditions took a toll on his health and he suffered several 'violent' colds. The letter goes on to break the news rather belatedly that he had married his Jean and boasts of her singing, 'the finest "wood-notes wild" I ever heard'.

Not far from the Cullies' cottage was the summer residence of the Dumfries lawyer, David Newall, who became a firm friend of Burns. In mid-October while the farmhouse was still being built at Ellisland, Burns accepted the offer of Newall's house for the winter. It was there on 7 December, Jean moved in with her husband, bringing her 17-year-old cousin Elizabeth Smith as a friend and servant – little Bobbie was to move from Mossgiel later the following year.

The building of the farmhouse at Ellisland took longer than expected. The Dalswinton stonemason Alexander Crombie built Ellisland under the guidance of the architect and stonemason Thomas Boyd.[10] It was a spacious, five-apartment, single-floor dwelling, with sufficient attic space to serve as temporary accommodation for servants. There was a well for drawing water situated halfway between the house and the River Nith, which ran close by and could be readily seen from the parlour window. A byre and stable had also been erected. (The farmhouse still exists but it was mostly rebuilt after being largely demolished in 1812.) Almost a year passed after taking the lease at Ellisland before Mr and Mrs Burns took up residence, bringing with them their four-poster bed (a gift from Mrs Dunlop) and furniture made mainly by Ayrshire carpenters. As superstitious ritual demanded, Elizabeth Smith was the first to enter the new farmhouse, carrying a Bible with a dish of salt on top to bless those who lived there with good luck.

In June, Burns was stunned at some unexpected news. Robert Ainslie contacted him to state that Jenny Clow was pregnant. His reply, from Ellisland, dated 30 June, briefly mentions 'I am vexed at that affair of the girl.'[11] Ainslie informed Burns also that a Mr Hamilton of Bangour, Ireland, cheated the poet out of money by sitting for Mr Miers, artist, in Edinburgh, and left Burns to pick up the tab. He promised to send Ainslie the money when he got to Mauchline, because 'there I have the Bank-notes in the house like salt-Permits'. (Creech had eventually stumped up the 100 guineas at the end of May.) A final comment in the letter to Ainslie suggests the poet wished to keep the affair with Jenny Clow as secret as possible now he was a married man: 'There is a great degree of folly in talking unnecessarily of one's private affairs.'[12]

Sometime in October, Jenny gave birth to a healthy boy, who took his father's name, Robert Burns. It is highly probable that Agnes McLehose helped Jenny to stay with friends somewhere near Haddington and Burns tried to visit his son without Jean's knowledge, as implied in the following phrase to Mrs Dunlop on 23 October: 'I may see you at Moreham Mains, if you do not leave it for two or three months; as a little business of the Devil's making, will some time soon drive me to Haddington.'[13] The business of the Devil's making was his own making, the pregnancy of Miss Clow. Later in 1788 a writ in *meditatione fugae* was taken out against Burns by Jenny Clow.

Ainslie had acted on behalf of Burns the previous year, when trouble had brewed with May Cameron. Now, Ainslie was caught in the middle of two friends, Agnes McLehose and Burns. Mackay is probably right to surmise that Ainslie played a part in the writ and, no doubt, was beginning to be embarrassed by his erstwhile friend's reputation in bastardy. McLehose's letters are silent on this issue in 1788, which does not mean she was ignorant of the affair but probably destroyed any letters she furbished to Burns on such a thorny subject. On 6 January 1789, Burns again wrote to Ainslie, stating he would be in Edinburgh sometime in February, hoping to see Jenny Clow to 'settle that matter with her, & free her hand of the process'.[14] The last phrase, 'free her hand of the process', would tend to suggest, given Burns' paternal attitudes, that he tried to arrange for baby Robert to be housed with friends or to take the boy himself at an agreed age, as he had done with his daughter to Elizabeth Paton. The efforts Burns made to finance the upbringing of his namesake are detailed within the unpublished private Burns–Ainslie Mss collection. By November 1788, Burns had only three children living: his daughter Bess, wee Bobbie and Jenny Clow's baby son, Robert.

Burns, conditioned to labour, could never be accused of being a lazy gentleman farmer. For all his romantic dreamy nature as a poet, he was no mean farmer. William Clark, who was taken on as a ploughman for six months by Burns in 1789, left a reminiscence for the biographer Dr Chambers stating that he was a friendly, hard-working employer.[15] However, on one occasion Burns had erupted in anger at a worker's incompetence, when one of his cows almost choked to death on a potato feed that should had been chopped into smaller pieces. Clark records that the poet kept around ten milking cows, some heifers and calves, plus a few pet ewes. Burns is credited with bringing Ayrshire cows into the Dumfriesshire area;

other farmers followed his lead once they realised they gave a higher milk yield.[16] If Ellisland farm eventually proved to be a ruinous bargain, to use the poet's phrase, it was not for want of trying to make it profitable.

Paying the rent proved problematic almost from the outset. A receipt dated 19 November 1788 shows that Burns paid David Cullie £36 1s. 6d as half of the total due for crops harvested that autumn. This was an overhead he could have done without. At Ellisland, for the first time, he was exposed to the harsh reality that he was on his own in the struggle to pay the rent. He lacked Gilbert's shrewdness and was by nature too generous to keep the purse strings tight over the first few years.

Things were looking difficult even before the onset of winter. Burns wrote to Beugo, on 9 September:

> I am here on my farm, busy with my harvest; but for all that most pleasurable part of Life called, Social Communication, I am here at the very elbow of Existence. – The only things that are to be found in this country, in any degree of perfection, are Stupidity & Canting.[17]

The most negative description of his first months at Ellisland is captured in his 'Epistle to Hugh Parker':

> Here, for my wonted rhyming raptures,
> I sit and count my sins by chapters;
> For Life and spunk like ither Christians,
> I'm dwindled down to mere existence,
> Wi' nae converse but Gallowa' bodies.

In the poem, even poor Jenny Geddes, his horse, sheds tears of home-sickness, looking towards Ayrshire.

Being of a gregarious bent, Burns thrived on social intercourse. The gap was partially filled by the poet's nearest neighbour, Robert Riddell of Glenriddell, the owner of Friar's Carse estate, which bordered Ellisland farm. Their friendship blossomed into one of the most important of the poet's life, the literary remains of which are captured in the Glenriddell manuscripts. Riddell, who was educated at the universities of Edinburgh and St Andrews, is remembered mainly as an expert antiquarian, although he was also an accomplished musical composer and musician. He had been a Captain during the American War and took a half pay pension after inheriting the family estate. Riddell had already published some of his original melodies with James Johnson in Edinburgh, so it is no surprise he and Burns hit it off. Burns eventually provided lyrics for some of Riddell's musical compositions. Riddell, like Lord Daer, was a Whig thorn in the flesh to the Tory administration in Scotland, particularly on the issue of Burgh reform. He wrote radical polemics which appeared in the *Glasgow Advertiser* under the Addisonian pen name 'Cato'; in some of these, he locked horns with the political theorist Edmund Burke, who was Rector of Glasgow University from 1783 to 1785.[18]

Riddell generously gave Burns a key to the hermitage on his estate and the first fruits of their friendship were 'Verses Written in Friar's Carse' a brilliant piece in the cast of 'Epistle to a Young Friend' but sadly neglected, because it is written in English. It is a remarkable tribute to Riddell that Burns said that he had enjoyed more entertaining discussion and pleasure at his table than among all the nobles and aristocrats of Scotland put together.

Over the summer, Burns had tried to find work for his brother William, sounding out Ainslie's connections in Edinburgh in the hope of finding him an apprenticeship as a saddler but to no avail. William stayed at Ellisland for a few short months before finding work as a saddler at Longtown, near Carlisle. He completed his apprenticeship in Newcastle upon Tyne and then moved to work as a saddler in London. William looked up to his brother as a father figure and Burns' advice to him in letters is always affectionate, although he did not take his own advice to 'Learn taciturnity.'[19] At one point he reassures William that he should get in touch if in financial straits, adding, 'You know my direction. – I shall not see you beat while you fight like a Man.'[20] Burns was always loving towards William and made him feel welcome in his home. Tragically, William died of a fever in London in July 1790.

Burns was never idle when it came to writing poetry or songs. As mentioned in the previous chapter, in the February 1788 edition of Johnson's *SMM*, 34 songs were contributed by Burns, most of them original, others, traditional lyrics he brushed up. As he informed Mrs Dunlop, his own lyrics were usually marked by the letters R, B or X.[21] Additional songs, notably of a Jacobite theme, were left anonymous, such as the beautiful lyric 'Strathallan's Lament'. From the spring of 1788 until early 1790,

Burns contributed at least 44 songs, which appeared in the third volume, in February 1790: these included the beautiful, deceptively simple lyric of heartbreaking loss, 'Ay Waukin O', the lyrics of the timeless love in old age 'John Anderson My Jo', the beautiful verses of 'Ca' the Yowes', an old battle song brushed up, 'Killicrankie', and the bacchanalian 'Willie Brew'd a Peck o' Maut'. The jewel of these early lyrics and one of the most beautiful songs in the Scots language was the heartmelting lyric, for Mrs Jean Burns, 'Of A' the Airts'. It is remarkable how many gems of song lyrics Burns threw out into the culture without appending his name as author.

A few other songs written during the 1788–89 period were not printed until after the poet's death: 'Where Helen Lies', 'O Mally's Meek', 'The Fête Champêtre' and the Jacobite lament in the voice of Prince Charles Edward Stuart after the defeat at Culloden, 'The Chevalier's Lament'. The leading English radical and friend of Samuel Taylor Coleridge, John Thelwall, thought 'The Chevalier's Lament' by far the best example of a song lyric conveying deep emotion in simple English language. 'The Fête Champêtre', a burlesque on corrupt politics in Ayrshire, where 'wine' and 'coin' were used to buy support, did not appear in print until 1834.

While at Ellisland, Burns also wrote his most famous song 'Auld Lang Syne'. An early draft was complete by 7 December. Its origin is often misunderstood, due to comments Burns himself made. It was probably Robert Riddell who furnished him with copies of the older, stuffy version from Ramsay's *Tea-Table Miscellany*. There was a broadsheet version, 'On old long syne my jo, / That thou canst never once reflect, / On old long syne', as cited by the editors Henderson and Henley in their centenary edition of Burns.[22] The poet's first draft is one he reworked and improved, dropping part of the original chorus, 'Let's hae a waught o Malaga, / For auld lang syne'. Burns used a time-honoured ploy in order to gauge Mrs Dunlop's true opinion, saying he had taken it down from an old man's singing.[23] When it was eventually published in December 1796 in the *SMM*, it was marked with a Z, which meant it was a song rewritten by Burns. In November 1788 he explained to Mrs Dunlop:

> Those marked Z, I have given to the world as old verses to their respective tunes; but in fact, of a good many of them, little more than the Chorus is ancient; tho' there is no reason for telling every body this piece of Intelligence.[24]

When he sent his first version to Mrs Dunlop – who was fortunate enough to be sent so many of his works hot off the cerebral press – he wrote, 'Light be the turf on the breast of the Heaven-inspired Poet who composed this glorious Fragment!'[25] In fact, apart from a couple of lines and phrases from the older versions, it was almost totally his work. As Daiches says: 'That the song as we have it is essentially Burns's cannot be doubted . . . We have only to set it beside the earlier extant poems of the same title to see the vast difference between Burns's version.'[26] There is no turf above the breast of the Heaven-inspired poet who wrote 'Auld Lang Syne'; there is a Mausoleum in Dumfries where Burns is buried.

It almost beggars belief that Burns' contribution to Scots song neither earned him a penny, nor enhanced his fame in his lifetime. Presciently, he repeatedly told Johnson that perseverance would bring them both immortal fame: 'You are a Patriot for the music of your country . . . let us go on correctly; and your name shall be immortal.'[27] Whether it was a tingle down the spine or an epiphany, Burns felt and knew his works would be immortal as long as Scotland survived. A sense of assured and deserved immortality as a poet pulsed in his veins but it was increasingly expressed in bitterness at the neglect and poverty he suffered. The poet's bitterness at the poverty he suffered can also be seen as an articulation of moral anger at the endemic poverty forced upon the mass of the population and of his abhorrence of a social structure in which birth determined wealth and status.

Many of the letters written during the Ellisland period are peppered with contempt for rank; in one, to Alexander Cunningham, dated 8 August 1788, he extols the excellence of Smollett's 'Ode to Independence', then lets rip:

> How wretched is the man that hangs on & by the favors of the Great! To shrink from every dignity of Man at the approach of a lordly piece of Self-consequence, who, amid all his tinsel glitter & stately hauteur, is but a creature formed as thou art – & perhaps not so well formed as thou art – came into the world a puling infant as thou didst, & must go out of it as all men must, a stinking corpse – & should the important piece of clay-dough deign to rest his supercilious eye over you, & make a motion as if to signify his tremendous fiat – then – in all the quaking pangs & staring terrors of self-annihilation, to stutter in crouching syllables

> – 'Speak! Lord! ! for thy servant heareth!!!' If such is the damned state of the poor devil, from my soul I pity him![28]

The same sentiments shaped his phrase in 'A Man's a Man': 'The coward slave we pass him by'. His contempt for the 'rattling equipage of some gaping blockhead'[29] is both specific and universal towards all men and women due to his egalitarian principles. Burns did not invent egalitarian principles nor was he the first to criticise the social Feudal order: in the radical magazines of the 1770s the phrase 'no ability' was synonymous with nobility (no a*bility*).

It clearly rankled with his principles when he was compelled to face the realities of his day and play the system of patronage. Seeking patronage was a form of social deference. Even in letters, he detested signing himself someone's 'humble servant' and often signed off with simply his name, or a throw away phrase such as the following 'I have just room for an old Roman Farewell! Robt. Burns.'

By September 1788, his concerns over the viability of Ellisland led him to write to Robert Graham of Fintry about getting formally into active service with the Excise sooner rather than later. After explaining to Graham 'the worn-out poverty' of the farm and the reality that the cash he ought to have set aside to 'supply the deficiencies of these hungry years' was consumed to save his family at Mossgiel, he informs Graham that he could not 'abstract my money from my brother' so would prefer to 'resign the farm, and enter immediately into the service of your HONOURS'. Explaining 'I am determined to stand by my Lease, till resistless Necessity compels me to quit my ground,' he continues:

> There is one way by which I might be enabled to extricate myself from this embarrassment . . . I live here, Sir, in the very centre of a country Excise-Division; the present Officer lately lived on a farm which he rented in my nearest neighbourhood; and as the gentleman, owing to some legacies, is quite opulent, a removal could do him no manner of injury; and on a month's warning, to give me a little time to look again over my Instructions, I would not be afraid to enter on business. I do not know the name of his Division, as I have not yet got acquainted with any of Dumfries Excise People; but his own name is, Leonard Smith. – It would suit me to enter on it, beginning of next Summer; but I shall be in Edinr to wait upon you about the affair, sometime in the ensuing winter.[30]

In the same letter, the poet shudders at his 'own Hardiesse' at asking such an apparently ruthless favour. He described the necessity of having to play the patronage game to a friend a little more bluntly but eloquently: 'To crouch in the train of meer, stupid Wealth & Greatness, except where the commercial interests of worldly Prudence find their account in it, I hold to be Prostitution in any one that is not born a Slave.'[31] In a further letter to Graham, he ponders on the possibility of being appointed as an Excise Officer in Dumfries 'if any of these officers could be removed with more propriety than Mr Smith'.[32] Fear of being unable to pay the rent at Ellisland and finding himself in his father's shoes, in the hell of litigation, was what drove Burns to chase employment in the Excise.

The situation vis-à-vis Leonard Smith has often been used to shed a bad light on Burns. Smith was not dismissed from the Excise to make way for Burns: he was moved to another division, suspended during 1790, then again in 1796, after which he was never re-employed. In courting Graham's friendship, Burns dedicated several poems to him. The first, in imitation of Pope's moral epistles, 'To Robert Graham of Fintry, with a Request for an Excise Division' is a subtle, clever attempt to explain to his patron (who had an interest in amateur dramatics) that a poet is often unfit for the world of commerce and bustle. 'To Mr Graham of Fintry, on Being Appointed to my Excise Division' was composed as a thank you poem. It took various letters to Graham of Fintry, in May and July 1789, after their meeting in Edinburgh in February, before the poet's string-pulling bore results. Even Mrs Dunlop petitioned Graham on the poet's behalf. Graham of Fintry's patronage was little more than a formal letter of introduction to the Collector of Excise in the Dumfriesshire area, John Mitchell, and the decision of whether or not to move Smith and replace him with the poet was left (ostensibly) at the discretion of Collector Mitchell.

In early November 1788, Burns had visited his local kirk for Sunday worship and was startled to hear a tirade of abuse against the Jacobite House of Stewart. The year 1788 was the centenary of the Glorious Revolution and various celebrations occurred throughout Britain. Burns firmly adhered to the principles of the Revolution but his indignation on hearing the Jacobite cause being attacked occasioned an immediate response which he forwarded to the *Edinburgh Evening Courant* on 8 November. This infrequently cited essay, signed 'A Briton', explains the bard's sentiments on Jacobitism and is therefore worth quoting substantially here:

> . . . I went last Wednesday to my parish church, most cordially to join in grateful acknowledgments to the Author of all Good, for the consequent blessings of the Glorious Revolution. To that auspicious event we owe no less than our liberties religious and civil – to it we are likewise indebted for the present Royal Family, the ruling features of whose administration have ever been, mildness to the subject, and tenderness of his rights. Bred and educated in revolution principles, the principles of reason and common sense, it could not be any silly political prejudice that made my heart revolt at the harsh abusive manner in which the Reverend Gentleman mentioned the House of Stuart, and which I am afraid, was too much the language of that day.
>
> We may rejoice sufficiently in our deliverance from past evils, without cruelly raking up the ashes of those whose misfortune it was, perhaps, as much as their crimes, to be the authors of those evils; and may bless God for all his goodness to us as a nation, without, at the same time, cursing a few ruined powerless exiles, who only harboured ideas, and made attempts, that most of us would have done, had we been in their situation.
>
> 'The bloody and tyrannical house of Stuart' may be said with propriety and justice, when compared with the present Royal Family, and the liberal sentiments of our days. But is there no allowance to be made for the manners of the times? Were the royal contemporaries of the Stuarts more mildly attentive to the rights of man? Might not the epithets of 'bloody and tyrannical' be with at least equal justice, applied to the house of Tudor, of York, or any other of their predecessors?
>
> The simple state of the case, Mr Printer, seems to me to be this. – At that period the science of government – the true relation between King and subject, like other sciences, was but just in its infancy, emerging from the dark ages of ignorance and barbarism. The Stuarts only contended for prerogatives which they knew their predecessors enjoyed, and which they saw their contemporaries enjoying; but these prerogatives were inimical to the happiness of a nation and the rights of subjects. In this contest between Prince and People, the consequence of that light of science which had lately dawned over Europe, the Monarch of France, for example, was victorious over the struggling liberties of the subject: With us luckily, the

Monarch failed, and his unwarrantable pretensions fell a sacrifice to our rights and happiness. Whether it was owing to the wisdom of leading individuals, or to the jostlings of party, I cannot pretend to determine; but likewise happily for us, the kingly power was shifted into another branch of the family, who, as they owed the throne solely to the call of a free people, could claim nothing inconsistent with the covenanted terms which placed them there.

The Stuarts have been condemned and laughed at for the folly and impracticability of their attempts, in 1715 and 1745. That they failed, I bless my God most fervently; but cannot join in the ridicule against them. – Who does not know that the abilities or defects of leaders and commanders are often hidden until put to the touchstone of exigence; and that there is a caprice of fortune, an omnipotence in particular accidents, and conjunctures of circumstances, which exalt us as heroes, or brand us as madmen, just as they are or against us?

. . . Who would believe, Sir, that in this our Augustan age of liberality and refinement, while we seem so justly sensible and jealous of our rights and liberties, and animated with such indignation against the very memory of those who would have subverted them, who would suppose that a certain people, under our national protection, should complain, not against a Monarch and a few favourite advisers, but against our whole legislative body, of the very same imposition and oppression, the Romish religion not excepted, and almost in the very same terms as our forefathers did against the family of Stuart! I will not, I cannot, enter into the merits of the cause; but I dare say, the American Congress, in 1776 will be allowed to have been as able and as enlightened, and, a whole empire will say, as honest, as the English Convention in 1688; and that the fourth of July will be as sacred to their posterity as the fifth of November is to us.

To conclude, Sir, let every man, who has a tear for the many miseries incident to humanity, feel for a family, illustrious as any in Europe, and unfortunate beyond historic precedent; and let every Briton, and particularly every Scotsman, who ever looked with reverential pity on the dotage of a parent, cast a veil over the fatal mistakes of the Kings of his forefathers.

This is a clear contextual historical analysis which shows the poet's limited sympathies for Jacobitism and also sets out his views on the flaws of the

Jacobite cause. The views expressed by Burns on the Stirling window were more a hit at the Hanoverians than a call to have the Young Pretender back on the British throne. Burns was first and foremost a poet, and an opinionated one at that, who felt it his duty to speak out on national affairs. Not to speak out would have probably been cowardice in his own terms. Burns' bent for controversy is probably best described in Daiches' phrase 'the tightrope walker'.[33]

As discussed earlier, the consistency of Burns' religio-political values is a powerful thread throughout his writings. His views were Deistic, that is, his faith was based on reason and nature. With varying levels of scepticism, many Deistic passages are found in his letters. In a letter to Mrs Dunlop on New Year's Day 1789, one passage is worthy of William Paley's famous analogy of the watchmaker, in the way it argues from nature to design by a Creator:

> We know nothing, or next to nothing, of the substance or structure of our Souls, so cannot account for these seeming caprices in them; that one should be particularly pleased with this thing, or struck with that, which on Minds of a different cast shall make no extraordinary impression. I have some favourite flowers in Spring, among which are the mountain-daisy, the hare-bell, the foxglove, the wild brier-rose, the budding birk, & the hoary hawthorn, that I view and hang over with particular delight. I never hear the loud, solitary whistle of the Curlew in a Summer noon, or the wild, mixing cadence of a troop of grey-plover in an Autumnal-morning, without feeling an elevation of soul like the enthusiasm of Devotion or Poesy. – Tell me, my dear Friend, to what can this be owing? Are we a piece of machinery, which, like the Eolian harp, passive, takes the impression of the passing accident? Or do these workings argue something within us above the trodden clod?[34]

For all the common mythology of the bard's supposed irreligiousness and the condemnation he suffered posthumously for being apparently anti-religious, the reality is vividly clear that he interpreted religion, faith and belief in God, through his own experience and rationality, in a holistic worldview.

In a personal letter to Peter Stuart of the *London Star* newspaper, Burns refers to the afterlife, hoping that Robert Fergusson was now enjoying pleasures he was denied in his short life:

> Poor Fergusson! If there be a life beyond the grave, which I trust there is . . . thou art now enjoying existence in a glorious world, where worth of the heart alone is distinction in the man; where riches, deprived of all their pleasure-purchasing powers, return to their native sordid matter; where titles and honors are the disregarded reveries of an idle dream.[35]

Burns was just about to learn bitterly that title and rank were not always levelled by death.

In a bizarre episode, Burns discovered that an aristocratic corpse still outranked him. In January 1789, at a friend's inn at Sanquhar, during a winter gale, he had just eaten and

> was sitting in a family way over a friendly bowl, glad that my weary body & soul had found out so comfortable a place of rest – when lo, the quondam Mrs Oswald wheeled into the courtyard with an immense retinue, and the poor Bard is obliged, amid the shades of night, bitter frost, howling hills & icy cataracts, to goad his jaded steed twelve miles further on to another stage.[36]

This experience was turned into the poem 'Ode, Sacred to the Memory of Mrs Oswald of Auchincruive'. Mrs Oswald was portrayed as a widow of Mammon due to her ill-gotten war riches courtesy of her late husband, Richard Oswald. Mary Oswald (a Ramsay of Auchincruive near Ayr) was known to Burns and 'detested with the most heart-felt cordiality' by her tenants and servants.[37] He sent the Pindaric poem to the *London Star*: it was published, under the pen name Tim Nettle, on 7 May (it was later collected in the 1793 Edinburgh Edition, with Mrs Oswald's name dashed out to maintain her anonymity).

Burns had no wish to be known publicly as the author. Peter Stuart, the editor, decided to print a personal note from him below the poem, so exposing his authorship, even although Burns had informed him 'I know not who is the author of the following poem.'[38] Newspaper journalism could be a murky business as it was in Stuart's self-interest (not in Burns') to let readers know a poet of literary fame was a correspondent. Indeed,

Stuart offered a small salary to Burns to continue submitting contributions, which the poet declined, although he agreed to make contributions for the newspaper if he obtained a free subscription.

Burns' projected visit to Edinburgh, to deal primarily with book subscriptions money owed to him by Creech, occurred from 19 February 1789 until the end of the month. He remarked in late 1788 that Creech owed him around £50 for books sold. Burns wrote to Jean from Edinburgh on 20 February saying he had settled matters with Creech 'greatly to my satisfaction . . . He is certainly not what he should be nor has he given me what I should have, but I am better than expected'.[39] The overall profit from the Edinburgh Edition was around £440 to £450 of which around £200 (Burns usually states £180, although he could have given more) went to Gilbert.

The sub-plot during this extended visit was, of course, to renew auld acquaintance, as he might have suggested to Jean, but there was a burning issue: to sort financial matters with Jenny Clow given the news of her pregnancy. Ainslie, of course, knew where Jenny and little Robert were living and had furnished the poet with information about the October birth (not November as some biographers state). Burns had promised to send money to Ainslie for Jenny, and for clothes for the baby and had given her a guinea when they parted. He also forwarded money to pay for the nurse and quarters for little Robert in Haddington, where he paid a visit to see his son while visiting Edinburgh. It is not known whether Mrs Burns knew anything of this matter. Mrs McLehose had told Ainslie to tell Burns she would not even go near her windows when he was in town 'lest even a glance of me should occur in the street'.[40]

In February 1789, Burns sent Mrs Dunlop, as usual, a first draft of his most recent work, 'Flow Gently Sweet Afton', explaining to her that the small River Afton falls into the River Nith near New Cumnock. It is one of his most touching love songs. In the same letter, he was forced to deny being the author of some bawdy material which had been brought to her attention and accused unnamed others for attributing the work to him, stating he doubted the verses were his. He did not deny writing such material and emphatically asserted it would be 'contemptible baseness' to give the details of 'thoughtless merriment . . . or intoxication, to the ear of cool Sobriety or female Delicacy'.[41] Burns' bent towards salty sexual honesty in bawdy lyrics was not part of the public persona he wished Mrs Dunlop to know about.

In what must have been a rather overwhelming package of prose, Burns also enclosed a copy of another polemical essay to Mrs Dunlop he had sent to the *Edinburgh Evening Courant* on the economic consequences of a tax which was hitting the Scottish distillers far more heavily than it did their English counterparts. The head note to the poet's own draft copy, kept for his records, reads as follows:

> At the juncture of the King's illness, while the Regency Bill was pending, & when everybody expected the Premier's downfall, Addresses crowded in to him from all quarters; & among the rest, the following appeared in a Newspaper. – The Addressers, the late Distillers of Scotland, has just been ruined by a positive breach of the Public faith, in a most partial tax laid on by the House of Commons, to favour a few opulent English Distillers, who, it seems, were of vast Electioneering consequence.[42]

After explaining to Mrs Dunlop the essay was sent for her amusement only, he mentioned 'Politics is dangerous ground to tread on.'[43] The prose essay, his second within a few months, written on behalf of the Scottish distillers, is a direct attack on the political chicanery of William Pitt. It illustrates the poet's patriotic sentiments and is a good example of how he was able to argue his views in prose, promoting the need for honesty, fairness and justice within politics:

> While pursy Burgesses crowd your gate, sweating under the weight of heavy Addresses, permit us, the quondam Distillers in that part of Great Britain called Scotland to approach you, not with venal approbation, but with fraternal condolence; not as what you are just now, or for some time have been, but as what, in all probability, you will shortly be. We will have the merit of not deserting our friends in the day of their calamity, and you will have the satisfaction of perusing at least one honest Address . . .
>
> . . . If Fame say true, and Omens be not very much mistaken, you are about to make your exit from that world where the sun of gladness gilds the path of prosperous men: permit us, Great Sir, with the sympathy of fellow-feeling to hail your passage to the realms of ruin . . . In this light, Sir, our Downfall may be again useful to you: though not exactly in the same way, it is not perhaps the first time it has gratified your feelings. It is true, the triumph of your evil star is exceedingly despiteful . . .

> . . . But turn your eyes, Sir, to the tragic scenes of our fate. An ancient Nation, that for many ages had gallantly maintained the unequal struggle for independence with her much more powerful neighbour, at last agrees to a Union which should ever after make them one people. In consideration of certain circumstances, it was covenanted that the former should enjoy a stipulated alleviation in her share of the public burdens, particularly in that branch of revenue called the Excise. This just priviledge has of late given great umbrage to some interested, powerful individuals of the more potent half of the empire, and they have spared no wicked pains, under insidious pretexts to subvert, what they yet dreaded the spirit of their ancient enemies too much, openly to attack . . .
>
> . . . In this conspiracy we fell; nor did we alone suffer, our Country was deeply wounded. A number of, we will say it, respectable individuals, largely engaged in trade, where we were not only useful but absolutely necessary to our Country in her dearest interests: we, with all that was near and dear to us, were sacrificed without remorse to the infernal deity of Political expediency! Not that sound policy, the good of the Whole; we fell to gratify the wishes of dark Envy, and the views of unprincipled Ambition! Your foes, Sir, were avowed; were too brave to take an ungenerous advantage; you fell in the face of day. On the contrary, our enemies, to compleat our over-throw, contrived to make their guilt appear the villainy of a Nation. Your downfall only drags with you your private friends and partisans: in our misery are more or less involved the most numerous and most valuable part of the Community – all those who immediately depend on the cultivation of the soil, from the landlord of a Province down to his lowest Hind . . .
>
> . . . We have the honor to be, Sir, your sympathizing fellow-sufferers, and grateful humble Servants, JOHN BARLEYCORN-Praeses.[44]

What is most remarkable about this second polemical essay is not so much the vivid anti-Pitt content or the poet's posture as the national voice of Scotland's whisky industry, it is the bewildering fact that it appears to be the last polemical essay ever written to the press by Burns. No later letters to the press, if written, have survived.

Given his obsession with political and religious topics and his bent for indignant outspokenness, it would appear to be very much out of character for Burns never to have written to the press again on similar matters. It is beyond question that he continued to write radical poetry in his last years and so why would he cease to write radical prose? If further radical polemical essays were printed by Burns under pen names in the press during his last years, it would seem that the censorial scissors of Dr Currie or other early biographers have denied us the right to them.

Moral outrage was the spark for 'On Seeing a Wounded Hare limp by me, which a Fellow had just Shot'. The context of this poem is the aggravated situation in which the son of a local farmer, James Thomson, shot a hare in late April 1789, during the time when hares have their young. Even those in the countryside who shoot hares do not break the country code that no one should shoot them *out of season*. This poem is simply outrage wrought into poetic form. On sending a copy to Alexander Cunningham, on 4 May, Burns wrote:

> You will guess my indignation at the inhuman fellow, who could shoot a hare at this season when they all of them have young ones; & it gave me no little gloomy satisfaction to see the poor injured creature escape him. – Indeed there is something in all that multiform business of destroying for our sport individuals in the animal creation that do not injure us materially, that I could never reconcile to my ideas of native Virtue & eternal Right.[45]

To amplify emotion, Burns uses the word 'individuals' of the animal kingdom. When he sent a copy of the poem to Mrs Dunlop he was aware her husband's father, old Major Dunlop, a gun-in-hand country aristocrat, might not be averse to the poem: 'I believe you may include the Major, too; as whatever I have said of shooting hares, I have not spoken one irreverend word against coursing them.'[46] James Thomson, who shot the hare, later recollected that the poet confronted him by the banks of the River Nith, making him quake in his shoes, as he believed Burns was going to physically throw him in the river.[47] It takes considerable courage to confront a man armed with a shotgun. Burns was opposed to the 'slaughtering guns' mentioned in his song 'Westlin' Winds' and found the aristocratic notion of shooting 'game' for sport repugnant.

During 1789 Burns saw four further radical works printed, three in newspapers and the satirical 'The Kirk's Alarm', as an anonymous broadside sheet. Just as he studied the Bible in minute detail and felt he could argue his views with anyone on ecclesiastical issues, Burns studied the political theory of the Enlightenment and current developments in Britain, Europe and America, as his poetry suggests, and was never shy of expressing his views. As he remarked to Mrs Dunlop in early April 1789, 'Politics is dangerous ground for me to tread on, and yet I cannot for the soul of me resist.'[48] In 'Elegy on the Year 1788', published in the *Caledonian Mercury* on 10 January, Burns employed the pen name 'Thomas A Linn'. As someone waiting on the Excise list, a pseudonym was essential. The first couplet 'For Lords or Kings I dinna mourn, / E'en let them die – for that they're born!' suggests, however, that Burns had no intention of sacrificing his sentiments for a career in the Excise. Indeed, from the plethora of radical compositions published from January 1789 onwards, it is clear he intended to have his say on political and religious matters as an underground radical poet.

Another known 'political Squib' by Burns was the more risky 'Ode to the Departed Regency Bill', published in the *London Star* on 17 April 1789 and signed 'Agricola'. The pen name usually signifies a farmer but there is also the possible connection to Dumfriesshire, since, as already mentioned, the Roman general Agricola encamped to the north of Ellisland. This time, though, Burns tried to throw a red herring to pretend the poem came from an Edinburgh poet by signing it as from the Scottish capital, 'Agricola, Edinburgh'. Anyone reading the poem would immediately think it was by an Edinburgh poet and, hence, could not have been written by Burns. Indeed, if it had been recently unearthed as a possible lost work of Burns, some critics would immediately leap to the wrong conclusion that the bard could not have written it.

The pacy, Pindaric ode parodies and satirises the clashing rhetoric of political manoeuvring among politicians vying for position during the constitutional Regency crisis of 1788–89, when King George was temporarily declared insane and it seemed that the Prince of Wales, who was supported by the Whig Party, would become Regent. Burns was receiving the newspaper free from Peter Stuart but his poem expressed views Stuart did not completely support, so Stuart modified some lines of the poem without Burns' permission, to suit his editorial policies and kept Burns from seeing the issue which contained his verses.[49] The line 'Paint Ruin, in the shape of high Dundas' would certainly have set Henry Dundas's hair a-bristle. The complex Pindaric Ode style employed by Burns was one a simple Heaven-taught ploughman would never have used or understood. So, along with the pen name and false locus of composition,

Burns was becoming an expert in disguising his radical Scottish muse.

To burlesque the day of public thanksgiving declared to celebrate King George III's recovery from a bout of insanity, Burns' 'A New Psalm for the Chapel of Kilmarnock on the Thanksgiving-Day for His Majesty's Recovery' appeared in the *London Star* on 14 May 1789.[50] Ten days earlier, he had sent a copy of the poem to Mrs Dunlop, stating:

> As I am not devoutly attached to a certain monarch, I cannot say that my heart run any risk of bursting . . . God forgive me for speaking evil of dignities! But I must say that I look on the whole business as a solemn farce of pageant mummery . . . as I am a little tinctured with Buff & Blue myself, I now and then help him to a Stanza.[51]

Buff and blue were the colours of the Whig party led by Charles James Fox. Once again, Burns employed the underground poet's modus operandi for publication, signing the poem under the pen name 'Duncan M'Leerie', who appeared to come from Kilmarnock. Once again he employed a false name and false place of composition to divert from his authorship. The metrical psalm-style poem mocks the 'new Jerusalem' of Prime Minister William Pitt. Poems such as these might have threatened his potential post in the Excise during 1789 but controversy in Church and State took on a more serious, ominous and darker side during the politically fraught 1790s when legal persecution under the sedition laws might have lost Burns his liberty, let alone his job.

Between 1787 and 1789, Burns monitored the progress of the persecution of the liberal minded cleric, the Reverend Dr William McGill, a friend of the poet's. McGill's theological views on the revolution of 1688 and the celebrations of 1788 differed greatly from the Auld Licht Calvinists in the Synods of Glasgow and Ayr. McGill's writings *A Practical Essay on the Death of Jesus Christ* (1786) and *The Benefits of the Revolution* (1789) were vehemently attacked by the minister at Newton-upon-Ayr, Dr Peebles. Writing to Mrs Dunlop in 1787 Burns told her if the persecution of his cleric friend continued he would 'keep no measure with the savages, but fly at them with the faulcons of Ridicule, or run them down with the bloodhounds of Satire, as lawful game, wherever I start them'.[52] In July 1789, he completed 'The Kirk's Alarm, or The Kirk of Scotland's Garland',

and informed Mrs Dunlop (who advised him not to print the song) that some of the Auld Licht 'lads, his opponents, have come thro' my hands before . . . I am thinking to throw off two or three dozen copies at a Press in Dumfries, & send them as from Edinburgh to some Ayrshire folks on both sides of the question'.[53] The phrase 'as from Edinburgh' means Burns planned to throw another red herring and make it seem the song was written by an Edinburgh poet. He was becoming a master at outfoxing his enemies.

Burns sent a copy of the ballad to Robert Aiken, working himself into a fervent froth of fury:

> Whether in the way of my trade I can be of any service to the Revd Doctor is, I fear, very doubtful . . . the worthy Doctor's foes are as securely armed as Ajax was. Ignorance, Superstition, Bigotry, Stupidity, Malevolence, Self-conceit, Envy – all strongly bound in a massy frame of brazen impudence – Good God, Sir! To such a shield, humor is the peck of a sparrow and satire the pop-gun of a school-boy. Creation-disgracing scelerats such as they, God only can mend and the devil only can punish. In the comprehending way of Caligula, I wish they had all but one neck. I feel impotent as a child to the ardour of my wishes! O for a withering curse to blast the germins of their wicked machinations! O for a poisonous Tornado winged from the Torrid Zone of Tartarus, to sweep the spreading crop of their villainous contrivances to the lowest hell![54]

The original 'Kirk's Alarm' contained 13 verses, compared to the final version of 20 verses. It was not printed under the poet's name until almost a century after it was first written. Alexander Tait, the sniding poet who thought himself at least the equal of Burns, decided to print 'The Kirk's Alarm' in his own *Songs and Poems* in 1790, and set up the Burns ballad in order to write a reply to it – a mediocre one at that. He made up a bizarre and malicious pen name that obviously pointed to Burns, 'Composed by Plotcock, the Foul Thief's Exciseman'. As mentioned earlier, Tait had already composed scurrilous verse in Scots, damning the poet's family as rogues, who had cheated the landlord McClure when they lived at Lochlie farm.[55] Tait's jealousy of the celebrated Burns is evident, as is his desire to square accounts because of a satirical song Burns had written about him, which, sadly, has not survived.

Burns sent a copy of the ballad to John Logan, a close intimate of Gavin Hamilton, and cautioned him to read it only to a 'few of us . . . I have enemies enow, God knows, tho' I should not wantonly add to the number'.[56] Burns did have enemies all right and Alexander Tait was added to the list of poets, including James Maxwell of Paisley, who detested Burns and his fame.

Burns was supportive at this time of the general thrust of the Whig opposition but, like many writers down the ages, he desired to keep his own views independent. He enclosed a draft copy of his dedication to the Whig leader, 'Inscribed to the Right Hon C.J. Fox' to Mrs Dunlop in early May 1789. Rather than being a hyper-laudatory poem of praise, it is a light-hearted eulogy to Fox, which debates whether the Opposition leader will be overwhelmed by passions rather than reason, or whether vice will win over virtue, in the struggle between ambition and power; in more general terms, it is a partly comic mini-dissertation on human nature and the chicanery of politics. There is no evidence that this poem was ever published in Burns' lifetime. It is known, however, that Fox was an admirer of Burns' poetry. Burns became an ardent supporter of Fox's anti-war policy from February 1793 onwards (when Britain was at war with France) and admired his pro-reform ideals.

Light is thrown on Burns' attitude to the slave trade in his response to a poem he received in the summer of 1789 from Helen Maria Williams, who worked for Dr John Moore in London. 'The Slave Trade' runs to 350 verses, four lines per verse. In August, he wrote to her, praising 'your excellent poem on the Slave-Trade'.[57] Burns was unequivocally in agreement with the sentiments it expresses, as is clear from the following comments:

> From the 115th verse to the 142d is a striking description of the wrongs of the poor African . . . The address to the advocates for abolishing the slave-trade, from verse 143rd to verse 208th is animated with the true life of Genius . . . The character & manners of the dealer in the infernal traffic is a well done though a horrid picture. – I am not sure how far introducing the Sailor, was right; for though the Sailor's common characteristic is generosity, yet in this case he is certainly not only an unconcerned witness, but in some degree, an efficient agent in the business.[58]

Burns was wholly opposed to the trafficking of human life in this ugliest of capitalist-imperialist developments. His lines inscribed for an altar to Independence at Kirroughtree in Galloway (1795) oppose anyone who would have a slave. The movement to abolish the slave trade had become a major issue throughout the 1780s, with upwards of seventy branches of the anti-slave trade movement set up in provincial towns and main cities of Scotland.

On 14 July 1789, with the storming of the Bastille, a revolution commenced in France in which the absolutist monarchy was ousted from power. A variety of factors had brought matters to a head, including famine among the populace, corruption in politics and mismanagement of public finances. Enlightenment political thought also undermined the absurdity of absolutist monarchy as a system of government. Absolutist monarchy had had its day. By 26 August a Declaration of the Rights of Man and Citizens and a set of principles modelled on the American constitution were drawn up to allow equal rights to all under the law, in principle at least. A new political dawn in America was followed by a new beginning in France. Even the great economic luminary of the Scottish Enlightenment, Adam Smith, was at first supportive of the bloodless change in 1789, as were most leading academics in Scotland and Whig supporters across Britain. Over the next few years, debates on the progress of French politics fused into debates within Britain at a politico-cultural level and it was only when events took on a much uglier and bloody aspect during 1792, that the British establishment reacted with panic as political tumult erupted. Burns was, at first, as he later remarked, a supporter of what seemed to be real democratic and, hence, human progress in France. In 1789, the Revolution represented a great symbol of hope to all progressive-minded individuals across Europe and America.

In early August 1789, Burns got the news he was to be offered the position of Excise Officer to cover the ten parishes of Upper Nithsdale in the division known as the First Dumfries Itinerary. The annual salary was now £50. The poet took up his post in the Excise on 7 September 1789, while still living at Ellisland. Rural Excise rides were always the hardest areas to cover, especially alone, in a highly dangerous job where smugglers, mostly armed, would not hesitate to shoot an Excise Officer if their own lives were at risk. He was leaving the farm pretty much in Jean's hands, changing it to mainly dairy work and probably hoped enclosure work by his seasonal workers could offset part of the annual rent in the first years. Jean's hands were largely full since, on 18 August 1789, she gave birth to a boy, Francis Wallace Burns, named in honour of Mrs Dunlop. Two months later, Burns described to her the 'open manliness of his infant brow', declaring with a dash of romantic idealism his baby son would 'one day stand on the legs of INDEPENDENCE and hold up the face of AN HONEST MAN'.[59] It is with some irony that Scotland's most celebrated poet felt himself grateful to enter the most despised profession in the country, that of a 'gauger'.

14

'Nature's Own Beloved Bard' at Ellisland – Gauging Ale-Firkins[1]

The new Excise Officer must have gritted his teeth as he swore an Oath of Allegiance to the Hanoverian king before a Justice of the Peace on 27 October, with his Excise superiors in attendance. In taking the oath, Burns had to declare he would, inter alia, oppose any 'foreign Prince, Person, Prelate, State or Potentate', who claimed to have any form of jurisdiction in Britain, 'or Authority, Ecclesiastical or Spiritual, within the Realm, so Help me God'. Burns could at least have comforted himself that he was in esteemed company. The fiery, radical essayist Thomas Paine had been obliged to do his share of boot-licking to get himself into the Excise.

For Burns, it was simply a job, a means to an end. He was fully aware of the 'certain stigma affixed to the character of an Excise-Officer', as he remarked to his favourite cleric, Bishop Geddes.[2] Writing to Peter Hill in Edinburgh shortly before commencing as a 'gauger', as Excise men were commonly termed, he blamed 'economy' and 'Prudence' for forcing him to put his pen to 'wretched paper originally intended for the venal fist of some drunken Exciseman, to take dirty notes in a miserable vault of an ale-cellar', continuing with vehemence:

> O Frugality! Thou mother of ten thousand blessings! . . . Lead me, hand me in thy clutching, palsied fist, up those heights, & through those thickets, hitherto inaccessible & impervious to my anxious, weary feet – not those damned Parnassian Crags, bleak & barren, where the hungry worshippers of Fame are, breathless, clambering, hanging between heaven & hell, but those glittering cliffs of Potosi where the all-sufficient, all-powerful deity, WEALTH, holds his immediate court of joys & pleasures; where the sunny exposure of Plenty & the hot-walls of profusion produce those blissful fruits of Luxury, exotics in this world and natives of paradise!!! . . . for the glorious cause of LUCRE I will do anything, be anything – but the horse-leech of private Oppression, or the vulture of public Robbery!!!!! – But to descend from heroics – what, in the name of all the devils at once, have you done with my trunk?[3]

It is widely believed Burns could not write great poetry in English – although the English passage in 'Tam o' Shanter' surely proves the contrary – but no one would doubt the bursts of genius in his prose. In his unbuttoned letters to Ainslie and Cunningham, for example, there are outbursts of what he sometimes terms 'nonsense', which, from today's perspective, can be seen for what they are: flights of creative expression that are far from being nonsense in the trivialising sense.

The very lifeblood of a poet is the desire to be original. Burns developed a knack of constantly losing himself in poetic composition, whether on horseback, or swinging back and forward over the melody of a song on his chair at Ellisland, working on the land, or walking the banks of the Nith. In this creative process, he often deployed poetic phrases first crystallised in his letters.

The poet expanded on his ambivalence to his new profession to several of his correspondents. Shortly after joining the Excise, he wrote to Ainslie:

> I know how the word, Exciseman, or still more opprobrious, Gauger, will sound in your Ears. – I too have seen the day when my auditory nerves would have felt very delicately on this subject, but a wife & children are things which have a wonderful power in blunting these kind of sensations. Fifty pounds a year for life, & a provision for widows & orphans, you will allow, is no bad settlement for a Poet.[4]

In a letter to the Earl of Glencairn's sister, Lady Elizabeth Cunningham, in late December, Burns again touched on the dilemma: 'People may talk as they please of the ignominy of the Excise, but what will support my family and keep me independent of the world is to me a very important matter, and I had much rather that my Profession borrowed credit from me, than that I borrowed credit from my Profession.' Committed to his path, he suggests that the knowledge it would give him of 'the various shades of Human Character' would assist him in his 'trade as a Poet'.[5] A talented, hardworking hyper-intelligent Excise Officer would be expected to rise through the ranks faster than most entrants.

Burns had just got through the door of entry to the Excise in time: as he later wrote to John Wilson, 'No man above thirty, or who has more than two children, is admissible'.[6] Possibly the rules were bent for Burns when he was placed in the Excise area where he lived, which was not normal practice. Excise Officers were often moved after three years in order to eliminate overfamiliarity with businessmen or smugglers. The first Dumfries Itinerary Division, which Burns covered, included the ten parishes of Upper Nithsdale, which were broken down into five separate areas known as 'rides'. As the sole Excise Officer, Burns was expected to survey one ride per day. Due to the extensive landmass of Upper Nithsdale, this meant, as he remarked to Mrs Dunlop: 'Five days in the week, or four at least, I must be on horseback, and very frequently ride thirty or forty miles ere I return; besides four different kinds of book-keeping to post every day.'[7]

Along with whatever element of smuggling Burns could detect, the businesses he had to deal with included tanners, brewers, tobacconists and spirit dealers. Rural divisions were often the toughest areas to survey. Officers did not keep to a predictable routine, giving them, theoretically, the element of surprise. Smuggling, generally of illicit brandy and other alcohol, was endemic in Scotland. In his native Ayrshire, there are legendary tales of cannibals who lived in coastal caves, which were merely a device intended to deter prying eyes while contraband was moved under cover of darkness – the exception being the real-life, flesh-tearing Sawney Bean and his notorious cannibal family from before Burns' time.[8]

As an Excise Officer, Burns was meticulous with paperwork and thorough in dealing with offenders. He reported to Graham of Fintry:

> I have found the Excise business go on a great deal smoother with me than I apprehended; owing a good deal to the generous friendship of Mr Mitchell my Collector, and the kind assistance and instruction of Mr Findlater, my Supervisor. – I dare to be honest, and I fear no labor.'

Burns, acutely aware that the letter of the law and justice are not always the same thing, was efficient without being officious. Typically, he acted with humanity:

> I took, I fancy, rather a new way with my Frauds. – I recorded every Defaulter; but at the Court, I myself begged off every poor body that was unable to pay, which seeming candour gave me so much implicit credit with the Hon. Bench, that with high Compliments they gave me such ample vengeance on the rest, that my Decreet is double the amount of any Division in the District.[10]

Indeed, so thorough was Burns (he was able to take a percentage of each seizure, or up to half of the total of fines imposed) that he began to make enemies among the untouchable aristocrats at the top of the contraband tree. After explaining to Collector John Mitchell that he had almost ridden his poor horse into the ground and had saddle sores on a nameless place from galloping around the ten parishes, he adds: 'I find that every Offender has so many Great Men to espouse his cause, that I shall not be surprised if I am committed to the strong Hold of the Law tomorrow for insolence to the dear friends of the Gentlemen of the Country.'[11] In the same letter to Mitchell, Burns quotes an old saying he picked up which aptly accords with his own values of honesty applied to his new job, 'Mercy to the Thief is Injustice to the Honest Man.'

An example of Burns giving the benefit of the doubt to the accused is seen in the case of a Robert Gordon, on whose behalf he wrote to the Justice of the Peace, Alexander Fergusson, citing the Metrical Psalms: 'Blessed be he that kindly doth / The poor man's case consider'.

> I have sought you all over the town, good Sir, to learn, what you have done, or what can be done, for poor Robbie Gordon. The hour is at hand when I must assume the execrable office of whipper-in to the blood-hounds of Justice, and must, must let loose the ravenous rage of the carrion sons of bitches on poor Robbie. I think you can do something

> to save the unfortunate man, and I am sure, if you can, you will. I know that Benevolence is supreme in your bosom, and has the first voice in, and the last check on, all you do; but that insidious whore Politics may seduce the honest cully Attention until the practicable moment of doing good is no more.[12]

Burns was not lax with the rules but he did square his professional duties with his conscience. In terms of seizure and fines, records show that he was twice the Exciseman Leonard Smith had been in the same area.[13]

A letter to Richard Brown on 4 November shows Burns was not used to having to ask permission to take a day off work: 'I cannot meet you anywhere. No less than an order from the Board of Excise, at Edinburgh, is necessary before I can have so much time as to meet you in Ayrshire.' He asked Brown to come visit him, if possible.[14] Within a few days it was apparent Burns had pushed himself perhaps too hard in his new job. By 8 November he was laid low with a 'violent cold' and a 'stuffed, aching head'.[15] In December, the illness was still dragging him down and he had to inform Nicol that he could not even step over the threshold of his own door and would not be able to inspect a farm for him.[16] (Nicol had come into some money through his wife and purchased Laggan farm in Dumfriesshire.)

November had been the third anniversary of the death of Mary (Margaret) Campbell. For Burns, to love someone once was to love them for ever. His thoughts were on her the following month, when he sent Mrs Dunlop 'Thou Lingering Star'. Falling into maudlin religiosity, he remarks on the benefits of the afterlife, where he would meet his father and, 'with speechless agony of rapture, again recognise my lost, my ever dear MARY, whose bosom was fraught with Truth, Honor, Constancy, & Love'.[17] Burns' romantic recollection turned only the best of the poet's memories of Mary into song, omitting her liaison with the soldier Montgomerie.

As an Officer of the Crown, Burns was called in to assist in monitoring the Dumfriesshire elections during the winter of 1789–90, which occasioned two songs, 'Election Ballad for Westerha' and the better known 'The Five Carlins – A Ballad'. In the latter, each shire is represented in the voice of an old woman, or carlin: Maggy by the Banks of Nith is Dumfries; Marjory o' the mony Lochs is Lochmaben, and so on. It was a characteristic of Burns in ballad-style songs like this, including 'John Barleycorn', to use 'was' rather than 'were', an unusual trait for the period:

There was five Carlins in the South
  They fell upon a scheme
To send a lad to Lon'on town
  To bring them tidings hame.

Sending both songs to Graham of Fintry, he vituperated against the Duke of Queensberry and the Whig candidate, Patrick Miller, son of his landlord:

> The Great Man here, like all Renegadoes, is a flaming Zealot . . . despised I suppose by the Party who took him in to be a mustering faggot at the mysterious orgies of their midnight iniquities, and a useful drudge in the dirty work of their Country Elections, he would fain this part of the world that he is turned Patriot . . . has the impudence to aim away at the unmistrusting manner of a Man of Conscience and Principle.[18]

Although Queensberry was a Whig, Burns saw through his false rhetoric pretending to be a 'Man of Conscience and Principle' and his condescension about caring for the 'welfare of his fellow-creatures', as he put it in his letter quoted above.[19] Like the majority of people, Burns had no vote. These two songs support the Tory candidate, Sir James Johnston – who lost. For Burns, honest principle always came before creed or ideology.

The prose and verse sent by Burns to Graham of Fintry during 1789 and 1790 illuminate his dual roles, as peasant-gauger and as the Bard of Caledonia. The openness with which he discusses politics implies considerable confidence in Fintry's tact. In his 'Epistle to Graham of Fintry', Burns' obsession with controversial topics is irrepressible:

Thus I break aff wi' a' my birr,
An' down yon dark, deep alley spur,
  Where Theologies dander:
Alas! curst wi' eternal fogs,
And damn'd in everlasting bogs,
  As sure's the Creed I'll blunder!

I'll stain a band, or jaup a gown,
Or rin my reckless, guilty crown
  Against the haly door!
Sair do I rue my luckless fate,

When, as the Muse an' Deil wad hae't
  I rade that road before. –

Suppose I take a spurt and mix
Amang the wilds o' Politics
  Electors and elected –
Where dogs at Court (sad sons o' bitches!)
Septennially a madness touches,
  Till all the land's infected. –
. . .
Your poor friend, the Bard, afar
He hears and sees the distant war,
  A cool Spectator purely:
So, when the storm the forest rends,
The Robin in the hedge descends,
  And, patient, chirps securely. –

Burns, the cute little robin hidden in the hedge of protection by his great patron chirping securely, is more of a political Robin Rousseau than a sweet little bird. The final stanza, though, shows the Bard of Caledonia on his pedestal of Independence, defying the world to have his say, come hell or high water:

Now, for my friends' and brethren's sakes,
And for my dear-lov'd LAND O' CAKES,
  I pray with holy fire;
Lord, send a rough-shod troop o' Hell
O'er a' wad Scotland buy, or sell,
  And grind them in the mire!!!

Joining the Excise had not clipped the wings of Burns the radical but his controversial poetry was largely published pseudonymously in newspapers or kept for private circulation among friends.

The first stone of the new theatre, being built by subscription in Dumfries, was laid in early February 1790. On 3 March, a 'Prologue' written by Burns was recited at the old theatre. (In a letter to William Nicol, Burns says he has 'given Mr Sutherland two Prologues' but the second Prologue has never been traced.[20]) The 'Scots Prologue' for Mrs Sutherland's Benefit Night was spoken at the theatre by her husband, George Sutherland. It is a piece of some quality, which ought to have been included in the 1793 Edinburgh Edition. Interestingly, Burns sent a copy to the Dumfries Provost, David Staig, to sound out his response before it was performed in public, remarking:

> . . . there is a dark stroke of Politics in the belly of the Piece, and like a faithful loyal subject, I lay it before You, as the chief Magistrate of the Country, at least the only Magistrate whom I have met with in the country who had the honor to be very conspicuous as a Gentleman; that if the said Poem be found to contain any Treason, or words of treasonable construction, or any Fama clamosa or Scandalum magnatum, against our Sovereign lord the King, or any of his liege Subjects, the said Prologue may not see the light.[21]

A mystery has surrounded what Burns meant by the 'dark stroke of Politics in the belly of the Piece' for over two centuries. Some dismiss it as rhetoric, while the scholar Kinsley lays the anxiety about the patriotic poem at Sutherland's door.[22] A close reading of the proper historical context of the verse suggests the subtle reference to the radical politics of a member of the Douglas family – the poet's friend Lord Daer is the 'dark stroke' in the poem. The Prologue invokes the historical importance of the Douglas family, famed for 'martial strife', then moves to a contemporary scene to suggest 'Perhaps, if bowls row right, and Right succeeds, / *Ye yet may follow where a Douglas leads!*' (My italics.) As previously mentioned, Lord Daer was an eloquent radical, who became one of the leading members of the pro-reform movement Friends of the People in 1792 and held the view that if there was not sufficient support in England to assist the Scottish radicals, then Scotland should form an independent republic.[23] The 'dark stroke of Politics' can therefore be interpreted as a reference to a new direction in Scottish politics under Lord Daer.

To a point, Burns was open about his radical sentiments, as in his 'Elegy on Captain Matthew Henderson', which first appeared in the *Edinburgh Magazine* in August 1790.[24] Its subtitle, a swipe at title and rank, describes Henderson as 'A Gentleman who Held the Patent for His

Honours Immediately from Almighty God!'[25] Henderson was a friend of Burns, an antiquarian and fellow Mason and member of the convivial, dissident Crochallan Fencibles. Burns sent the poem to Dugald Stewart, commenting, 'The inclosed Elegy has pleased me beyond any of my late poetic efforts'.[26] It contains this breath of democratic air:

> Go to your sculptur'd tombs, ye Great,
> In a' the tinsel trash o' state!
> But by thy honest turf I'll wait,
>   Thy man of worth!
> And weep the ae best fellow's fate
>   E'er lay in earth.

The depth of his Scottish patriotism is something Burns never hid from close confidants. He was far from being Anglophobic, yet he clearly felt that the dominant role of London was suffocating Scottish politics and cultural expression and did not permit a healthy equality between Scotland and England. He remarked in a letter to Mrs Dunlop in April 1790:

> You know my national prejudices. – I have often read & admired the Spectator, Adventurer, Rambler, & World, but still with certain regret that they were so thoroughly and entirely English. – Alas! have I often said to myself, what are all the boasted advantages which my Country reaps from a certain Union, that can counterbalance the annihilation of her Independence, & even her very Name![27]

Those who signed the Treaty of Union are condemned in his anonymous song 'Such a Parcel o' Rogues in a Nation'. The poet's pragmatic acceptance of the Union of Parliaments in 1707 was at variance with the rather different emotions he felt regarding the slaughter at Culloden in 1746 and the Duke of Cumberland's subsequent brutal suppression of the Highland clan system, which included banning the playing of pipes and wearing Highland dress.

Burns' pro-Jacobite sentiments were the spark for 'Lament of Mary Queen of Scots, on the Approach of Spring', written in 1790, in the lamenting voice of Mary herself. In a letter addressed to 'Mrs Graham of Fintry' on 10 June, Burns remarks that he thought it one of his finest songs. Another of his Jacobite songs written at this period, the mournful 'There'll Never be Peace Till Jamie Comes Hame', recalls the death of seven sons killed in fighting for the Jacobite cause. Burns sent it to Alexander Cunningham with the observation, 'When Political combustion ceases to be the object of Princes & Patriots, it then, you know, becomes the lawful prey of Historians & Poets'.[28] Burns knew that, in heightening awareness of Scotland's past, his poetry might influence the present and help shape the future. Whether he would have agreed with Shelley's bombastic view that poets are the unacknowledged legislators of the world is uncertain. Certainly, like every great radical poet, his dream was to help to make the world a better place by his writings.

In July 1790, Burns was transferred to the Dumfries Third Division 'footwalk' area as it was termed, which boosted his salary to £70 per annum. Until 11 November 1791, when he moved his family into Dumfries, he travelled to and from work from Ellisland on his new horse named Pegasus. He had been lobbying Mrs Dunlop to use her influence on his behalf with William Corbet the Supervisor-General of the Excise, who lived near Stirling. His ambition for promotion prompted a friendly lampoon by William Nicol, in a letter to Robert Ainslie:

> As to Burns, poor folks like you and I must resign all thoughts of future correspondence with him. To the pride of applauded genius is now superadded the pride of office. He was lately raised to the dignity of an Examiner of Excise, which is a step preparative to attaining that of a *supervisor*. Therefore we can expect no less than that his language will become perfectly Horatian – 'odi profanum vulgus et arceo'. However, I will see him in a fortnight hence; and I will find that Beelzebub has inflated his heart like a bladder with pride, and given it the fullest distension that vanity can effect, you and I will burn him in effigy, and write a satire, as bitter as gall and wormwood, against government for employing its enemies, like Lord North, to effect its purposes. This will be taking all the revenge in our power.[29]

Writing this in August 1790, Nicol was misinformed about the promotion – it was not until a few days after the poet's birthday in 1791 that Burns was added to the list of candidates eligible to become Supervisor or Examiner. The reality was that, had Henry Dundas been favourable towards him, even the elevated level of Collector could have been his at the great man's nod.

In a letter to Graham of Fintry at the start of September 1790, Burns mentions that he would like to be transferred to a Port Division, in Dumfries, Port Glasgow or Greenock, mainly because of the extra income this would bring and also because he would need a more rounded experience in the Excise if he was to obtain promotion to Supervisor, indicating that such a position somewhere in the North of Scotland would appeal.[30]

During his stay at Ellisland, Burns became involved with Robert Riddell and was instrumental in setting up the Monklands Friendly Society reading library. Books were the lifeblood of Burns' own education and he in turn was a keen educationalist. Riddell acted as President of the library and gave many of his old books to start the club. Burns became Secretary and asked Peter Hill to furnish it with additional books (Hill, formerly Creech's assistant, had started his own book shop. He and Burns corresponded regularly and the poet usually sent Hill and his wife a New Year present of a Nith salmon or a ewe-milk cheese). The Monklands Friendly Society met on every fourth Saturday. Members paid a one-off fee of five shillings, then six pennies at every meeting. It was democratically decided which books were purchased from the common funds. At one point the society owned as many as 150 books, many of them works recommended by Burns. The poet saw that their reading society could be replicated all over Scotland and wrote to Sir John Sinclair of Ulbster, who was at the time working on his *Statistical Account of Scotland*, to explain how the society operated, saying it was 'so simple, as to be practicable in any corner of the country'.[31]

Although Burns was a liberal-minded educationalist for his day, he was less so judged by modern standards: for example, he once sarcastically told a member of the society to walk to and from the library with books strapped to his back to absorb the knowledge, later commenting, 'In a dozen pilgrimages, [he] acquired as much rational Theology as the said priest had done by forty years perusal of the pages', a throwaway remark that was probably meant in jest.[32]

On 17 January 1791, Burns sent Peter Hill a polemical rant on the issue of poverty, in a style he himself described as 'heroics': in the Scottish traditional of flyting, it is an artistic rant in creative prose. It was published in the *Glasgow Advertiser*, in the issue of 29 April – 3 May, under the headline 'Fragment – On Poverty':

> POVERTY! Thou half-sister of Death! Thou cousin-german of Hell! Where shall I find force of execration equal to thy demerits? By thee, the venerable Ancient, though, in thy invidious obscurity, grown hoary in the practice of every virtue under Heaven, now laden with years & wretchedness, implores from a stony-hearted son of Mammon, whose sun of prosperity never knew a cloud, a little, little aid to support his very existence, and is by him denied & insulted. – By thee, the Man of Sentiment, whose heart glows with Independence & melts with sensibility, inly pines under the neglect, or writhes in bitterness of soul under the contumely, of arrogant, unfeeling Wealth. – By thee the Man of Genius, whose ill-starred ambition plants him at the tables of the Fashionable & Polite, must see, in suffering silence, his remark neglected & his person despised, while shallow Greatness in his idiot attempts at wit, shall meet with countenance & applause. – Nor is it only the family of Worth that have reason to complain of thee. The children in Folly & Vice, tho' in common with thee, the offspring of Evil, smart equally under thy rod. – Owing to thee, the Man of unfortunate disposition & neglected education, is condemned as a fool for his dissipation; despised & shunned as a needy wretch, when his follies as usual have brought him to want & when his unprincipled necessities drive him to dishonest practices, he is abhorred as a miscreant, & perishes by the justice of his country. – But far otherwise is the lot of the Man of Family & Fortune. – His early extravagance & folly, are fire & spirit; his consequent wants are the embarrassments of an Honest Fellow; & when, to remedy the matter, he sets out with a legal commission to plunder distant provinces & massacre peaceful nations, he returns laden with the spoils of rapine & murder – lives wicked & respected – and dies a Villain & a Lord. – Nay, worst of all, alas! For hapless Woman – the needy creature who was shivering at the corner of the street, waiting to earn the wages of casual prostitution, is ridden down by the chariot wheels of the CORONETED RAPE – hurrying out to the adulterous assignation. She, who, without the same necessities to plead, riots nightly in the same guilty trade!!![33]

This critique on poverty and social oppression, with a kick at colonial plundering, was printed anonymously. It was discovered during my researches in the 1990s and the text exactly as it appeared in the *Glasgow Advertiser* has not been reproduced in any previous biography of Burns. In versions of the poet's complete letters the phrase 'CORONETED

RAPE' has been censored to read 'CORONETED REP'. It is possible from this discovery there are other anonymous passages from Burns' prose writings yet to be found in newspaper archives. Certainly, it constitutes further evidence of his drive to have his radical sentiments made public, despite the danger this involved for him as an Excise Officer.

In mid-1791, Burns leapt to the defence of the principal schoolmaster of Moffat, James Clarke, who faced an inquiry into his conduct by the Town Council, Magistrates and Ministers of Edinburgh who were the Patrons of the school. He told Cunningham frankly:

> He is accused of harshness to some perverse dunces that were placed under his care. God help the Teacher, a man of genius & sensibility, for such is my friend Clarke, when the blockhead Father presents him his booby son, & insists on having the rays of science lighted up in a fellow's head whose scull is impervious & inaccessible by any other way than a positive fracture with a cudgel! A fellow, whom in fact it savours of Impiety to attempt making a scholar of, as he has been marked 'A Blockhead', in the book of fate at the Almighty fiat of his Creator. You know some good fellows among the Magistrates & Council, though, God knows, 'Tis generally a very unfit soil for good fellows to flourish in.[34]

He asked Cunningham to use his influence with his acquaintances on the School Board and petitioned the Reverend William Moodie on Clarke's behalf, declaring in fustian exuberance, 'I would go down on my knees to the rocks & the mountains, & implore them to fall on his Persecutors & crush their malice & them in deserved destruction!'[35] Burns persuaded Robert Riddell to add his support. Clarke eventually won his case and kept his job.

On 9 April 1791, Jean presented Burns with another son, who was named William Nicol after the poet's Classics teacher and Jacobite friend. A few weeks before the birth, Burns had reaped the whirlwind of his visits to the Globe Inn, Dumfries, where his celebrity and gift of the gab led him into an affair with the landlord's niece, his only known affair during his marriage. Golden-haired Anne Park, who gave birth to their child Elizabeth on 31 March, inspired one of his best love songs:

Yestreen I had a pint o' wine
    A place where body saw na;
Yestreen lay on this breast o' mine
    The gowden locks of Anna. –
The hungry Jew in wilderness
    Rejoicing o'er his manna,
Was naething to my hinny bliss
    Upon the lips of Anna.

Nothing is known of what became of Anne Park after the birth. However, before the end of 1792, the baby came to live with her father and Jean in Dumfries and was brought up by them as one of the family. Burns, in the unpublished Burns–Ainslie Mss collection, tells Ainslie in comic self-mockery that he proposed a Bill of Reform regarding his amours with the opposite sex but he feared stiff opposition from the Lower House.[36]

Working in Dumfries, Burns formed a strong bond of friendship with his immediate superiors in the Excise, John Mitchell and Alexander Findlater. The latter was promoted to Supervisor in Dumfries in 1791. Findlater was interested in Burns' work as a poet and received several letters, poems and songs from him. Their close friendship served Burns well over the next few years. On being reprimanded in June 1791 because of an error in surveying the quantity of stock owned by a local brewer, William Lorimer, Burns wrote to him in terms that show how sensitive he was to criticism of his professional standards:

> I know, Sir, & regret deeply that this business glances with a malign aspect on my character as an Officer; but as I am really innocent in the affair, & as the gentleman is known to be an illicit Dealer, & particularly as this is the single instance of the least shadow of carelessness or impropriety in my conduct as an Officer, I shall be peculiarly unfortunate if my character shall fall a sacrifice to the dark manoeuvres of a Smuggler.[37]

In mid-June, Burns wrote to Collector Mitchell asking for leave to attend the wedding on the 20th of the month of his only surviving brother, Gilbert, to Jean Breakenrigg, at Mauchline.

It was through the friendship of Robert Riddell that Burns met Francis Grose, the larger-than-life antiquarian who was travelling Scotland working on *The Antiquities of Scotland.* During the few months Francis Grose stayed with Riddell, the poet met him regularly at Friar's Carse. Burns wrote a few poems on the antiquarian, an epigram and, following Grose's death, 'On the Late Captain Grose's Peregrinations Through Scotland'. Burns asked him if he would include a sketch of Alloway's haunted kirkyard in his book, explaining his family connection to the place and that his father was buried there. Grose agreed to do so only if Burns would furnish him with ghost stories concerning the church. The result was a prose piece of some 750 words recounting two different tales:

> Upon a stormy night, amid whirling squalls of wind and bitter blasts of hail, in short on such a night as the devil would choose to take the air in . . . approaching a place so well known to be a favourite haunt of the devil and the devil's friends and emissaries, he was struck aghast by discovering through the horrors of the storm . . . a light . . . plainly shewed itself to proceed from the haunted edifice . . . the immediate presence of Satan . . . he ventured to go up to, nay into the very kirk . . . heads of unchristened children, limbs of executed malefactors . . .
>
> Another story which I can prove . . . On a market day in the town of Ayr, a farmer from Carrick, and consequently whose way lay by the very gate of Aloway kirk-yard in order to cross the river Doon at the old bridge, which is about two or three hundred yards further on than the said gate, had been detained by his business, till by the time he reached Aloway, it was the wizard hour, between night and morning. Though he was terrified, with a blaze streaming from the kirk, yet as it is a well-known fact that to turn back on these occasions is running by far the greatest risk of mischief, he prudently advanced on his road. When he had reached the gate of the kirk-yard, he was surprised and entertained, through the ribs and arches of an old gothic window which still faces the highway, to see a dance of witches merrily footing it round their old sooty blackguard master, who was keeping them alive with the powers of his bag-pipe. The farmer stopping his horse to observe them a little, could plainly descry the faces of many old women of his acquaintance and neighbourhood . . . the ladies were all in their smocks: and one of them happening unluckily to have a smock which was considerably too short

> to answer all the purpose of that piece of dress, our farmer was so tickled that he involuntarily burst out, with a loud laugh, 'Well luppen Maggy wi the short sark!' and recollecting himself, instantly spurred his horse to the top of his speed . . . no diabolical power can pursue you beyond the middle of a running stream. Lucky it was for the poor farmer that the river Doon was so near, for notwithstanding the speed of his horse, which was a good one, against he reached the middle of the arch of the bridge, and consequently the middle of the stream, the pursuing, vengeful, hags, were so close at his heels, that one of them actually sprung to seize him; but it was too late, nothing was on her side of the stream but the horse's tail, which immediately gave way to her infernal grip, as if blasted by a stroke of lightning; but the farmer was beyond her reach. However, the unsightly, tailless condition of the vigorous steed was to the last hour of the noble creature's life, an awful warning to the Carrick farmers, not to stay too late in Ayr markets.[38]

Burns took both ghost stories and merged them into the epic masterpiece 'Tam o' Shanter'. He more than kept his end of the bargain. It was in June 1790 that Burns sent Grose the ghost stories. On 1 December, he furnished him with the complete poem. What Grose ended up using was 'Tam o' Shanter: A Tale' presented, astonishingly, as a footnote to a drawing of Alloway Churchyard. It is probably still the longest footnote in Scottish history. The poem first appeared in the *Edinburgh Herald* on 18 March, 1791 and was included in the 1793 Edinburgh Edition. Between the version of the poem printed by Grose in April 1791 and the 1793 edition of Burns, there are 60 differences in words and punctuation, clear evidence of reworking by Burns.

It is part of Scotland's mythology to believe 'Tam o' Shanter' was composed in one day. Burns could make some bizarre claims about the origins of his songs, but never suggested his greatest work was out of the kiln, dried and polished in one effort. It was R.H. Cromek, in 1808, who started this glorious, seductive lie. Some have said, with nationalist relish, that the poem is the best day's work done in Scotland since the Battle of Bannockburn – making the composition seem like a miracle performance. (It also fits perfectly with the myth of the 'Heaven-taught ploughman' poet, whose poetry arrives by pure inspiration.) In reality, like all great poems, its finesse was the result of a process of revision and considerable polishing. It is indeed possible that Burns wrote a considerable part of the poem in one day, but not the entire poem. Proof of early reworking is to be found in a letter Mrs Dunlop wrote to Burns, after she received part of the poem anonymously from him, which prompted her to state it was a poem 'no hand other than yours' could have written. Here are the lines from the early draft she quoted back to Burns:

> Kings may be blest, but thou art glorious,
> O'er a' the ills of life victorious;
> As bees fly home laden with treasure,
> By thee the moment's winged with pleasure.
> But pleasure will not always last;
> They're like the rainbow in the blast:
> Awhile it shows its lovely form,
> Then vanishes amid the storm . . .

Mrs Dunlop sent the above to Burns in early November and, as already stated, he forwarded the completed poem to Grose on 1 December. Burns is supposed to have composed much of the poem while walking back and forth near the River Nith. This is almost certainly true, given his trait of going over and over poetry in his head, lost in contemplation as his rhyming mania took over. Corrections, changes and further work would have been committed to paper at his Ellisland desk and gone over again and again, until he milked the best from each line his genius could muster. Not even Burns could have written 'Tam' in one day.

In the passage where Burns changes from the vernacular Scots to English, he shows his ability to switch from one language to another with remarkable ease: this is from the final version:

> But pleasures are like poppies spread,
> You seize the flower, its bloom is shed;
> Or like the snow falls in the river,
> A moment white – then melts for ever;
> Or like the borealis race,
> That flit ere you can point their place;
> Or like the rainbow's lovely form
> Evanishing amid the storm. –
> Nae man can tether time or tide;

It was this passage which prompted Samuel Taylor Coleridge to remark that no one could ever again watch snow falling on a river without a 'new feeling from the time that he has read Burns' comparison of sensual pleasure'.[39] Indeed, as I have argued above, 'Tam o' Shanter' proves the notion false that Burns could not write great poetry in the English language as well as in Scots.

There is no debate among literary critics about this masterpiece. Reading it is one thing; to hear it performed live is an experience no one forgets and its effect must have been amplified during the poet's lifetime, when superstition and belief in the powers of the Devil were so potent.

Professor Alexander Fraser Tytler, son of William of Woodhouselee, and a member of the Edinburgh literati, sang its praises on reading it in March 1791, although his advice to Burns was to omit four lines from the original poem. Burns agreed reluctantly, writing 'the hit at the lawyer and priest, I shall cut out'.[40] About a third of the way into the poem, Burns cut the four lines: 'Three Layers' tongues, turned inside out, / Wi' lies seamed like a beggar's clout; / Three Priests' hearts, rotten black as muck, / Lay stinking, vile, in every neuk'; he replaced them with: 'Wi' mair of horrible and awefu', / Which even to name wad be unlawfu'.' Otherwise, Tytler's heartfelt response was entirely accurate:

> Had you never written another syllable, [this poem] would have been sufficient to have transmitted your name down to posterity with high reputation. In the introductory part, where you paint the character of your hero, and exhibit him at the ale-house ingle, with his tippling cronies, you have delineated nature with an honour and naiveté, that would do honour to Matthew Prior; but when you describe the unfortunate orgies of the witches' sabbath, and the hellish scenery in which they are exhibited, you display a power of imagination, that Shakespeare himself could not have exceeded.[41]

It is still unsurpassed as the greatest poem by any Scots author.

On 15 October 1791, Robert Ainslie paid a visit to Ellisland farm. There is nothing in the poet's letters regarding this visit. Moreover, the correspondence of the two men effectively stops for over two years following this visit. Ainslie conveyed his impressions of the Burns ménage in a letter to Mrs McLehose, which loudly proclaims his own snobbery.

According to his report, Burns still associated with 'Great', important people but no one took notice of Jean. The farmhouse, he says, is 'ill contrived – and pretty Dirty'. Mrs Burns is 'Vulgar & Common-place in a high degree – and pretty round & fat . . . a kind Body in her own way, and the husband Tolerably Attentive to her.' The friends of Burns he met are dismissed as human dirt: 'a Vulgar looking Tavern keeper from Dumfries; and his wife, more Vulgar – Mr. Millar of Dalswinton's Gardiner and his Wife – and said Wife's sister – and a little fellow from Dumfries, who had been a Clerk.' The latter would probably be John Drummond, who had worked as a clerk in Dumfries. For Ainslie, the fame and wealth of Burns in his heyday in Edinburgh were gone and the bard had sunk in his estimation.

Also in October, Burns wrote to Graham of Fintry, 'I have no longer a choice of Patrons: the truly noble Glencairn is no more!'[42] James Cunningham had spent the winter in Portugal, hoping to recuperate from illness, but died sometime after landing at Falmouth on 30 January 1790. Burns read his obituary in the press during early March and heard the funeral would be at the family burial grounds. He attended the funeral and later promised the Earl's sister, Elizabeth, that he would name his next child, if a boy, after her brother. A few years later Burns kept his word and named a son James Glencairn. He composed his 'Lament for James, Earl of Glencairn', a work of intense genuine devotion, and sent a copy to 'Lady Betty'.[43]

In early 1790, when the annual rent rose to £90, Burns decided to untangle himself from his lease at Ellisland. It took almost a year for arrangements to be worked out. After some wrangling with Miller, he renounced the lease on 10 September 1791 and arranged for the crops and livestock to be auctioned at two different sales. The crop sale was favourable. He received a guinea an acre and sold above the expected price. A letter to Thomas Sloan of Wanlockhead, whom Burns met during travels to and from Ellisland and Ayrshire in 1788, tells the story of the first auction and the aftermath, a drunken brawl:

> After the roup was over, about thirty people engaged in a battle, each man for his own hand, & fought it out for three hours. – Nor was the scene much better in the house. – No fighting, indeed, but folks lieing drunk on the floor, & decanting, until both my dogs got so drunk attending

> them, that they could not stand. – You will easily guess how I enjoyed the scene as I was not further over than you used to see me.[44]

It is surprising that Burns did not turn this episode into poetry. The second sale resulted in an argument about the value of a pile of manure with the new owner of Ellisland, James Morin, Laird of Laggan. Burns felt cheated at the price he received but did nothing about the dispute until he moved his family into his new lodgings in Dumfries, which he furnished during October and early November 1791. To take vengeance on James Morin, Burns sent Jean's brother, Adam Armour, to smash every windowpane at the farmhouse on which he had inscribed verses with his diamond stylus pen. As a law enforcer, Burns did not mind being a lawbreaker if he felt a personal injustice.

There was a degree of inevitability in Burns getting rid of Ellisland farm once he had joined the Excise. The farm needed full-time dedication. He was saying farewell to the worry of not being able to pay the rent and the Excise offered at least a modest financial stability. Yet, as country folk born and bred, it would have been with some sadness that Robert, Jean and family left Ellisland on 11 November 1791 to start a new phase of life in Dumfries.

Part Five

From Enlightenment to Tyranny

15

WHEN THE LIGHTS OF LIBERTY CAME ON ACROSS SCOTLAND

THE DUMFRIES YEARS OF THE POET'S LIFE HAVE only been partially understood by previous biographers due to inadequate understanding of changes which occurred in Scotland during these years. There has been a tendency to view the French Revolution of 1789 as the major international event that triggered a demand for parliamentary reform in Britain. The demand for reform pre-dates the French Revolution. What occurred during the last years of Burns' life was, in essence, an ideological war of ideas which witnessed the emergence of the roots of British democracy. For Burns and his radical generation, the loss of the fierce ideological wars of the 1790s were felt as an unmitigated disaster, and the anguish of this permeates his prose and poetry.

Burns, as later evidence will show, had his finger on the pulse of international and domestic events. There is significant evidence to show that Burns took part in reform activity, both as an author and as an individual participant in the Dumfries branch of the Friends of the People, the Scottish pro-democracy movement. A spy, known only to historians by his initials 'JB', infiltrated the Scottish Friends of the People in Edinburgh.[1] He confirmed to government sources, in his very copious reports, that a delegate from the Dumfries branch of the reform group attended the National Convention in Edinburgh in late 1793.[2] This research, combined with a new historical perspective, casts a fresh light over the poet's last years in Dumfries.

On 11 November 1791, the Burns family moved into a second floor flat in the Wee Vennel in Dumfries – now called Bank Street. It contained three small rooms and a kitchen. Below the flat was the office of John Syme, the Distributor of Stamps for Dumfries and Galloway, who was to become a firm, intimate friend of the poet until his death. It was a relatively cramped flat, compared to the more spacious dwelling-house of Ellisland. Jean probably found the town more amenable than the isolation of Ellisland farm. She had been used to the life of a small town at Mauchline. She had hoped she could keep one cow for milk and graze it out at the back of the flat but the area was too small and they were forced to sell her pet cow.

With a population of just over 5,000, it has been estimated that there was an inn to every 90 people in Dumfries. The town was prospering: the new Theatre Royal was being built and it already had its own infirmary. The River Nith winds through Dumfries, running by the main open market area known as the White Sands. The Vennel runs down towards the White Sands from the Mid Steeple on the High Street. Dumfries was the social hub for the local gentry, who were prominent at the local theatre and were always on show at Tinwald Downs, horse-racing with the Dumfries and Galloway Hunt and the Caledonian Hunt, or at the cattle and horse fairs. During the 1790s, the south area of the river was deep enough to be navigated from the Solway to bring in imports of coal, tobacco, tea, sugar and take local produce such as grain and potatoes elsewhere to be sold.

In Britain, shipping was the main form of transport for commerce, via sea, rivers and man-made waterways such as the Forth and Clyde Canal, then under construction. Before the advent of the railway network during the nineteenth century, shipping was the lifeblood of the economy. Unlike today, Dumfries was a relatively busy shipping port. During time of war, when trade blockades were imposed on shipping, the consequences for economic stability were potentially serious for the Dumfries area.

In late November 1791, Burns received news from Nancy McLehose concerning Jenny Clow's health. Nancy took no prisoners. She told him Jenny was dying, was alone, 'untended and unmourned', and had no one to turn to but the father of her child. Burns had little option but to take immediate action and arranged time off from work to visit Jenny in Edinburgh from 29 November until 11 December 1791. He wanted to do what he could for Jenny and make payments from the Ellisland roup towards their son's upbringing. He had wanted to take the boy from Jenny previously but she would not allow him to. Burns had already made contributions for a nurse during young Robert's first years. No details are known of his contribution on this visit. He stayed at the White Hart Inn in the Grassmarket, which was owned by a Mr Mackay. Exactly how Burns explained to Jean why he needed to be away in Edinburgh is not known.

Burns also heard from Ainslie that Nancy McLehose was due to set sail for Jamaica, hoping to make up with her estranged husband. It was now a few years since Clarinda and Sylvander's overheated, platonic romance and she allowed Burns to visit to say goodbye before she left Scotland. Having visited Jenny and his illegitimate son first, then renewed old acquaintances, probably among the Crochallan Fencibles, Burns put off his visit to Nancy, until his last day in Edinburgh, 6 December. Deep love for someone never truly goes away, and the two parted with a kiss after exchanging locks of hair like a pair of adolescent romantics. Nancy, in a sense, represented another life Burns could have lived. At least, from his viewpoint, he had to some extent patched up a friendship from the ruins of past dreams.

On his way home to Dumfries, Burns sent Nancy a copy of his 'Lament of Mary Queen of Scots'. On 27 December, he wrote again, enclosing three songs written for her. These were 'Ae Fond Kiss', 'Behold the Hour, the Boat Arrive' and 'Ance Mair I Hail Thee, Thou Gloomy December'. The latter two are mediocre works. 'Ae Fond Kiss', though, is one of the great jewels of songwriting, probably one of the best songs of love and loss ever written. From the dead stem of an old song – 'One fond kiss before we part, /Drop a tear and bid adieu' – Burns crafted another glittering jewel. 'Ae Fond Kiss' stands comparison with any song of heartache by the greatest modern lyricists of our time. Can we truly doubt his love for Nancy after hearing this song?

It was probably during the poet's stay at Ellisland that he was introduced to another married woman who would feature large over the Dumfries years. Robert Riddell's brother Walter had made a considerable amount of money overseas. After the death of his first wife, he met and married Maria Banks Woodley, in Antigua. He returned to Britain and purchased the Goldielea Estate, four miles from Dumfries, and eventually changed its name to Woodley Park in honour of his young wife. While overseas, Maria had made sketches and notes of her journey, including some comments on natural history. On meeting Burns, she enquired after a publisher and was put in touch with William Smellie, who also happened to be Scotland's leading expert in natural history; Smellie was in the process of writing his second volume on that subject when Burns wrote a letter of introduction to him for Maria – cautioning the caustic wit Smellie that Mrs Riddell was apt to be blunt with those she did not like. Through this connection, Maria later published her work *Voyages to the Madeira and Leeward Caribee Islands*. Maria was, like Mrs McLehose, a bit of a poetess. Burns' relationship with her replicates in its social, creative and sexual tensions his earlier one with Mrs McLehose.

Covering the foot walk Excise division in Dumfries professionally paid dividends in late February when Burns was moved to the more lucrative post at the Dumfries Port Division. He was happy to inform 'My Dear Friend', Maria Riddell, of the good news: 'I have just got an appointment to the first or Port Division as it is called, which adds twenty pounds per annum more to my Salary.'[3] It was Mrs Dunlop he had to thank for getting the nod towards his new post. She had, as he had hoped, petitioned William Corbet, Supervisor General of Excise, suggesting a Port Division for Burns. Findlater also spoke to Corbet on the poet's behalf, stating Burns was interested in the move, and Burns himself wrote to Corbet, mentioning Mrs Dunlop's intervention. Burns hoped his perquisites would add at least another £15 per year to his salary and 'as much rum & brandy as will easily supply an ordinary family … My Glass is run'.[4] With his growing family to support, it was beginning to look as if the Excise was a prudent career choice.

On 29 February, Burns was involved in an incident with the Excise, which became national news in the Scottish press. A 100-ton schooner, the *Rosamond*, was engaged in smuggling along the shallow Solway coast. The smuggling ship had been spotted supplying shore-based dealers a few days before. Those on board were heavily armed. The smugglers, who knew Customs Officers could call on dragoons and Excise Officers to board their ship at any time, played a foxy game for a few days, moving from near Palnackie Bay down towards Annan and the River Sark estuary, where it met the Solway. Burns was one of three Excisemen involved in the incident, the other two being Walter Crawford and John Lewars. On becoming aware that there were around 24 armed smugglers on board the *Rosamond*, Crawford and Lewars went off to get reinforcements, leaving Burns to keep them under observation. A total of over 40 dragoons were rallied, to support the Customs Officers and Excise Officers who spearheaded the operation. The plan was to wade into the Solway to draw swords and fire a volley of shots as they boarded the ship. The dragoons were split into three groups, one commanded by Burns. When they boarded the ship, they found her abandoned and a hole blasted in the hull. All the contraband goods were still on board. The proceeds from the ship were subsequently sold at auction and both Customs and Excise preened themselves on a major smuggling bust. Burns and his colleagues were hailed as heroes.

The poet's next action was cavalier in the extreme. He decided to purchase the four four-pound carronade guns from the *Rosamond* at auction. He then wrote a dedicatory letter of support for the Legislative Assembly in France and despatched them to the new republic. The purchase cost him three pounds. How and by what method Burns sent the weighty guns to France is not known, although a story exists via later investigative work by Sir Walter Scott (with no corroborative evidence), that the guns were seized by Customs at Dover. It is more likely that Burns contacted the Glasgow group, who were then raising considerable funds to aid the new French government, and despatched the guns to Port Glasgow (or Leith Docks) for shipment to France, rather than use landward haulage to Dover. Britain did not go to war with France until the end of January 1793, so there is no reason why the carronades would be seized at all. Indeed, in early 1792, Prime Minister William Pitt received emissaries from the French government and there seemed no likelihood of hostilities between the two countries at this time. Whether Burns' senior employers knew of the carronade affair is not known. A year later, when Britain went to war with France, sending guns to France would have been deemed an act of treason.

The song Burns composed about the *Rosamond* incident, 'The Deil's Awa wi' the Exciseman', was sent to his Edinburgh Excise bosses after he had sung it at an Excise Court dinner in Dumfries. A copy was sent to John Leven, the General Supervisor in Edinburgh. It was probably Burns' heroic part in the *Rosamond* incident which prompted Alexander Cunningham to put the bard's name forward to be honoured with a diploma from the Royal Archers of Scotland in Edinburgh, on 10 April. It is noteworthy that Dr William Maxwell, who later moved to Dumfries and became an intimate friend of Burns, instigated a public call to aid revolutionary France by funding the manufacture of thousands of daggers for the impoverished French army. By the end of 1792, Dr William Maxwell was publicly described by one loyalist newspaper as Britain's most wanted, dangerous Jacobin sympathiser.

❖ ❖ ❖

William Creech had shown some interest, in 1791, in bringing out another edition of the poet's work. He contacted Burns in the spring of 1792, requesting new poetry written over the last few years, to enhance the appeal of the proposed new edition. Burns informed him on 16 April that he could add a good 50 pages of new material and told him emphatically, 'These said fifty pages you know are as much mine as the thumb-stall I have just now drawn on my finger,' going on to add 'A few books which I very much want, are all the recompense I crave, together with as many copies of this new edition of my own works as Friendship or Gratitude shall prompt me to present.'[5] He could have pressed for pro rata payment for all original material written since he sold his copyright. Creech only owned the copyright of the material purchased, not poetry written thereafter. A new edition without new poetry would have been worthless. When the next Edinburgh Edition appeared in 1793, Burns allowed Creech once again to exploit his talents and did not receive a penny for the new poetry he provided. Burns once remarked to Mrs Dunlop, 'devil take the life, of reaping the fruits that another must eat,'[6] in relation to a farmer paying rent, but he foolishly allowed Creech to exploit him when his family could have benefited from his creative work.

During the early summer of 1792, political events slowly came to the boil in Scotland. The parliamentary petition for Borough Reform on 18 April – which meant every town of Scotland – was dismissed out of hand by Henry Dundas. This led, in mid-May, to mobs burning effigies of Dundas in Aberdeen, Brechin and Dundee. The high hopes of the many anti-slave trade organisations throughout Scotland also hit Dundas's stonewall rejection. Then, on 21 May, the government issued a proclamation against 'wicked and seditious writings', targeting mainly Thomas Paine's *The Rights of Man*. The proclamation empowered magistrates to find any authors, publishers, printers and distributors of radical writings they thought might cause civil and political unrest. Paine's publisher was jailed for over a year for publishing the book. The radical attorney John Frost was incarcerated for 18 months for the remark, 'I am for equality . . . no kings!' The proclamation had the effect of petrol to flames. Rather than subdue interest in Paine's book, it ignited interest and made people enquire as to why they should not read it. Sales of *The Rights of Man* rocketed in Scotland to over 15,000 copies by the end of the year. It was open season on radical writers in Britain and their publishers. Burns is reputed to have taken and hidden his copy of Paine's book with a friend.

Colonel Norman McLeod, a leading Scottish MP, was sympathetic to the calls for reform. In a letter to Charles Grey dated 30 November 1792, he looked back at the attempt to silence radical protest in Scotland:

> . . . The Proclamation acted like an Electric shock! It set people of all ranks a-reading and as everybody in this Country can read, the People are already astonishingly informed.[7] Farmers, ploughmen, peasants, manufacturers, artificers, shopkeepers, sailors, merchants are all employed in studying and reasoning with great deliberation on the nature of Society and Government . . . The present Ministry is extremely odious from three causes: the Proclamation; the resistance to the Borough Reform; and the firing on the Mob on the King's birthday here, for burning Dundas in Effigy. The pension of £100 a year given immediately to Pringle the Sheriff who ordered the troops to fire and creating the Provost a Baronet, have greatly aggravated the insult to the people. The conduct of Government seems to be a mixture of timidity and cunning; they are really afraid of insurrections on the one hand and on the other they court and provoke them. On the slightest occasion the troops are put in motion. On the 4th June, before there was the slightest appearance of riot, the dragoons paraded thro' all the principal streets of Edinbr. with drawn swords, the Regiment in the castle were furnished with ball cartridges, a signal by cannon and flags from the Castle was concerted to make the Men of War in Leith roads land their Marines, and another for a regiment of Dragoons to gallop into the city: and all this to rescue the Secretary's effigy which had been threatened in anonymous letters. A few days ago some boys assembled at Dundee to plant the tree of liberty: one of the Magistrates immediately announced an Insurrection and it was industriously given out here that the inhabitants of that town had risen, had seized the Customs House and Excise Officers and refused to pay taxes . . . Dundas's person was in some degree of danger for their hatred and contempt of him is beyond all bounds. . . The People are everywhere associating, reading, deliberating and corresponding . . . the result of this steady calmness of consultation may be great and aweful.[8]

The King's Birthday riots of 4–6 June were precipitated by handbills and placards put up around the city declaring Henry Dundas would be burned in effigy. A proclamation issued around the city tried to prevent political disturbance and banned the throwing of various objects, not just bricks and stones; bizarrely, the list included 'dead cats'. The houses of Robert and Henry Dundas were besieged. Fourteen arrests were made on the first night and on 6 June two volleys of shots were fired at the assembled crowd after the reading of the Riot Act failed to disperse them. Six protesters were wounded and one killed. The riots were symptomatic of a growing widespread feeling of radical discontent. The heavy-handed reaction by the establishment inflamed the situation and generated further grievances among the non-voting majority as news spread of the excessive use of force.

Without the foregoing historical context, it would be almost impossible to comprehend the significance, or even the subject matter, of a missing work by Burns, known only by its title, 'The Lucubrations of Henry Dundass, May 1792'. The double 'ss' is, of course, deliberate, presumably for comic effect. The title of the work is all that remains of more than three-quarters of a page cut away from the poet's Interleaved *Scots Musical Museum*. This was a special printed copy of the *SMM*, with extra blank pages added for the poet to write up notes. Had it been a work in praise of Dundas, it would have been certainly preserved. It may have been written a few months after the events, given the way Burns transmuted news data into poetry or song. From the title, it can be deduced the work was about the midnight drinking worries of the Home Secretary Dundas, as he was deluged by the growing tide of seditious writings and the rising clamour of political demands in Scotland. It was almost certainly written in the first person, which would make it a work possibly similar to 'Holy Willie's Prayer'. The censorial scissors were probably taken to the satirical poem to protect the memory of Henry Dundas. Other similar radical songs of the time pilloried these same events, songs such as 'Wha Wants Me'. Although only known by its title, 'The Lucubrations of Henry Dundass, May 1792', has hitherto, strangely, never been mentioned by previous biographers. A copy may yet survive in private hands.

On 26 July 1792, a meeting occurred in Fortune's Tavern in Edinburgh out of which was born the Scottish reformist group, the Friends of the People. This acted like a beacon among other dissenting groups throughout Scotland and in August and September the lights of Liberty were coming on all over Scotland. Branches of the Friends of the People appeared in Perth, Dundee, Glasgow and Paisley. In Edinburgh and Glasgow, several sub-branches were

formed, because the original branches were too large to meet in one hall or pub. By the end of the year, there were almost 100 branches of the pro-democracy movement, demanding a wider extension of the franchise, more regular parliaments and an end to political corruption. The Scottish Friends of the People aimed to keep their demands strictly within the remit of the Constitution and all declared their loyalty to Britain and to King George. As the first mass movement in Scotland for democratic reform, it is remarkable that there is almost no popular memory in modern history regarding the struggle of so many Scots for political change.

That said, recent historical work has, at long last, provided literary Burns scholars with the necessary political and historical context in which to fully understand Burns' life and poetry. Dr J. Brimms' thesis on the Scottish democratic movement marks a watershed in our understanding of the period. Significantly adding to this are the publications of Professor Bob Harris, including his *The Scottish People and the French Revolution* (2008), which contains revelations regarding Robert Graham of Fintry.

The significance for Burns' life story is that new evidence proves there was a branch of the Friends of the People in Dumfries and that Burns himself was almost certainly a covert member. One would assume a modern democracy such as Britain would now be proud of its early democratic forebears and that their struggle would be widely known, along with the story of the Chartists and Suffragettes. The pro-democracy movement is of importance to Burns' radical writing in the 1790s, because he articulated the radical sentiments of the movement in songs such as 'A Man's a Man', which was, in its time, a seditious song he could only publish anonymously.

◈ ◈ ◈

As well as correcting and collating material for Creech's proposed new edition of his works, Burns was heavily involved in writing and correcting songs for the fourth volume of the *SMM*. He informed Mrs Dunlop near the end of August, 'These two or three months, besides my own business, I have been writing out for, & correcting the Press-work of, two Publications. One was for a friend; the other is, my own Poems,'[9] which Creech proposed to publish in a two-volume edition. Burns contributed almost 50 songs to Johnson's *SMM* between 1790 and early August. The fourth volume appeared on 13 August 1792. Burns is also credited with writing the Preface of the *SMM*. The songs included 'Cragie-Burn Wood', 'Cock Up Your Beaver', 'The Whistle', 'My Collier Laddie', 'Ye Jacobites By Name', 'Ye Banks and Braes o' Bonie

Doon', 'Willie Wastle', 'Such a Parcel of Rogues in a Nation', 'The Slave's Lament', 'The Song of Death', 'Flow Gently Sweet Afton', 'The Carls of Dysart', 'The Deil's Awa Wi' the Exciseman' and 'Ae Fond Kiss'. Two versions of 'Ye Banks and Braes' were written by Burns, the second and best after he heard a melody by his Edinburgh friend Allan Masterton. 'Such a Parcel of Rogues' was overtly political and Jacobite in sentiment and, wisely, Burns did not sign it. For any lyricist, to compose one or more songs that continue to be sung over two centuries after their death is a remarkable achievement.

Burns did not live in an era where successful 'hit' songs could produce instant fame and wealth as they do nowadays. By his songwriting and ballad 'hobby-horse', as he called it, he was laying in store his own fame as a songwriter. One of the major differences in perception between today's culture and his own era is that then Burns was hardly known as a songwriter among the general public. The full cultural value of his contribution to Scots songs was not known, therefore not fully appreciated, during his lifetime.

Two further song collection projects were underway in Edinburgh. One had already been published earlier in the year, *A Selection of Scots Songs*, by Professor Peter (or Pietro) Urbani, who later met Burns on a tour of Galloway and requested his assistance to write lyrics for his collection. Burns gave only limited help. In mid-September, George Thomson wrote to Burns requesting his cooperation in a new venture, which was more ambitious than Johnson's *SMM*. The former lawyer's clerk and bit-part musician had on board the celebrated musician Joseph Pleyel and planned to add a flavour of continental music to the Scots airs he selected for his project, including some music provided by Beethoven. Whereas Johnson had allowed complete editorial control to Burns, Thomson thought himself a better arbiter of musical and lyrical taste than Burns. The volume of correspondence which exists between the two men shows Thomson as an megalomaniac meddler, who believed he could improve not only the lyrics of Burns but also on the music of Beethoven.

Burns promised Thomson he would send him around 25 songs before early 1793 and he kept to his word. He made several stipulations regarding his involvement. One was that he would not be hurried, nor would he have any truck with composing purely English lyrics for Scots music. That was non-negotiable. Burns insisted on the freedom to sprinkle Scots words into any old ballads he chose to amend. Burns' passion for songwriting was such that it made him altruistic in giving his lyrics to Thomson for free:

> As to any remuneration, you may think my Songs either above, or below price; for they shall absolutely be the one or the other. – In the honest enthusiasm with which I embark in your undertaking, to talk of money, wages, fee, hire, &c. would be downright Sodomy of Soul![10]

This was, of course, an emotional reaction to the idea that any song could be priced or valued in pounds shillings and pence. In one letter of 8 November, Burns illustrated with musical annotation the problems of joining lyrics to music, showing Thomson he was not a fool when it came to music per se. The syllables of lyrics had to match to the 'feature notes' of the melody, according to Burns. Jean reminisced after the poet's death that he could play a fiddle well enough to perform slow airs but no one ever danced to his playing, which meant he was not practised enough to perform a jig, reel or the most distinctive Scots tune, a strathspey. Trained fiddlers in Scotland have always had a dislike of those who play by ear, those who cannot read music by the black dots – people they still quaintly term as 'lug merchants'. Among the first songs sent to Thomson were 'Will You Go to the Indies, My Mary' and 'The Lea-Rig'.

A further song posted to Thomson related to an experience in mid-August, when Burns met with a Mr Baillie, his two daughters and a friend, Mr Hamilton of Grange. The Baillies, from Mayfield, Ayrshire, were neighbours of Mrs Dunlop. They called on Burns on their way through Dumfries into England. Burns was delighted to meet friends of Mrs Dunlop and was so transfixed by 'Miss Leslie Baillie, the most beautiful, elegant woman in the world', he conveyed her and her family 15 miles out of Dumfries towards Annan.[11] Such was his infatuation, by the time he dined and spent most of the day with them, he did not reach home until around 9 p.m. Like an obsessive photographer who must photograph everything he deems beautiful, Burns got to work on a ballad for Miss Baillie. Although a few verses are of some merit, he fell into the trap of stealing from his own earlier work, using phraseology employed in 'Ae Fond Kiss' – 'To see her is to love her / And love but her forever'. This reveals a lack of inspiration and an extempore, patchwork mediocrity quite uncommon to his songs.

As the beacons of Liberty burned across Scotland and the 'Swinish Multitude' (in Burke's elitist phrase) clamoured for representation in parliament, the fear and insecurities of the British government went a few notches up the Richter scale during August and September. This was also due to events in France. The French monarchy were tolerated by the new republic until a counter-revolutionary plot was discovered, which provoked a defensive act of brutality by French leaders and led to the infamous September massacres. The blood of the guillotine now became a symbol of French Jacobinism to other nation states, where royalty and nobility feared for their own future. The British government, who had been working since 1791 to create loyalist propaganda in the press to subdue any form of unrest here, now began to tar and feather all reformers in Britain as evil, bloodthirsty Jacobins, hell-bent on overthrowing legitimate government authority. This was, of course, a hysterical lie to intimidate and stem the tide of reform. After further political unrest and riots during November in various parts of Scotland, in Dundee and Perth in particular, the fear of a potential uprising or political insurrection spread in government circles. Britain was in the grip of an ideological war and the feudal order was beginning to crack at the seams.

If Dumfries was a rural Scottish backwater, it still pulsed with news of events in Britain and Europe. Scotland's national press was mostly sympathetic to the pro-democracy movement in 1792. People would gather at town centres – at the Mid Steeple, in the case of Dumfries – to meet the Mail Coach to hear news of London, Paris, or home. Most newspapers were twice weekly, only a few were daily. Two fed into the new reform movement, the *Caledonian Chronicle* and the *Edinburgh Gazetteer*. Only one issue of the former has survived. There may have been works by Burns in the *Caledonian Chronicle* which have never seen the light of modern day. The *Edinburgh Gazetteer*, though, is still mostly extant. Burns burst with enthusiasm when he read its 'Prospectus', which was circulated among the branches of the Friends of the People in Scotland. He wrote to the proprietor, Captain William Johnston, on 13 November:

> I have just read your Prospectus of the Edinr Gazetteer. – If you go on in your Paper with the same spirit, it will, beyond all comparison, be the first Composition of the kind in Europe. – I beg leave to insert my name as a Subscriber; & if you have already published any papers, please send me them from the beginning. – . . . Go on Sir! Lay bare, with undaunted heart & steady hand, that horrid mass of corruption called Politics & State-Craft! Dare to draw in their native colors these 'Calm, thinking VILLAINS whom no faith can fix' whatever be the Shibboleth of their pretended Party.[12]

The newspaper was the most political broadsheet ever published in Scotland and represented a highly articulate, pro-democracy movement. Burns' support for the newspaper and the reform movement are obvious proof of his disdain towards hermetic, nepotistic, corrupt parliamentary politics.

One of the first poems he sent to Captain Johnston was 'The Rights of Woman', written for Miss Louisa Fontenelle for her benefit night at the Dumfries theatre on 26 November. Burns was a regular theatre-goer in Dumfries, although few facts exist about how often he attended and what performances he saw. The older Assembly Rooms had been used for theatrical performances until the new theatre was opened on 29 September. Burns gave a belt-and-braces compliment to Miss Fontenelle: 'To you Madame, on our humble Dumfries boards, I have been more indebted for entertainment, than ever I was in prouder Theatres' when he enclosed a copy of 'The Rights of Woman'.[13] It is a lightweight piece, not to be compared with Mary Wollstonecraft's magisterial work, *The Vindication of the Rights of Woman*, from which the title alone springs. The poem contains a wicked, troublemaking aspect in the first couplets and an incendiary ending, wrapped around an illustration of liberal-minded, gentlemanly manners towards women at the time – protection, decorum and admiration. It begins, 'While Europe's eye is fix'd on mighty things, / The fate of Empires and the fall of Kings' and moves on to a line that would have had Henry Dundas slamming the table in fury: 'And even children lisp, The Rights of Man'. The idea of a generation of children learning Paine's banned book by heart would have been a nightmare image for any reactionary politician. Burns, too, would have known that the theatres in most cities in Britain had become notorious for conflict between reformers and loyalist factions during the preceding months, when the traditional 'God Save the King' was normally played but was regularly chanted down by reformers calling for the French revolutionary song 'Ça Ira'. Hence, to end the poem 'Ah! Ça Ira! The MAJESTY OF WOMAN!!!', was deliberately provocative and likely to prompt reformers in the audience to chant down the traditional loyalist song. The poem was published anonymously on 30 November.

When Burns sent a copy of 'The Rights of Woman' to Mrs Dunlop on 6 December, he mentioned the confrontation of reformers and loyalists in the Dumfries theatre but carefully did not implicate himself in the business:

> We, in this country, here have many alarms of the Reform, or rather the Republican spirit, of your part of the kingdom. – Indeed, we are a good deal in commotion ourselves & in our Theatre here, 'God save the king' has met with some groans & hisses, while Ça ira has been repeatedly called for. – For me, I am a Placeman, you know, a very humble one indeed, Heaven knows, but still so much so as to gag me from joining in the cry.[14]

In a small town where Burns himself was known by his fame and as a gauger, there was little he was able to do that would not escape public attention, especially in a small theatre of a couple of hundred seats. Likewise, he would have known any reformers in the area, given his republican sympathies towards France and his pro-reform views, although he may have tried to be discreet in openly expressing such views.

With the flood of French loyalist refugees into Britain after the September massacres, the passing of the Alien Act in December and the demand by Pitt's administration that all town and city magistrates and burgesses should hold meetings to sign a petition of loyal declaration to King George III, political ferment was at fever pitch. Loyal declarations were printed from every corner of Britain by town magistrates, including Dumfries. Thomas Paine was tried in his absence on 18 December and found guilty of sedition. Paine knew a guilty verdict was guaranteed, so fled to France. On 11 December 1792, a National Convention of the Scottish Friends of the People met in Edinburgh. The government decided to take action against the Scottish reformers, by whatever means possible, to crush the movement. They considered the Scottish Convention to be a Jacobin-influenced government-in-waiting and saw red at the very term *Scottish National Convention*, named after the French National Convention, which took over from the National Assembly when the monarchy was deposed and imprisoned.

Lord Daer attended the Scottish Convention and declared his own hereditary title as a lord to be part of the corrupt practice of an outdated feudal order which held back progress in Britain. Daer denounced all hereditary titles, insisting delegates should address him as Citizen Daer. To use the term 'citizen' was fighting talk in these paranoid times – a barber called John Citizen was arrested, suspected of being a Jacobin, purely on the basis of his name and, when declared innocent, was told to change his surname. The leading spokesperson for the Convention was a young advocate, Thomas Muir of Huntershill in Glasgow. Although Muir read out a letter of support from the United Irishmen, which incensed the Dundases when it was published, he made it very clear that the Convention of the Friends of the People was a non-violent movement, whose ambitions were universal suffrage for all taxpayers, more regular parliaments and an end to corrupt political practices. The Scottish National Convention made their loyalty to King George III known and emphasised their loyalty to the constitution of 1688. Any members who advocated Jacobin-style violence were to be expelled. Despite this, Robert Dundas was gunning for Thomas Muir and privately wrote in mid-December that he would 'lay Muir by the heels on a charge of High Treason'.[15] At the start of 1793 members of the reform movement in Scotland saw themselves as British patriots. Over the next few years they were damned as enemies of Britain and the pro-government loyalists claimed to be the only true British patriots.

The Dundas dynasty in Scotland wanted the names of every political activist involved in seditious writings or activity deemed to be a threat to the status quo. Government fear and paranoia in Scotland led to a mixture of systematic professional and amateur monitoring of radicals up and down Scotland. Probably the most famous political spy from the time of the 1707 Union was Daniel Defoe, who acted as an agent of the English crown by wandering the streets of Edinburgh in disguise, lobbying for the Union and taking notes on people's views. A full-time, professional intelligence service did not exist at this time, although some spies were employed and paid by government on an ad hoc basis. It was Sir William Maxwell from Dumfriesshire who employed two servants to gather information on radical agitators in and outwith Dumfries and one of his reports – seven pages in length – was sent addressed to Henry Dundas on 19 November 1792.[16] Government demanded the names of every recipient of *The Edinburgh Gazetteer* and this was supplied by spy intelligence.[17] The cold hand of authority was soon on the poet's shoulder.

It has generally been assumed that someone reported Burns to his Excise bosses in Edinburgh, instigating an investigation into his political sentiments. It is more likely, in the custom of the times, that the report was sent to Henry or Robert Dundas, who then passed the intelligence over to the Excise Board to deal with their wayward employee. The identity of the informers who reported Burns in December 1792 is not known (it may have been spies paid by Sir William Maxwell). The list of charges levelled at the poet threatened to have him sacked from his job. On discovering he had been reported for his radical activities, Burns wrote to Graham of Fintry to save him from being sacked:

> I have been surprised, confounded & distracted by Mr Mitchel, the Collector, telling me just now, that he has received an order from your Honble Board to enquire into my political conduct, & blaming me as a person disaffected to Government. Sir, you are a Husband – & a father – you know what you would feel, to see the much-loved wife of your bosom, & your helpless, prattling little ones, turned adrift into the world, degraded & disgraced from a situation in which they had been respectable & left almost without the necessary support of a miserable existence . . .
>
> To the British Constitution, on Revolution principles, next after my God, I am most devoutly attached![18]

General Supervisor Corbet led the investigation into the poet's political sentiments. Fortunately for Burns, Collector Mitchell and Supervisor Findlater saw him as a professional Excise Officer and both, as work colleagues and as close friends, obviously did not wish to see him lose his job.

The list of charges aimed at Burns was extensive. The original documentation has been destroyed. We only know of the charges through Burns' response to them. The informer(s) accused him of being a member of a political group and its leader in Dumfries; of receiving copies of and sending poetry and prose material to the *Edinburgh Gazetteer*; of being part of a rabble in the Dumfries theatre who yelled out 'Ça Ira' and chanted down 'God Save the King'; of uttering an invective or drinking a toast critical of King George III. Burns was caught between a rock and a hard place. The radical poet's cavalier actions and outspoken nature now threatened the livelihood of Burns the Exciseman. Were the charges true and he admitted to them, he was out of a job forthwith. He had little option but to save his own skin and preserve his family from beggary and ruin.

In a plucky and clever piece of self-defence Burns wrote to Graham of Fintry to rebuff every charge of which he was accused:

> It has been said that I not only belong to, but head a disaffected party in this place . . . if there exists such an association, it must consist of such obscure, nameless beings, as precludes any possibility of my being known to them, or they to me.

I was in the Playhouse one night, when, ÇA IRA was called for. – I was in the middle of the Pit, & from the Pit the clamour arose. – One or two individuals with whom I occasionally associate were of the party, but I neither knew of the Plot, nor joined in the Plot; nor ever opened my lips to hiss, or huzza, that, or any other Political tune whatever. – I looked on myself as far too obscure a man to have any weight in quelling a Riot; at the same time as a character of higher respectability, than to yell in the howlings of a rabble. – This was the conduct of all the first Characters in this place; & these Characters know, & will avow, that such was my conduct. –

I never uttered any invectives against the king. – His private worth, it is altogether impossible that such a man as I, can appreciate; and in his Public capacity, I always revered, & ever will, with the soundest loyalty, revere, the Monarch of Great Britain, as, to speak in Masonic, the sacred KEYSTONE OF OUR ROYAL ARCH CONSTITUTION. –

As to REFORM PRINCIPLES, I look upon the British Constitution, as settled at the Revolution, to be the most glorious Constitution on earth, or that perhaps the wit of man can frame; at the same time, I think, & you know what High and distinquished Characters have for some time thought so, that we have a good deal deviated from the original principles of that Constitution; particularly, that an alarming System of Corruption has pervaded the connection between the Executive Power and the House of Commons. – This is the truth, the whole truth, of my Reform opinions; opinions which, before I was aware of the complection of these innovating times, I too unguardedly (now I see it) sported with: but henceforth, I seal up my lips. – However, I never dictated to, corresponded with, or had the least connection with, any political association whatever. Of Johnston, the publisher of the Edinr Gazetteer, I know nothing.- One evening in company with four or five friends, we met with his prospectus which we thought manly & independent; & I wrote to him, ordering his paper for us. – If you think that I act improperly in allowing his Paper to come addressed to me, I shall immediately countermand it. – I never, so judge me, God! wrote a line of prose for the Gazetteer in my life. – An occasional address, spoken by Miss Fontenelle on her benefit-night here, which I called, the Rights of Woman, I sent to the Gazetteer; as also, some extempore stanzas on the Commemoration of Thomson: both of these I will subjoin for your perusal. – You will see that they have nothing whatever to do with

> Politics. – At the time when I sent Johnston one of these poems, but which one, I do not remember, I inclosed, at the request of my warm & worthy friend, Robt Riddel Esq of Glenriddel, a prose Essay signed Cato, written by him, & addressed to the delegates for the County Reform, of which he was one for this County . . .
>
> As to France, I was her enthusiastic votary in the beginning of the business. – When she came to shew her old avidity for conquest, in annexing Savoy, &c to her dominions, & invading the rights of Holland, I altered my sentiments. –
>
> To this statement I challenge disquisition. – Mistaken Prejudice, or unguarded Passion, may mislead, & often have misled me; but when called on to answer for my mistakes, though, I will say it, no man can feel keener compunction for his errors, yet I trust, no man can be more superior to evasion or disguise.[19]

Burns may have tried thereafter to 'seal up his lips' but he did not throw away his quill. It is interesting that Burns ordered the radical paper the *Edinburgh Gazetteer* on behalf of a group of his associates in Dumfries, merely four or five people. Who were they and what was the purpose of their meetings? Bearing in mind that the prospectus of the *Edinburgh Gazetteer* was mailed out to leading members of the Friends of the People, it puts Burns in the frame as a possible leading member in Dumfries, if the accusations were true. The newspaper, which Burns latched on to so enthusiastically, was the primary organ and voice of the Scottish radical group. Whether or not a Dumfries branch was formally or informally set up prior to this investigation is not known. That he held a meeting of 'friends' who supported the newspaper and *ipso facto*, reform, he does not deny and that he ordered the paper on behalf of the group he affirms. What is now known, as mentioned earlier, is that a branch of the Friends of the People was in existence during late 1793 when a Dumfries delegate was sent to the National Convention of the Friends of the People in Edinburgh.[20] Did the branch exist earlier, that is, during December 1792? An independent witness or witnesses who made the report on Burns certainly thought so and named him as its leader. Why would they invent such an accusation? We can accept the bard's denial to Fintry at face value, that he was not a member of such a political group, or can set his denial in context, aware that he had little choice but to rebuff the accusations due to his family predicament.

The members of the Dumfries radical association are described by Burns as 'obscure, nameless beings', who could not know of him. This is improbable, even if Burns had no connection with the group. Any radical pro-democracy sympathisers would have been pulled towards their local articulate bard, whose cavalier expressions and wit were legendary and magnetic. Dumfries was a small rural town, where everyone knew Burns, the local celebrity. The spy report by 'JB' lists a Mr 'Drummond' as the Dumfries delegate to the National Convention in late 1793. This may, of course, have been any Mr Drummond from Dumfries and might indeed have been someone Burns did not know. Did Burns know a Mr Drummond? A close intimate friend of Burns was the young John Drummond. The poet tried to find work for Drummond via Mrs Dunlop in the new Royal Bank of Scotland being opened in Glasgow, to no avail. Burns called Drummond 'an uncommonly clever worthy young fellow, an intimate friend of mine'.[21] Drummond had worked for four years as a clerk in the Paisley bank based in Dumfries, which closed down. He was an ideal candidate to send to Edinburgh. So, if we put together both spy reports and the evidence they provide is valid – that is, one report identifies Burns as an active member of the Dumfries radical group and the later report confirms the existence of such a group in the town, then the delegate in all probability was his friend John Drummond. Further circumstantial evidence from a nineteenth-century biographer refers to a pub in which Burns and friends met which 'required closed doors'.[22] If this references the meetings of the Dumfries Friends of the People, no matter how small a group, it would have been wise after the investigation into the poet's views to do so in strict privacy. During the next few years Burns and his coterie of radical friends were branded the 'Sons of Sedition' by the loyalist Pitt supporters of Dumfries, a topic dealt with in the next chapter. All the branches of the Friends of the People were disbanded from early 1794 onwards when the central organisation of the movement was crushed by government oppression. Indeed, many years after the poet died, Robert Ainslie confirmed that the poet had been a covert 'friend of the people' while in Dumfries.[23]

Evidence from Charles Sharpe, who was at the Dumfries theatre during the heated squabble, as mentioned by Burns, suggests the poet was among the rebel rousers in the theatre and sat, arms folded, with his hat on, during the rowdy chanting down of 'God Save the King'.[24] The invective against the king uttered by Burns is supposed to have been 'Here's the last verse of the last chapter of the BOOK of KINGS!'

Burns was largely guilty of almost every charge levelled against him and did not deny his radical values outright. One allegation was inaccurate. Burns was alleged to have written and sent a prose essay signed under the pen name 'Cato' to *The Edinburgh Gazetteer*: it was written by Robert Riddell of Friar's Carse, although Burns did 'frank' and post it on his behalf. His letter of apology to Fintry was passed on to the Board of Excise and his superiors were ordered to document to him that his 'business was to act, not to think; & that whatever might be Men or Measures, it was my business to be silent and obedient'.[25] The Excise records of this episode, if made, were destroyed, as was the original spy report.

Was Graham of Fintry, as history has cast him, the loyal patron to Burns who saved the bard from being thrown adrift to want and ruin? Evidence I unearthed during the 1990s casts some doubt on his loyalty towards Burns. Fintry himself received a payment from a central government spy network fund amounting to £26 6s. 0d and wrote a series of letters to Robert Dundas about radical activists in his home area.[26,27] The spy network was funded from London under the auspices of Henry Dundas's Home Office staff, where his Scots-based associate John Spottiswood paid out £1,000 on 8 February 1793 to the Edinburgh Sheriff Depute, John Pringle, from which Fintry received his payment. The vast majority of this was paid to pro-Pitt newspapers in Scotland for loyalist anti-radical propaganda. Professor Harris's most recent research reveals that Fintry 'was employing informers' around the Dundee area to expose active radicals and names three of these individuals actively under his charge.[28] It turns out that in the cauldron of late 1792, Fintry was a diehard establishment man, a fact that would have shocked Burns.

Luckily for Burns no one detected the publication in the *Edinburgh Gazetteer* of 'Here's A Health to Them That's Awa', a triumphalist celebration of the leading lights of reform in Scotland, including Colonel McLeod, Thomas Erskine – celebrated brother of Henry and defence counsel for Thomas Paine – and the Earl of Lauderdale, James Maitland. The lines 'May Liberty meet with success' and 'There's nane ever fear'd that the Truth should be heard, / But they whom the Truth wad indite', ring of sedition. The song is not within the extant copies of the radical paper in The Mitchell library, but a column is ripped out of an issue in late December and the poetry page is missing from the edition of 15 January,

1793. It is fortunate for Burns this radical song saluting the leading Scottish reformers did not form part of the Excise investigation.

John Syme, the Stamp Collector, informed Alexander Peterkin that he sat for dinner twice with Corbet, Findlater and Burns during the investigation into Burns' alleged misconduct in supporting democratic ideals. Such informality suggests it was the poet's excellent professionalism as an Exciseman, his fame as a poet and his bond of friendship with his superiors, taken together, which saved his skin. He was, after all, an asset to the service even if the Dundas dynasty wanted him, like other radicals, silenced.

Burns' situation was potentially serious. His was not an isolated example. Over the next few weeks, James 'Balloon' Tytler, a friend of the poet, was to be tried for seditious writings – he fled the country. Thomas Muir, a young advocate, on his way to Edinburgh from Glasgow to defend Tytler, was arrested for sedition and a date for trial set. On hearing the news of the impending execution of the king and queen of France, Muir realised the reaction to such an event in Britain would not be in the interests of Scottish reformers and went to Paris in January 1793 to plead for a stay of execution for the French monarchy. (The spy 'JB' reported to government Muir's fear that 'the death of the King would disgrace the cause of Freedom for ever.')[29] Three men were arrested at Edinburgh Castle for inciting soldiers to leave their post and join the reform movement: they were sentenced to nine months' imprisonment. The printer of the *Edinburgh Gazetteer* was arrested for publishing details of an address by the United Irishmen to Scottish reformers and jailed. A letter by Professor Richardson of the University of Glasgow was passed on to government authorities, stating, 'I tread on dangerous ground. Many things may be said which cannot be written . . . there is not a literary man in Glasgow with whom I can speak freely on the topic of the times.'[30] The postal system was being monitored for radical content. In Edinburgh, Henry Mackenzie reported to George Home that some of the literati were sympathetic to reform: 'From my Communication with Men of Letters here, I can perceive that they are generally on the side of the Malcontents.'[31] Edinburgh's literati were being turned into establishment men by the governing elite. The Scottish Enlightenment was entering its darkest days.

Troops were dispatched to Perth and Dundee in late November 1792 and three battalions of dragoons marched on Hamilton and Kilmarnock. Major Waller's regiment were sent to Dumfries on 25 November and reported 'a disposition to good order . . . all is peace & quiet' but, two days later, reported that 'Riot and Disturbances would follow' if the troops were withdrawn.[32, 33] Another letter to Henry Dundas of late November referred to large meetings of weavers and cotton spinners in Cumbernauld and Kirkintilloch, which should be checked immediately otherwise most of Scotland would be 'withdrawn from the Dominion of Great Britain' to 'form a State by itself'.[34] It was the close friend of Henry Dundas, Henry Mackenzie, who boasted to the ultra-loyalist George Chalmers that a policy of not employing 'Jacobin' or pro-reform traders was proving a success in Scotland.[35] Reform sympathisers were to be squeezed from employment wherever loyalist government employers and landowners found them. Henry Dundas ordered a stock-check of all arms and weapons available in Scotland if a rebellious rising occurred.[36] The wave of oppression during December and January was based on the establishment fear that there might be a national rebellion or potential revolution in Scotland. Government policy was intended to curb ringleaders of the radical movement. Burns' freedom of speech was a casualty in the British government's war against the pro-reform movement in Scotland. The notion that the formal investigation into the poet's sentiments was merely an isolated 'storm in a tea-cup which Robert, with his propensity for self-dramatisation, had greatly magnified and distorted out of all proportion' completely misses the reality of the times.[37] It was a tumultuous political storm which engulfed leading radicals of Scotland, including its outspoken radical bard.

The poet was quick to try and settle matters with his superiors and show he still had ambitions and loyalty to the service. Professionally, he tried to put the matter behind him as soon as possible. On 7 January, he wrote to Graham of Fintry to ask if there was any possibility he might be able to cover the district of Galloway until a Mr McFarlane recovered from illness.[38] It was a non-starter. He informed Mrs Dunlop his future hopes of promotion were 'blasted'.[39] Later in January, he showed he was more than capable of promotion and could think on his feet, by pointing out to the Provost of Dumfries, David Staig, a way by which the town council could raise extra local revenue by including brewers around Dumfries, who were hitherto able to get away without paying taxes levied on other town brewers. This involved the 'Twa pennies' tax on beer. 'The Brewers & Victuallers within the jurisdiction pay accurately; but three Common Brewers in the Bridgend whose consumpt is almost entirely in Dumfries, pay nothing.' He also listed 'an Annan Brewer, who daily sends in great quantities of ale, pays nothing'. This anomaly was due to the fact that 'Ale Certificates are never asked for.'[40] As a result, with Ale Certificates issued in Dumfries for the first time, the town raised extra needed revenue. The psychological conflict between Burns the professional civil servant 'gauger' at work and being a radical democrat in private was intensifying.

Around the time of Burns' 34th birthday on 25 January 1793, John Syme, one of the poet's closest confidants, tried to suggest he keep his nose out of politics and turn his muse to lighter topics. This led to an incident at his home in Rydale, near Dumfries, when he advised Burns to keep his head down for his own good. They had been drinking and a row erupted in which the bard was about to pull out his Excise sword on Syme but stopped short of doing so.[41] In Syme's recollection, Burns' eyes were red like coals in fury and it was only when he realised he was almost ready to run his sword through his close friend that he sank to his knees in apologetic remorse. Syme may have exaggerated this drunken squabble between friends but it reveals that the Excise rebuke to silence Burns was a very touchy subject for him. He did take Syme's advice and find a lighter topic than politics, which resulted in a lovely poem, 'Sonnet – On Hearing a Thrush Sing on a morning Walk in January'. The sweet-singing thrush, though, is symbolic of an oppressed age 'in bleak Poverty's dominion drear', where it sits with 'meek Content', quite unlike the poet's agitated state of mind.

Pitt's government went on a war footing with France following the execution of King Louis XVI and the Queen of France on 21 January 1793. Pro-democracy activists of all ranks in Britain were blamed as dangerous, bloodthirsty Jacobins from the August counter revolution in France. Such a comparison was exaggerated, unjustified and paranoid. France became the symbol of all things to be detested, hated and destroyed within the mindset of the British establishment, who feared for their wealth, posts, positions and status. The primary source of the loyalist elite's fear was not from France. It was the British reform movement. Reform threatened the existence of the feudal order. The home-grown democracy movement was vilified as a foreign import, a disease of the mind, to be extinguished domestically and attacked at its 'evil' source, France. As an act of provocation, Britain kicked out the French ambassador in London. This led France, as expected, to declare war on Britain. In turn, Henry Dundas, drunk at the dispatch box in the House of Commons, gleefully declared on 1 February that Britain was now at war with France. The war against France was, in effect, an inflected war against the pro-democracy movement in Britain, to cow a rebel generation of the British public clamouring for reform.

Any letters or poetry that may have been written by Burns about the outbreak of war have not survived. The immediate effect of the war on Burns was financial: the war virtually stopped all imports and reduced seizures, thus his wages were cut in real terms. His view of British politics in February 1793 is tempered with cynicism. He defined politics in a new catechism to Alexander Cunningham on 20 February:

> Quere, What is Politics?
> Answer, Politics is a science wherewith, by means of nefarious cunning, & hypocritical pretence, we govern civil Polities for the emolument of ourselves & our adherents. –
> Quere, What is a Minister?
> Answer, A Minister is an unprincipled fellow, who by the influence of hereditary, or acquired wealth; by superior abilities; or by a lucky conjuncture of circumstances, obtains a principal place in the administration of the affairs of government.[42]

The lists of pensions and gongs dished up to politicians was openly printed in the press and always led to condemnation of the flagrant cronyism integral to British politics at this time. The apostate Edmund Burke, for instance, received £2,000 per year for switching to the Tory party. His pensions totalled £3,700 per year.[43] Loyalty to government paid handsome dividends. Had Burns become a loyalist Hanoverian bard and Pitt-Dundas supporter and employed his pen on their behalf he would have been, like Robert Heron and others, handsomely paid.

News spread of Burns' humiliating apology to keep his job. William Nicol, acting as John Syme had done, wrote to Burns on 10 February to scoff at the poet's reckless support for reform: 'Dear Christless Bobbie . . . if the reports concerning thy *imprudence* are true. What concerns it thee whether the lousy Dumfriesian fiddlers play "Ça Ira" or "God Save the King"? Suppose you had an aversion to the King, you could not, as a gentleman, wish God to use him worse than He has done.' The highly political Nicol suggested Burns be wise and not resist the 'Higher Power' which was shaping events.[44] Robert Ainslie gave an interesting insight into the situation, written a few years after the death of Burns:

> The Commissioners of Excise, irritated at his opinions, wrote him a formal official letter, sealing with the large seal of office, informing him that a 'petty officer' had 'no business with politics'. The proud heart of Burns did not like this humbling; after a few wrathful words in secret to one of his friends, he took a pencil and wrote these lines on the envelope.[45]

The lines referred to by Ainslie are a cynical, biting quatrain known as 'The Creed of Poverty':

> In politics if thou would'st mix,
> And mean thy fortunes be;
> Bear this in mind, be deaf and blind,
> Let Great folks hear and see.

Not only did the Excise reprimand fail to silence Burns, it provoked him to immediately write the above radical poem, an admission that Burns was politically active. There can be no doubt it was reckless of Burns to be politically active while employed as an Exciseman. Any normal person in the Excise would have knuckled down for the sake of his family. His actions over the ensuing years are only comprehensible if judged as the actions of a national poet who felt he had a duty to his country, as well as to his fame and reputation, *as well as to his family*, to do whatever he could for the pro-democracy movement, even if this meant he would continue to write radical, seditious songs under a pen name or print such material anonymously.

A story was peddled around Edinburgh that Burns had been sacked due to his radical sentiments. Mrs Dunlop also heard the rumour he had been sacked. John Francis, Erskine of Mar, wrote to Robert Riddell after hearing the rumour that Burns had been dismissed from the Excise, offering to head a subscription to raise funds for the poet among the 'friends of Liberty'. Burns wrote to Mar stating 'You have been misinformed, as to my final dismission from the Excise: I still am in the service.' He went on, 'but for the exertions of . . . Mr Graham of Fintry . . . I had, without so much as a hearing . . . been turned adrift, with my helpless family, to all the horrors of Want,'[46] He goes on to assert boldly that he would have resigned and saved them the trouble, if he had the finances to support his family. Burns then emphasised the crucial importance of his fame and reputation as a poet, and, in a flash of prescience, rightly anticipated the hireling scribbles of Robert Heron's politically motivated, posthumous character assassination:

> Still, my honest fame is my dearest concern; & a thousand times have I trembled at the idea of the degrading epithets that Malice, or Misrepresentation may affix to my name. I have often, in blasting anticipation, listened to some future hackney Magazine Scribbler, with the heavy malice of savage stupidity, exulting in his hireling paragraphs that 'Burns, notwithstanding the fanfaronade of independence to be found in his works, & after having been held forth to Public View & Public Estimation as a man of some genius, yet quite destitute of resources within himself to support this borrowed dignity, he dwindled into a paltry Excisemen; & slunk out the rest of his insignificant existence in the meanest of pursuits & among the vilest of mankind.[47]

Burns had no idea just how vicious Heron's character assassination would be, with its accusations of whoring and death by alcoholism.

In April 1793, when Burns wrote to Mar, it is clear his radical sentiments were galvanised, not subdued. Also, he makes clear his views about the sedition laws curbing his own personal freedom and the freedom of others being silenced by the despotic government of Pitt:

> BURNS was a poor man, from birth; & an Exciseman, by necessity: but – I will say it! the sterling of his honest worth, no poverty could debase; & his independent British mind, Oppression might bend, but could not subdue![48]

'Oppression' had forced him to apologise for his democratic views and plead for his job. To say he lied to his employers is too strong a term, since he was saving his own skin and his family's livelihood, as anyone would have been compelled to do in the circumstances. It was a humiliation too far. In the midst of a burst of British patriotism – 'independent British mind' – are overtones of Scottish patriotism which led to 'Bruce's Address to his Troops at Bannockburn' ('Scots Wha Hae'). He then goes on to affirm he would rather die before he would be 'silent and obedient'. To be silenced would have been cowardice in Burns' own eyes. The Pitt government represented the opposite of his every principle and core values.

Burns wanted reform and his ideals appear to have been more radicalised by the Oppression he experienced:

> Have not I, to me, a more precious stake in my Country's welfare than the richest Dukedom in it? – I have a large family of children, & the probability of more. – I have three sons, who, I see already, have brought with them into the world souls ill qualified to inhabit the bodies of Slaves. – Can I look tamely on, & see any machination to wrest from them, the birthright of my boys, the little independent Britons in whose veins runs my own blood? – No! I will not! – should my heart stream around my attempt to defend it![49]

This fighting talk was written in April. Burns makes it evident that it was *for the very sake of his children and their future* that he would not be silenced. Burns the Exciseman might be 'silent and obedient' during his workday but the Bard of Caledonia was in the fray and up for the fight:

> Does any man tell me, that my feeble efforts can be of no service: & that it does not belong to my humble station to meddle with the concerns of a People? – I tell him, that it is on such individuals as I, that for the hand of support & the eye of intelligence, a Nation has to rest. – The uninformed mob may swell a Nation's bulk; & the titled, tinsel Courtly throng may be its feathered ornament, but the number of those who are elevated enough in life, to reason & reflect; & yet low enough to keep clear of the venal contagion of a Court; these are a Nation's strength.[50]

Burns asked Erskine of Mar to burn the letter, but he made a fair copy, which is to be found in the Glenriddell Mss collection. Burns clearly was not going to lie down at the dictates of his Edinburgh employers, whose strings were being pulled by the Dundases.

The notion that Burns became a loyalist Hanoverian bard – that is, a supporter of Pitt and George III – is a myth.[51] The idea that Burns suddenly changed his sentiments and threw out his radical principles has been repeatedly promulgated in the modern press. In 1996, Mackay (although his biography states otherwise) made the claim that the bard did not write anything radical or controversial from 5 January 1793 onwards.[52] Nothing could be further from the truth. The letter to Erskine of Mar itself breathes a seditious air of democratic rage at the oppression Burns felt by his Edinburgh employers trying to silence him. Burns was not an Orwellian Winston Smith who eventually loved Big Brother; he had a touch of the Covenanter about him and took his principles and beliefs to the grave.

◈◈◈

As he began to feel the pinch financially, Burns cashed in on his status within Dumfries as a Freeman of the Borough, by writing to the Lord Provost and town council to have them quash the school fees his children would have to pay. His wish was duly honoured.

Creech brought out a new edition of the poems of Burns in April 1793, printing every new poem written since 1787 gratis. Burns duly received a few copies of his new edition and forwarded signed copies as gifts to friends – the Earl of Glencairn's brother John and sister, Lady Elizabeth; Patrick Miller, Mrs Graham of Fintry, Robert Riddell, John McMurdo of Drumlanrig and a few others. It was the last edition of the works of Burns to be published in his lifetime. It contained no more than a fifth of the actual poems and songs he composed. Creech's greed even extended beyond the poet's death, when he tried to claim damages against new editions published. Burns' copyright was discussed in the House of Lords in 1811 when Charles Grey emotively accused the Pitt government of a policy of starving Burns to death in Dumfries

In March, General Charles Francois Dumouriez deserted from the French republican army and at the end of the month was declared a traitor by the National Convention for joining Austria, then at war with France. Dumouriez planned to lead the Austrian army into Paris and establish a new monarchy and end the Revolution. Dumouriez was made out to be a hero in the British press and eventually, in June 1793, he came to London, where he toured in a hackney carriage before large crowds and visited the House of Commons as a guest. Burns learned of the General's defection in early April and parodied the Scots song 'Robin Adair' by writing 'You're Welcome to Despots, Doumouriez'. The 'Despots' against France were Austria and Britain who would 'fight about' until 'Freedom's spark is out'. The song reveals Burns' opposition to the war and his sympathies for the French cause. Mackay's remark is apt, that 'even after Britain was at war Robert was recklessly espousing the republican cause.'[53]

Burns was a risk-taker but he did not send 'You're Welcome to Despots, Dumouriez' to George Thomson. He did not know Thomson personally so was uncertain of trusting him, albeit with a few lapses of indiscretion. When Thomson dared to ask Burns in late January if he would help collect a volume of Jacobite songs, alarm bells rang. Burns tactfully asked Thomson if such a collection might not cause offence to some and ignored his request. It is possible Thomson suspected Burns to be the author of some of the Jacobite songs in the *SMM*. Thomson also asked Burns to send him a copy of the potently anti-establishment cantata, *The Jolly Beggars*, which Burns had suppressed. Aware it would now be considered highly seditious, Burns cautiously told Thomson he had forgotten almost every line of the cantata and had not kept a copy. It would seem Thomson wished to test the poet's apparent pledge of political silence.

During this period, Burns was aware suspected radicals had their mail monitored and, therefore, often used a special carrier he could trust if sending material he did not wish to be intercepted. It was not paranoia to do so, it was wisely cautious.

In April, Burns wrote to a friend of Maria Riddell's, Deborah Duff Davies, who had been living at Beeswing, near Dumfries, for several years.[54] She was petite, attractive, educated and shared Maria's armchair radical sentiments. The song 'Bonie Wee Thing' was written for her and enclosed in the letter of 6 April, in which Burns goes into a bombastic rant:

> Out upon the world! says I: that its affairs are administered so ill! They talk of REFORM – My God! What a reform would I make among the Sons, and even the Daughters, of men! Down, immediately, should go Fools from high places where misbegotten Chance has perked them up; and through life should they sculk, ever haunted by their native insignificance, as the body marches accompanied by its shadow.[55]

Maria Riddell asked Burns if he would be able to obtain a pair of French gloves for her, since they were now contraband. She was aware he was duty-bound to seize French gloves and might have access to a pair. Burns, in comic mode, responded that he had put 'all the haberdashers . . . on the alarm as to the necessary article of French gloves', then told Maria:

> You must know that French gloves are contraband goods, and expressly forbidden by the laws of this wisely-governed realm of ours. A satirist would say this is the reason why the ladies are so fond of them; but I, who have not one grain of Gall in my composition, shall alledge that it is the patriotism of the dear goddess of man's idolatry that makes them so fond of dress from the land of Liberty and Equality.
>
> . . . one haberdasher . . . will clothe your fair hands as they ought to be, to keep them from being profaned by the rude gaze of the gloating eye, or – horrid! – from perhaps a [kiss] by the un-hallowed lips of Satyr Man . . .[56]

For such a trivial favour to be taken as the opportunity for such a cleverly facetious statement of political irony shows how Burns' mind was simmering after the war with France started. His radical sentiments boiled over in his letters. In a letter to Thomson, written in June, he launches a tirade about the 'Ambition' of politicians in waging war and the human consequences of war:

> Have you ever, my dear Sir, felt your bosom ready to burst with indignation on reading of, or seeing, how these mighty villains who divide kingdom against kingdom, desolate provinces, & lay nations waste out of the wantonness of Ambition, or so often from still more ignoble passions?
>
> The air of Logan Water, probably had its origin from the plaintive indignation of some swelling, suffering heart, fired at the tyrannic strides of some Public Destroyer; & overwhelmed with private distresses, the consequence of a Country's ruin.[57]

The first sentence of this letter, a rhetorical question, might not be deemed seditious but the thrust of the comment is. Here Burns' radical zeal overtakes common sense and he becomes dangerously outspoken to a correspondent with whom he might have done better to keep his own counsel. Peter Hill, however, was a trusted friend and Burns did not mind opening up to him:

> I hope & trust that this unlucky blast which has overturned so many, & many worthy characters who four months ago little dreaded any such thing – will spare my Friend. –
>
> O! May the wrath & curse of all mankind, haunt & harrass these turbulent, unprincipled miscreants who have involved a People in this ruinous business!!![58]

The sentiments expressed by Burns to Thomson and Hill are echoed strongly in several pseudonymous poems unearthed by my recent archival research, which have been endorsed by leading literary scholars as lost works of Burns, and were included in the new complete edition of his poems in 2001.[59] The full extent of Burns' underground activities in favour of the reform movement during these last, darker and dangerous times, is still to be fully investigated, in both prose and poetry.[60]

It was early April when Burns told Thomson 'Ballad-making is now as compleately my hobby-horse.'[61] After Excise duty was done, when he had time, Burns would croon over his ballads, matching lyrics to melodies by swinging back and forth on his armed chair at his desk. This allowed him to get the rhythm of timing to each melody and marry it to the syllables and stresses of ballads he mended, rewrote or composed. At 34 years of age, he was the most accomplished songwriter of the era.

Stephen Clarke, an Edinburgh musician who met Burns in 1787 and worked on the musical annotation of Johnson's *SMM* collection, would visit Dumfries to go over tunes with him and test out songs. Burns was musically intelligent in matching quavers and dotted crochets to the cadence of Scots lyrics. He had frequently contended with song-collector Thomson's innate snobbery against the 'native features' of some Scots songs which Burns wanted to preserve and he to discard. The bard argued that many Scots songs possessed a naturalness 'unreduceable to the modern rules; but on that very eccentricity, perhaps, depends a great part of their effect'.[60]

The poet's first work to appear in print under his name after being chastised by the Excise was a song which appeared in the loyalist newspaper, the *Edinburgh Advertiser*, 16–19 April 1793. The song, 'On the Commemoration of Rodney's Victory on 12th April', is a brilliant example of Burns' tightrope-walking: he dares to say what he should not say and, using ironic assent, toasts what he is, in reality, attacking. The song is published in a manner which makes it appear as though it was not Burns who sent it to the press and that he sang it extempore – that is, he made it up on the spur of the moment. Readers were meant to believe he just stood up and the words appeared out of his mouth. The myth of the Heaven-taught ploughman was thus continued. The song celebrates the victory of Admiral George Rodney over the French navy at Dominica on 12 April 1782, which secured British control of the Atlantic during the American Wars of Independence. This song, therefore, can be viewed as a statement of Burns' loyalty to Britain and can be viewed as a celebration of a French defeat in war. The Dundas dynasty in Edinburgh would have been delighted, unless, of course, the song is read closely. It gives a nod of loyalty to the king, then trenchantly affirms the extent of Burns' British patriotism, founded on 'OUR FREE CONSTITUTION, / As built on the base of THE GREAT REVOLUTION'. It flics above the head of those who might expect sedition from Burns by stating that extremist politics should be cursed and damned, 'Be anarchy curs'd – and be Tyranny damned'. Finally the last remark is given to 'Liberty', that those who would betray the light of reform should be hanged by their offspring (since to betray reform would be to deny the next generation the right to vote). In short, Burns cleverly got away with stating he did not mind giving due respect to the king if he had to, but he considered the British government to be tyrannical. Burns was never a simple poet – he could outsmart opponents with words and deliver a seditious fist in a loyal coloured glove. Burns was showing loyalty to what he deemed the best of British Liberty which was by this time, still burning, although struggling to flicker to a flame.

When the lights of Liberty came on over Scotland, the branches of the pro-democracy movement, the Friends of the People, represented a cultural phenomenon of optimism for a generation who wanted progressive reform. It was not an avaricious, self-seeking generation wishing to topple the Pitt-Dundas government like a bunch of revolutionary wolves. It was a mix of democratically minded people from all social classes. Industrial and agrarian revolution had created a society pregnant for reform. British radicalism came not from France; it was the result of the Enlightenment, of reason and common sense. The real war fought by Pitt and Dundas was not against France per se. Their battle was an ideological war against the domestic pro-democracy movement in Britain and in Scotland in particular, where they feared a mass rebellion or outright revolution.

16

WHEN TRUTH IS TREASON, FREEDOM DIES[1]

IN MAY 1793, THE BURNS FAMILY MOVED INTO 24 Mill Hole Brae, a detached, three-bedroom house with a kitchen. A more spacious dwelling was essential, what with the arrival to stay of Anne Park's daughter Betty and the birth of Elizabeth Riddell Burns on 21 November. The oldest of the children, Robert, was now seven years old. The front door often stood open during summer months and passers-by regularly saw Burns attending to the education of his children. The landlord, Captain John Hamilton of Allershaw, charged a modest rent of eight pounds per year. Lacking the money to splash out on new furniture, they moved their possessions, in time-honoured fashion, on a horse and cart. The coal fire always required a protective fireguard, to ensure safety for the children and to prevent sparks landing on the living-room carpet – a very unusual domestic appurtenance in such a modest household.

Relatively speaking, Burns was still a poor man but his profession provided financial stability and the surge of income from the Edinburgh Edition and gifts from Mrs Dunlop allowed the family to have possessions many could not afford. Friends sometimes popped round with a Nith salmon, or some fresh game for the pot. Burns was innately tuned to rural customs, such as collecting wild hazelnuts or picking apples, blackberries and gooseberries. Home-made produce, including cheese, jam and home baking, helped keep the wolf from the door.

If Burns had a modicum of the trappings of wealth, he was not the type to lord it over others. His identification with the homeless mouse thrown to the ravages of winter (in 'To a Mouse') was not an empty gesture, it was an oblique commentary on the economic fragility of so many people's lives.

The war with France stopped many imports, especially French brandy and wine, and even imports of American tobacco were affected. This cut Burns' real income from the Excise by around £20 per year. On at least two occasions, the poet fell behind with his rent and, being hypersensitive to debt, avoided his landlord until he could afford to square accounts. Burns was severely apologetic to Hamilton, who showed considerable forbearance and never once threatened eviction.[2]

That spring, Burns added many new songs to Thomson's *Select Collection*, marrying some from the *SMM* to tunes for Thomson's new edition. Several sent to Thomson during this period, such as 'Young Jessie' (inspired by Provost Staig's daughter), 'Farewell Thou Stream', 'Lord Gregory', 'Blythe Hae I Been on Yon Hill' and 'Logan Braes', were not printed by Thomson in Burns' lifetime. In fact, Thomson, the meddler, refused to print 'Logan Braes' because of its anti-war sentiments. Burns justified the lyrics, set in a female voice, as the 'indignation of some swelling, suffering heart, fired at the Tyrannic strides of some Public Destroyer; and overwhelmed with private distresses, the consequence of a Country's Ruin' – a veiled hit at the consequences of Pitt's war with France.[3] He was beginning to be less cautious towards Thomson and let his radical views pour out briefly in their correspondence.

When Thomson's *Select Collection* appeared in May 1793, there were only a few new songs by Burns, although the collection did duplicate some lyrics from Johnson's *SMM*. The new songs were 'Wandering Willie', 'Braw Lads o' Galla Water', 'Auld Rob Morris', 'Open the Door to Me' and the best of the pack, 'The Sodger's Return'. With his usual alacrity, Burns ensured copies of the *Select Collection* were subscribed to by friends such as Robert Riddell, John McMurdo and Patrick Miller. Having gained financially from the project, Thomson kindly sent Burns five pounds, which, if the poet had been honest about his circumstances, he would have happily pocketed with thanks. Prickly pride got the better of Burns and, although he kept the money, he launched into a tirade:

> by that HONOUR which crowns the upright Statue of ROBT Burns' INTEGRITY! . . . I will indignantly spurn the by-past transaction, & from that moment commence entire Stranger to you! – Burns' character for Generosity of Sentiment, & Independence of Mind, will, I trust, long outlive any of his wants which the cold, unfeeling, dirty Ore can supply: at least, I shall take care that such a Character he shall deserve.[4]

A friend from the poet's Ayrshire days visited him on 19 June: Archibald Lawrie of Newmilns met Burns in company that evening and spent a fair bit of the next day with him, walking along the banks of the Nith in conversation and dining. They met up with the celebrated oboe player and composer Thomas Fraser of Edinburgh – associated with his wooded instrument, a hautboy – who was now temporarily in Dumfries with the Breadalbane Fencibles. It was Fraser, playing his hautboy in a wood by Dumfries, probably Lincluden, who caused Burns to hear 'Hey Tuttie Taitie', a slow, moving air which made him cry with sadness. Burns always wore his heart on his sleeve and felt the sadness in many old Scots airs. As a composer of words, he had an affinity with musicians who had the creative skill to compose original music, such as Allan Masterton, Stephen Clarke, Niel Gow and Thomas Fraser.

There is little evidence in the poet's letters of his brief tour of Galloway, made with Syme, in the summer of 1793. Most of the information on this excursion is based on Syme's reminiscence for Currie's 1800 *Life and Works* of Burns; if the poet kept a journal of their jaunt, it has not survived.

Riding on Sheltie ponies over the narrow roads of Galloway, Burns and Syme headed westward on 27 July. They stopped for lunch with the Glendinning family at Parton, between Castle Douglas and New Galloway. After a visit to Airds, they continued northwards to the grand Kenmure Castle, home of John Gordon, whose family were active in the Jacobite rebellion of 1715, and spent three days there. Syme left no record of what Burns recited to his hosts – merely stating that he composed an (uninspired) quatrain on the death of Mrs Gordon's dog, Echo, and that he ruined his new pair of boots after carrying the local minister ashore, after a trip on a rowing boat on Loch Ken.

When they left Kenmure, they headed towards Gatehouse of Fleet, over a rugged, stony, moor pathway, through some of the wildest forestland of hilly

Galloway, past tumbling burns and a waterfall. At one point, in a pelting shower, Syme saw Burns charge away on the pony, as if hurtling into battle with Bruce against the English army at Bannockburn. Syme's tale gave birth to the legend of Burns composing 'Scots Wha Hae' either on his way to Gatehouse, or that night, in the Murray Arms Hotel, where, he says, Burns insisted on them getting 'utterly drunk'. A tipsy poet might compose a song after a few drinks but a drunk poet would not compose 'Scots Wha Hae'. Syme's recollections put the proverbial cart before the horse – Burns later confirmed in a letter he had no idea of composing lyrics for the tune 'Hey Tuttie Taitie' until he met Peter Urbani at the Earl of Selkirk's home at St Mary's Isle, near Kirkcudbright, after they left Gatehouse of Fleet. The great anthem of Scottish freedom was not written in the Murray Arms.

On their way to Kirkcudbright, Syme pointed out Garlieston House, the grand residence of the Earl of Galloway, who was notorious for being mean to the local peasantry – he was known to send a servant round the local hamlets and villages with a whip to clear the streets before he rode round his lands on his horse and carriage. Syme suggests the poet was still seething from ruining his new boots, which fell apart on him the next day, when he tried to pull them on. Whatever the motivating factors, he vented his spleen on the Tory Lord:

What dost thou in that mansion fair?
  Flit, Galloway, and find
Some narrow, dirty, dungeon cave,
  The picture of thy mind!

Burns (without his boots) and Syme dined at the Heid Inn in Kirkcudbright with a friend of Syme, John Dalzell. It was here, according to folklore, that Burns wrote and recited 'The Selkirk Grace', those tea-towel lines famed the world over. Burns may have indeed recited it. The lines, however, are not his. Probably a Covenanter grace, they were around long before Burns was born. Another tale suggests Burns recited 'The Selkirk Grace' at St Mary's Isle, seat of Dunbar Douglas, the fourth Earl of Selkirk – father of Lord Daer – where the travellers arrived early in the evening. As mentioned above, it was at St Mary's Isle that Burns met Peter Urbani and it was the Italian composer who requested Burns write 'soft verses' for 'Hey Tutti Taitie'.

Towards the end of August, Burns wrote to Thomson, enclosing a copy of 'Bruce's Address to His Troops at Bannockburn', or 'Scots Wha Hae' as it is best known. The poet explained the origin of the song thus:

> There is a tradition, which I have met with in many places of Scotland, that it was Robert Bruce's March at the battle of Bannock-burn. – This thought, in my yesternight's evening walk, warmed me to a pitch of enthusiasm on the theme of Liberty & Independence, which I threw into a kind of Scots Ode, fitted to the Air, that one might suppose to be the gallant ROYAL SCOT'S address to his heroic followers on that eventful morning.[5]

The song, in the voice of King Robert the Bruce, is more than a simple reference to a past Scottish victory against tyranny: it is loaded with reference to the struggles for 'Truth and Liberty' in Scotland in 1793. Burns spells this out:

> I shewed the air to Urbani, who begged me to make soft verses for it; but I had no idea of giving myself any trouble on the subject, till the accidental recollection of that glorious struggle for Freedom, associated with the glowing ideas of some other struggles of the same nature, not quite so ancient, roused my rhyming Mania.[6]

The 'other struggles . . . not quite so ancient' were the struggles of the Friends of the People for freedom and democratic rights. Freedom of speech no longer existed in Britain, due to the draconian sedition laws.

At this time, an intense drama was unfolding. The young Advocate Thomas Muir was arrested at Portpatrick on 2 August, in the Rhins of Galloway, and dragged in chains through Gatehouse of Fleet on his way to face trial in Edinburgh. His return from France was made problematic after war broke out with France on 1 February and his only passage home was via Ireland. (He was supposedly taken through Gatehouse on the same day Burns and Syme were visiting the town.) This was the beginning of the notorious sedition trials and the turning point which led to the crushing of the pro-democracy movement in Scotland. Read in historical context, 'Scots Wha Hae' was clearly forged in the radical, dissenting culture of the pro-democracy movement.

Robert the Bruce was one of the poet's greatest heroes. 'Bruce's Address to His Troops at Bannockburn' was, as Burns remarked, written about both past and present struggles. The notion of the king of a free Scotland rising up and speaking to the events of Burns' time predates his great anthem 'Scots Wha Hae' by just over a month. In the radical *Edinburgh Gazetteer*, a poem entitled 'The Ghost of Bruce' was printed on 16 July 1793 with an image of the ancient king, appearing, in splendid armour, amid smoke and fire, to give advice about the contemporary struggles. The image, representing the organic spirit of Scotland's suppressed freedom, rises in 'Freedom's cause' to save the people of Scotland from being enslaved by the sedition laws and urges the nation to renew its Liberty. The poem, written in Shakespearian blank verse, is signed under the pen name 'Agrestis'.

Although the subject of press debate in 1996 after I discovered this poem, it has been widely accepted now as a work of Burns by eminent literary experts including the late Professor Daiches, Carol McGuirk, Andrew Noble, and Thomas Crawford.[7] Indeed, McIlvanney, in *Burns: The Radical*, discusses both versions of 'The Ghost of Bruce' as Burns' work. There is, however, no definitive provenance to place his authorship beyond doubt without manuscript authority. Poems without manuscript have, though, already been accepted as works of Burns in the past.[8]

Interestingly, a second poem of the same name 'The Ghost of Bruce' features in the same paper on 24 September. It too has been accepted by the literary experts abovementioned. Not only are its sentiments and language in the mould of Burns at this time, it also reveals, in the body of the poem, a four-line quotation from his favourite English poet, Addison. Could it be merely coincidence that, when Burns sent a copy of 'Scots Wha Hae' to Captain Miller in December, he added a three-line quotation from Addison? It was the Addison–Robert the Bruce link which first convinced me of its likely provenance, having not believed, initially, that it could be by Burns. 'Scots Wha Hae' is one of three works written a few months apart in the voice of Robert the Bruce. The origin, therefore, of 'Scots Wha Hae' is a little more complex than was first thought by biographers.

'Scots Wha Hae' eventually appeared, anonymously, in a London newspaper, the *Morning Chronicle*, on 8 May 1794. The song's underlying sentiments, that it is better to fight for Liberty and Freedom, rather than live the life of a coward under oppression, would have been regarded as seditious, particularly with the triple exclamatory ending 'Let us do or die!!!', which echoes a key French revolutionary oath of 1789. As Burns remarked to Erskine of Mar, he did not want his sons to grow up to be slaves. In 'Scots Wha Hae', the line 'See the front o' battle lour' is echoed strongly in the second 'Ghost of Bruce': 'Bid all my Sons be firm; and when the storm / Shall gather thickest, boldly show their front'. The lexical similarities between the poems and the great patriotic song are detailed elsewhere.[9] 'Scots Wha Hae' is one of the finest lyrics Burns ever wrote.

Responding to Thomson's suggestion that 'Scots Wha Hae' would be better set to the tune 'Lewie Gordon', Burns rewrote the song for the new tune in September. This meant adding a double syllable stress at the end of the refrain, changing 'Or to victory' to 'Or to glorious victory'. The result was a turgid version of the great patriotic anthem, with a stuttering, syllabic stagger, which almost ruined the song. Burns eventually went back to his original lyric and tune, and ditched Thomson's recommendation. When he published the song after the poet's death, Thomson egotistically chose to present the weaker version, with a cheeky note to suggest lyrical changes that would make the song a pro-British, anti-French anthem.

Some have suggested that the trial of Thomas Muir was the spark which provoked the composition of 'Scots Wha Hae'. This is not so: the trial took place *after* the song was written. The judgement of the trial was, however, probably the spark which led to the second version of 'The Ghost of Bruce', a more indignant poem than the earlier version. Muir's trial opened on 30 August in Old Parliament House in Edinburgh. Supporters of the Friends of the People in Scotland travelled from all over the country to attend. Scotland's reactionary establishment intended to make an example out of the young lawyer. Muir appeared before five Law Lords, including the notorious Lord Braxfield, who spoke from the bench in broad Scots. The indictment, drawn up by the Lord Advocate, Robert Dundas, charged him with feloniously and wickedly committing the crime of sedition on over a dozen occasions, between September 1792 and January 1793. Muir's acts of sedition, according to his accusers, bordered on treason and, during the trial, the Law Lords remarked several times that he was lucky not to be facing the death penalty. The 'crime' of sedition was a catch-all, wrapped in legalistic mumbo-jumbo, which included: inciting others to question or show disloyalty to government or king; arranging meetings of reformers; addressing reformers; recommending or possessing Thomas Paine's banned book, *The Rights of Man*; and much more. Muir denied that he, or anyone among the Friends of the People, wished to overthrow the government and argued all reformers in Scotland were law-abiding and loyal to government and king. But demanding reform was, in the eyes of the court, disaffection to government per se. The Law Lords knew from their man on the inside of the reform movement, the meticulous spy 'JB', that the Friends of the People were loyalist and wholly opposed to any illegal form of protest.[10] Hence, they knew the charges against Muir were largely based upon their own hysteria to silence the person they deemed to be the Scottish ringleader of reform.

Muir, acting in his own defence, declared:

> I admit that I exerted every effort to procure a more equal representation of the People in the House of Commons. If that be a crime, I plead guilty to the charge. I acknowledge that I considered the cause of Parliamentary reform to be essential to the salvation of my country; but I deny that I ever advised the people to attempt to accomplish that great object by any means which the Constitution did not sanction.[11]

Every member of the hand-picked jury belonged to the loyalist Goldsmith Association. To a man, they were sworn enemies of reform and believed it would lead to rapine, murder and the end of title and rank by the blood of the guillotine. The verdict was a foregone conclusion.

Finding Muir guilty on all charges and sentencing him to 14 years' transportation to Botany Bay, Lord Swinton declared that the sentence was intended to 'deter others from committing the like crime in times coming' and 'serve as an example and *terror* [my emphasis] to others'.[12] On strict points of law, Muir's defence was exemplary but he knew from the outset that he would be found guilty and faced his accusers with defiant dignity, hoping future generations would expose the judgement against him.

Muir's trial was, in effect, much more than the trial of one young advocate: it was the reform movement on trial. As Lord Swinton admitted, it was government policy to spread fear and terror among the people to stem the tide of reform activity. The pro-democracy movement was to be crushed at all costs.

It is not known if Burns attended Muir's trial. Lord Daer, the poet's friend, was cited as a witness for Muir. Details of the trial filled Scottish newspapers. Pamphlet editions of Muir's defence were printed and reprinted over the next months. Mackay suggests in his biography that Muir's sentence 'served as a salutary warning' for Burns to keep his head down and stay out of controversial politics: 'We examine Robert's letters in vain' during this period for 'political indiscretions', he says.[13] While it may be partly true, that Burns became more cautious about writing his views down, it is also likely that his views on Muir's trial have either not been collected, or were censored. It is well known that letters to radicals such as Mary Wollstonecraft, William Roscoe and William Smellie were destroyed. It was in mid-September that Burns inscribed a political quatrain in a copy of John Syme's *The British Album*, a book of Della Cruscan poets led by Robert Merry:

PERISH their names, however great or brave,
Who in the DESPOT's cursed errands bleed!
But who for FREEDOM fills a hero's grave,
Fame with a Seraph-pen, record the glorious deed!

The 'despot' was, of course, William Pitt.

Burns would certainly have had views on Muir's trial. If he commented on it in his correspondence, no such letters have survived. There was a widespread belief in the radical press that the verdict against Muir was illegal under Scots law and unconstitutional. Burns was evidently aware of this debate in the press. He himself studied De Lolme's *The British Constitution* during September 1793, perhaps to find any points of law upon which such a punishment could be based. He afterwards handed the book into the Dumfries library, with the inscription, 'Mr Burns presents this book to the Library & begs they will take it as a Creed of British Liberty – until they find a better.' Thinking this remark might be misconstrued as seditious, he went into the library the next day and stuck down the page with glue.

British newspapers sympathetic to reform were horrified at the sentence of 14 years' transportation. While Muir waited to be transported to Botany Bay on one of the 'Woolwich hulks' (prison ships), he was kept in the Tolbooth in Edinburgh. Many leading radicals visited him there. At one point, a guard overheard a digging sound from a lower part of the Tolbooth and raised the alarm that radical weavers and miners from Paisley and Kilmarnock were tunnelling from Glasgow to liberate Muir. Despite the obvious fact that such a lengthy tunnel would have taken a few years to dig, a few dragoons of troops were sent to circle the Tolbooth. The sound was later found to have been a rat scratching in a hole. The response shows that political hysteria was at fever pitch. For a short period at least, the sentence against Muir galvanised the Scottish reform movement and had the opposite effect of crushing the Scottish Friends of the People: it rallied the Scottish radical movement, albeit temporarily.

Muir's trial was swiftly followed by the trial at Perth of the Reverend Thomas Fysche Palmer, a Unitarian minister from Dundee, whose radical activities had been monitored for almost six months. Described as a 'bankrupt butcher from Birmingham', he was alleged to be a former member of the English radical group of Dr Joseph Priestley, who had fled England for America after being set upon by loyalist mobs. Two of the jurors at Palmer's trial were William Creech and Peter Hill. Burns must have known this from the press reports but there is no indication he stopped writing to Hill after reading the verdict. Palmer was sentenced to seven years' transportation. Within the next few months, leading radicals such as James Thompson Callander and the poet James Kennedy were fugitated and left the country.

Robert Dundas, fearing 'an Insurrection' in Scotland, pushed for the ringleaders of the next National Convention of the Friends of the People in late December to be arrested and charged with sedition.[14] The three leaders, Maurice Margarot, William Skirving and Joseph Gerrald, were all tried and sentenced to fourteen years' transportation. At the end of January 1794, the *Edinburgh Gazetteer* was shut down and the proprietor arrested for sedition. The ringleaders of the Friends of the People and their newspapers were going down like ninepins.

Burns' creative escapes from the heady politics and tumultuous drama of the period were ballad-making and his family. He told Thomson in late September, if he did not know a tune he could not compose for it:

> My way is: I consider the poetic Sentiment, correspondent to my idea of the musical expression; then chuse my theme; begin one Stanza; when that is composed, which is generally the most difficult part of the business, I walk out, sit down now & then, look out for objects in Nature around me that are in unison or harmony with the cogitations of my fancy & workings of my bosom; humming every now & then the air with the verses I have framed: when I feel my Muse beginning to jade, I retire to the solitary fireside of my study, & there commit my effusions to paper;

> swinging, at intervals, on the hind-legs of my elbow-chair, by way of calling forth my own critical strictures, as my pen goes on.[15]

He went on to chastise Thomson, who always thought he knew better than Burns about matching lyrics to music, for his remarks upon the tune 'Dainty Davie'. Burns told the meddler he had heard the tune sung:

> ... nineteen thousand, nine hundred, & ninety-nine times, & always with the chorus to the low part of the tune; & nothing, since a Highland wench in the Cowgate once bore me three bastards at a birth, has surprised me so much as your opinion on this subject.[16]

This was, of course, iconoclastic Burns writing for effect, not a statement of fact regarding triplets, although, given his exaggerated reputation in relation to fathering children, it is surprising that some biographers have not searched for evidence of the mother. Indeed, the rather stuck-up Thomson may himself have taken the remark literally and fuelled Edinburgh's elite with gossip of the bard's illegitimate triplets.

Although Burns' songwriting now focused mainly on producing material for Thomson's *Select Collection*, he did send 41 songs to James Johnson for the fifth volume of the *SMM* by February 1794. Thomson's second edition appeared in January 1794. Burns informed Thomson he intended collating all his own songs and publishing them in a small volume, not so much for pecuniary gain but to make a volume of all the songs he wished to be publicly known as the author – bar, of course, the bawdy material and politically controversial lyrics. It would have greatly facilitated Burns scholars if the poet had done so.

For whatever reason, Dumfries became a military garrison town during the poet's last few years. The Breadalbane Fencibles were first in the town, followed by a battalion of Royal Ulster Volunteers in the winter of 1794–5 and then the Cinque Ports Cavalry in 1796, led by the future prime minister, Robert Banks Jenkinson. It is possible Dumfries was considered the soft underbelly to an invasion force from France, or that local radicals might rebel and cause trouble. Culloden was still living memory to some people and the fear of a Scottish rebellion was uppermost in the mind of the Dundas dynasty. Two spy sentries were posted to monitor the incoming flow of people and commodities at Portpatrick harbour, and precise notes were relayed to Edinburgh on everyone entering the country. Names were taken and the purpose of their visit established. Charles Ogilivie of the Customs at Greenock reported to government that French troops landed for food supplies at Greenock dock and were assisted by local tradespeople.[17] Luke Mullen of the radical United Irishmen group visited Burns, although it is not known if this was reported to the authorities. The eyes and ears of government were finely tuned and regionally placed to monitor any suspected movement by radicals. Dumfries was becoming, for Burns, more and more claustrophobic and – due to the increased confidence of jingoistic loyalists – intolerant of radicals, who were unjustly blamed as Jacobin enemies of Britain.

Some of the soldiers appear to have had an inbuilt bias against anyone suspected of being sympathetic to the French Jacobin cause; Burns himself detected this among many of them and preferred to avoid them. The poet was due to meet Maria Riddell at the Dumfries theatre, one evening in November, but found her attention was taken by a few of the town's resident soldiers:

> I meant to have called on you yesternight, but as I edged up to your Box-door, the first object which greeted my view was one of those lobster coated PUPPIES, sitting, like another dragon, guarding the Hesperian fruit.[18]

Maria did not mind the attention of the soldiers and could openly make her armchair republican remarks with impunity. She was an aristocrat. Burns, though, had a reputation for being an opinionated radical and a handful of the soldiers appear to have sought him out to cause provocation, knowing all too well that he risked his job by public declarations of his sentiments.

On two different occasions, Burns was provoked into making a toast on the topic of national affairs by Dumfries loyalists. Drinking a toast to various leaders or to a certain topic, such as the Freedom of the People, was all the rage from 1788 onwards. After the start of hostilities with France in February 1793, few radically minded people dared to voice their sentiments, unless among like-minded radicals. Newspaper articles often mention up to 20 toasts being made at political meetings in London. Such behaviour reflects the hard-drinking exuberance of the times. In January 1794, Burns appears to have been ready for the provocation and had an ambivalent toast ready. When Captain James Dods threw down the gauntlet to test his loyalty, Burns thought he could walk the tightrope by declaring, 'May our success in the present war be equal to the justice of our cause!' The implication was obvious: Burns thought the war against France unjust and hoped the campaign would not be a success. An ugly scene erupted in the King's Arms and stopped just short of violence. It is clear from Burns' letter the next morning to the young Dumfries lawyer Samuel Clark, that the poet had been drinking and was not going to flinch in the face of an arrogant loyalist. Burns was concerned the incident would be reported to the Excise and blown out of proportion:

> I was, I know, drunk last night, but I am sober this morning. From the expressions Captn Dods made use of to me, had I had nobody's welfare to care for but my own, we should certainly have come, according to the manners of the world, to the necessity of murdering one another about the business. – The words were such as generally, I believe, end in a brace of pistols; but I am still pleased to think that I did not ruin the peace & welfare of a wife & a family of children in a drunken squabble. – Farther, you know that the report of certain Political opinions being mine, has already once before brought me to the brink of destruction. – I dread lest last night's business may be misrepresented in the same way. – YOU, I beg, will take care to prevent it. – I tax your wish for Mr Burns' welfare with the task of waiting as soon as possible, on every gentleman who was present, & state this to him, & as you please, shew him this letter. – What after all was the obnoxious toast? – 'May our success in the present war be equal to the justice of our cause' – a toast that the most outrageous frenzy of loyalty cannot object to.[19]

There was no balanced rationality to the loyalist cause: in Captain Dods' view, Burns was either pro-British or pro-Jacobin. There was no middle way. Democracy was an evil, French creed, according to loyalists. Burns was lucky an earlier toast he made was not reported to his superiors. The toast he gave followed a loyalist one, 'Gentlemen, Our Prime Minister William Pitt', to which Burns stood up and countermanded with, 'I give you a better man, General George Washington!' For British radicals, Washington was symbolic of Liberty. It was a daring toast for an Exciseman to make. It was safer for Burns to employ his pen and write radical material he could publish anonymously or under a pen name, than open his mouth in public.

An example of Burns being used as the butt of a joke by aristocratic friends when he had too much claret occurred near the end of December 1793 at Friar's Carse. This notorious incident has become known as the Rape of the Sabine Women. Burns attended a dinner party hosted by Robert and Elizabeth Riddell, which included many other guests, including Maria, whose husband Walter was away in the West Indies at the time. Robert Riddell's partiality for drunkenness is enshrined in Burns' song about the legendary drinking contest 'The Whistle'. In the middle of the drunken debauch, Burns did not realise that a few soldiers and gentry had hatched a prank to embarrass him. Each of the male company – the 'Roman' males in the original scene – was allocated one of the women in attendance, that is, one of the Sabine maids. When the signal was given, the men were to charge through to their allocated target – in the case of Burns, it was Maria – grab their maid and hug and kiss them. Being somewhat infatuated by Maria, Burns fell for the prank. Indeed, it was probably due to his infatuation that the joke was hatched. On the signal, Burns led the charge and landed on Maria, who was outraged at his advances. To add insult to injury, the gentry and soldier friends of Riddell acted in feigned horror and Burns was ejected from Friar's Carse in disgrace. Burns was a shrewd observer of 'men and their manners', when sober. When drunk, his own generosity of spirit blinded him to the chicanery of those who sought to publicly humiliate him.

Hypersensitive to his own foolish, extravagant behaviour and justifiably angry at being set up, Burns sought to repair his friendship with the Riddells by writing to his hosts, 'the first epistle you ever received from the nether world'. Burns strained every nerve to be allowed a fair hearing and be reinstated in their good books but he waxed a little too lyrical for Mrs Riddell, who appears to have been ready to think the worst of him. It did not matter that Burns was tortured with guilt at his lack of etiquette or that he, in the end, suffered most from the preposterous prank. Writhing in angst, he told Elizabeth he was 'laid on a bed of pitiless furze, with my aching head reclined on a pillow of ever-piercing thorn', which tormented him, in recollection, 'with a whip of scorpions'. He then went on to point out the guilty parties: 'To the men of the company I will make no apology. – Your husband, who insisted on my drinking more than I chose, has no right to blame me; and the other gentlemen were partakers of my guilt.'[20] Two of the women present tried to intercede on his behalf before he was ejected from Friar's Carse; he appealed to Mrs Riddell to believe them. Had his erstwhile conspiratorial friends of the night been honest and admitted their part in setting Burns up, he would, in all probability, have been exonerated.

Burns knew of the 'caprice' in Maria Riddell's nature. She was bluntly honest. He had valued her friendship considerably. The Riddells, though, stuck together in cutting Burns from their circle of friends. He sought Maria's forgiveness but was met with a wall of silence. In several letters, which would have melted the heart of any feeling individual, Burns suggested that, if offences 'come only from the heart', then he was 'guiltless'. He tried to build bridges to reinstate their friendship but her 'cold neglect & contemptuous scorn' continued.[21] Maria's ongoing silence eventually engendered reciprocal contempt. This, he turned into epigrammatical satire, to mock her stuck-up superiority, including works such as 'Monody on a Lady Famed for Her Caprice' and 'Extempore, Pinned to a Lady's Coach'. Burns knew these lines were 'ill natured'. It took until after the death of Robert Riddell, on 20 April 1794, at only 39 years of age, for Burns and Maria to get back on speaking terms.

Burns remarked that he had spent more enjoyable hours at Robert Riddell's table than among all the gentry in Scotland put together. His sense of loss at Robert's early death was heart-wrenching. It was made worse by the fact that he had been estranged from his close friend. The sonnet, 'On the Death of Robert Riddell', featured in the *Dumfries Journal* of 22 April, then in the *London Star*, the *Morning Chronicle* and the *Gentleman's Magazine*.[22]

With Riddell's death, Burns felt uneasy for the collection of manuscripts he had compiled for his erstwhile friend, possibly due to some of the controversial material therein. He returned Maria's own Commonplace Book, thinking their friendship was over, and sought and obtained his own collection of writings from Friar's Carse. If Riddell had a copy of Burns' 'The Lucubrations of Henry Dundass, May 1792', then the poet was right to retrieve his collection, to exclude the possibility that a friend of the Riddell family might expose such material. It was probably fear of his continued radical composition and publications being exposed which caused Burns to write, in 'From Esopus to Maria':

> The shrinking Bard adown the alley skulks,
> And dreads a meeting worse than Woolwich hulks,
> Though there, his heresies in Church and State
> Might well award him Muir and Palmer's fate.

DeLancey Ferguson believed it was almost a miracle that Burns did not share the same fate as Muir and Palmer, given his radical poems post-January 1793.[23] Burns' description of himself as a 'shrinking Bard' skulking down an alley is an image of how the grip of political hysterical loyalty which enveloped Britain affected radicals of the era, curbing their freedom of expression. Burns was indeed lucky he did not share the same fate as Muir and Palmer.

It is possible the rumour of Burns' drunken lapse of decorum at Friar's Carse went as far as the Edinburgh Excise office. A few months after the incident, he wrote to Samuel Clark and mentioned rumours he had heard from the Excise office in Edinburgh. Clark knew the Supervisor General Mr Corbet and Burns may have been trying to mend fences:

> Some of our folks about the Excise Office, Edinr had, & perhaps still have conceived a prejudice against me as being a drunken dissipated character. – I might be all this, you know & yet be an honest fellow; but you know that I am an honest fellow, and am nothing of this.[24]

It is possible such negative rumours harked back to Burns' reputation in his Crochallan Fencibles days. It only took one or two incidents in Dumfries to reinforce the negative view of him falling into dissipation. Had he been a habitual drunk, he would have been unable to do his work professionally and would have eventually been sacked. Moreover, we know from the volume of his correspondence that he was at home almost every night with Jean and his family. The 100-plus songs and as many letters composed in his last years did not write themselves while the ram-stam boy of popular myth raked the bars of Dumfries for loose women. He had told Mrs Dunlop his association with the hard-drinking aristocrats of Dumfries area did him mischief. In reality, Burns could not hold his drink alongside them. He was a lightweight, out of his league. He neither had the stomach nor the constitution to be a regular drinker. In his teens and early twenties, he never had the income, even if he had had the inclination. Thus, when he did get drunk and some indiscretion occurred, not only did his conscience exaggerate the offence, his fame amplified any minor escapade to become the talk of the town.

As a public servant, Burns' professionalism in the Excise was, as the evidence confirms, always exemplary. There was never a contradiction between his radical principles and his work ethic. He had been brought up to labour and it was part of his nature to work hard and from his father's inculcation in youth, to be prudent with money. This attitude was transferred to the Dumfries Excise area. Burns wrote to Graham of Fintry in January 1794, suggesting that the Second Division of Excise be 'annihilated' and its duties 'divided among the others'. With the dramatic drop in imports due to the war (and hence less work for Excisemen in Dumfries), he was concerned that no public servant should 'eat the bread of idleness'. Even in busier times, his Division was the largest, with the heaviest workload, which he coped with readily. He informed Fintry he felt it a duty to report any possible way to save public money and reassured him that the 'Duties will be equally well charged, & thus an Officer's appointment saved to the Public.' He then went on to 'beg of you, Sir, should my plan please you, that you will conceal my hand in it, & give it as your own thought'.[25] This was slightly imprudent, as the suggestion should have been made through his immediate superior, but it shows Burns was already promotion material and would have seen options his superiors did not. The gauger in the Second Division, John McQuaker, might have been transferred elsewhere if the suggestion had been followed through. It was not. Burns' manoeuvring, which has sometimes been used to cast him in a negative light, was symptomatic of a highly intelligent officer not wishing to pass his management ideas to superiors who might use the idea for their own self-advancement in the service.

With Fintry apparently unable or unwilling to find promotion for Burns, he looked to find himself another powerful, protective patron during 1794–95. This was the primary motive behind his second Galloway tour, in late June 1794. The three-day trip took him as far west as Kirroughtree estate, near Newtown Stewart, to meet Patrick Heron, a Whig, whom Burns sought out as a potential patron. No doubt he had hopes that Heron would be elected to parliament over the next few years. John Syme was on business in Galloway and was scheduled to meet the bard in Gatehouse of Fleet at the Murray Arms. Another friend due at Gatehouse was the young radical, David McCulloch, who had been in France for a few years after the Revolution. McCulloch, a renowned tenor singer, hailed from the small hamlet of Ardwall, near Gatehouse, which was walking distance from the meeting place. Earlier that year he had joined the Dumfries St Andrew's Masonic Lodge, the same lodge to which Burns belonged. The singer and poet were the usual synergy of lyricist and vocal talent: Burns got to hear his songs sung by a young man with a reputation and McCulloch had the privilege of singing Burns' finest lyrics. Although this was a holiday excursion, Burns was conscious of the political xenophobia of the times and informed McCulloch he wanted him along: 'I will need all the friends I can muster, for I am indeed ill at ease whenever I approach your Honorables & Right Honorables.'[26] To stand his ground and debate topics with the literati in 1786–87 was one thing; to speak unguardedly on the controversial issues of the day in mid-1794 would have been foolish. The poet was not losing his self-confidence; he was being wisely circumspect.

Burns made the first part of the journey on his own in the Mail Coach as far as Castle Douglas, where he stayed overnight at the Carlinwark Inn. From the quiet inn, he wrote two letters, one to Nancy McLehose and the second to Mrs Dunlop. Writing to Nancy, he let the recollection of their love wash over him. A few glasses of claret took him back in his imagination. Her very name invoked so many memories, 'Recollection ruins me,' he wrote, and, a 'host of Memory's tenderest offspring crowd on my fancy'. He bemoaned Ainslie's dwindling friendship, stating the last letter from him was 'so dry, so distant, so like a card to one of his clients, that I could scarce bear to read it, & have not yet answered it'. Burns half mocked his own self-pity, describing the scene: 'a solitary hermit, in the solitary room, of a solitary inn, with a solitary bottle of wine'.[27] Nancy never replied. The same alliterative 'Solitary confinement' in a solitary village oozed to Mrs Dunlop. Burns enclosed part of a poem on the theme of Liberty for her. It mentioned her once removed heroic ancestor William Wallace. He introduced the passage thus:

> I am just going to trouble your critical patience with the first sketch of a stanza I have been framing as I passed along the road. – The Subject is, LIBERTY: you know, my honored Friend how dear the theme is to me. I design it as an irregular Ode for Genl. Washington's birth-day. – After having mentioned the degeneracy of other kingdoms I come to Scotland thus.[28]

The lines Burns forwarded to Mrs Dunlop form the final stanza of the 'Ode'. They were polished later to become:

> Thee, Caledonia, thy wild heaths among,
> Fam'd for the martial deed, the heaven-taught song,
> To thee, I turn with swimming eyes. –
> Where is that soul of Freedom fled?
> Immingled with the mighty Dead!
> Beneath that hallow'd turf where WALLACE lies!
> Hear it not, Wallace, in thy bed of death!
> Ye babbling winds in silence sweep;
> Disturb not ye the hero's sleep,
> Nor give the coward secret breath. –
> Is this the ancient Caledonian form,
> Firm as her rock, resistless as her storm?
> Shew me that eye which shot immortal hate,
> Blasting the Despot's proudest bearing:
> Shew me that arm which, nerv'd with thundering fate,
> Braved Usurpation's boldest daring!
> Dark-quench'd as yonder sinking star,
> No more that glance lightens afar;
> That palsied arm no more whirls on the waste of war. –

Burns had raised the redeeming spirit of Bruce in 'Scots Wha Hae' the previous year. By mid-1794, the pro-democracy movement was being trampled underfoot in Dundas's despotic Scotland. Wallace was a buried corpse, whose spirit would be violated by what had happened. Optimism had turned to pessimism. Scotland was a nation broken by the sedition laws, silenced and brought to its knees by oppression and war. Many of the brightest minds of the country were forced into quiet, disgruntled loyalty to the Dundas dynasty, or into exile; they had either fled to America or been transported to Botany Bay. Academics were afraid to speak out. Reformers were systematically suffocated, silenced or driven, like Burns, underground.

General George Washington was born on 22 February, so the poem was probably written to celebrate American freedom on 4 July. Washington was an iconic figure of Liberty and Independence for British reformers.

During 1793–94, there are letters by Washington printed in the Scottish radical press. Burns probably knew of Washington's Scottish ancestry and the American's passion for the Scots people, stridently expressed in the following:

> If all else fails, I will retreat up the valley of Virginia, plant my flag on the Blue Ridge, rally around the Scotch-Irish of that region and make my last stand for liberty amongst a people who will never submit to British tyranny whilst there is a man left to draw a trigger.[29]

It would seem from this last sentence, that Washington had not only fought alongside the Scots and Irish but had read a copy of the Declaration of Arbroath, which he appears to echo.

Mrs Dunlop would not have been too keen on the sentiments expressed in the first part of the 'Ode', which are seditious and treasonable. Burns, wisely, did not copy these lyrics to her. The 'Ode' begins with a celebration of American freedom:

> No Spartan tube, no Attic shell,
> No lyre Æolian I awake;
> 'Tis Liberty's bold note I swell,
> Thy harp, Columbia, let me take.
> See gathering thousands, while I sing,
> A broken chain, exulting, bring,
> And dash it in a tyrant's face!
> And dare him to his very beard,
> And tell him he no more is fear'd,
> No more the Despot of Columbia's race.
> A tyrant's proudest insults brav'd,
> They shout, a People freed! They hail an Empire saved.

In the second part of the 'Ode', Burns vaunts 'The Royalty of Man' as opposed to that of monarchy and shows his strident views were far from those of a 'silent and obedient' public servant:

> Where is Man's godlike form?
> Where is that brow erect and bold,

That eye that can, unmov'd, behold
The wildest rage, the loudest storm,
That e'er created Fury dared to raise!
Avaunt! thou caitiff, servile, base,
That tremblest at a Despot's nod,
Yet, crouching under the iron rod,
Canst laud the arm that struck th' insulting blow!
Art thou of man's Imperial line?
Dost boast that countenance divine?
Each skulking feature answers, No!
But come, ye sons of Liberty,
Columbia's offspring, brave as free,
In danger's hour still flaming in the van,
Ye know, and dare maintain The Royalty of Man.

Burns then invokes the 'freeborn' Briton and damns Pitt's tyranny:

Alfred, on thy starry throne
Surrounded by the tuneful choir,
The Bards that erst have struck the patriot lyre,
And rous'd the freeborn Briton's soul of fire,
No more thy England own. –
Dare injured nations form the great design,
To make detested tyrants bleed?
Thy England execrates the glorious deed!
Beneath her hostile banners waving,
Every pang of honour braving,
England in thunder calls — 'The Tyrant's cause is mine!'
That hour accurst, how did the fiends rejoice,
And Hell thro' all her confines raise th' exulting voice,
That hour which saw the generous English name
Link't with such damnèd deeds of everlasting shame!

This remarkable poem was only known by the final passage sent to Mrs Dunlop and would have remained a casualty to the censorship after the poet's death had it not surfaced in manuscript in 1874, 80 years after composition. It was printed in full in the *Glasgow Herald* the same year. This was almost certainly a newspaper poem and may have featured among the pages of the *Glasgow Advertiser* missing for late 1794 or later. Or it may have appeared within the missing issues of the periodical the *Glasgow Magazine*, where 'A Man's a Man' was first printed anonymously. Had Burns been discovered as the author of the Ode he would almost certainly have been arrested and tried for sedition. It constitutes further evidence to support the simple truth that Burns did put his liberty and possibly life on the line for the democratic cause in these dangerous times.

Interestingly, Mrs Dunlop's reply to the letter containing the last section of the 'Ode' refers to the 'many devious paths' the letter had taken before it reached her. She jokingly remarked the handwriting looked like it came from 'Oberon the fairy', the Shakespearian character. Burns did not risk sending a letter through the normal postal system with this type of radical poetry.

My primary researches also show that a hitherto unknown variant of the first stanza of the Washington 'Ode' was sold in manuscript at auction in London in May 1862. It shows that Burns employed the phrase 'Thy harp, Hibernia, let me take', rather than Columbia. The harp is more a natural symbol for Ireland than for America. This minor change is of some significance. It shows support for the Irish radical movement, an even more politically explosive stance. There were many links between the Scottish and Irish reform movements and, as already mentioned, Luke Mullen of the United Irishmen made a personal visit to Burns in Dumfries. The possibility of links between Burns and Irish radicals still engenders heated controversy. (I was warned in 2001, when this reference to Burns praising Irish radicals was first made public, to check my life insurance and monitor the post for a silver bullet similar to that sent to Catherine Carswell in the 1930s, after her biography of Burns was published.)[30] Newly discovered facts about Scotland's bard are not always welcome to those who prefer an anodyne myth to the real man.

At Kirroughtree, Burns presented Lady Elizabeth Heron with a copy of the lyric 'Here is the Glen', which was composed for her to the old tune 'The Banks of the Cree'; the River Cree ran through Kirroughtree estate and John Syme, a friend of the Heron family, passed the melody to Burns from Mrs Heron, who was herself an accomplished musician. Patrick and his brother Major Basil Heron later subscribed to Johnson's *SMM*. Nothing else is recorded of Burns' visit to Kirroughtree.

In March Burns had received a letter from Captain Patrick Miller junior, the Whig MP for the Dumfries burghs, son of his landlord at Ellisland farm. Miller was a close friend of James Perry, the editor of the Whig paper the *Morning Chronicle*. A Scot, originally from Aberdeen, Perry requested Miller to offer Burns a guinea a week to write for the newspaper. Burns declined, in a letter of 1 May:

> Your offer is indeed truly generous, & most sincerely do I thank you for it; but in my present situation, I find that I dare not accept it. – You well know my Political sentiments; & were I an insular individual, unconnected with a wife & a family of children, with the most fervid enthusiasm I would have volunteered my services: I then could & would have despised all consequences that might have ensued.[31]

The *Morning Chronicle* offer for literary services represented at least the equivalent of his Excise salary. Burns did not wish to move his family to London and the Exciseman's Oath of Allegiance did not allow payment for any services or employment outwith the Excise, let alone of a controversial, political nature. Despite saying no to the cash itself, Burns offered to write for the paper and enclosed 'Scots Wha Hae', asking them to publish it anonymously:

> . . . they are most welcome to my Ode; only, let them insert it as a thing they have met with by accident, & unknown to me . . . if Mr Perry . . . will give me an address & channel by which anything will come safe from these spies with which he may be certain that his correspondence is beset, I will now & then send him any bagatelle that I may write. – In the present hurry of Europe, nothing but news & politics will be regarded; but against the days of Peace, which Heaven send soon, my little assistance may perhaps fill up an idle column of a Newspaper.– I have long had it in my head to try my hand in the way of little Prose Essays, which I propose sending into the world through the medium of some Newspaper . . . to these Mr Perry shall be welcome.[32]

'Scots Wha Hae' duly appeared *anonymously* in the paper on 8 May 1794 and Burns' song 'The Sutor's Dochter' featured on 10 May.

It is noteworthy that Burns promised to send not just poetry. He proposed to send prose essays to the leading Opposition newspaper. To facilitate this, he requested a safe means of sending material to London which could not be detected by 'spies'. What we have here is a window into the way in which Burns actively sought to publish his underground radical views during these last years of his life. If he was going to send controversial material to the leading Opposition paper, he wanted the risk of his being identified as the author to be minimal and such material would not be sent using the normal post. As Professor Lucylle Werkmeister remarked in her seminal research work of the mid-1960s, it was an open secret among London radicals that Burns was covertly publishing controversial material under pen names during this period.[33]

My archival research also reveals that in August 1794, Burns significantly updated a poem from his Edinburgh Edition of 1787 and republished it under his initials in *The Gentleman's Magazine* of that month. The earlier poem 'A Winter's Night' reappears under a new title, 'Humanity: An Ode', and is very different from the earlier version.[34] Gone are the Scots vernacular stanzas which introduce the body of the poem as a 'voice' heard by the poet. The poem is more forcibly radical and the lines, 'See stern Oppression's iron lip, / See mad Ambition's gory hand, / Sending, like bloodhounds from the slip, / Woe, Want and Murder, o'er a land!' carry more resonance in the context of late 1794 than they did in 1787. The revised version is an improved work containing a sharper sentiment and better rhythm and ending than the earlier version, as David Daiches remarked on reading the new variant.[35] Only Burns himself could have undertaken such fine-tuning.

The murky business of government spying on radicals exploded into the Scottish media with the trial for High Treason of Robert Watt, during August and September. Watt had been paid as a government spy on and off from 1792. He was accused of being a turncoat involved in a planned insurrection; who his co-conspirators were is uncertain, although a David Downie was tried alongside him. Watt was found guilty and his sentence, reported in the press, spelled out he would be hanged by the neck and while still alive, his heart would be ripped out and his bowels burned before his face before his body was dismembered. In reality, he was beheaded and then his head held up by the hair to public view with the cry, 'So die all traitors.' Watt was found in possession of large metal spikes, which might have formed part of a large country estate gate made by a blacksmith. The spikes were deemed to be part of an arsenal of weapons, prepared for a political rebellion. Spikes for a single large gate do not constitute weapons of mass rebellion. Whether or not Watt was involved in a planned rebellion is far from conclusive – it may have been that he had become sympathetic to the cause of reform but knew too much about the government's spying activities. The elusive spy 'JB', who infiltrated the Edinburgh radicals, began to fear his cover would be blown when he spotted Watt attending a few of the same meetings of radicals.[36] James Boswell of Auchinleck, Ayrshire, (on a rare visit to Scotland from London), was beaten up by Paisley radicals who thought him to be the infamous 'JB' spy. Whether Robert Watt was an agent provocateur or not, the government needed some proof of the rebellion they so feared, to justify their paranoid crackdown. His public execution was part of the Scottish terror aimed at eradicating reformist activity.

In September, Burns wrote his third letter of the year to Mrs Dunlop. It contained a burden of cares. He had been feeling poorly and complained of a 'diseased Spirit' for which there was no cure. 'Poverty,' he remarked, 'is to be my attendant to the grave.'[37] He bemoaned the money he had lent to Gilbert, as he was now in need of it for the sake of his children. Gilbert, who was back in financial trouble, could not repay him. Since December 1793, Burns had been haunted periodically with a premonition of how fragile his life was. Now he was in his thirties and the fear of dying, leaving his 'little flock' helpless without a stay in the world, troubled him deeply. Elizabeth, his youngest daughter, had been seriously ill for a few months at the end of 1793 and on 12 August he was a father again when Jean gave birth to another boy, James Glencairn Burns, named after James, Earl of Glencairn.

In the same letter to Mrs Dunlop, Burns mentions a new friend who had recently moved to Dumfries sometime in 1794. Dr William Maxwell, son to James Maxwell of Kirkconnell, was the same 'Dr Maxwell whom Burke mentioned in the House of Commons about the affair of the daggers'.[38] Burns extolled the virtues of his radical associate: 'Maxwell is my most intimate friend, & one of the first characters I ever met with; but on account of his Politics is rather shunned by some high Aristocrates.'[39] This remark alludes to Maxwell's reputation: a former member of the French National Guard, he was reputed to have dipped his handkerchief in the blood of the guillotined French king and queen. In 1792, while resident in England, Maxwell had been named as Britain's most notorious Jacobin for raising a subscription to purchase thousands of daggers for the impoverished French army. After being interviewed personally by Edmund Burke, it was reported that he was not the bloodthirsty Jacobin his reputation suggested. Maxwell was in fact a medical doctor and, when Provost David Staig's 16-year-old daughter was diagnosed as terminally ill by the family physician, it was his intervention, as a last option, which saved her life.

Mrs Dunlop replied to Burns saying his muse's reputation was now stained, by association with Dr Maxwell, with the blood of the guillotine. As Lord Braxfield had quipped to Thomas Muir, 'if ye fly wi' the craws ye'll get shot wi' them' – meaning in modern parlance, a person is known by the company he or she keeps. Burns had shared the early enthusiasm of Maxwell for the French revolution and had sent carronade cannons to the French army in 1792. With their bond of cannons and daggers, the two radicals were brothers-in-arms, both now wary not to be seen, or, at least, publicly known to indulge in radical controversy. Burns was a master at appearing to be the 'silent and obedient' public servant, while having his say via subterfuge newspaper publications.

In January 1794, the Dumfries Loyal Natives, an ultra-loyalist, jingoist group modelled on Reeves' Association for Preserving Liberty and Property Against Republicans and Levellers, attacked Burns' radical coterie in verse:

> Ye Sons of Sedition, give ear to my song,
> Let Syme, Burns, and Maxwell, parade every throng,
> With Cracken the attorney, and Mundell the quack
> Send Willie the monger to Hell with a smack.

Burns responded with a satirical assault on their 'intemperate Loyalty' in two quatrains. The first includes the barb: 'From envy and hatred your corps is exempt, / But where is your shield from the darts of contempt?' The second likens them to brainless savages: 'The ignorant savage that weather'd the storm / When the man and the Brute differed but in form'. Burns also composed an eight-verse song, now lost, which is mentioned in a manuscript sales catalogue of 1861, 'Here are we Loyal Natives . . . Song in 8 verses, 2 pages folio.'[40]

The small knot of Burns' radical friends was far outnumbered by the loyalist supporters of Pitt in Dumfries. By late 1794, the Dumfries group of the Friends of the People was probably little more than an informal association – the 'Sons of Sedition' – now that the national movement had been virtually crushed.

❖❖❖

From late summer 1794 onwards, Burns, in sometimes manic bursts of activity, sent so much material to George Thomson for the *Select Collection* that Thomson could hardly keep up with the inundation, merely confirming parcels received. A clutch of the songs furnished to the prudish Thomson were love songs, many written with Jean Lorimer in mind. They were not love songs to woo her. Jean Lorimer is referred to either under her own name, Jeanie, or as the Arcadian 'Chloris'. Burns tried to explain his fascination with Jean Lorimer as a heroine of song, making it clear she was 'one of the finest women in Scotland'; that his devotion to her was like something from a novel, or 'in the guileless simplicity of Platonic love'. He went on to pre-empt gossip by wagging his finger at Thomson, asserting 'don't put any of your squinting construction on this, or have any clishmaclaver about it'.[41] Yet, the more Burns opened up his creative process to explain how he wrote a love song, the more biographers have shaken their heads, thinking he protested far too much. Burns explained to Thomson that he held up to his creative eye, the object of his idolatry – in this case, Jean Lorimer – based on Platonic love or friendship, and by the cogitations of fancy (or what we might term imagination nowadays), he poured his feelings into his lyrics with her in mind.

In 1794 she was a stunning 19-year-old with flaxen hair. Burns was not alone in being struck by her looks. She was the pin-up of the Dumfries Excise. She had had a fling a few years earlier with Burns' colleague John Gillespie, who had since been moved to Portpatrick. Burns wrote to Gillespie enclosing the first copy of the song 'Craigieburnwood' in 1791. The song was meant to help Gillespie woo Jean Lorimer. Burns, though, stated to Gillespie that the Excisemen John Lewars and James Thomson were also smitten by her.

Jean had been a near neighbour at Ellisland when her father, William Lorimer, rented the farm of Kemmishall. She became a close friend of Mrs Jean Burns. The one who won Jean Lorimer's heart was a David Whelpdale who, in a burst of teenage euphoria, eloped with her to Gretna Green and married her, only to go on the run back to England to escape creditors within a few months of marriage. She was married to the absent rake for the remainder of her life but used her maiden name till she died.

The Ettrick Shepherd, James Hogg, claimed Jean Lorimer told him she and Burns had a physical affair although the poet's letters suggest otherwise. And, if such an affair occurred, the lyrics might have been expected to be more passionate. The songs 'Craigieburnwood', 'Sleepest Thou, or Wak'st Thou'; 'Lassie Wi' the Lint-White Locks' and other lyrics for 'Chloris' are largely stock-in-trade lyrics, lacking in genuine passion. Burns would have turned out many love songs whether or not he knew Jean Lorimer. Had he not been temporarily estranged from Maria Riddell it is likely she would have been the name employed in the songs.

Maria and Walter Riddell sold their property after Robert's death and moved to London. By the end of the year, Maria was back in Dumfriesshire, living at Tinwald House, just outside the town. She appears to have either forgiven Burns' poetical lampoons in epigram, or was unaware of them. The poet and poetess renewed their friendship by the close of the year, even if it was couched in cool, third-person prose from Burns, when he first heard of her return.

The best lyrics penned by Burns in the latter part of 1794 were two songs, 'A Red Red Rose', which he sent to Cunningham in Edinburgh, and 'Ca' the Ewes to the Knowes', which was sent to Peter Hill. The former is a magical reworking of a stuffy old ballad; the few inspiring lines it contained Burns kept and redrafted into a new song, like a green-fingered gardener who has rescued the living stem from a dying old shrub. Here, for instance, are some of the older words:

Her cheeks are like the Roses
   That blossom fresh in June
O, she's like a new-string instrument
   That's newly put in tune;

Altho' I go a thousand miles
   I vow thy face to see,
Altho' I go ten thousand miles
   I'll come again to thee, dear Love
I'll come again, to thee . . .

The Day shall turn to Night, dear Love,
And the rocks melt wi' the Sun,
Before that I prove false to thee.[42]

Burns' reworking keeps the sentiment and a touch of the original phraseology:

O my Luve is like a red, red rose
That's newly sprung in June;
O my Luve's like the melodie
That's sweetly played in tune.

As fair art thou, my bonny lass,
So deep in luve am I;
And I will luve thee still, my dear,
Till a' the seas gang dry.

Till a' the seas gang dry, my Dear,
And the rocks melt wi' the sun;
I will luve thee still, my Dear,
While the sands o' life shall run.

And fare thee weel, my only Love,
And fare thee weel, awhile!
And I will come again, my Love
Tho' it were ten thousand mile.[43]

The symbol of the rose may be English, but in song lyric, on the basis of this remarkable song, it is forever Burns'. Only the greatest of songsmiths can distil emotions down to their most powerful simple imagery that touch the heart, as he does here. The fragility of love and the immortality of love shine together in this crowning gem. By the end of 1794, Burns had written almost all the greatest love songs he would ever produce.

An endemic 'want of cash' prompted Burns to nudge Graham of Fintry once more, in the hope that his patron would lobby for a promotion on his behalf. The rumour was out that Corbet might be promoted in Edinburgh and the Supervisor General's job would fall to Alexander Findlater. This would create a vacancy for a Senior Officer in Dumfries, which Burns, by dint of seniority alone, might expect to fill. Nothing came of the request. It was only when Findlater fell ill during December 1794 that Burns received temporary promotion as Acting Supervisor. Burns threw himself into the role to show he was up to the job, doing more hours than required.

The year 1794 came to a close and the poet's hoped for resurrection of the Scottish spirit of freedom embodied in 'Scots Wha Hae' never materialised. There were few radicals in the vanguard daring to maintain 'The Royalty of Man', the virtues of the general public. Burns felt a desolation across Scotland, a nation where even the very 'soul of Freedom' itself had fled. Britain had become a country where to speak the truth about governmental tyranny was to commit sedition or treason. A generation with its head down afraid to speak out in public was for him a generation without freedom. As a committed democrat, Burns had no intention of capitulation.

17

THE POET LAUREATE OF DEMOCRACY

Arm'd alone with Truth and Reason,
  Mammon's venal slaves we dar'd;
Short of triumph was the season: –
  Virtue, view the base reward.

Anon, 1795

JANUARY 1795 STARTED WELL FOR BURNS THE EXCISEMAN. He was Acting Supervisor for the Dumfries Divisions and felt his 'political sins' had been forgiven by his Edinburgh employers. The year did not begin so well for Burns the poet. As usual, at the start of a new year, he wrote to his Mother Confessor, Mrs Dunlop. In the hurry of business as Acting Supervisor he could only find time for a start-stop letter, commenced on 20 December and completed on 12 January. The letter reveals the intensity of the political drama of the time and his views on the unfolding events:

> *Entre nous*, you know my Politics; & I cannot approve of the honest Doctor's whining over the deserved fate of a certain pair of Personages. – What is there in the delivering over a perjured Blockhead & an unprincipled Prostitute to the hands of the hangman, that it should arrest for a moment, attention, in an eventful hour, when, as my friend Roscoe in Liverpool gloriously expresses it –
>
> 'When the welfare of Millions is hung in the scale
> And the balance yet trembles with fate!'
>
> But our friend is already indebted to People in power, & still looks

> forward for his Family, so I can apologise for him; for at bottom I am sure he is a staunch friend to Liberty. – Thank God, these London trials have given us a little more breath, & I imagine that the time is not far distant when a man may freely blame Billy Pit, without being called an enemy to his Country.[1]

The phrase, a 'perjured Blockhead & an unprincipled Prostitute', must have almost given Mrs Dunlop a heart attack. The execution of the king and queen of France in January 1793, as a result of the counter-revolutionary coup, which failed, was history to Burns. The entire future of Europe was in the balance, in the poet's view. He had coldly referred to the French regicide in 'The Tree of Liberty' with the line 'Cut aff his heid and a' man'.[2] The slight on John Moore (referred to as 'the honest doctor') must have also hurt Mrs Dunlop. Moore, once a pro-liberty supporter, had become an anti-Jacobin British loyalist.

'These London trials' refers to the trials of Thomas Hardy, Horne Took, John Thelwall and others, for High Treason, which returned verdicts of Not Guilty. Thomas Hardy, a Scot, originally from near Stenhousemuir, was the leader of the London Corresponding Society, the equivalent of the Scottish Friends of the People. The final lines of the letter reveal the crucial strand of the poet's British patriotism. Mrs Dunlop would not have identified with the phrase that the treason trials had 'given us a little more breath': by 'us', Burns means all supporters of the pro-democracy movement in Britain. In the last sentence of the letter, Burns spells it out that his criticisms of Pitt do not make him an enemy of Britain: it was considered anti-British and pro-Jacobin for supporters of reform to keep their demands for democratic change alive during a time of war. The song quoted by Burns is William Roscoe's 'O'er The Vine Covered Hills and Gay Regions of France', a leading reform anthem; it is highly regrettable that all the letters between Roscoe and Burns were destroyed.

Although Burns tried on several occasions to elicit a reply from Mrs Dunlop, she never again wrote to him. She must have felt her dearly beloved bard, whom she had tried to advise and guide, had become a bloodthirsty Jacobin. Burns once again paid the price for expressing his radical principles.

Mrs Dunlop was an avid admirer of the bard's poetry but was no literary expert. On one occasion, she asked him to read passages from mediocre poetry by Jenny Little, the Scottish Milkmaid poetess. Burns had offended her by making it plain that he was utterly bored at the prospect. He had also once offended her by giving a present of a volume of poetry directly to her daughter, something Mrs Dunlop informed him he was not meant to do. It was a bizarre snub to Burns' generosity.

Her kindness, though, to Burns and his family, generally knew no bounds. He made exceptions for her and she, likewise, for him. She had a soft spot for the wayward bard but warned him more than once about his opinionated remarks against King George III and his support for reform. Mrs Dunlop was an aristocrat to the bitter end and expected Burns to show fealty to her rank, something he never did. He often signed his letters to her as a friend, not in the style of 'your humble servant'. The poet's association with William Maxwell was bad enough; to slight her good friend Dr Moore and callously consign French royalty to the trash-bin of history was going too far. Burns had fallen off the social tightrope.[3] Even his heart-melting letter in January 1796, informing her of his daughter Elizabeth's death, did not budge her, nor did his last scrawl, telling of his terminal illness, in late July 1796, break Mrs Dunlop's resolve to keep her distance.

A few days after sending this fateful letter to Mrs Dunlop, Burns sent another stop-start letter, this time to Thomson, enclosing three songs: a bawdy, amusing piece on the theme of spring ('The wild-woods sang, the echoes rang, / While Damon's arse beat time Sir'), an improved version of 'Craigieburnwood' and one stated not to be 'for your book, but merely by way of vive la bagatelle; for the piece is not really Poetry', introduced thus:

> A great critic, Aikin on songs, says that love & wine are the exclusive themes for song-writing. – The following is on neither subject, & consequently is no Song; but will be allowed, I think, to be two or three pretty good prose thoughts, inverted into rhyme.[4]

This song, now famed all over the world, is 'A Man's a Man'. In its progressive, democratic sentiments, it was a rebellious, seditious piece in the oppressive social context that gave it birth, when many radicals had lost heart and democracy must have seemed a remote possibility. Burns told Thomson the song was not to be included in his collection. It was wise for an Exciseman to keep it from public view, although, once more, a little risky trusting a copy to the prudish loyalist, Thomson.

The version sent to Thomson would have been the first, which contains only four verses, and begins with, 'What tho' on hamely fare we dine', which was later moved to the second verse. The final song contains five verses. The verse beginning 'Is there for honest Poverty' did not exist in January 1795. My own recent research reveals that Burns reworked the song considerably: I traced at least five different versions, one of which has the line 'A King can mak a belted knight' rather than the softer, modified 'A prince can mak a belted knight'. To criticise the king, even in a general way, was fighting talk in 1795. (Daniel Isaac Eaton, editor of the journal *Politics for the People*, had been tried for sedition the year before, for publishing a prose passage by John Thelwall in which a cockerel struts around mistreating chickens in the coop; the prosecution argued the theme of the poem was that King George III, the cockerel, was a tyrant and the public were the abused chickens.) An early variant line of 'A Man's a Man' refers to the 'honest man' as 'Chief o' men for a' that', strongly echoing a phrase from newly attributed Burns poem 'The Ghost of Bruce', in which Bruce is described as 'The Chief of Men'. Another version printed by Peter Urbani in 1798 contains the well-known first verse, modified somewhat: 'Wha wad for honest poverty'. The last three lines of the verse printed by Urbani end thus: 'Their purse-proud looks and a' that, / In ragged coats ye'll often find, / The noblest hearts for a' that'. The first published version of the song appeared anonymously in the *Glasgow Magazine* of August 1795.

Given the poem's seditious nature, it is rather sinister that further publication occurred on 2 June 1796 in the Pitt-supporting *London Oracle*, this time with Burns named as the author. Burns, who was seriously ill at the time, would never have authorised his name being used. The song was copied and printed in the *London Star* the following day, again, disturbingly, with Burns named as author. It may be that only the poet's illness prevented his Excise bosses from taking action against him. It is certain that the Dundas power elite would have pressed them to do so or arrested him for sedition had Burns survived.

'A Man's a Man' is still the greatest democratic anthem penned in Britain. Although Burns was right to believe democracy would eventually win the day and the feudal order would disintegrate, he might have been surprised to see with what tenacity the remnants of landed title and rank would survive and co-exist within the modern democratic British state.

◈ ◈ ◈

In January 1795, Burns wrote a letter to the *Morning Chronicle* to inform the editor that, as a subscriber for the previous nine months, some issues had not been delivered, specifically one in which an anti-war speech by the Marquis of Landsdowne was reported: 'That paper, Gentlemen, never reached me; but I demand it of you.' Asserting, 'I am A BRITON; and must be interested in the cause of Liberty,' Burns goes on to emphasise 'that the humble domicile in which I shelter my wife and children, is the CASTELLUM OF A BRITON'.[5] As usual, he made a fair copy of this letter, and kept it. A peculiar aspect is the emphatic stress placed on being 'A BRITON' and this is of especial interest because 'A BRITON' is a pen name Burns had used when he sent a letter to the press in 1788. In 1794, it should be recalled, Burns had offered to write 'prose essays' for the paper.

Within the 1 January 1795 issue of *The Morning Chronicle*, in which the Marquis of Landsdowne's speech is reported, a prose essay signed 'A BRITON' is to be found. Is this simple coincidence? Burns writes to the London Opposition press, demanding a copy of a newspaper, which contains an essay under a pen name we know for certain he employed before, and screams at the editor, in the letter of complaint demanding that very newspaper, that he is 'A Briton'? It would be remiss to ignore such a triangulation of evidence pointing at Burns' possible authorship.

It is certain that if Burns had written radical prose for the newspaper, he would have published it under a fictitious name, as with his previous controversial essays. He would naturally have been irritated not to receive the paper containing his essay (a few issues of the *Star*, which contained his poetry in 1789, were also never received by him). The textual argument to suggest Burns is the author of the prose essay has been presented elsewhere and has been accepted by leading literary experts.[6] It is important to stress that the evidence in attributing the prose essay to Burns is far from being purely based on the pen name 'A Briton'. It does not automatically follow that anything discovered under this pen name would be by Burns. A pamphlet, 'An Address to the Inhabitants of Great Britain Shewing the Inevitable Consequences of A Revolution in this Country', written in 1795 and signed 'A Briton', is almost certainly not the work of Burns. It is discussed in Appendix 2, along with a letter signed 'a Briton' (BL: Reeves Papers), which is, in my view, not by Burns either. Neither the pamphlet nor the letter contains textual similarities with the prose of 1 January 1795 considered here, or contextual evidence pointing towards Burns.

The prose essay from the *Morning Chronicle*, if by Burns (as the evidence suggests), would go a long way to clarifying his views on national and international affairs at this time and clear up some of the debate between biographers over the last centuries. For that reason, it is presented here for readers to make up their own minds. It begins by contrasting the development of the theory of government with the current reality experienced in Britain:

> It is a melancholy reflection, that in an age when the theory of Government and legislation has been so well developed by a long succession of celebrated writers, mankind still struggle with the imperfections experienced in more unenlightened days.

This is followed by a balanced and critical appraisal of the mistakes made by the leaders of the French Revolution and the extreme reaction in Britain:

> The People of France, in endeavouring to unshackle themselves from the oppression of their Government, and trusting to the theories of philosophers, have fallen a prey to an oligarchy, who hold unbalanced every branch of government; this they have undergone, although theory has often said that the same persons must not be Legislators and Judges, and the dread occasioned by the misfortunes of that country, induced the people of this to fall into the opposite extreme – the adoration of Regal Power.

The next passage exposes the undemocratic abuse of power in Britain and makes comparisons with Roman history and the lives of various Caesars; such classical history formed part of the poet's education in Masson's radical school textbook, although, of course, it would be common to the education of many:

> The Alarmists have cried down all Reform in Parliament as dangerous, and Parliament has given into the hand of the Crown our dearest rights. Nothing now remains, but to renew that act of Henry VIII by which the King's Proclamation may have the force of an Act of Parliament; for

> as the majority of our House of Commons is not elected by a majority of the People, nor by a majority of those, who, under the present system have a right to vote, we have no security for its speaking the sense of the People; and, like the Romans in the days of Augustus Caesar, are insulted, with the forms of a free Government, while, in some of the most important parts, the substance is lost.
>
> To tell us that Reform is dangerous, is to say, my children, be good and don't complain, you will have all you desire granted you at a more convenient time. Will anyone who knows the history of mankind assert, that any liberty or privilege we shall have lost, will be ever spontaneously restored, even by the wisest and best of Kings? During the prosperous reigns of Nerva, Trojan, and the Antonines, the Roman world was governed with wisdom and equity; but those Emperors, although they knew the miseries which the People had suffered under their predecessors, never put one bar on the omnipotence of their own authority; and the succession of Commodus shews, that though a good Prince need not be shackled, those shackles ought to exist, as no Sovereign, let him be ever so good and just, can become immortal but in the page of history.

After a critique on the wantonness of ambition in war – a critique repeated in Burns' letters of 1793–94 – the next passage reveals a British patriotism and the concern that the government has become so despotic it might trigger a rebellion:

> It therefore is proper, that every man who has a love for his King and country, should wish to see the Government brought back to the spirit of its institution: because every free man should hold his privileges dear; and because, when he sees ministers endeavouring, under insidious pretexts, to increase the power of the Crown at the expense of those privileges, he should foresee the most terrible consequences; for either the Government must become absolutely despotic, or the bulk of mankind, not properly sensible of the fine texture, and intrinsic value of our Constitution, may one day join in a general cry against Kings, and overturn the regal part of the Government.

The phrase 'insidious pretexts' is one Burns used in his first known essay signed 'A Briton'. The next section contains echoes of sentiments found in two radical poems by Burns: in 'The Tree of Liberty', no trees of liberty can be found between London and the Tweed – meaning there is no longer any liberty or freedom in England; and in 'Scots Wha Hae', an early version contains an image of children in iron chains, enslaved. The poet's letter, already quoted, to Erskine of Mar, contains similar imagery of the poet's children possibly being enslaved:

> The present time seems to be the crisis which is to determine whether England is to remain a free country or not. At this moment you and I are subject to be seized and confined without having a right to demand a trial; for when a Minister can send his *marechausee* into your house, and take you in silence to a dungeon, what security can you have against a transportation to some distant region? This has not been the case as yet, but what does the annihilation of your dearest privelages tend to but this; will not our children, perhaps, be subject to such an iron sceptre?

This is followed by a detailed argument that contrasts and condemns both anarchy and tyranny, in the same way Burns does in the song he published in the press in early 1793, 'Be anarchy curs'd and tyranny damn'd':

> This prospect of our future condition, whether we be overwhelmed by tyranny, or become the victims of anarchy, is alarming to men who value, and who understand the British Constitution. Ministers continually warn us to dread innovations, while we daily see the encroachments made on the free part of the Government, which, although they have not yet been called by that name, are not to be stopped by having the word innovation retaliated on them. I will briefly declare what reflection I have made on the subject of our Government, and if I am guilty of errors, shall hope to stand corrected through the medium of your paper.
>
> The spirit of the British Constitution seems to consist in this: That the House of Commons are the deputies of the separate districts of this island, who meet to deliberate for the common good; while the House of Peers, forming the Aristocratical part of the Constitution, may be a check on the Tribune of the People, and, at the same time, constitute the highest Court of Judicature; from the Crown, we are insured in the quick execution of our laws, and we blend with the advantages of a Republic, all those of a Monarchy. But when the servants of the Crown are at the same time permitted to be Tribunes of the People; when the vassals of

> Nobles enjoy the same pre-eminence, on what do the bulk of this nation rest the bulwark of their liberty? The same parliament that has continued the suspension of the Habeus Corpus may establish a Committee of the House of Commons to take cognisance of cases of High Treason; the Tribunal of the Star Chamber may be renewed; and should that be the case, how are we to help ourselves, when so great a military force exists in these kingdoms?

The conclusion brings the argument to a sharp focus in the context of France having beaten most of her warring enemies at the close of 1794. The allies against France were in disarray hoping for peace and in Britain the alarm was spreading of a possible French invasion. There is an equal condemnation of both the bloody slaughter of Robespierre and the Pitt government's callousness in pursuing an unjust war: the hint is made plain that the French Revolution has sunk into anarchy and the British government has become tyrannical – a situation which can be remedied by peace in Europe and reform at home:

> Our present situation is critical: we are involved in a war without properly knowing why! Do we propose to ourselves to re-establish the regal authority in France? That were a vain hope, all our Allies have nearly abandoned us. Do we wish to defend Holland? The Dutch are better disposed towards France than towards us. What object do we propose by the war? The Minister acquires great patronage, and he is thus enabled to keep his place, at the public expence, and by the lives of his fellow-subjects. How many have already been the victims of his ambition; and he tranquilly holds his place, though he knows that his countrymen daily bleed to keep him there? This might, one would think, better become a Robespierre; but before we feel abhorrence at the cruelty of the Convention, let us ask ourselves, Whether those who vote for the continuance of the war be not as unfeeling? What signifies it to the sufferers, whether they fall by the guillotine of Robespierre, or by the massacres which the Great Catherine and the King of Prussia have committed for the sake of good order, Religion, & c. Will Poland feel any better effects from those, than France from the former? Does not the same hold good with regard to the subjects we daily lose on the Continent? The true medium between anarchy and tyranny ought to be strictly kept in view, for extremities touch; and therefore, so far

> from its being dangerous to reform our Parliament, we ought to rouse from the present infatuation, and before it is too late, before every trace of our Constitution be effaced, bring it back to those principles on which it is established: that is, make the theory and practice tally better together.

All this ties in with the views expressed in fragmentary outpouring throughout the poet's letters during the 1793–95 period. That, of course, does not automatically mean it is his work. As compared with this essay, the views Burns sets out in his private letters are more developed, as we would expect. Rather than being a revolutionary firebrand, it shows a highly politically astute Burns, well read in ancient history and far from being semi-confused and contradictory in political sentiments, as some biographers have suggested. The leaders of the French Revolution are condemned as much as Pitt and Dundas. From the vantage point of the twenty-first century, the essay reads as a highly articulate, hyper-intelligent view, argued cogently, although in the teeth of the political tumult of the era; such a perspective was anathema to loyalist jingoism.

This essay shows that Burns was no bloodthirsty 'Jacobin'. Without manuscript proof, there is likely to be further debate on its provenance but circumstantial evidence has convinced many leading literary experts, including the late Professor Daiches, that it is the work of Burns.[7]

On 31 January 1795, Burns walked into the lions' den of the loyalists in Dumfries by attending the inaugural meeting of the Royal Dumfries Volunteers, knowing full well he was associating with most of the local rabidly jingoistic Loyal Natives. This did not signify the poet's conversion to the Pittite cause. It was probably seen as a duty of all Excisemen to join the Volunteer corps then being formed up and down the country. John Syme was one of the first to join with Burns, and his Excise colleagues Lewars and Findlater joined up at the next meeting. Such a Volunteer army would never have been raised in the winter of 1792 or during 1793, when government fears of home-grown radicalism was at its peak. The pro-democracy movement had now been effectively crushed and the greater fear was of a French invasion force, given the disarray and defeat of allies united against France. A host of the poet's friends also joined up, including Thomas White, schoolteacher; his landlord, Captain John

Hamilton; William Hyslop, proprietor of the Globe Inn; the lawyer and owner of the Isle, near Ellisland, David Newall; and Samuel Clark. Burns was not a pacifist per se. He opposed the rightward swing of French politics towards the cult of the personality, embodied by the emerging young Napoleon Bonaparte. As Burns later wrote in the song 'The Dumfries Volunteers', British problems ought to be fixed by British solutions, not by an invasion force. During 1795, Burns also made a toast which sums up his position on the Volunteers. 'Gentlemen, may we never see the French, nor the French see us.'

On 20 February, the Volunteers chose Colonel Arent Schuyler De Peyster, the oldest and most experienced soldier in the corps, as its Major Commandant. De Peyster was married to Provost David Staig's daughter Rebecca and resided at Mavis House, a few miles outside Dumfries. Burns was a regular visitor there during 1795 and the two men became good friends. De Peyster shared an interest in poetry and admired Burns' work.

Under De Peyster, the Dumfries Volunteers were split into First and Second Company, for drilling and target practice with muskets at the Dock park area by the River Nith. Captain John Finnan was placed in charge of the Second Company, which included Burns, John Syme, John Lewars and James Gracie. Government funding covered purchase of muskets and bullets for the Volunteers but not of uniforms. Volunteers were unpaid for their time and services, and were fined if they did not turn out for drilling and practice when mustered.

A Volunteer, local tailor David Williamson, was chosen to supply the uniforms. There was no standard design for Volunteer corps uniforms and the Dumfries Volunteers ended up with ones that had the dandyish look of eighteenth-century military garments: a round hat, turned up on the left with a cockade and black feather; blue coat, with red cape lapels and cuffs; white cassimere vest, trousers and stockings; and black shoes with a black tie band. When the Management Committee decided to place advertisements in the local press petitioning the public to deffray uniform costs, Burns and his fellow privates protested to the committee that such an act was an embarrassment to the Dumfries Volunteers. Burns is believed to be the author of the letter to the Committee, addressed to Commandant De Peyster, dated 18 May:

> From what we have learned of the proceedings of our Committee today, we cannot help expressing our disapprobation of the mendicant business of asking a public contribution for defraying the exps of our Association . . . That the Royal Dumfries Volunteers should go a begging, with the burnt out Cottager and Ship-wrecked Sailor, is a measure of which we must disapprove. –
>
> Please then, Sir, to call a meeting as soon as possible, and be so very good also as to put a stop to the degrading business, until the voice of the Corps be heard.[8]

It would be typical of Burns the democrat to insist on the voice of the corps being heard. This letter, although not in the poet's handwriting, is widely accepted as being by Burns. It was signed by Burns and 25 privates. The circumstantial evidence of Burns' authorship is simply the notion that no other person among the corps would have been asked to write it other than the famous author. Although the Volunteers did raise some funds for their uniforms, ignoring the privates, Burns insisted on paying for his own. It was a stubborn, independent stance he would rue when he was terminally ill. Pride, as they say, comes before a fall, and Burns had a knack of creating problems for himself.

The impact on Burns' income resulting from the restriction on imports since February 1793 has already been mentioned. Now, moreover, his temporary promotion exploited his enthusiasm to shine in the position of Acting Supervisor. The Excise did not increase the pay of an Officer elevated to a temporary promotion until the sick Officer was off for several months. He was effectively doing Findlater a favour and increasing his own chances of a genuine promotion into the bargain but at a cost. Burns had extra travel and accommodation costs to pay out of his already reduced salary. In mid-January, he wrote to William Stewart of Closeburn a 'painful, disagreeable letter', asking him for 'three or four guineas'.[9] The three guineas obtained from Stewart were forwarded to Captain John Hamilton to reduce rent arrears. Burns was indeed lucky his landlord was a patient friend, who understood the precarious situation of Excise Officers dependent upon imports for up to a third of their salary. Debts were a humiliating embarrassment to Burns. Owing what he could not pay was, to him, a living nightmare. He could not avoid Captain Hamilton, his landlord, since they were now fellow Volunteers. The notion that Burns was a wealthy man living a sort of middle-class life in Dumfries is a myth. The biographers who have used the poet's extensive library as an index of his wealth during these last years, neglect the reality that books cannot be eaten during a food shortage or used as currency in lieu of rent.[10]

Remnants of the poet's Excise diary from his time as Supervisor have survived. They show the dedication Burns had in covering Findlater's duties, during a brutal winter period of severe gales and freezing weather. A few examples of his daily routine give an indication of his determination to show he was promotion material. On visiting Sanquhar Division he rose at 5 a.m., worked through until 7 p.m., covering a variety of tobacco and tea dealers, a maltster, a tanner, twelve victuallers and a chandler. Each required different monitoring and paperwork. Monitoring each Division meant docketing the local Excise Officers books for accuracy. In the Dumfries First Division, his first post, Burns was back around Dunscore and Ellisland, covering five additional parishes in a day's ride, which included docketing James Hossack's books with nothing untoward to report. Burns arrived home after his first ride round his old haunt at 11 p.m., having worked almost 16 hours that day. Dumfries Divisional staff were shuffled around to cover the poet's absence. His stead was covered by John Lewars, while a new trainee, Adam Stobie, covered Lewars' Division. The only critical remarks made by Burns on a fellow Officer relate to Leonard Smith, who had made a series of basic errors in entering figures for a local maltster. Collector Mitchell then endorsed the poet's Excise diary, commenting in his report to Edinburgh that Burns was in every Division of the area at least once a day and on one day, 5 January, he visited two Divisions. Mitchell highly commended Burns for his enthusiasm and professionally discharging the 'duty entrusted to him'.[11] The only ambiguity was a minor misunderstanding relating to the Dumfries Divisions Wine Account figures, which Burns did not submit for the simple reason that he was in the process of collating these when Findlater returned to work. John Edgar, the Excise administrator in Edinburgh, wrote to alert the Dumfries Collector of the figures being late for the Wine Account. Burns replied to Edgar on 25 April, explaining that Findlater was back at work and that he had assumed the duties would fall to him. The delay was caused primarily by a late return of figures from the Sanquhar Division Officer, John Graham. Collector Mitchell asked Burns to deal with the situation and he duly obtained the figures from Graham and made the submission, without being formally censured. To cover costs of a horse, accommodation and subsistence during his period as Acting Supervisor, Burns received an extra £12 pay. Given that Findlater received upwards of £200 per annum for the work Burns was temporarily doing, his extra pay towards costs was a dismal, demoralising sum.

Burns had pushed himself to his physical limits. From May onwards, his health declined and a variety of ailments started to erode his constitution. Regular parading and drilling along with the Dumfries Volunteers had added to his strenuous efforts to cover for Findlater as Supervisor.

An idea of how biting the winter weather had been is given in a letter to Thomson from Ecclefechan on 7 February, when Burns wrote:

> I came yesternight to this unfortunate, wicked, little village. – I have gone forward – but snows of ten feet deep have impeded my progress: I have tried to 'gae back the gate I cam again', but the same obstacle has shut me up within insuperable bars.[12]

The poet's humour was still intact, even if his bones were shivering by the fireside. An amateur fiddler decided to impress him with his skill and, oblivious to how terrible he was, kept 'torturing Catgut, in sounds that would have insulted the dying agonies of a Sow under the hands of a Butcher'.

It is almost certain Burns did his own health some permanent damage during this four-month period. There can be little doubt that if he suffered from rheumatic heart disorder it would have been exacerbated. The bitter experience of being Acting Supervisor taught Burns that the position he should aim for was that of Collector, which was less physically demanding and mainly entailed overseeing Divisional paperwork. It would allow him more leisure time for writing, whereas being a Supervisor was almost a bar to writing, as it sucked the vitality and energy from him.

The election for the Stewartry area of Kirkcudbright triggered by the death of the Tory MP was postponed until the spring due to the severe weather. The Tory candidate, Thomas Gordon of Balmaghie, was a nephew of the notoriously immoral rich landowner James Murray of Broughton, MP for Wigtownshire. By the end of March, Burns had written a couple of political ballads to assist Patrick Heron's campaign, lampooning his opponents. Burns printed the ballads as private broadsheets and circulated them privately to cause a stir:

> I enclose you some copies of a couple of Political Ballads; one of which, I believe you have never seen . . . I have privately printed a good many copies of both ballads and have sent them among friends all about the country.
>
> To pillory on Parnassus the rank reprobation of character, the utter dereliction of all principle, in a profligate junto, which has not only outraged virtue, but violated common decency; which, spurning even hypocrisy as paltry iniquity below their daring; – to unmask their flagitiousness to the broadest day – to deliver such over to their merited fate – is surely not merely innocent, but laudable; is not only propriety, but virtue.- You have already, as your auxiliary, the sober detestation of mankind on the heads of your opponents; and I swear by the lyre of Thalia to muster on your side all the votaries of honest laughter and fair, candid ridicule![13]

Not even Thomas Muir or his Botany Bay compatriots had dared raise such a pitch of invective against the Pitt government as the declamation made here by Burns.

Heron had written to John Syme to ask how he could help Burns if he was elected as a local MP. The poet explained he would need a political friend if promoted to Supervisor, in order to reach the position of Collector, which was 'always a business purely of political patronage'. Such a promotion would allow him 'A life of literary leisure' and was 'the summit of my wishes'.[14] Regrettably, Opposition MPs never have the political clout of ministerial influence and although Burns was backing the most honest, principled candidate, he was naïve in his optimism that the Whigs would oust Pitt at a general election. Burns also sent the Whig MP Richard Oswald some 'songs of triumph' and informed him 'In these days of volunteering, I have come forward with my services as poet-laureate to a highly respectable Political party, of which you are a distinguished member.' But the Poet Laureate of reform and democracy was, in the short term, backing the losing horse; all the smart money was in the Treasury coffers, buying support and silencing extra-parliamentary opposition.

Penning poetic propaganda for an Opposition candidate was yet more reckless behaviour for an employee of the Crown, even if Burns was not openly proclaimed as the author. The contest was close to home and Thomas Gordon and his supporters must have known Burns was the political squib-merchant, even if they could not prove it. Whether the songs by

Burns helped Heron's victory is impossible to determine, although most biographers tend to inflate their importance in winning votes. There is no means of truly gauging the influence Burns had at this time.

The Heron ballads were ephemeral, mediocre verse, which Burns would never have published under his name for that reason alone. The first, with touches of 'A Man's A Man', lauds Heron as the 'independent Patriot, / The Honest Man, and a' that' and the 'independent Commoner'. Then a hit at the Tory opponent follows: A 'Lord may be a gowk, / Tho' sprung fae kings and a' that' and 'A Lord may be a lousy loon, / Wi' ribbon, star, and a' that'. The song appeals to the people of the Stewartry not to be bought and sold like cattle at a market, although the majority could not vote.

The second ballad is a ten-verse array of scathing, epigrammatic stings at every Tory supporter of Gordon. Two clerics, the Reverend Dr James Muirhead and George Maxwell were also casualties of the poet's wit. Muirhead, who had no illusions that Burns was the author, snarled back in a clever, highly personal quatrain, calling him a 'pimp' and hitting a raw nerve by asking why he was 'poor as a church-rat'. (Could it be that the accusation of Burns being a 'pimp' is the origin of the notion the poet was a 'whore maister'?)

The third Heron ballad is a mocking lament for the defeat of the Tory candidate, put into the mouth of the leading Tory supporter, John Bushby, the Sheriff Clerk in Dumfries – hence the title, 'John Bushby's Lamentation'. To win a single ally, Burns was prepared to make a dozen or more powerful enemies.

His next composition may have been partly motivated to throw detractors off the scent and display the threadbare British patriotism he held onto during these turbulent times. An early draft of 'The Dumfries Volunteers', which has not survived contained a satirical attack on a 'ci-devant Commodore'. Burns wrote to Mrs Dunlop, enclosing a copy of 'The Dumfries Volunteers', stating, 'Miss Keith will see that I have omitted the four lines on the ci-devant Commodore which gave her so much offence. Had I known that he stood in no less connection than the Godfather of my lovely young Friend, I would have spared him for her sake.'[15] It is bizarre that recent biographers seem oblivious to the early variant stanza of 'The Dumfries Volunteers'. Referring to the phrase a 'ci-devant Commodore', Mackay remarks 'No poem answering this description has survived,' even though the letter to Mrs Dunlop states 'The Dumfries

Volunteers' was enclosed and the remark relates exclusively to the song.[16] McIntyre is a little more in tune with the sentiments, cynically stating the bard's radicalism did not change overnight with this veneer of apparent loyalty. If 'haughty Gaul' threatens to invade Britain, the song suggests the Volunteers will stand against such an invasion and calls for an end to political wrangling and demands Britain should stay true to Britain's ideals, an oblique reference to the Glorious Revolution of 1688. The implication is also that parliament has the power to bring Pitt and Dundas back to the letter of the constitution. Verse three admits there are problems within 'Kirk and State' but domestic problems are not for foreigners to fix. The final verse condemns tyrants and the mob, both, as extremes. The song declares that 'while we sing God Save the KING, / We'll ne'er forget THE PEOPLE'. Hence, the display of loyalty to king and country (not Pitt) finally comes down, with a loud, seditious ring, on the side of 'THE PEOPLE'.

If Burns wanted 'The Dumfries Volunteers' to draw attention away from the Heron ballads, publication on 4 May in the *Edinburgh Evening Courant* did the job. The poet's fealty to King George was always threadbare tokenism. Kingship is the source of title and rank. To oppose the tinsel show of gentry and title is to oppose its source, monarchy. In the chaos of war, though, Burns had no problem with making a symbolic gesture of loyalty to an entire system he wished to see reformed. It was not the king who was tyrannically oppressing the people, it was a handful of ministers. The various royal proclamations published in the press since early 1792 were known to be the work of Pitt's government; King George III was effectively a puppet during Pitt and Dundas's abuse of power. The king made a notorious speech in December 1792 stating it was a time of great peace and stability – the country was in political meltdown. Such was the mood of hysteria, that, on one occasion, when a stone flew up from the wheels of his carriage and hit his window, news spread of an assassination attempt on the king.

Burns stepped forward to assist Patrick Heron once again during the general election of 1796 and composed the fourth Heron ballad, 'Buy Braw Troggin: An Excellent New Song'. This time, the Tory candidate was the son of the Earl of Galloway, Montgomery Stewart. The brevity of the radical song does not detract from its satirical point. It employs the image of a trogger for the Tory candidate, who is shown as a hawker, peddling worthless election promises. The Earls of Galloway played a role in selling out Scotland in 1707, so Burns uses that as one of the satirical barbs of the song. Once more, as in the earlier Heron ballad, the Reverend James Muirhead of Urr, near Castle Douglas, is castigated as a sour crab-apple 'rotten at the core', while the Reverend George Maxwell is named as a gin addict. The song ends with a hilarious scoff at the Tory candidate: the Devil turns 'chapman' to 'buy a' the Pack!' – that is, all the false promises of Montgomery Stewart. The propaganda song was written sometime in May or early June, 1796, when the poet's health was failing.

Burns' spirits appear to have been buoyed up in August 1795 by a visit from Robert Cleghorn of Saughton Mills, Edinburgh, a fellow Crochallan Fencible and partaker of the 'turtle feast' of naughty bawdy lyrics. Burns arranged for Cleghorn and a farming compatriot of his to join him and William Lorimer, Jean's father, at the Globe Inn for 'a plateful of hotch-potch, and a bottle of good sound port'.[17] The poet's convivial social nature could still sparkle wit among likeminded intimates.

During the late summer of 1795 and into that winter, Burns kept up his correspondence with George Thomson and James Johnson for both collections of Scots songs, altering and amending songs, while also sending a few new compositions. Burns took pains to go through the old collection of songs in the *Orpheus Caledonius* and the *Tea-Table Miscellany*, the two primary sources of Scots songs for the poet's contemporaries. He was able to recommend to Johnson that he simply reprint some of the old songs without tinkering, since Johnson's was more of an antiquarian collection than Thomson's. In September, Burns asked Johnson to design and print a bill for his friend Hyslop, proprietor of the Globe Inn, the poet's favourite howff. It was not until February when the proofs for the Globe Inn bills were ready and required correction due to spelling errors. In early January, Thomson sent Burns a copy of Peter Pindar's recent collection of songs. Peter Pindar was the pen name of Dr Peter Wolcot, an English satirical poet whom Burns admired, although very few of his works have any lasting merit. Pindar is best remembered for his satirical hits at King George III. Even when Burns began to suffer periodic bouts of illness during the winter, his dedication to songwriting was unshaken, albeit his enthusiasm was tempered by low spirits.

The horrendous toothache Burns suffered in early summer, in the days before proper painkillers and anaesthetics – which led to his penning an 'Address to the Toothache' – paled in significance to the awful news from Jean, who was in Mauchline during September. The death of Elizabeth Riddell Burns shook the poet to his very core. She had been severely ill the previous year but recovered, although her health was precarious during the summer months. Her death occurred while at Mauchline with her mother and relations. She was nearing her third birthday.[18] To make matters worse, Burns himself was too ill to attend her funeral. It was a crippling psychological blow to lose his only remaining girl. Whatever has been said of Burns' love for Jean or other women he knew, he was a doting father, who glowed with warmth and unconditional love for his children. He wrote to Maria Riddell telling her, 'A severe domestic misfortune has put all literary business out of my head.'[19] His letters to his Edinburgh friend Robert Cleghorn were normally jovial, with free, unbuttoned wit and bawdy lyrics: in January 1796 Cleghorn was informed of Elizabeth's death and the poet's intermittent illness in a manner which must have concerned him. Burns told him he had

> scarcely began to recover the loss of an only daughter & darling child, I became myself the victim of a rheumatic fever, which brought me to the border of the grave. After many weeks of a sick-bed, I am just beginning to crawl about.[20]

It was not until 31 January that the poet informed Mrs Dunlop, 'The Autumn robbed me of my only daughter & darling child.' He wrote of meeting Mrs Dunlop's son John in Dumfries, then repeated the description of his illness, adding that he was in such a delirium of fever that he had 'been before my own door in the street'.[21] As has been stated, the bard's plea for their friendship to be rekindled elicited no response.

❖ ❖ ❖

In late November 1795, Josiah Walker paid Burns a visit. They had not met for several years. Walker left a detailed description of the meeting in his memoirs, telling of seeing Burns reading at a window at his house with the front door wide open to the street and the children busily playing near the bard. They chatted at length, then Burns amiably acted as host, taking Walker down to the Nith and on to Lincluden Wood. They spent part of the afternoon at an inn, probably the Globe. The lengthy anecdote is full of judgement on the poet's character and an assessment of the correctness of his behaviour and manners, to the point of being nauseating. Walker was disappointed in Burns and the 'interview not so gratifying as I had expected'. The prudish visitor, so used to the cocoon of aristocratic cotton wool, condescended to rap the poet's knuckles for daring to repeat 'fragments of an "Ode to Liberty" with marked and peculiar energy, and showed a disposition . . . to throw out peculiar remarks of the same nature for which he had been reprehended'.[22]

Walker knew of the Excise investigation and Burns' chastisement and public humiliation. The 'Ode to Liberty' mentioned was probably 'The Irregular Ode for General Washington's Birthday'. On the second day of Walker's visit, he refers to their being at the inn until three in the morning. Walker then basks in his own frothy condemnation of Burns' conversation being too elaborate, interspersed with weakened expressions and a tendency to make witty, epigrammatic points purely for applause. His reminiscence reads like a half-term school report on a wayward pupil. If Walker was unimpressed by Burns, it is certain Burns was unimpressed by the pompous superior ass patronising him, to paraphrase DeLancey Ferguson.[23] In his reminiscence of Burns, Walker did little more than join up the dots of the picture of the supposed decline into dissipation of a once great poet.

During the poet's last year, there were periodic problems with food supply in Dumfriesshire. Provost Staig wrote to Robert Dundas on 4 February 1796, requesting help due to the extreme shortage of oatmeal: 'The enclosed memorial was handed to me this morning by our Magistrates . . . under this alarm of scarcity . . . it is impossible for me as Collector for the Customs, to give the wished for relief.'[24]

Dumfries bakers and grain dealers petitioned Robert Dundas, complaining that grain from the area, essential for local survival, was being shipped out of Scotland and not enough was left to allow them to make a living or feed local people.[25] It is surprising there are no newspaper reports of food riots in Dumfries in early 1796 when shortages due to grain and oatmeal being exported to London caused prices to become so exorbitant that many people could not purchase the staple food they required.[26] The spectre of famine hung over various places across Britain, due to the government prioritising the supply of grain to feed troops overseas and in the major cities, before the needs of the general public.

In a letter written in January 1796 to Mrs Dunlop, (which she once again ignored), Burns recounted:

> I know not how you are in Ayr-shire, but here, we have actual famine, & that too in the midst of plenty. – Many days my family & hundreds of other families, are absolutely without one grain of meal; as money cannot purchase it. – How long the Swinish Multitude will be quiet, I cannot tell: they threaten daily.[27]

On 12 March, food riots erupted in Dumfries due to the shortage of meal, two days after the king called for a general fast throughout Scotland. The town granary was broken into and cart-loads of potatoes were stolen. The Angusshire Fencibles and Dumfries Volunteers were dispatched to patrol and calm the streets. A few nights of unrest were followed by another outburst of looting for meal. The leading Scottish academic radical of this period, Professor John Millar of Glasgow University, who was forced underground to express his views (using the pen name 'Crito'), lamented the terrible irony in Pitt's policy to starve Paris to its knees through force and famine: 'What a dreadful reverse of fortune we have sustained!'[28] Lack of nutrition almost certainly contributed to Burns' declining health in 1796.

During his illness in January, he kept himself active in the radical cause, writing the ballad 'The Dean of Faculty', a eulogy to the Whig supporting Henry Erskine, who had lost his office as Dean of the Faculty of Advocates in Scotland to Robert Dundas, nephew of Henry. Robert Dundas is colloquially referred to as 'Bob' while Henry is 'Hal' in the satirical song. Henry Erskine was effectively voted out of the post for his sympathies with the radical cause of the era, so often championed in London by his brother Thomas Erskine. It was during the 1840s when the final stanza surfaced, after being censored by Cromek in 1808, when the song was first published. The slight against the Tory administration and King George III are in the last lines of the song:

> With your honours and a certain King
>   In your servants this is striking –

The more incapacity they bring,
The more they're to your liking. –

The song, set to the tune 'The Dragon Of Wantley', was probably written as a newspaper poem and may have featured under a pen name, in issues, now missing, of the *Glasgow Advertiser*.

Although punctuated by temporary pockets of respite, a cycle of ill health dominated the poet's life during 1796. His state of health was further undermined by stress both at what might be the cause of his illness and by the negative impact it had on his income. At the close of 1795, Burns wrote a poetical epistle to Collector Mitchell mentioning his failing health – 'You've heard this while how I've been licket, / And by fell Death 'maist nearly nicket' – and asking for a guinea advance on his wages. Burns was unable to resume his Excise duties full-time until February. Thereafter, the extant Excise records of his salary payments show illness prevented him from drawing full wages in April and July, when his normal wages of £6 were reduced to £3 and £2 respectively. The basic salary of £50 applied only when Officers were at work. During illness it was reduced to £35.[29] It irritated Burns considerably he could not draw his full wages while ill. He even went as far as writing to Alexander Cunningham in early July to ask his lawyer friend to petition the Excise board to grant him his full salary. It is possible some of the Excise staff in Edinburgh, unaware of the poet's true illness at this time, pieced together the rumours they had heard about Burns over the years and jumped to the conclusion his illness was a result of alcoholism. With his declining income and the demands of a large family to feed and rent to pay, Burns could not afford to drink excessively on a regular basis. He was often too ill to lift the claret jug.

The final letters from Burns to Thomson are laced with remarks about the poet's illness. In April, Burns told Thomson:

> Almost ever since I wrote you last, I have only known Existence by the pressure of the heavy hand of Sickness; & have counted time by the repercussions of PAIN! Rheumatism, Cold, & Fever have formed, to me, a terrible Trinity in Unity, which makes me close my eyes in misery, & open them, without hope.[30]

By May, Burns was hoping the coming summer months might help rejuvenate him, remarking he could not yet 'boast of returning health.

I have now reason to believe my complaint is a flying gout'.[31] It seems Burns was beginning to think his illness was due to past excesses, which were few and periodic.

The last two letters from Burns to Thomson, both of which were delivered to Edinburgh by friends of the poet, rather than by the post, were written from the poet's sea-bathing quarters at the Brow hamlet, ten miles southeast of Dumfries, on the Solway coast, where he was making a last desperate attempt to convalesce. His situation was deteriorating by the week: 'I am here at a sea-bathing quarters. – Besides my inveterate rheumatism, my appetite is quite gone, & I am so emaciated as to be scarce able to support myself on my own legs.'[32] By mid-July, the poet's physical illness was no better. His psychological health was in tatters after he found out David Williamson was legally pursuing him for the cost of his Dumfries Vounteers uniform, for a sum of just over £7. Burns did not have the money to spare and feared the want of it would result in his incarceration in a debtor's jail. The fear of debtors' jail that had haunted his father to the grave was upon him. It broke his stubbon pride, causing him to beg friends for money in a frenzy of panic. Thomson opened the letter and read:

> After all my boasted independence, curst necessity compels me to implore you for five pounds. – A cruel scoundrel of a Haberdasher to whom I owe an account, taking it into his head that I am dying, has commenced a process, & will infallibly put me in jail. – So, for God's sake, send me that sum, & that by return of post. Forgive me this earnestness, but the horrors of a jail have made me half distracted. –
>
> I hereby promise & engage to furnish you with five pounds' worth of the neatest song-genius you have seen.[33]

Thomson came through for him and acted promptly, borrowing the money after reading the cry for help. It was the last letter of their lengthy correspondence.

A scrawled letter for financial help was also sent to James Clarke, who was now a schoolmaster in Forfar, after moving from Moffat. Clarke still owed Burns money and a debt of gratitude for his support when his professional future was in jeopardy. After asking for the money, Burns added:

> were you to see the emaciated figure who now holds the pen to you, you would not know your old friend. –
>
> As to my individual Self, I am tranquil; – I would despise myself if I were not: but Burns' poor widow! & half a dozen of his dear little ones, helpless orphans, there I am weak as a woman's tear. –
>
> Enough of this! 'Tis half my disease![34]

In 1796, it was customary to throw debtors in jail. The increase in bankruptcies and debtors being jailed after the start of war with France was dramatic, in some regions upwards of 500 per cent. Burns could probably have asked some Dumfries friends to pay the £7 4s. owed to Williamson for the Volunteers uniform but his pride deterred him and, alone at the Brow Well, the fear of being jailed festered in his mind.

He appealed in despair to his cousin James Burness to send him ten pounds: 'O, James! Did you know the pride of my heart, you would feel doubly for me! Alas! I am not used to beg!'[35] Williamson's pursuit of Burns to the grave does not place him in a favourable light, nor the wealthy Royal Dumfries Volunteers, who could have paid the demand on the poet's behalf due to his illness; but the loyalist, Pittite Tories had no liking for Burns and showed no such magnanimity. Had Williamson any consideration for his fellow Volunteer, he might have waited until the poet's health improved rather than trying to get blood from a stone. Burns was being kicked because he was down.

It was on the advice from his friend Dr Maxwell that Burns tried sea-bathing to help his condition. (The family's doctor, though, was a Dr Brown, whose bill after the poet died amounted to £2 3s.) The Brow hamlet, however, was not on the balmy Mediterranean coast; it was a bleak expanse of a sandy bay and bathing involved walking up to half a mile from his lodgings to the water, then wading out to a place deep enough, in the very shallow Solway waters, for it to reach chest-high. In late July, the Solway coast is still cold, which would have debilitated the poet's health further, possibly causing an additional complication, pneumonia.[36] The water from the Brow Well spring was believed to have healing properties, possibly iron. The poet's condition was too far gone to be alleviated by fresh sea air, sea-bathing or healing wells. He knew it was over. His last letters are painful to read, the final farewells of a distraught genius, despairing for his wife and little flock of dependants.

Cunningham, whose role in helping the poet's family after his death was exemplary, obtained the sombre news that Burns' illness was terminal, first-hand:

> Alas my friend! I fear the voice of the Bard will soon be heard among you no more! For these eight or ten months I have been ailing, sometimes bedfast & sometimes not; but these last three months I have been tortured with an excruciating rheumatism, which has reduced me to nearly the last stage . . . Pale, emaciated, & so feeble as occasionally to need help from my chair.
>
> When an Excise-man is off duty, his salary is reduced to 35£ instead of 50£. – What way, in the name of thrift, shall I maintain myself & keep a horse in Country quarters with a wife & five children at home, on 35£?
>
> I had intended to beg your utmost interest & all friends you can muster, to move our Commissrs of Excise to grant me the full salary . . . If they do not grant it me, I must lay my account with an exit truly en poete, if I die not of disease I must perish with hunger.[37]

There was little chance of the Board granting such a wish and the meagre pension available for widows and children was barely enough to keep a large family from beggary. Jean was once more in the final stages of pregnancy. The birth was expected within a few weeks. Being more and more unable to eat or keep food down, Burns could add malnutrition to his catalogue of woes.

Maria Riddell, who was herself ill at this time, received a brief letter from Burns in June, when he wrote to her to say he was unfit to attend the town's celebration of the King's birthday. After asking her if he should copy out a love song for her he answered his own question with the retort: 'No! if I must write, let it be Sedition, or Blasphemy, or something else that begins with a B, so that I may grin with the grin of iniquity, & rejoice with the rejoicing of an apostate Angel.'[38] His health may have been broken but his spirit and humour were intact. Maria sent her carriage to collect Burns from the Brow to visit her. After their last meeting she described his condition –

> The stamp of death was imprinted on his features. He seemed already touching the brink of eternity. His first salutation was: 'Well, madam, have you any commands for the other world?'[39]

Burns told her of his pride in his eldest boy and how remarkably well his education was going on; of his deep concerns for Jean and the children if he were to die and leave them almost penniless. 'His anxiety for his family seemed to hang heavy upon him,' she recalled. Burns anticipated his detractors' posthumous outpouring of 'shrill-tongued malice or the insidious sarcasms of envy'and 'venom to blast his fame'.

On 10 July, Burns wrote three letters. He asks his father-in-law for assistance during Jean's pregnancy, signing the letter, 'Your most affectionate son'.[40] To Mrs Dunlop, in hope of a final reconciliation, he tells her that her friendship was the 'dearest to my soul'.[41] She had been his longest correspondent and a difference of political principles was meagre in the bard's eyes compared to a long, heartfelt friendship. Mrs Dunlop enquired of Gilbert if the gravity of the poet's claims was true but Gilbert had only just been informed of the same news. The third letter of the day was to Gilbert himself, with the news his eldest brother was 'dangerously ill, & not likely to get better . . . my appetite is totally gone, so that I can scarcely stand on my legs'. He again expressed his fears for Jean and their children and asked Gilbert to 'Remember me to my mother.'[42] On Thursday 14 July, Burns wrote to Jean, trying to keep her spirits up by suggesting he had benefited from sea-bathing and promised to be home by Sunday. 'No flesh nor fish can I swallow: porridge and milk are the only things I can taste.'[43] Burns was too weak to ride a horse to Dumfries so he borrowed a carriage from John Clarke of Lockerwoods to make his way home.

John Syme visited Burns on his arrival home and immediately wrote to Cunningham in Edinburgh to apprise him of the situation. The emaciated Burns he met at the Mill Hole Brae shocked him greatly. 'Today the hand of Death is visibly fixed upon him. I cannot dwell on the scene.' Syme was the poet's most intimate friend in Dumfries; he was close to tears telling Cunningham to prepare for the worst: 'It overpowers me . . . He had life enough to acknowledge me – And Mrs Burns said he had been calling on you and me continually . . . we must think on what can be done for his family.'[44] Jean later left testimony to say the fever of delirium made her husband call out during his last night for his brother Gilbert, while William Maxwell sat by his bedside, watching over him. A couple of hours after the sun rose on the morning of 21 July 1796, Scotland's greatest ever poet died of a prolonged, agonising illness. The exact cause of death has never been definitively determined. It is believed by modern medicine to have been a combination of rheumatic heart disorder and endocarditis.

John Syme took charge of most of the funeral arrangements on behalf of the family. Although treated merely as an ordinary peasant gauger in his last years, the funeral arrangements were almost stately, as the people of Dumfries and from many parts of Scotland bid a last farewell to a genius, who was already known the world over when he died. Burns was buried on 25 July. His body was taken to the Town Hall early in the morning before the funeral. Syme's arrangements went ahead precisely, as he told Cunningham in a letter dated on 23 July. The funeral took place on Monday 25 July at one o'clock. The Cinque Port Calvary lined one side of the road towards the kirkyard, while, on the other side of the street, stood the Angusshire Fencibles. The Dumfries Vounteers carried Burns and were led by other Volunteers, who marched solemnly before the coffin. The Cinque Port Calvary played 'The Dead March in Saul' to a muffled drum as he was taken into the kirkyard. The town bells pealed out as the huge crowd progressed. The poet had asked his fellow Volunteer, John Gibson, to not 'let the awkward squad fire over me'. The awkward squad, the Dumfries Volunteers, out of respect, fired three volleys into the air as the poet's coffin was lowered to its resting place in the far corner of St Michael's Churchyard. The *Glasgow Mercury* of 2 August 1796 reported, 'The whole ceremony presented a solemn, grand and affecting spectacle; and accorded with the general regret for the loss of a man whose like we scarce shall see again.'

While the sombre funeral moved slowly to its destination, Mrs Jean Burns, a widow at 31 years, gave birth to a son she named after William Maxwell, who delivered him. Robert was denied seeing his last child, Maxwell Burns, who sadly died on 25 April 1799, aged two years.

Robin was not quite in his last lair. After several years of a somewhat embarrassing cool start in raising funds for the family's aid – through the primary help of John Syme and Alexander Cunningham and a biography by Dr James Currie of Liverpool in 1800 – the body of Burns was eventually moved in September 1815 to the grand mausoleum, paid for by public subscription, where his remains still lie. His 'delicious armful', Jean, was laid to rest with him in 1834.

One of the last lyrics Burns wrote, a gem more poignant due to the illness he suffered while composing it, was 'O Wert Thou in the Cauld Blast'. It was dedicated to young Jessy Lewars, daughter of his Excise colleague John Lewars. Jessy tended Jean in her last stages of pregnancy and helped out in the Burns family home when the poet was ill. Burns may have been physically dying when he wrote it but, as the lyrics reveal, his generosity of spirit and creative genius were undimmed:

O wert thou in the cauld blast,
  On yonder lea, on yonder lea;
My plaidie to the angry airt,
  I'd shelter thee, I'd shelter thee:
Or did Misfortune's bitter storms
  Around thee blaw, around thee blaw,
Thy beild should be thy bosom,
  To share it a', to share it a'.

Or were I in the wildest waste,
  Sae black and bare, sae black and bare,
The desert were a paradise,
  If thou wert there, if thou wert there.
Or were I monarch o' the globe,
  Wi' thee to reign, wi thee to reign;
The brightest jewel in my crown,
  Wad be my queen, wad be my queen.

Burns remarked a few years before his untimely death that he would readily give £20 to have written a lyric as good as the Scots song 'Come Under My Plaidie'. With 'O Wert Thou in the Cauld Blast', he surpassed the earlier lyric and added yet another priceless jewel to the tapestry of Scots songs he left us to marvel at.

In celebrating Burns, we celebrate the humanity of the people enshrined within his writings and, in a sense, the best of human nature the world over. As we have seen, during his own lifetime he was the major radical poet of the late Enlightenment period. One of the greatest songwriters of all time, who stood firm, unbowed, against a storm of political tyranny, the crucible out of which 'A Man's a Man' was written, Burns won his spurs to be celebrated annually in many an immortal memory. Two hundred and fifty years after his birth, Robert Burns, the *Patriot Bard*, remains unrivalled as the greatest poet Scotland has ever produced.

Appendix I

A Prose Essay, Signed 'Agricola'

THE FOLLOWING PROSE ESSAY IS PRESENTED AS A possible work of Burns. It is included here for discussion. The essay features in the *Morning Post* newspaper, 1 February 1795 and is signed 'Agricola'. It is known Burns used the pen name Agricola for a poem 'Ode on the Departed Regency Bill' in 1789. This is not a common pen name in the press during this period. It was found again within the *Gentleman's Magazine*, in September 1790, with an epitaph, 'On the Late Death of Dr Adam Smith':

> Death and Hermes of late in Elysium made boast,
> That each would bring thither what earth valued most:
> Smith's *Wealth of Nations* Hermes stole from his shelf;
> DEATH just won his cause – he took off Smith himself.
> Agricola

This epitaph has subsequently been accepted by literary scholars such as professors David Daiches and Carol McGuirk as a work of Burns and was included in the 2001 edition of his complete works I co-edited. The prose essay does, on a first reading, appear rather dry and laborious for Burns, although some passages reveal a poetic flair for language, displaying flashes of indignant, over-the-top energy indicative of Burns. He knew the works of Adam Smith well and the author here employs Smith to advance the argument. If it is the work of Burns, it further enhances our view of his sentiments and beliefs in his last years. It may be worth recalling Dr James Currie's description of Burns, as a man who 'might have influenced the history of nations', before reading this essay. From my detailed trawling of archival sources, the pen name 'Agricola' is rare indeed. I believe it to be the work of Burns due to the rarity of the pen name and the language and sentiments expressed. I would be happy to accept the considered views of senior literary experts.

THE PAPER OF THE PEOPLE

Mr Editor

Such have been our National misfortunes and so numerous our Wars, that we are apt to imagine that even the present extravagance cannot exhaust our capital or reduce our Country to misery and distress: placing a rash and unbound confidence in a weak and desperate Administration, we think it neither prudent nor respectful, to reflect a moment on our situation, and buoyed up with the idea of an inexhaustible treasury, we despise and regret every salutary advice, suggested by those competent to form an opinion of our danger.

The annual produce of Land and Labour being the true Wealth of every Nation, no Country can encrease in wealth, without increasing its number of productive labourers, or the power of those Labourers, who had been before employed. Whatever then prevents their increase, strikes at the rising prosperity of the Country, whatever cause conspires to diminish their number; gradually accomplishes the Ruin of the Nation. This Proposition carries such truth and conviction, that it requires no sophistry or ingenuity to expound it. Many times the number of productive labourers have been occasionally diminished in this Country; but was there ever a period, in which so great a number of productive hands have been drawn away from productive industry. Does the page of History shew an instance of the political state of this Kingdom, maintaining such a number of unproductive hands as it does at this moment. The greater the encrease the greater the dimunition of the National Capital; as, since the commencement of this memorable Crusade, the number has encreased in an extraordinary proportion; in such extraordinary proportion must we expect to hear of the expenditure of the Public Money, and of course the nearer do we approach the unfortunate point at which we seem industrious to arrive, National Bankruptcy. Innocent men in private life, consider Bankruptcy as the most humiliating calamity, they shudder at the idea of encroachment on their Capital; they endeavour by frugality, by temperance and moderation, to avert this melancholy catastrophe. In society we too often find those speculative Ruffians, who, having no regard for their own property, or that of others, by dissipation, extravagance, avarice or ambition, plunge themselves and their connections into misery and woe; but can History, can Experience, can Observation shew a frugal and saving Ministry in any [but] the most economical Country in Europe. Do we not observe our former Ministers extorting praise, not for diminishing, but keeping our debt in the same situation in which they found it, never considering the danger of encreasing the National Expenditure, and no way alarmed at living on the National Principal. We on the contrary behold our present Ministry annually adding to the grievance, and careless of the Country's interest, provided they can retain their office and continue their career, they stake and sport with that which should be kept till time of emergency, and madly and foolishly flatter their Princes into wanton Wars, endangering the security of the Crown, and striking at the happiness of the People. Did we behold the Revenues of Countries in promoting the National Interest, instead of supporting a number of hands; taxes would not fall so oppressively on the Poor, and misery and wretchedness would not be the portion of a harassed People; in Despotisms, in Absolute Monarchies, we find National Misery, Poverty and Woe, the portion of the unfortunate subjects. – Why, because to support a system of such infamy, and such iniquity, we find the Prince obliged to govern by a systematic Corruption, to attach to his interest, by the oppression of his subjects, a numerous and splendid Nobility, to maintain, at an extravagant and profligate expense, an unnecessary number of Ecclesiastics, whose sycophantic tongues are employed in flattering the virtues of their Princes, inculcating the dastard principles of Passive Obedience and Divine Right; and who being paid in proportion to their servility, cringe and fawn, and pay an implicit respect to the Inquisitorial Tyranny of their Master; nor are these the only leeches by which the People are tormented; such governments find great Armies and great Fleets, which in Peace produce nothing, and which never can gain in War what will compensate for the Blood which is spilled and the Treasure which is expended. Such People, says Smith, as they produce nothing themselves, are all maintained by the produce of other men's Labour; should they be extravagantly numbered they may consume so great a share of this produce, as not to leave a sufficiency for those productive labourers to reproduce for the next occasion. The unproductive hands, who should be maintained on the open Revenues of the Country, may consume so great a share of the whole Revenue, and thereby oblige so great a number to encroach on their capital upon the Funds destined for the maintenance of productive labour, that all the frugality and good conduct of the individuals may not be able to compensate the waste and degradation of produce occasioned by this violent and forced encroachment!! Everyone must allow that this Country exhibits a singular instance of the great burthen which a Nation is capable of enduring; and the boasted internal happiness of the People, is a proof, it is said, of the trifling manner in which it is felt, to support the farcical DATUM of this Country, being able to bear up against a regular encrease in debt. We must be told where her extraordinary resources are? – To what do the People look for safety and relief in the day of Necessity? – Where is the stronghold to which she can retire, when her strength is inadequate to the preservation of her extensive fortifications? Prudence should suggest the propriety of her having her citadel so well provided with every necessary as to enable her to withstand, with success, the impetuosity of her [illegible]. She surely should not permit her Generals infrugality, to waste and consume, in the hour of Plenty and Peace, that which is essentially necessary for preservation, in the hour of such danger and of trouble; she should not permit a number of idle and unproductive hands to come within her walls, as shall eat up that which should be alone kept for those employed in her defence: she should be careful, frugal, economical and watchful, thus by adding to her own security, she thwarts the designs of her enemy, and perhaps prevents her falling a victim to its fury. When time impairs the strength, and repeated shocks endanger the machine, he is a bad and unskillful workman, who does not advise prudence in its management, care in its use; and above all, who does not warn the Artist to beware how he makes use of it, lest he should tear away the screws and break the planks of his rickety system; he must tell the Artist, that anything which puts the smallest clog on its operation, ought to be sedulously avoided, that in the attempt to repair the breach which may be made, he may probably endanger the withered sides. Old and worn as it is, it may however, last for some time by proper care and attentive management. Just so is it with an Old Government, which has continued for years periodically weakening itself by Extravagance and Corruption. The uniform constant attention of every man to better his condition, is so powerful as to maintain it with sufficient resource; and not withstanding the prodigality of the Governors, it supplies a sufficient fund for the ordinary occurrence. But let certain branches of Industry be injured, let Commerce be suspended, let the foreign credit of the Merchant be affected and let a considerable supply of money, or money's worth, be sent out of the Country to support large unprofitable Armies and a large Navy, then we must take care, lest the old worn-out System should sink and fall beneath its burthens. – Retrenchment within, is ever indispensably requisite, when there is an exorbitant external expenditure. The prudent father when he is fortuning off his Daughter, or settling his Son in honourable industry, contracts and limits his domestic expences; in every department of his family he strenuously urges the necessity of economy. Thus he indures a great drawback from his income, without inconvenience; but were he extravagant in his arrangement, were he profusely hospitable, were he even to continue his former expence, he might have felt the miseries of bankruptcy, or the chilling damps of a prison. What then can be said of a Minister, who is profusely prodigal at home, and shamefully extravagant of the public money abroad? Who encroaches on the Public Stock to reward his Myrmidons, his Sycophants, and his Satellites, and maintains thousands in the Field to gratify his pride, his caprice, or his ambition. To say he is wise, would be to contradict every idea of common sense. Fools might well call him prudent, but wise men must tremble for the consequences his temerity may entail on his country.

AGRICOLA. Jan 27 1795.

Appendix 2

A PROSE ESSAY, SIGNED 'A BRITON'

THIS SECOND PROSE ESSAY IS PRESENTED AS A possible work of Burns purely for discussion. It was unearthed by Dr G. Carruthers from within the radical publication *Politics for the People*, part 2, no. 2, 1794. Dr Carruthers does not believe it to be the work of Burns. Having closely studied the poet's key educational school book, Masson's *Collection of Prose and Verse*, I humbly differ in opinion, mainly because of the reference to Demosthenes and the sentiments expressed about the ruin of the nation – an expression repeated in the poet's letters of 1793 and 1794. The pen name 'A Briton' is one Burns employed in 1788. It does not automatically follow everything signed 'A Briton' is the work of the bard. In my detailed archival scan of contemporary newspaper occurrences of this pen name, I only found two such examples for prose essays, one of which was Burns himself in 1788. The second example is the prose essay placed within the biography as an essay attributed to Burns which has been widely accepted. Dr Carruthers' find is therefore fascinating and deserves a wider readership to determine its provenance.

A 16-page pamphlet, 'An Address to the Inhabitants of Great Britain shewing the Inevitable Consequences of A Revolution in this Country', written in 1795 and signed 'A Briton', is almost certainly not the work of Burns. It is a Pittite loyalist polemic contrary to the sentiments and language of Burns and may have been written by a government hack in response to the 'A Briton' essay on page 300. A copy is in the British

Library. The pamphlet was printed in London and sold throughout Britain. There is insufficient space to reproduce the text here.

A further brief letter, signed 'a Briton', was identified by Professor Bob Harris in the British Library's Reeves Papers (folios 113–14) and, in my view, this is not by Burns. The following short prose essay, though, perfectly matches the poet's views in late 1793–94. As Dr Carruthers shows, Burns had access to the radical periodical, *Politics for the People* and copied a quatrain on Edmund Burke from the magazine, so we know the poet had access to the monthly magazine. Professor Harris's recent historical work has shown that copies of *Politics for the People* were distributed throughout the west of Scotland. Dr Andrew Noble's view, after close scrutiny of the essay, is that it is almost certainly by Burns. The essay may or may not be the work of Burns.

ON THE DUTY OF SPEAKING OUR SENTIMENTS FREELY IN TIMES OF THE MOST IMMINENT DANGER.

'SELL NOT THE TRUTH.' PROV. XXIII.23.

This precept, *Sell not the Truth*, regardeth, with others, the politician, who, by a timid circumspection, useth an artful concealment, when he ought to probe state wounds to the bottom, and to discover the real authors of its miseries, and the true causes of its decline. In these circumstances, it is not enough to mourn over public calamities in secret; they must be spoken of with *firmness* and *courage*: the politician must be the mouth and the voice of all those *oppressed people*, whose only resources are *prayers* and *tears*: he must discover the fatal intrigues, and unveil the mysterious springs of the conduct of HIM, who, under pretence of public benefit, seeks only his own private emolument – he must publish the shame of him who is animated with no other desire, than that of building his own house on the ruins of the nation – he *must* AROUSE *him from his indolence, who deliberates by his own fire-side*, when imminent dangers require him to adopt bold, vigorous and effectual measures; he must, without scruple, sacrifice him, who himself sacrificeth to his own avarice, or ambition, whole societies: he must fully persuade other senators that, if the misfortunes of the times require the death of any, it must be that of him *who kindled the fire*, and not of him who is ready to shed the last drop of his blood to extinguish it. To keep fair with all, on these occasions, and by a TIMID SILENCE to avoid incurring the displeasure of those who convulse the state, and of those who cry for vengeance against them, is a conduct not only *unworthy of a Christian*, but unworthy of a *good Patriot*. Silence is an atrocious crime, and to *suppress* truth is to *sell* it: to *betray* it.

How doth an orator merit applause, my brethren, when, being called to give his suffrage for the public good, he speaks with that fire, which the love of his country kindles; and knows no law but equity, and the safety of the people! With this noble freedom the heathens debated: their intrepidity astonisheth only those, who are destitute of courage to imitate them. Represent to yourselves Demosthenes speaking to his masters and judges, and *endeavouring to save them in spite of themselves*, and in spite of the punishments, which they sometimes inflicted on those, who offered to draw them out of the abysses into which they had plunged themselves. Represent to yourselves this orator making remonstrances that would now-a-days pass for FIREBRANDS of SEDITION, and saying to his countrymen; *Will ye then eternally walk backward and forward in your public places, asking one another, What news?* Imagine you hear this orator blaming the Athenians for the greatness of their enemy, and crying, *War, immortal war with every one, WHO DARES TO PLEAD FOR PHILIP*. Such an orator merits the highest praise. With whatever chastisements God may correct a people, he hath not determined their destruction, while he preserveth men who are able to shew them in this manner, the means of preventing it.

A BRITON.

In the absence of manuscript authority to prove beyond doubt the provenance of the above prose essay, the onus falls on textual and contextual evidence either way. The best published exposé of Burns' radical sentiments is Professor McIlvanney's *Burns: The Radical* (2002), where he writes, 'Couched in the language of prayers and curses, his letters at this period are full of the impotent anger of the frustrated reformer.'[1] If academic consensus attributes the essay to Burns, the praise for discovering the new prose is due to Dr Carruthers.

NOTES

NB BURNS' LETTERS HAVE BEEN NUMBERED AS IN *The Letters of Robert Burns* edited by J. DeLancey Ferguson (1931) and labelled 'CL' in the notes section.

INTRODUCTION

1 *Times Online* report, 15 August, 2008.

2 See *Scotland's Magazine*, 1951.

3 Andrew O'Hagan, *A Night Out With Robert Burns: The Greatest Poems*, Canongate, 2008, p. xiv.

4 Dr Currie to James Syme, *Burns Chronicle*, 1919, pp.11–12.

5 I was delighted and congratulated my then colleague at the University of Strathclyde, Dr G. Carruthers, when he discovered that two of the poems I had thought might be by Burns turned out to be by the radical, London-based Scottish poet Dr Alexander Geddes. By the time of Dr Carruthers' fine work, I no longer maintained that the two poems might be by Burns, a fact Gerry was aware of as we were working together on a book project. They had already been rejected the previous year by Professor David Daiches, Professor Carol McGuirk and Thomas Crawford, who endorsed many other poems as Burns' work. I myself found that two poems in the 'B' section of *The Lost Poems* were the work of Anna Latitia Barbauld.

6 See the chapter on 'Anonymous and Pseudonymous' writings by Burns in *The Canongate Burns*, 2001.

7 Fine research by Chris Rollie reveals Burns tried to find the whereabouts of his early flame, Ellison or Alison Begbie, in 1787, during his tours. She is the recipient of his letters addressed to 'My Dear E', CL 5–9.

CHAPTER 1

1 CL 125.
2 CL 125.
3 James Mackay, *A Biography of Robert Burns*, p.335.
4 CL 125.
5 CL 377.
6 A handwritten copy of the religious manual was copied out by the family tutor Murdoch and printed during the nineteenth century. William is credited as author.
7 CL 125.
8 CL 125.
9 CL 10.
10 CL 125.
11 Tom Devine, *The Scottish Nation, 1700–2000*, Allen Lane, 1999.
12 David Daiches, *Robert Burns: The Poet*, p.303.

CHAPTER 2

1 Mackay op. cit., p.34.
2 CL 125.
3 J. DeLancey Ferguson, *Pride and Passion*, 1939.
4 CL 125.
5 Burns puts these lines together but they are not together in the poem – he puts a dash to show he is dropping several lines of the poem.
6 Mackay (ed.), *The Complete Letters of Robert Burns*, Index, p.812, Alloway Publishing, 1987.
7 A copy of the Peterhead Burns Club booklet is in the Mitchell Library, Glasgow.
8 Liam McIlvanney, *Burns: The Radical*.
9 McIlvanney op. cit., p.50.
10 See Masson's *Collection*, p.8.
11 See McIlvanney op. cit., p.53 for further discussion. Mrs Dunlop wrote to Burns stating her London friends did not like 'A Dream'.
12 McIlvanney op. cit. p.61.
13 See Masson op. cit. p.170.

[14] CL 649.
[15] The list of Scotch MPs praised by Burns is in 'Here's a Health Tae Them That's Awa'.
[16] CL 125.
[17] J. DeLancey Ferguson, *Pride and Passion,* p.35.
[18] CL 403.

CHAPTER 3

[1] J. DeLancey Ferguson, op. cit., p.51.
[2] Voltaire and other Enlightenment authors are listed among the poet's library after his death.
[3] CL 13.
[4] The comment by Gilbert was in a letter to Mrs Dunlop, the lifelong correspondent of Burns.
[5] C. McGuirk. *Robert Burns: Selected Poems*, p.xix.
[6] CL 125.
[7] CL 125.
[8] CL 125.
[9] See CL 1, 2 and 3.
[10] CL 125.
[11] CL 125.
[12] CL 125.
[13] CL 125.
[14] CL 14.
[15] CL 125.
[16] This is from Burns' 'Humanity: An Ode', an update of his earlier poem 'A Winter's Night'.
[17] See *The Canongate Burns*, op. cit., p.160.
[18] CL 125.
[19] The Tarbolton Batchelors' Club is now preserved as a museum in Tarbolton.
[20] First attributed to Burns in *The Canongate Burns*, p.544 – from my research.
[21] CL 12.
[22] The poet joined the St Andrew's Lodge. Dumfries on 27 December 1792.
[23] Quoted in various biographies from Cunningham onwards. See Mackay op. cit., p.76.
[24] Research by Chris Rollie reveals that Burns annotated Begbie's name in his Borders Tour journal and planned to look her up somewhere in Glasgow. See *Times Online*, 9 January 2005.

[25] CL 125.

[26] CL 125.

[27] In 1783, Burns was awarded a £3 prize for flax raising at Lochlie, by the Trustees for Fisheries Manufactures and Improvements, for flax he grew in 1781.

[28] CL 125.

[29] CL 125 A reference to the poem 'The Poet's Welcome to His Bastart Wean'.

[30] CL 4.

[31] Quoted in Ferguson, *Pride and Passion*, p.91.

[32] CL 14.

[33] CL 125.

CHAPTER 4

[1] CL 125.

[2] This was written at Lochlie farm.

[3] This stanza is taken from a manuscript sold by Puttock and Simpson, May 1862; a copy of the saleroom catalogue is in the Mitchell Library.

[4] CL 125.

[5] J. DeLancey Ferguson, 'Burns and Hugh Blair', *Modern Language Notes*, xlv., 1930, pp.441–43.

[6] A detailed discussion of the dispute is provided in Mackay op. cit., pp.162–66.

[7] CL 586.

[8] Daiches op. cit., p.195.

[9] Quoted in Cunningham, *The Life of Robert Burns*, p.62.

[10] Scott Douglas's edition of Burns p.104, which mentions the plagiarism of Lapraik. Also J.L. Hempstead, *Burns Chronicle*, February, 1994, pp.94–101.

[11] Burns' note from the poet's own *Interleaved Scots Musical Museum*.

[12] Currie op. cit., vol. 3, p.32.

[13] CL 420.

[14] A statement to this effect was made by Jeremy Paxman, August 2008.

CHAPTER 5

[1] See Crawford's detailed critical views, *Burns: A Study of the Poems and Songs*, pp.183–92.

CHAPTER 6

[1] CL 21.

[2] CL 125.

3 See J. McDiarmid, *Widow of Burns: Her Death, Character and Funeral*, Dumfries, 1834.

4 CL 265.

5 First Commonplace Book.

6 CL 21.

7 CL 25.

8 Mackay's treatment of this subject is excellent, see pp.209–25.

9 Quoted from the *Interleaved Scots Musical Museum*. See also J. DeLancey Ferguson's article in *Philological Quarterly*, July 1930.

10 Mackay op. cit., p.217 contains a quote from the Train Mss.

11 CL 21.

12 CL 25.

13 Quotation from Milton's *Paradise Lost*, book IX.

14 CL 29.

15 CL 31.

16 CL 31.

17 CL 34.

18 CL 36.

19 This document is collected among the poet's complete letters, CL 35 and is still extant.

20 CL 125.

21 CL 125.

22 CL 125.

23 CL 40.

24 CL 43.

25 Mackay op. cit., p.195.

26 CL 46.

27 CL 48.

28 The first line is adapted from Addison's *Cato*, a seminal work for Burns.

29 This quatrain has never been entered in the collected works. All editors of his letters state the lines are by Burns.

30 CL 53.

31 This work is part of the Kilmarnock Edition and was not written in August, as Mackay erroneously states. See Mackay op. cit., p.237.

32 CL 53.

33 Quoted in Donald Low, *Robert Burns: The Critical Heritage*, p.61.

34 CL 125.

35 Currie op. cit., vol. 1, p.137.

36 From Thomson's The Seasons: Autumn, line 901.

37 CL 55.

CHAPTER 7

1 Donald Low, *Robert Burns: The Critical Heritage*, pp. 63–64.

2 The original Latin is *Rusticus abnormis sapiens, crassaque Minerva.*

3 This was a theme developed by David Daiches in his keynote address to the *Burns Now* conference, University of Strathclyde, 1996.

4 Donald Low op. cit., pp.70–71.

5 William Wallace, *Robert Burns and Mrs Dunlop*, p.11, London 1898.

6 CL 98.

CHAPTER 8

1 The description of Burns as a 'tightrope walker' is taken from the keynote speech by David Daiches at the *Burns Now* conference, University of Strathclyde, 1996.

2 CL 61.

3 CL 77.

4 CL 62.

5 CL 62.

6 CL 65.

7 CL 60.

8 CL 65.

9 CL 68.

10 Eliza Burnett is possibly the lady referred to in the newly attributed work, 'Verses Written Upon a Blank Leaf in COWPER's POEMS Belonging to a Lady'.

11 Adam Smith, *Theory of Moral Sentiments*, quoted in R. Heilbroner, *The Essential Adam Smith*, p.86.

12 Second Commonplace Book.

13 Adam Smith, *Theory of Moral Sentiments*, p.87.

14 Letter to Mrs Dunlop, 4 March 1789.

15 The Crochallan Fencibles still exist today as a club.

16 CL 455.

17 Chambers-Wallace, vol. 2, pp.52–53.

18 Chambers-Wallace, vol. 2, pp.52–53.

19 This comment is highly allusive of the fables in Masson's *Collection of Prose and Verse.*

20 A letter by Stewart to Currie, printed by Currie op. cit., vol. 1, pp.133–34.

21 Sarah Tytler and Jean Watson: *The Songstresses of Scotland*, Edinburgh, 1811.
22 Letter quoted in Chambers-Wallace, op. cit., vol. 2, pp.79–80.
23 Mackay op. cit., pp.266–67.
24 CL 77.
25 CL 70.
26 Low op. cit., p.81.
27 CL 90.
28 CL 66.
29 CL 97.
30 CL 79.
31 CL 82.
32 CL 64.
33 CL 77.
34 It was my suggestion to Colin Fox, then an MSP, to submit an early day motion to the Scottish Parliament to create the post of Scottish National Poet with an annual stipend. The then First Minister, Jack McConnell, created the post but there was no money attached. Edwin Morgan was duly appointed.
35 CL 72.
36 CL 76.
37 CL 80.
38 CL 84.
39 CL 102.
40 James Nasmyth, *Autobiography*, London, 1883, p.34.
41 CL 88.
42 J. DeLancey Ferguson, *Pride and Passion*, p.100.
43 CL 80.
44 CL 98.
45 CL 81.
46 CL 321.
47 This line is from Thomas Gray's *Elegy in a Country Churchyard.* On the headstone in Edinburgh's Canongate cemetery erected by Burns, the quote from Gray is not in inverted commas, which makes it seem to the non-literary eye that the verse is all by Burns.
48 John Home's tragedy *Douglas* (1756) was seen by many Scots as an improvement on Shakespeare; Harley was the leading character in MacKenzie's *The Man of Feeling*.
49 The quotation is from lines 25–30 of Mrs Elizabeth Scott's poem dedicated to Burns.

50 I. McIntyre, *Dirt and Deity*, pp.118–20.

51 Edinburgh University Library, Laing Mss Collection, folio 269, letter dated 6 November 1793, and folios 500–501.

52 CL 96.

CHAPTER 9

1 McIntyre op. cit., states erroneously that it was Creech who made the typesetting error, p.132, footnote 4.

2 CL 107.

3 Other biographers go on to mention the Deed of Assignment made between Burns and his brother Gilbert in 1786 regarding the poet's copyright. It was a deal between brothers and obviously no longer stood.

4 CL 170.

5 CL 95.

6 E.C. Mossner, *David Hume*, 1954, pp.413–14.

7 CL 102.

CHAPTER 10

1 Mackay op. cit., p.306.

2 Mackay op. cit., p.307.

3 Quoted in Raymond Lamont Brown, *Robert Burns, Tour of the Borders*, Boydell Press, 1972, p.35.

4 CL 110.

5 CL 110.

6 CL 112.

7 Chambers-Wallace op. cit., vol. 2.

8 CL 246.

9 Mackay op. cit., p.317.

10 CL 114.

11 CL 114.

CHAPTER 11

1 CL 113.

2 CL 114.

3 CL 116.

4 The Burns–Ainslie Mss Collection in private hands was examined in detail by Professor David Daiches and Hamish White, manuscript expert at the Mitchell library before his retirement.

5 CL 117.
6 CL 119.
7 CL 112A.
8 CL 127.
9 CL 130.
10 Burns inscribed an appropriate verse on a window, piqued at the lack of hospitality.
11 CL 131.
12 CL 132.
13 Walker met Burns in Edinburgh and later received the post of Collector of Stamps at Perth before being made Professor of Humanity at the University of Glasgow in 1815.
14 CL 140.
15 CL 145.
16 CL 147.
17 CL 137.
18 I am indebted to Dr James McGregor for this information from Lord Balfour, Robert Bruce.
19 The Burns–Ainslie Mss collection is in private ownership.
20 CL 175.

CHAPTER 12

1 CL 144.
2 CL 146.
3 CL 145.
4 CL 147.
5 Burns did request money from George Thomson just before his death due to debts owed for his Dumfries Volunteers uniform – not for songs written.
6 CL 168.
7 CL 159.
8 CL 160.
9 CL 161.
10 Mackay op. cit., p.373.
11 CL 168.
12 CL 166.
13 CL 170.
14 CL 441.
15 CL 164.

16 CL 172.
17 CL 172.
18 CL 189.
19 CL 192.
20 CL 171.
21 CL 175.
22 CL 179.
23 CL 187.
24 CL 185.
25 CL 227.
26 CL 228.
27 Grierson Mss notes, in Mackay op. cit., p.396.
28 CL 207.
29 CL 210.
30 CL 220.
31 CL 215.
32 I discussed this matter with two midwifery experts who do not think the unborn children would have been hurt.
33 CL 226.
34 CL 230.

Chapter 13

1 CL 236.
2 CL 237.
3 See Mackay, op. cit., p.416, in relation to Joseph Train's documentary evidence of the marriage.
4 The *Glasgow Advertiser* of 18 December 1788.
5 CL 238.
6 CL 254.
7 CL 242.
8 CL 243.
9 CL 272.
10 He later designed and built the new bridge over the River Nith in Dumfries, and the Theatre Royal.
11 CL 252.
12 CL 252.
13 CL 280.
14 CL 295.

[15] See Chambers-Wallace op. cit., vol. 3, pp.397–79.
[16] Mackay op. cit., p.442.
[17] CL 268.
[18] The forerunner to *The Glasgow Herald*, started in June 1783.
[19] CL 318.
[20] CL 391.
[21] CL 280.
[22] Henderson and Henley (eds), *The Poetry of Robert Burns*, vol. 3, p.408.
[23] CL 290.
[24] CL 285.
[25] CL 290.
[26] Daiches op. cit., p.315.
[27] CL 288.
[28] CL 263.
[29] CL 319.
[30] CL 269.
[31] CL 284.
[32] CL 273.
[33] Daiches, from his keynote speech at the *Burns Now* conference, University of Strathclyde, 1996.
[34] CL 293.
[35] CL 361.
[36] CL 305.
[37] CL 322.
[38] CL 338.
[39] CL 315.
[40] CL 320.
[41] CL 310.
[42] CL 311.
[43] CL 310.
[44] CL 311.
[45] CL 336.
[46] CL 330.
[47] Quoted in Mackay op. cit., p.462.
[48] CL 326.
[49] Lucylle Werkmeister, 'Burns and the London Daily Press', in *Modern Philology*, 1966.

50 Mackay op. cit., p.354 makes the error of stating the poem was printed in the *Edinburgh Star* – no such newspaper existed.

51 CL 335.

52 CL 121.

53 CL 352.

54 CL 354.

55 The two poems by Alexander Tait are 'Burns at Lochly' and 'Burns in his Infancy'.

56 CL 356.

57 CL 358.

58 CL 358.

59 CL 363.

CHAPTER 14

1 The description is taken from Samuel Taylor Coleridge's poem on Burns, 'To a Friend', written to help raise a subscription for the poet's family in late 1796, after Burns' death.

2 CL 308.

3 CL 325.

4 CL 367.

5 CL 379.

6 CL 420.

7 CL 363.

8 It was in Ayrshire, near the Bennan Head, where Sawney Bean and his family of cannibals lived in a cave: they were eventually caught by soldiers and put to death in Edinburgh.

9 CL 373.

10 CL 419.

11 CL 417.

12 CL 364.

13 See Graham Smith, *Robert Burns, the Exciseman*, Darvel, 1990, p.47. Smith had been suspended several times and was known to be lazy.

14 CL 369.

15 CL 371.

16 CL 375.

17 CL 374.

18 CL 373.

19 CL 373.

20 CL 390.

21 CL 394.

22 J Kinsley, *Poems and Songs of Robert Burns*, vol. 3, p.1341.

23 For further reading on Lord Daer's views, see *Scottish Historical Review*, vol. 35, 1956, pp.26–41.

24 The poem subsequently appeared in the 1793 edition of the poet's works.

25 This point was quoted by the leading London radical of the pro-democracy movement during the 1790s, Thomas Hardy, when he wrote his autobiographical notes in 1832 – that the true rank of a man was a patent from God, not from the feudal order.

26 CL 410.

27 CL 397.

28 CL 441.

29 Chambers-Wallace op. cit., vol. 3, p.200.

30 CL 419.

31 CL 469.

32 CL 561.

33 CL 430.

34 CL 456.

35 CL 498.

36 Burns–Ainslie Mss. This is a paraphrase of an unpublished passage in a letter not collected in the complete letters.

37 CL 460.

38 CL 401.

39 Samuel Taylor Coleridge, on Burns in *Biographia Literaria*, p.49.

40 CL 445.

41 Currie op. cit., letter cvi, 12 March 1791.

42 CL 467.

43 CL 467 The poem was composed sometime in 1791 and a copy sent to Lady Cunningham in September 1791.

44 CL 466.

CHAPTER 15

1 The identity of the spy 'JB' has been a mystery to historians for two centuries. In my view, he was Claude Irvine Boswell, Depute Sheriff of Fife and cousin of James Boswell. In early December 1792, Claude Irvine Boswell offered his services to spy on the Edinburgh Friends of the People in a letter to government and he is named as the source of a report on Edinburgh radicals in papers

RH2/4/64 f.255. (b) The mystery surrounding his identity has been largely down to his signature where he employed only two initials, his middle name and surname only. Claude Irvine Boswell signed his name with a long slanted old fashioned 'I' for Irvine, which looks like a capital J. His signature was simply 'IB', for Irvine Boswell. The 'I' has been mistaken for a 'J' and his identity has remained a mystery until now – if I am correct.

2 The infiltrator of the Friends of the People in Edinburgh, the spy 'JB' provided intelligence to government for just over a year, from late December 1792 until early 1794. His reports are archived in Register House, Scottish Record Office in Edinburgh. See, for example papers RH2/4/69 f.270, f.234–90 and RH1/4/65 f.60–61. For the name and evidence for the Dumfries branch delegate see papers relating to the National Convention of the Friends of the People.

3 CL 497.

4 CL 493.

5 CL 502.

6 CL 510.

7 Proclamation against so-called 'wicked and seditious' writings.

8 From the *Edinburgh Gazetteer*, Jan 1793.

9 CL 505.

10 CL 507.

11 CL 506.

12 CL 515.

13 CL 519.

14 CL 524.

15 RH 2/4/66 f.340.

16 Scottish National Archive files, RH 2/4/65/ ff.54–57.

17 The recipients of the *Edinburgh Gazetteer* in Edinburgh are listed at RH2/4/69 f.231.

18 CL 528.

19 CL 530.

20 See footnotes 1 and 2 above, relating to the reports by 'JB', Irvine Boswell, the spy.

21 CL 579.

22 Cunningham op. cit., p.278.

23 See Ainslie's letter, quoted as a footnote, Cunningham op. cit., p.725.

24 A letter by C. Sharpe, quoted in Cunningham op. cit.

25 CL 558.

26 RH 2/4/65 f.84–5 lists the total spy network fund for £1,000, out of which £975

was spent in the first quarter for secret-service spying activities.

27 For letters from Fintry to Robert Dundas see Laing Mss 500, ff404–405 and Laing Mss 500, folios 734, 747, 751 and 753.

28 Professor Bob Harris, *The Scottish People and the French Revolution*, Pickering & Chatto, 2008, p.118.

29 RH 2/4/69/ f.234.

30 RH 2/4/65/ ff.84–85.

31 H. Mackenzie's *Letters*, no 94, p.175.

32 RH 2/4/65/ f.104.

33 RH 2/4/65/ f.163.

34 RH 2/3/65/ f.117.

35 H. Mackenzie's Letters, op. cit., no. 96.

36 RH 2/4/65/ f.66.

37 Mackay op. cit., p.521.

38 CL 533.

39 CL 529.

40 CL 534.

41 Cunningham op. cit., p.310, 1834. Syme's version of the story is given and also a version embellished by Sir Walter Scott where he states that Burns made an actual attempt to stab Syme with his sword – which seems highly improbable.

42 CL 536.

43 Footnote in Oxford edition of S.T. Coleridge, pp.80–81.

44 Chambers-Wallace op. cit., vol. 3, p.394.

45 Cunningham op. cit., footnote on p.725.

46 CL 558.

47 CL 558.

48 CL 558.

49 CL 558.

50 CL 558.

51 This is the view argued in the press by James Mackay early in 1996.

52 David Daiches wrote a personal letter to me in late 1995, stating the 'Burns establishment believe the bard did not write anything radical or controversial' in his last years, pointing out that this view was a barrier to understanding Burns' last years and a primary motive to dismiss new poems out of hand.

53 Mackay op. cit., p.503.

54 Burns penned three letters to her, dating from autumn 1791.

55 CL 556.

56 CL 599.

57 CL 566.

58 CL 553.

59 Hogg and Noble, *The Canongate Burns* op. cit., pp.425–529.

60 Hogg and Noble op. cit., pp.456–530.

61 CL 557.

62 CL 559.

CHAPTER 16

1 The phrase is from my own song 'The Wigtown Martyrs' or 'The Twa Margarets'.

2 Four letters are documented between tenant and landlord between 1794 and 1795.

3 CL 566.

4 CL 569.

5 CL 582.

6 CL 582.

7 These include David Daiches, Carol McGuirk, Thomas Crawford, Liam McIlvanney, Andrew Noble, Cairns Craig and Rory Watson.

8 For example, 'The Tree of Liberty' is generally accepted as from Burns without manuscript provenance.

9 Hogg and Noble op. cit., pp.461–72, contains a detailed discussion of the provenance of 'The Ghost of Bruce', versions one and two.

10 The spy reports signed 'JB' in the Scottish Record Office, document discussions and meetings in which reformers openly declare their loyalty to the king and constitution.

11 MacMillan, *Handful of Rogues*, p.70.

12 MacMillan op. cit., p.99.

13 Mackay op. cit., p.541.

14 Government papers, RH 2/4/74 f.76.

15 CL 586.

16 CL 586.

17 RH 2/4/74/f95.

18 CL 594.

19 CL 631.

20 CL 608.

21 CL 611.

22 An obituary to Robert Riddell published throughout Britain is believed to have been written by Burns.

[23] J. DeLancey Ferguson's essay, 'They Censored Burns' in *Scotland's Magazine*, vol. 51, January 1955, pp.29–30.
[24] CL 618.
[25] CL 610.
[26] CL 627.
[27] CL 629.
[28] CL 628.
[29] Quoted by Duncan A. Bruce in *George Washington at Valley Forge*.
[30] This was a casual remark made by a Masonic friend, who commented that many Burns supporters nowadays would not tolerate any link between Burns and Irish radicals then because of political problems in our times. He thought my life might be at risk from a few fanatical Burns supporters due to finding material some would not want to know about.
[31] CL 622.
[32] CL 622.
[33] Werkmeister, 'Robert Burns and the London Daily Press', *Modern Philology*, 1966.
[34] *The Canongate Burns* op. cit., pp.494–97 for the poem text.
[35] Professor David Daiches sent a personal note to me about this new variant version of the known Burns poem, stating it was an improved version of the older poem.
[36] Hector MacMillan's fine book on Thomas Muir makes the error, in my view, of convoluting these two separate people into one person, thinking Robert Watt was the spy 'JB'.
[37] CL 638.
[38] CL 638.
[39] CL 638.
[40] Edward C. Bigmore, Sales Catalogue, p.8, 1861.
[41] CL 658.
[42] Kinsley op. cit., vol. 3, pp.1454–45.
[43] Peter Urbani printed 'A Red Red Rose' in his selection of Scots songs, 1794, without Burns' permission.

CHAPTER 17

[1] CL 649.
[2] Precisely when Burns wrote 'The Tree of Liberty' is uncertain, although it was certainly after events mentioned in the poem which occurred in January 1793.
[3] David Daiches, keynote speech, op. cit.

4 CL 651.

5 CL 654.

6 *The Canongate Burns* op. cit., pp. 516–24.

7 In several newspaper articles, Professor Daiches affirmed his view that around twelve of the provisionally attributed poems in *Robert Burns: The Lost Poems*, were, in all probability, the work of Burns. His views were made public on STV News, 21 July 1997. His views were also expressed to me in private conversation at his Edinburgh home, and in one letter and a postcard, which I retain.

8 CL 666.

9 CL 652.

10 Mackay op. cit., cites the poet's extensive library as proof of his wealth.

11 Mackay op. cit., p.599.

12 CL 657.

13 CL 660.

14 CL 660.

15 W. Wallace, *Robert Burns and Mrs Dunlop*, p.419, London, 1898.

16 Mackay op. cit., p.586.

17 CL 678.

18 Mackay erroneously states she died at four years of age; her birth was in November 1792.

19 CL 685.

20 CL 687.

21 CL 688.

22 Josiah Walker's *Memoirs*, pp.lxxxiv-v.

23 J. DeLancey Ferguson, *Letters of Robert Burns*, Oxford, Appendix II.

24 RH 2/4/78/ f.25.

25 RH 2/4/78/ ff.27–28.

26 RH 2/4/79/ f.3.

27 CL 688.

28 The *Scots Chronicle*, 2 September 1796.

29 McIntyre op. cit., p.392.

30 CL 693.

31 CL 694.

32 CL 699.

33 CL 706.

34 CL 698.

35 CL 705.

[36] This is from personal experience, having been brought up the son of a Galloway fisherman and having knowledge of the coastal waters.

[37] CL 700.

[38] CL 697.

[39] Chambers-Wallace op. cit., vol. 4, pp.267–67.

[40] CL 701.

[41] CL 702.

[42] CL 703.

[43] CL 708.

[44] Syme–Cunningham Correspondence, in *Burns Chronicle*, vol. x, p.40, 1935.

APPENDIX 2

[1] McIlvanney, op. cit., p.215.

BIBLIOGRAPHY

Broadie, Alexander (ed.) *The Scottish Enlightenment: An Anthology*, Canongate, Edinburgh, 1997.

Chambers, Robert and Wallace, William *Life and Works of Robert Burns*, 4 vols, Edinburgh, 1896.

Coleridge, E.H. *Coleridge: Poetical Works*, Oxford University Press, London, 1973.

Crawford, Thomas *Burns: A Study of the Poems and Songs*, Canongate, Edinburgh, 1994.

Currie, James (ed.) *The Complete Works of Robert Burns* (new edition), London, 1824.

Daiches, David *Robert Burns: The Poet*, Saltire Society, Edinburgh, 1994.

Ferguson J. DeLancey 'They Censored Burns', *Scotland's Magazine*, vol. 51, 1955.

Pride and Passion: Robert Burns, Oxford University Press, New York, 1939.

Ferguson, J. DeLancey and Ross Roy, G. (eds) *The Letters of Robert Burns*, second edition, 2 vols, Clarendon Press, Oxford, 1985.

Harris, Bob (ed.) *Scotland in the Age of the French Revolution*, John Donald, Edinburgh, 2005.

Harris, Bob *The Scottish People and the French Revolution*, Pickering & Chatto, 2008.

Heron, Robert *Memoir of the Life of the Late Burns*, 1797.

Hogg, Patrick S. *Robert Burns: The Lost Poems*, Clydeside Press, Glasgow, 1997.

Hogg, Patrick S. and Noble, A.J. *The Canongate Burns*, Canongate, Edinburgh, 2001.

Hutchinson, Thomas (ed.) *Wordsworth: Poetical Works*, Oxford University Press, Oxford, 1936.

Keane, John *Thomas Paine: A Political Life*, Bloomsbury, London, 1995.

Low, Donald A. (ed.) *Robert Burns: The Critical Heritage*, Routledge and Kegan Paul, London, 1974.

McGuirk, Carol (ed.) *Robert Burns: Selected Poems*, Penguin, London, 1993.

McIlvanney, Liam *Burns: The Radical*, Tuckwell Press, East Linton, 2002.

McIntyre, Ian *Dirt and Deity*, HarperCollins, London, 1995.

Mackay, James A. *A Biography of Robert Burns*, Mainstream Publishing, Edinburgh, 1992.

MacMillan, Hector *Handful of Rogues*, Argyll Publishing, Glendaruel, 2005.

O'Hagan, Andrew *A Night Out With Robert Burns: The Greatest Poems*, Canongate, 2008.

Ross, Ian S. *The Life of Adam Smith*, Clarendon Press, Oxford, 1995.

Simpson, Kenneth *Love and Liberty: Robert Burns – A Bicentenary Celebration*, Tuckwell Press, Edinburgh, 1996.

Thornton, Robert D. *James Currie: The Entire Stranger and Robert Burns*, Oliver and Boyd, Edinburgh, 1963.

Thornton, Robert D. *William Maxwell to Robert Burns*, John Donald, Edinburgh, 1979.

Werkmeister, Lucylle 'Robert Burns and the London Daily Press', *Modern Philology*, New York, 1966.

Werkmeister, Lucylle 'Robert Burns and the London Newspapers', *Bulletin of the New York Public Library*, vol. 65, Oct. 1961.

ARCHIVAL SOURCES

Laing I, or II manuscripts, University Library, Edinburgh.

Mitchell Library, Glasgow.

National Library of Scotland, Edinburgh.

Public Record Office, Kew, London.

RH: Registry House papers, Scottish Record Office, Princes Street, Edinburgh.

TS: Treasury Solicitors Papers, Public Record Office, Kew, London.

University Library, Edinburgh.

University Library, Glasgow.

University Library, Strathclyde.

INDEX